Home Was
Wherever We Were

Home Was
Wherever We Were

---

*The story of the lives and marriage of
Elton and Doris Geist*

Doris Geist

To order additional copies of this book, contact:
Xlibris Corporation
1-888-795-4274
www.Xlibris.com
Orders@Xlibris.com
34485

CONTENTS

Dedicated to my beloved daughter and granddaughters
Daille Geist Pettit,
Kristin Pettit Sheppard and Karin Pettit Sullivan

And in memory of our grandparents and parents, our son Gregg David,
our brothers and sister and all the friends and relatives who have
helped to make our lives interesting and exciting

Enjoy when you can, and endure when you must.
Johann Wolfgang von Goethe

ACKNOWLEDGMENTS

My thanks go to all those who have made my life memorable and especially to those who encouraged me to keep writing. Special thanks to Lyn Cameron and Christina von Biedermann for their help in editing my manuscript, sorting photographs and doing all the jobs necessary to get this book printed; and to my sister-in-law, Ramona Johnson, who kindly shared with me material relating to Elton's early life and that of the Geist family.

PROLOGUE

Sometime in the 1990's, one of my granddaughters asked me, "What was it like during the depression?" In thinking about the many changes that had taken place over sixty years, I decided to write a comparison of the differences in life in the thirties and life now. I used such topics as clothing, hair styles and popular music and worked my little essay into a twenty-page article which turned out to be of more interest to people of my age than to those the ages of my granddaughters. While working on that project, I realized how little my family knew about my life, so I decided a few years ago to write my life story.

As a result, this book relates in detail my life history but more particularly the lives and marriage of Elton and Doris Geist. Although I've described our personalities and characters throughout the book, I believe Elton deserves a more comprehensive biography than I've given him. Married couples often dwell on the faults and errors of their mates. I was also guilty of this, but since his death in 2004, I've been able to think more about Elton's virtues and have greater insight into the man he was, an interesting and complex person.

Elton had several distinctive characteristics which made him a cut above most people. He had extraordinary determination and perseverance learned, to some extent, from his father who taught him that "when you get knocked down, you get up and get going again." He never moaned or spent any time wondering what he could have done differently or expressed any regret. Instead, he would immediately decide on the action he should take as the result of what had occurred. The Parkinson's disease he suffered for 13 years was especially difficult for him once it had reached the point where he could do nothing but accept it. And this he did, calmly and patiently. Another special characteristic, and a reason for Elton's success as a consultant, was his ability to see every aspect of a project, including the small, but necessary, actions that others missed. He had, also, a rare grasp of time. Many people live largely in the past, others in the future and still others in the present. He saw time as a continuum, an important factor when considering long-term plans or actions. He was a very good father and boss, demanding hard work, discipline and effort, but never asking the impossible; he was unfailingly fair in his treatment of others. He was always calm and controlled and rarely became angry, but if angry, he spoke quietly. He was rarely judgmental and he liked people, all people, and enjoyed their company. One of Elton's most important qualities, perhaps, was his sense of humor. He would see the humor in any situation and we both loved a good joke—even a bad one—and were always anxious to share a new joke with each other; we also enjoyed silently sharing a mutual reaction to someone's unintended humor. All of these qualities were developed during Elton's very difficult early life. He had a poor start, and lived in straitened circumstances throughout most of his youth, with an inadequate education. But he had an in-born good character and a great blessing in having loving and caring parents and maternal grandparents.

Elton learned to work at an early age and to adjust to whatever circumstances he found himself in. He also learned the importance of money early in life. His family was very poor, but also very proud. Their one experience with a long unpaid bill at a grocery store left him with a lifelong abhorrence of debt. When, early in our marriage, we finally had a steady income and no refrigerator or washing machine, I wanted to buy them on "time," but he refused. I went without until we'd saved enough to pay cash. He was horrified to learn several years later that money he had received for help in college from a missionary friend of our pastor was a loan, not a gift, as he had thought. When we learned of it, we repaid it promptly. Until we bought our condo in 1976 we never incurred any debt. Elton was not parsimonious and he enjoyed spending money for "nice" things, especially good clothes (for both of us), fine restaurant meals, expensive cars and trips.

In addition to learning the importance of money, Elton learned the importance of proper language and manners. When he started out for college, someone arranged for him to live in the home of a family for whom he did odd jobs. The woman of the house was so appalled at his lack of good manners and poor grammar that her husband soon arranged for other quarters for him. Over time, I was able to help him with his grammar and his manners, but he remained concerned about behaving properly in company and speaking correctly.

I met Elton when I moved to Custer as a high school junior. I was very impressed because he was a senior and a football star (and good looking) and I had no idea of his poverty. During the depression, everyone was poor, but other than the movies, there was no place to spend money and none of us had much. A class ring and a class photo, for instance, were expensive then and it must have been very difficult for the Geist family to fund these purchases, but somehow they did.

Because of his ambition and awareness of the importance of money, his willingness to marry at age nineteen was nothing less than remarkable. It is a kind of testimony in itself to the deep affection we felt for each other almost from the time we met and our determination to make a commitment to each other. Our marriage was foolish, perhaps, but it was inevitable. We were fortunate in having families who were willing and able to help us in any way they could; with their help, we managed most of our expenses with what little we had, especially while Elton was in the service. It wasn't until we'd been married for six years, with two toddlers, that we had an income that covered more than the bare necessities.

Elton was determined to get a college education and managed to work at jobs that gave him funds for two years. He became a metallurgical engineer in mining, partly because that was one of the very few activities a young person in the Black Hills was aware of and it was a major field at the School of Mines. But he loved mining and would go anywhere any time to visit a mine, see the machinery and look at the treatment process. Although raised to do carpentry and serving in ordnance in the army, he disliked doing anything with his hands. But he understood and loved all machinery and would spend hours figuring out some mechanical process.

Elton was exceedingly ambitious and really wanted to achieve an important position in a big company. Although he became successful as a plant manager and later as a well-known and highly respected consultant, he did not reach his major goal. This was always a disappointment to him, but it did not keep him from continuing to work hard and move forward and I believe he felt he had lived a good and full life. With his calm demeanor, his enjoyment of people and his sense of humor, he was a wonderful person to live with. He deserves much credit for his acceptance of life and what it brought him, and for his efforts to do the best he could in whatever situation or place he found himself. He will always be remembered well by those who knew him.

I concluded my narrative with Elton's death in July, 2004 because the story of our marriage was at an end. My life is not over and there is no knowing when it will end, or what I might do in the interim, but it is now my life, not our life, and if the rest of my life should deserve it, it must be another story.

CHAPTER 1

Our Families

Doris' Family—the Roesers

My Father's Father, Jacob Roeser, was born in Hessen, Germany on September 3, 1868. His parents died when he was very young and he lived with an uncle, a farmer. He came to the U.S. in 1882 when he was fourteen. He went first to Baltimore where there was a sizable group of his Schweitzer relatives, one of whom was his sister whose husband owned a saloon. Grandpa didn't want to be a bartender and decided to become a baker's apprentice instead—not because he didn't drink! He became a U.S. citizen in 1890. Apparently, he worked in Baltimore for a while and then went to St. Louis with a lifelong friend, Wilhelm Flam, whom we always knew simply as "Flam." They were both bakers, and before too long my grandfather had his own bakery, with an apartment above, in the German section of town. St. Louis had a very large German population and my father, his brother and sister went to a German-speaking church and school and spoke little or no English until he was in high school.

My grandmother, Frieda Eugenia Huber, was born in Furtwangen, Baden, Germany on September 23, 1872. Her father had a good business building stoves, but unfortunately, he had a partner who absconded with the insurance premiums. When a fire destroyed the business, they had no insurance and lost everything. Instead of rebuilding, the family left for the U.S. For some reason, Grandma remained behind with an aunt and uncle. After a few years the family sent for her to join them in St. Louis, which she did, and in a few years she and Grandpa were married.

This began a stormy, 55-year relationship that ended only when he died in 1949. Although they were separated several times, they always got back together. They fought constantly, in German, usually about religion, since Grandma was Roman Catholic and Grandpa was Missouri Synod Lutheran. They were married in a Catholic chapel and the children were to be raised Catholics. When the children arrived, however, Grandpa insisted that the boys were to be Lutheran, but the girls could be Catholic! Grandma never missed Mass, and my father, Jacob, Jr. (born January 3, 1894) and Edmund (born February 15, 1896) became familiar with the Roman church, but they remained Lutheran; Aunt Jo (Josephine) (born December 28, 1901) ended up as an Episcopalian.

Apparently, over time, Grandpa bought and sold several bakeries as well as residential property. About 1909 he, Grandma and Jo took a trip to Germany, leaving the boys in Baltimore with relatives. When they returned, they either bought another bakery, or they may have made their first trip to Colorado. It is possible that they went to Colorado because Edmund was so thin that they thought he might have tuberculosis—he did have asthma all his life. Or, they may have been persuaded to do so by Grandma's brother, Egon, who lived in Manitou (after a stint in Georgetown, Colorado, as a barber), and her brother, Otto, who by then lived in Denver.

When the First World War ended in 1918, Grandpa got his affairs in order in preparation for a return to Germany. When both Grandma and Jo refused to go with him, he went anyway, intending to stay. He found such disruption and terrible inflation in Germany that he came back to the U.S. in disgust and never returned. He was, however, quite a fan of Hitler after he first came to power, and talked admiringly about *Mein Kampf*. Like many Germans, he did not like Jews.

After Grandpa returned from Germany, the family seems to have done a lot of moving back and forth between St. Louis and Manitou Springs. He had several different bakeries in St. Louis and at least two in Manitou before settling down in the bakery on Manitou Avenue. He ran this bakery until he retired, with help from Ed and his wife Ruth. It's possible that the reason for their being in Manitou, rather than St. Louis during World War I, was the anti-German feeling that was rampant in the U.S. It must have been strong in St. Louis with the many Germans living there, but this was never mentioned to me.

The family seems to have been in St. Louis long enough, however, for Jo to finish her Catholic schooling. Ed, who had also become a baker, lived in St. Louis before and after his marriage to Ruth in 1917, with his only child, Mary Jane, born there in 1918. Dad told the story of going home to St. Louis after finishing his second year at the University of Missouri in 1914, and finding no one there. They seem to have forgotten to notify him of their move!

Dad had completed two years at Missouri U. with letters in baseball, football and track, but transferred to Colorado College in Colorado Springs for his final two years. He graduated in 1916 with a B.S. in Forest Ecology. He loved all sports, especially baseball, and while they were growing up, he and Ed spent every possible minute at the baseball stadium—Dad was a confirmed St. Louis Browns fan and Ed was a fervid Cardinals booster. They both knew all there was to know about baseball stats up until the time they died—Ed in 1967 and Dad in 1971. Dad was so entranced with baseball when he was a kid that playing baseball was what he thought he really wanted to do when he grew up. However, when he had to write a paper in high school about what he wanted to do, the teacher refused to allow baseball as a choice and, having read an interesting article on forestry, he chose forestry as his future goal.

In addition to their love of baseball, the brothers shared a love of singing. They both had good voices and were lucky enough to attract the attention of someone who arranged for them to take singing lessons. Though not around the house, Dad always sang a lot—on early radio programs, for many different organizations, and in many churches, often with Uncle Ed. He also appeared in minstrel shows whenever asked. These were shows with music and comedy, featuring actors in blackface as stumbling bumpkins, ignorant clowns. This was the way everyone thought of blacks in those days, and the minstrel shows were certainly racist to the nth degree. Dad was not racist, but he loved doing the shows that were part of the culture of the time. When I was old enough to sit alone, I often went with him when he sang in some church other than the Congregational Church to which we belonged. Mother's family was also Lutheran, but I think they did not attend church often, and apparently, my folks agreed on the Congregational Church as a compromise.

It's likely that Dad chose to transfer to Colorado College because he was recruited for a forestry program, begun by Gifford Pinchot of the U. S. Government's Division of Forestry—a pet project of Theodore Roosevelt. The Government had not been interested in preservation of forests until 1881 when this division was added to the Department of Agriculture. Some people had begun to realize that the country's forests were not infinite, although many still felt they were, as witness the Hinckley fire 13 years later. By 1900, four state universities, but not Missouri, and a few private colleges, including Colorado College, offered courses in Forestry. But it was not until Pinchot came aboard under Roosevelt that real action was taken.

One of Pinchot's plans was an extremely far-reaching, long-lasting and comprehensive program to study and analyze the U.S. forests and their ecology. Two of the locations chosen as study centers for this program were Coeur d'Alene, Idaho, and Colorado Springs. The fact that Dad went to Coeur d'Alene for his first job out of school, with a stint in Arizona at another center, makes me think that he may have signed into this program earlier. In 1917, he went into the Army. When he was discharged, he was assigned immediately by the U.S. Forest Service to the Fremont Forest Experiment Station on Mt. Manitou (we referred to it as *the Mountain*), outside Colorado Springs, part of the Pike National Forest.

When Dad enlisted in the Army he was sent to officers' training camp at Camp Funston, Kansas. He and Mother had become acquainted while he was still in college, and both of them were living in Manitou with their parents. While he was at Funston, Mother went to visit him and they were married secretly on December 29, 1917—secretly, because married women were not then employed as teachers and she would have lost her teaching job if they were to discover that she was married. When he completed training, Dad was sent to Ft. Belvoir in Virginia, and in the spring, my mother joined him and rented a room in Alexandria. She became pregnant and, after the Armistice on November 11, 1918, she returned to Colorado, stopping in St. Louis on her way home. Aunt Jo and Uncle Ed were still living there, and perhaps other family members were there too. Alan Huber Douglass was born on April 24, 1919, in Colorado Springs, and on May 3, Dad was assigned to work on the Fremont project, first in Denver where Mother and Alan joined him, and after two years, at the Station itself. Since this was just outside Manitou, the small family moved south, but this time, back to Colorado Springs.

Dad worked full time on the project and was Supervisor from about 1926 until the station closed in 1936. He spent as much time as possible on the Mountain, but had an office in Colorado Springs, and spent considerable time out in the woods, mainly at various tree plantings. He was on the Mountain when I was born on October 17, 1922, and he climbed down hurriedly to greet his daughter. From September to June, the only way to get to the Station was to hike up and, of course, down Mt. Manitou, so it wasn't possible for his family to live there all year. In the summer, however, we could drive to the foot of Mt. Manitou and ride up the front of the Mountain on the Incline. This was a funicular railroad, or cable car, run in the summer as a tourist attraction. It ran from 8:00 in the morning, until 6:00 in the evening. Since my family notoriously ran late, we did a lot of rushing to catch the last car which the operator reluctantly held for us if he knew we were coming. At the top, we had to walk a mile to the Station.

There were four houses at the Station, only two of which were inhabited that I recall—an office building with a lab in the basement, a greenhouse, barn and storage shed, and a large building which incorporated a small sawmill and a warehouse. There was also a small concrete building that we called "the bomb shelter", evidently built for that purpose, since it was never used for anything else, and it was never bombed! The houses were frame and had running water supplied by the Station's own water system, power transmitted from Manitou, and bathrooms, though quite primitive. We had no refrigeration and no electric appliances, though few existed in the 1920's. We did have an electric iron that Mother took along each summer. She did the laundry in a hand-operated, wooden-tubbed "machine." She cooked with a wood stove, using mostly aspen which burns very quickly, requiring constant filling of the wood box. My brother, Alan, was charged with keeping the box full—but he often didn't.

In 1935, the lives of the family changed. The forestry research project was closed down by the government for lack of funds, and that summer was the last we spent there. The shut-down was probably wise from a fiduciary standpoint, with nationwide demands for employment and drought relief, but very sad in many ways. The forest project had not run nearly long enough to begin a real forestry experimentation program, and the valuable work begun was never adequately appreciated, nor was it ever completed (as far as I know). Dad was transferred that fall to Ft. Collins to the Forest Service Branch, associated with the Colorado A&M College.

The Skamsers

Unfortunately, I know less about my Skamser grandparents than I do about the Roesers. My Mother's parents came from Norway, that is, my grandfather, Christ Skamser, came from Norway. He came to the States in about 1885 as a young man of 22, seeking his fortune, like so many others at the time. His name was originally Christ Jacobson, which he changed to the name of a farm in Norway, because there were so many Jacobs' sons. He was from a peasant family and, incidentally, was born out of wedlock, on September 17, 1863. He was a skilled shoemaker, a skill I assume he learned in Norway. What was the immediate incentive for his emigrating? What did he do when he got here, or how did he manage to survive with no money and no English? He had neither relatives, nor close friends here. No one will ever know, but it is safe to assume he worked at whatever he could and he learned the necessary English. I remember him telling the story of eating ham and eggs for every meal for a long time because those were the only English food words he knew.

At some point he worked in North Dakota in the wheat fields; he then went to Wisconsin where timber was the big industry. There he met and married 18-year old Clara Ladum. Clara had been born in Merideen, Wisconsin, on June 17, 1873. Both her parents were born in Norway, and her mother, at least, never learned English. I believe they ran a boarding house, which is where she met Christ. Soon after their marriage, they moved to Hinckley, Minnesota, in the heart of timber country, where he began a little shoe store and repair shop. There they had the first two of their five children. Richard was born in 1892, and Cora, my mother, was born on July 1, 1894. They did not live long in Hinckley, because a raging forest fire drove them out.

The summer of 1894 was terribly hot and dry and forest fires burned intermittently all summer over the northern Great Lakes region. In that day of abundant, uncut forests, with few inhabitants, no one was concerned about forest fires burning out of control. Rain would often extinguish them. It was believed by most people that the forests were inexhaustible and no damage would be done to the sparse population. In late August, however, a long-smoldering fire was fanned by hot winds into a major conflagration that in a few days presented a great enough threat to Hinckley that the population began a hasty evacuation on September 1. Many of the residents went to a nearby gravel pit, believing they would be safe below the fire, but they all suffocated when the fire jumped across, pulling all the air out of the pit. My grandparents were among those who took their children on the last train north, over burning bridges, with the fire visible on all sides, and the walls of the cars too hot to touch. My mother was two months old, Dick was two years; the shoe store was lost, with no hope of repaying the debts incurred, or replacing the losses suffered.

Grandpa found work in the booming iron-mining town of Virginia, Minnesota, but after a few years, migrated to Colorado. Family tradition has it that this was because of Grandma's poor lungs. At that time, it was believed that living in the high altitude and rarefied air of Colorado was one of the few ways lung ailments could be treated. Colorado was also in the midst of a silver boom, and it seems likely that Grandpa thought he could turn some of that silver into gold. They settled briefly in Boulder, but then moved to Manitou where they lived until my mother was about fifteen. Grandpa worked as a shoemaker, and they rented rooms to summer tourists—not exactly gold, but a living.

Like most Colorado towns at the time, Manitou was inhabited mainly by Anglo-Saxons from the eastern and southern U.S. My mother was embarrassed to be foreign and different, and she was painfully aware of her parents speaking a foreign language (which she refused to learn), and subscribing to a foreign-language newspaper which she had to pick up for them at the post office. She was so aware of being different that when she had her first menstrual period she assumed that this was just another Norwegian difference that set her apart. She was much relieved when she heard a girl whom she knew to be Irish talking about having the same problem. She never ceased trying to avoid being Norwegian. She never cooked Norwegian foods, and I learned to cook lefse (a flatbread made from mashed potatoes), and fattigman (crisp fried sweet cookies) from my grandmother and Uncle Dick's wife, Phoebe. We certainly never ate lutefisk (Norwegian dried and smoked fish) in our house.

In about 1909, the family moved once again—this time to Paonia, Colorado, on the Western Slope. They now had three more children, Clara Eunice (always known as Eunice) born in 1900, Carl, born in 1902 and Thelma, in 1906. I believe that this move, too, was made to cash in on a boom—a fruit-raising boom. They might have bought, but probably rented, a fruit farm. The two older children stayed home for a year because the town and high school were too far away. The next year, they drove a buggy into town and my mother graduated from the eighth grade in Paonia in 1914 and had some high school. Unfortunately, my grandfather had another stroke of bad luck with nature—a drought and a late frost destroying one year's crop. In about 1916, they moved back to Manitou and their old life. Mother taught school in two very small (2 or 3 pupils) county schools until 1917 when she married my Dad. Her only other paying job was during World War II in Custer, South Dakota, when she sorted mica. Heat resistant mica was plentiful in the Black Hills and, before the age of plastics, large pieces were used in place of glass in some instruments. During the war, sorting the mica employed much of the available labor force in the Hills.

I knew all my grandparents until I was 18, when Grandpa Scamser died as a result of a fall in February, 1941, and Grandma until I was 23, when she died on October 17, 1945 of ulcerated varicose veins and kidney problems. Because I knew them as my "grandparents", not as "people", I knew very little about their histories or their personalities. They always seemed to have a very happy relationship, with lots of private jokes, and I know Grandpa had a good sense of humor. Grandma, however, always seemed stern and forbidding toward me and my brothers. Mother said this was because she was afraid of spoiling us. This may have been so—we were pretty undisciplined. But she was certainly puritanical and disapproved of anything modern. When she visited my parents in September 1944, before my daughter was born on November 17, she was shocked that I would go out of the house at all in my condition. She would most certainly have a lot of trouble with today's society!

The Skamsers had some very difficult times in their lives, in addition to the events above, with which I can now sympathize more than I could when they were alive and I was young. Their daughter, Thelma—the whole family's precious baby and our adored aunt—died in 1931 at age 24, after suffering a siege of only three or four days of spinal meningitis. Eunice died in 1940 at the age of 40, after a long and painful stomach cancer. Carl married a woman named Gladys (I remember her as a typical flapper). They had a baby, Orpha Glee, born November 18, 1928, and they were divorced two years later. Gladys kept the baby and had no further contact with the family. Carl himself never amounted to much, but worked in the shoe shop and lived with his folks until after WWII. My grandparents survived their losses, worked hard and, in retrospect, I realize they epitomized the many immigrants who were self-supporting, hard working, good citizens.

My Parents

My parents were married for 54 years in what was apparently a good relationship in the earlier years. They both liked to read, loved dancing and parties and being with other people. Mother was a good homemaker, while Dad was a good provider. He loved sports of any kind, and Mother liked playing cards. They were both honest and decent people, active in the Congregational Church and pretty Victorian in their ideas. Since they were also law-abiding and apparently didn't care much for liquor, they observed prohibition and we kids never saw any alcoholic beverages until we were teen-agers, except the home-made wine all four of our grandparents kept on hand for "emergencies." Grandpa Roeser must have had a tough time with prohibition. He wanted his pail of beer every day and maybe found a way to get it. Uncle Ed apparently served a short term in prison for bootlegging, but all such information was carefully hidden from us.

As in most marriages, there were fissures in my parents' marriage, and these grew more and more pronounced as they grew older. Their later years were not very happy. Dad didn't like responsibility, and although he managed the money (in that generation, of course he did!), he left most other areas of responsibility to Mother, including child-rearing. She had a hard time dealing with us and could have used some help. She was a person who simply couldn't reason. She was not stupid, but we could always out-think her and wear her down. Mother wanted badly to be "somebody" and, as a consequence perhaps, she was very envious. She was very proud of Dad's job. She tried hard to teach us all proper manners and a "nice" way of life so we always had the table set with a tablecloth, napkins, silver properly arranged and no milk or ketchup bottles on the table. Mother was not as smart as Dad, but she was an avid reader and was very knowledgeable about some things—wild flowers, for instance. And she was an excellent speller. She had a great sense of humor and could laugh at herself. We almost always had an atlas and/or dictionary close at hand for settling discussions about spelling and geography.

Mother was almost always cheerful, except during the period in the mid-thirties when Dad was involved to some extent with another woman. Apparently, he suggested divorce, which Mother believed to be a major sin and wouldn't consider. When that period was over, they seemed to get along well enough and were reconciled. Dad didn't have much of a sense of humor, but he was always interested in other people and enjoyed being with them. He was comfortable with anyone. Everyone liked him and enjoyed his company. He tended to be pessimistic, but he was so involved with other people and whatever he was doing that he never became really low in spirit. Only when his physical condition deteriorated in the two or three years before he died, keeping him from singing in the church choir, going out, or doing things away from home, did he become unhappy. As his frailty increased, he was even less able to deal with things, and Mother couldn't deal with his condition. She nagged him more and more until, I believe, he was really desperate to get away from her.

Dad had Parkinson's disease, which showed up in 1969. He was taking medication for it, but this was very early in the history of treatment for Parkinson's. The disease appeared to worsen after he had surgery for lung cancer in the fall of 1970, although he seemed to do quite well after the surgery. During the next year he must have grown much worse, unbeknown to us, and apparently ignored by my brother, Jack, and his wife, Betty, who lived in Colorado Springs. When Elton and I went to Colorado Springs at the end of September, 1971, we were shocked at his condition. He couldn't speak, and he had trouble eating and making himself understood. He could move only with difficulty, and seemed miserable. He needed help desperately, either at home or in a nursing home, but Mother seemed to feel he could pull himself out of it if he would try, and was annoyed at him for being so difficult.

While Elton went off on a business trip, I spent a week trying to prepare Mother for the future, but I made no dent at all in her conviction that he would be getting better and they needed to make no changes. On Friday night I fervently prayed God to help her understand, or to take my Dad from his evident misery. Early Saturday morning, Mother came in to tell me something was wrong with Dad and we called an ambulance (no 911 at that time). He was taken to the hospital, but I was sure he was already dead. He was. I knew he was ready to go, but I loved him dearly and have missed him ever since. Was my prayer answered, or was it just said at the appropriate time? I believe it was heard and answered, and since then I've believed completely in the power of prayer.

Mother lived until 1983, but not happily. All her family was gone, except Carl's widow from his second marriage in 1945, and they were not very close. She sold the house within a year and moved into an apartment. She moved two more times before realizing that her problems wouldn't be solved with a new place to live. She had adequate income, mostly from Dad's Government pension and Social Security. Although Dad left little more than their house, she managed what she had well enough to leave an estate of around $100,000. Mother was always lonesome, but wouldn't consider going into a retirement home where she'd have people with whom to talk and play cards. She didn't want to be with "all those old people." She wanted a husband, and she dated her lifelong friend, Pete Young, for a while, but broke up with him—he wanted sex but not marriage!

I went to see her as often as I could get away from work and other demands, believing she had Jack and Betty to look out for her. Although Mother always put on a cheerful front and was good company, we had trouble getting along because she was so independent (shades of my future, when my daughter complains about my being too independent) and it was impossible to reason with her. Early in February 1983 she had either a stroke or a heart attack and was taken first into the hospital, and then into a nursing home. I had planned to visit her at home on the week she was in the hospital, but went instead to visit her in the nursing home. Two things were immediately apparent. Jack and Betty had been pretty indifferent to her gradual deterioration, and she was not going to be able to go back to her apartment. Consequently, I spent a week visiting with her, getting her things sorted, packed and disposed of, and moved out of her apartment. I left for Cleveland on February 15. As soon as I got home, I got word that she had died that day.

Elton's Family—The Geists

The Geists were not recent immigrants, like my family. Elton's father's family was Pennsylvania Dutch, having settled in Pennsylvania in its early years. His grandparents were both from Schuylkill County, Pennsylvania. His grandfather, Timothy Geist, and grandmother, Ella Amanda Moser, were married on August 11, 1883. Their first child, Nevada, was born two days later on August 13, 1883! There was always speculation in the family about Nevada's parentage. By a previous marriage, Timothy had three sons whose mother died. These boys must have been raised by other relatives because they did not go west with Ella and Timothy when they took Nevada and moved to Nebraska—also in 1883. There appears to have been little contact with the older half-brothers after that move, although at least one of the boys spent some time in Nebraska with his father.

Things were booming in Nebraska because of the Homestead Act, and Timothy took out a homestead in Beaver Crossing where he farmed and worked as a carpenter, along with his sons, as soon as they were old enough to work with him. They had thirteen children, after Nevada. Persis was born in 1885, Katie in 1886, Olive May in 1886-who died at eight weeks; Samuel (Elton's father) was born in 1889, Earl in 1891, Gertie in 1893, Carrie in 1895, Glenn in 1897, Timothy in 1899, Ella in 1901, Ord in 1906, and Irene in 1908. In 1907 the family moved to a farm in Potter County, South Dakota, and in about 1921 moved to Lebanon, South Dakota. They had some sixty grandchildren. Occasionally, someone has enumerated all of them, but the exact number is always forgotten, and at this point (2004), it's unlikely that we could count all of them, much less the great grandchildren.

Grandma Geist was illiterate, but she made up for it by making quilts. She made a hand-pieced and hand-quilted quilt for each of her children and each of her grandsons and a silk quilt for each of the granddaughters. Unfortunately, she made Elton's quilt during WWII. Since we were married in 1941, and good quality material wasn't available, much of the material she used shredded in a few years and the quilt has not been usable, though we kept it. No doubt she made many additional quilts. She sewed all her life and died at the age of ninety. Her husband often read the Bible to her while she was sewing. They were not church folks, but were of Quaker background. Later in life, when many of her children and grandchildren had moved away, she traveled often to see them.

Sam served in the Navy in World War I, but got no further than the Great Lakes Naval Training Station in Chicago. Somewhere along the line he contracted syphilis, not surprisingly, perhaps, as he was known to be quite a ladies' man. He was not aware of having contracted the disease, but it eventually caused the heart problems that killed him in 1944—on D-day, June 6. It was never transmitted to his wife or children. After his naval service, he was a farmer, particularly raising horses. In the late twenties, when heart problems limited his activities, he was able to do only an occasional odd job as a carpenter.

The Geists were down-to-earth, sensible, gregarious, humorous people who enjoyed having a good time and playing practical jokes. While I've never met them all, I liked all of those whom I did know, and think of them as among those who are the real backbone of this country.

The Mesicks

There was quite a contrast between the Geists and Elton's maternal grandparents, the Mesicks. The family of Harry Mesick was descended from the early Dutch settlers in New York. His ancestors gradually moved west and settled first in upstate New York and then in Princeton, Wisconsin, where they farmed. Harry was the fourth child, younger by nearly twenty years than the other three. Judging from that fact and the way he expected to be waited on when he was old, he was obviously spoiled rotten. One of his older brothers drowned at an early age while his father was drinking in a saloon. As soon as he heard about his son's death he swore off liquor and the family became teetotalers. Harry remained one, and disapproved of the family drinking until his eighties when a doctor told him a little nip at night would be good for him. Thereafter, he faithfully took a nip of whatever had been bought and left at the house by children and grandchildren, mixed with his nightly grapefruit juice.

Harry attended Ripon College for a couple of years and married Sarah Werner, daughter of an Evangelical minister, two years older than he and apparently better educated. Her family had lived in Chicago until moving to Princeton sometime in the 1880's. They were evidently pious and strait-laced. The impression of Sarah, passed down through the family, is that she considered herself above the Mesicks, and Elton always believed that she married Harry only because she was 24 years old and an OLD MAID! They lived on the farm in Princeton, but one of Harry's older brothers, Oliver, moved to South Dakota in the 1880's or 1890's, invested heavily in land and became (on paper) very wealthy. Either the rest of the family pushed them out, or Oliver persuaded Harry and Sarah to move to central South Dakota. They moved with Ethel May, born on November 28, 1898, and Elton who was born in 1900, and arrived in Gettysburg (South Dakota) in March 1902. Ruth was born in November 1902. In August 1904, another son was born who lived only one month.

Another of Harry's brothers, David Mesick, homesteaded what later became Harry's farm in 1902. David died soon after. The farm was in Harry's name, but in 1917, it was changed to the names of Ethel and Ruth, Harry and Sarah's daughters, with life usage by Harry. Harry and Sarah moved to that farm in 1918. While they lived in Gettysburg, Harry worked for International Harvester, selling and freighting to the Cheyenne Indian Reservation. He also dug water and sewer lines in Gettysburg, and in 1914 was a mail carrier. The family lived on or near the Sioux reservation near the Missouri for some time, as well as in Gettysburg for several years, before settling on the farm. Ethel had happy memories of their life on the reservation where they did a lot of horseback-riding and running games. One of the Indians, Smoky Dunn, whom she mentioned occasionally, even when she was in her eighties, called her "Running Deer." By the age of eleven she was also working in the hay fields, driving a hay rake with her brother, Elton.

When Elton contracted tuberculosis (TB), they moved to the tiny town of Forest City because there was a doctor. He died there, at home, on March 9, 1917, having been bed-ridden for six months. A sentence from Ethel's reminiscence tells a lot about the times and the way they lived. "He would lie on one side and cough up a quart of pus, then turn over and do the same thing. I used to wash the rags he coughed in and I imagine that is where I started having TB." It's impossible to imagine this kind of life without cleansing tissues, plastic bags, and all our other paraphernalia and sanitary equipment. They didn't even have newspaper to wrap the waste in (since they took a weekly paper), or disposable rags, as clothes were worn and linens used until they were threadbare. It was probably Ethel's task to do all the washing, which meant getting the water, building a fire, heating the water on the stove, putting it in a tub and using a scrub board, then hanging clothes on the line to dry. No wonder Ethel got TB, but, apparently, neither of her parents or Ruth did.

Elton's death at 17 was a terrible loss to the family, and Sarah never really recovered. And, no doubt, neither did the girls. Four years later, Ethel's first baby, the first grandchild, was named Elton in memory of his uncle, but Sarah couldn't bear to call him by that name and he became "Sonny" to the entire family.

From Forest City, the family moved back to Gettysburg, but Ethel had not finished high school when they moved to the farm and she could not return to school. This was always a great disappointment to her, although she did get her GED when she was in her sixties. She was nine years younger than Sam whom she met at one of the many dances in the area. Although this was largely farming country with only a few very small towns, the young and single people of the area did a lot of partying and dancing. The dances were held in barns and meeting halls, in some cases involving very long drives by horse and buggy. It was at one of these dances that Sam and Ethel met in the fall of 1918. Sam was one of the most popular young men, and Ethel was little, blonde and pretty. Their courtship seems to have been brief but serious—they were married in January, 1919, and rented a farm to begin their life together.

Elton's Parents

Like my folks, the Geists got together because they both loved dancing and, I'm sure, because Ethel was young and pretty and Sam was old enough to want to settle down. He loved playing cards and would play cribbage, or any other card game, at the drop of a hat. He loved having people around, and they were around—dropping in, or moving in for a time, throughout their marriage. During the depression, this was common. Many lost their homes and wandered from place to place, looking for work, or they simply couldn't make it where they were and moved in with relatives or friends who stretched their own meager means to help them. Unemployment insurance and homeless shelters didn't exist. Although there were some minor forms of relief from charities and governments, many would, literally, die before they would accept charity.

Ethel, having contracted TB when her brother died, was ill most of the time. In 1920, she went to Pierre, the capital of South Dakota, with Sam's sister, Ella, and went to a doctor there. She was pregnant and so ill that the doctor performed an abortion because he thought she would not live long.

She and Sam moved in with the Mesicks. She became pregnant again and spent her entire pregnancy in bed. Their son, Elton, was born at home, prematurely, on March 5, 1921. His grandmother kept him warm and alive by placing him in the oven. In the days of wood—and coal-burning stoves, this was possible. Ovens could be kept warm without being too hot, and he managed to survive the hazards of premature birth.

Ethel, still ill with TB in 1922, was told by the doctor that he thought she should go to the TB Sanitarium (always known as "The San") in the Black Hills. This suggestion was vetoed by Grandpa Geist. He thought this was charity, and his family could not accept charity. Ethel spent another year with her folks, and Sam moved to a new place. In 1923, she had another son who lived only one day. In 1924, they moved to Sam's parents' place, and again, Ethel was pregnant, this time having a miscarriage. They moved in 1928 to Charlie Cross' place. Charlie was Sam's brother-in-law. While they were there, Grandpa Geist died on November 23, and Ramona was born the next day. Throughout the twenties, when she was not with her family, Ethel helped Sam with the farming, as well as taking care of the children and home duties. All of this must have been extremely hard for her because she was always ill. In 1930 they built a place near Ethel's folks, and after a family fight, Sam put her into the San.

According to Ethel's memoirs, written when she was well into her eighties, Sam was extremely jealous of every man who came their way—with no provocation on her part, of course. It is hard to see how she might have philandered much in her condition. Ethel also remembered Sam having several different stills on their farms, and selling the bootleg products. They obviously had a very stormy marriage, but none of us ever heard Sam's side, so it's hard to tell how accurate Ethel's memories were.

After all of the foregoing, it's no wonder that Elton spent a great deal of his early childhood with the Mesicks. Sarah adored him, helped him learn to read, and inculcated in him a life-long desire for learning and getting ahead. Sam, too, was a great influence on his life. He was one of those "people" persons who liked, and could get along with, everyone (except, perhaps, his wife) and he really loved his two kids. Meantime, Ethel, although she certainly loved the kids, was probably always tired and ill and often in a violent temper, demanding and impatient with them, and making life quite difficult. For example, she complained strongly enough about Elton's singing voice that he never sang any place for the rest of his life; neither did he ever nod 'yes' or 'no,' in response to a question.

Both Elton and Ramona grew up with a real horror of people who lose their tempers.

The Geists never owned a farm, but leased. Consequently, they moved often, sometimes to barely livable houses. Sam farmed and raised horses, and although they were never well-off, they apparently did well enough—from bootleg sales?—until Sam became ill in 1928. He went to the V.A. hospital in Kansas City for a stay of a month or two. Here, syphilis was diagnosed, and Sam was made aware that little could be done about his heart. I think it interesting that neither Elton nor Ramona ever tested positive for TB or for syphilis, and neither of them ever suffered from either. My personal belief is that they developed antibodies which protected them, not only from those two diseases, but from others as well. They were both very healthy until they were in their seventies.

Ethel and Elton went along with Sam to Kansas City and stayed in a rooming house. This visit to a city was a memorable time for Elton. They returned to the farm shortly before Ramona was born. Before going to the V.A. hospital, Sam turned over the horse-raising business to his brother, Tim, who somehow managed to lose the business. Because Sam was unable to do as much as he once had, things grew more difficult, and these developments coincided with the beginning of the Great Depression and the drought. In February 1932, Ethel was in the San, in Sanator, near Custer in the Black Hills, and Sam went back to the V.A., this time in Hot Springs, South Dakota. The kids went to stay with the Mesicks.

The next year and a half was a difficult and unpleasant period for the entire family. The Mesicks' farmhouse was very small, and shortly after Elton and Ramona moved in, Ruth Mesick Smith also moved in with her husband, Bud, and at least two or three of the six children she would eventually have. As the oldest of the children, though only 11, Elton did chores and helped his grandfather, including milking 22 cows, while Bud *rested*. I think Elton had not found farm life too unpleasant before, but this period was enough to convince him that it was not for him. He always said that the trouble with farm animals was that you had to take care of both ends—feed the front and clean up after the back—something he didn't want to do ever again.

He also didn't want to be poor ever again. Like everyone else in eastern South Dakota, they were poor. The Depression hit with poor prices for farm products, and from 1933, the state suffered a severe drought. Both of these conditions affected farmers very severely. One winter, for instance, they were obliged to use the corn they raised for fuel because they couldn't get enough for the corn to pay for coal. The drought hurt pasturage so badly that the desperate cows were reduced to eating tumbleweed, which made their milk bloody. With little or no money, the population got by as best it could. Truck-farm type farms (those that produce vegetables for the market) are never possible in South Dakota because of the climate and the wide spread of population over a large area, but they did have chickens, eggs and some garden vegetables. Everything else fell by the wayside, like Christmas gifts and new clothes. Elton remembered going to Pierre with one of the Geist families to the swearing-in of a new governor and really feeling his poverty. He had nothing to wear but overalls. He never forgot this, and as an adult, he loved to buy and wear expensive clothes.

In the fall of 1933, Ethel and Sam were released from their hospitals, Ethel apparently cured, but Sam with a bad heart which could not be helped. This was before nitroglycerin tablets, but there was a nitrogen pill he could take. He had intermittent angina attacks which could be relieved only by heat. With only wood-burning stoves and no electricity, generating heat in the middle of the night in a cold climate was difficult to achieve. From the time Elton was twelve, he was often called upon during the night to build a fire to relieve his Dad's pain. Ramona would take over if he were not there.

When they left their hospitals, the family went to a spot on French Creek near Custer where they and a family named Husaboe staked out a mining claim and collaborated on building two houses. Mrs. Husaboe had been a fellow patient of Ethel's at the Sanatorium. These houses were little more than shacks, but the Geists' house had a pleasant living room, a kitchen and two bedrooms. There was no electricity or plumbing, and Elton had to carry the water from a well some distance away. They had a car—a necessity, since their place was more than a mile from Custer. The Mesicks had taken Elton and Ramona to join their parents in October, 1933, and the family was together again.

A year after Sam and Ethel moved, the Mesicks came to visit, and while there, Sarah died. Harry continued to live on the farm in the eastern part of the state, but in later years he spent the winters with the Geists. On French Creek, the Geists continued to struggle mightily. Sam got an occasional small job painting or doing carpentry work, but he was not physically able to do much, even when work was available. There was precious little work available for anyone in those years. Ramona started school in the first grade, but contracted whooping cough and didn't get back to school until the next fall. Meantime, she was very frail and tiny; they decided to buy a goat so that she could have goat's milk. Sam had to sell his rifle to pay for the goat and Elton, of course, had another job—milking the goat!

Sam's health was always a worry and attracted a lot of attention. It's no wonder then that, after her brother's death and Sam's illness, Ethel equated the attention of others during illness with affection and went out of her way to be, or seem to be, ill around her kids. Nevertheless, she pitched in and did whatever she could, and brought home as much as possible, which was still very little, by doing some practical nursing and working at the dime store. Although she had little education or training, she was given work by the Civilian Conservation Corps (CCC), as a teacher, and she taught music—which her mother had taught her—and English. Many of the enrollees were uneducated; many were probably illiterate, and she enjoyed helping some of them find their way. At the same time, she worked hard to keep her kids clean and neat and, as through most of her life, it was difficult for her but she managed to come through. It is really amazing, and a tribute to her courage and determination, that she was able to do all that she did. After we were married, I got along with her, but I always complained a lot about her. Only in recent years have I realized what a really hard life she had, and how much she is to be admired for her hard work, her courage, and her ability to manage under extremely difficult conditions.

In August 1941, the CCC's were phasing out after the draft was instituted, and with Elton going to the School of Mines, the family thought it would be a good idea to move to Rapid City and board and room Mines students. So they moved to Rapid and rented a house with four bedrooms and one bath. This was a wonderful house for all, especially for 13-year old Ramona—with electricity! plumbing! a refrigerator! and an electric washing machine! Ethel still worked at the one CCC camp near Hill City, and got a job with the Red Cross.

Meantime, Sam did the cooking for the Miners, who put up with unimaginative food because they all loved Sam. After the war began, the fellows left one by one to go into the service. The Geists then rented rooms to soldiers' wives, but did not board them. Sam liked the company and they liked him, but he got a little frailer all the time, and died on June 6, 1944.

Things became a little easier, especially after the Air Force opened its base near Rapid. As the wife of a veteran, Ethel had the advantage of finding a job and was assigned to the publications department, where she worked until she retired in 1967. She worked hard, received several awards for her work and was proud of her job. We all got pretty tired of hearing about publications, but were glad she had the job and enjoyed it.

Ethel, Ramona and Granddad stayed on until the war was over, then the family, with Elton's help, built a house which Ethel lived in until 1968. After she retired, Elton taunted her about the fact that Grandma Geist had made quilts all her life, and Ethel took up quilt making. She made several for each member of the family. After a brief try at city living in Cleveland in 1969, she returned to Rapid and bought a very small house which was a perfect place for her to spend the rest of her days. She was a very good housekeeper and a very good money manager. She died in July 1989, owning some nice things, and leaving an estate of about $50,000.

CHAPTER 2

OUR CHILDHOOD AND TEEN-AGE YEARS—DORIS

1921-1941

When my Dad was transferred to the Colorado Springs Office of the Forest Service, located on the upper floor of the Post Office, he moved the family to Colorado Springs rather than Manitou where their families lived. The Springs, as we always referred to the city, was considerably larger than Manitou, with about 35,000 people. It is 6,000 feet above sea level, at the base of Pike's Peak on the Front Range of the Rockies. Its economy was based largely on tourism, but there were also some coal mines and large pottery and printing businesses, as well as Colorado College. A considerable number of wealthy people lived in the Springs, many of whom were there only in the summer months when it was cooler in the mountains. Most of the population was white Anglo-Saxon, but there was a small community of blacks who, at that time, were either household help or were employed in menial jobs in the town. There were many large, old houses in the city, as well as good middle class neighborhoods, and on the west of the city, at the foot of Cheyenne Mountain, stood the Broadmoor Hotel with its lake and elegant homes. It was a lovely town and everyone had a view of Pike's Peak.

We had very little rain, and rainstorms never lasted long—I don't remember ever seeing an umbrella. We certainly didn't have very much rain or snow during the mid-thirties. All the western states suffered from the severe drought that made life so difficult in the Rocky Mountain Empire, including South Dakota. The drought also contributed to the destructive dust storms that blanketed the plains and extended west to the foot of the

Rockies. These dust storms were largely the result of plowing up the plains in the preceding half-century, and it was during the thirties that the science of soil conservation began. When we had one of these dust storms in the Springs, the wind-blown dust collected inside windows and doors, no matter how tightly they fitted.

We used water very sparingly in those days, watering plants with rinse water from dish-washing and clothes-washing. We limited the water we used for everything, because the city's water source was not from the mountains, but from deep wells that were not being rapidly replenished. In a footnote on water it might also be noted that Colorado Springs has a small part in medical history. The well water was heavy with minerals, one of which was fluorine. It was finally determined that this was responsible for the excellent condition of the teeth of those of us born there. The result was the universal fluoridation of water.

Despite drought, rain, or snow, the Springs was an easy town in which to live. We could walk almost anywhere, though there were streetcars, and later buses, too, and there were movie theaters with Saturday matinees. The mountains were there for climbing and there were great open spaces for kite-flying and bicycling, and few restrictions about where or how far we could go.

Although far from the action in World War I—The Great War, it was called—it had an effect on Colorado Springs. My Dad was very active in the American Legion and Mother in its Auxiliary. Both Memorial Day and Armistice Day (November 11) were holidays with parades. I will never forget the veterans marching in these parades—a great many with severe disabilities, including one man whom I particularly remember, whose nose was missing. There was no such thing as plastic surgery or rehabilitation. In my youth, people still spoke of WWI as "the war to end all wars." I think there was some optimism about the League of Nations, but all of that was before the Roeser children arrived.

I was born on October 17, 1922, when my brother, Alan Huber Douglass, was three and a half. When I was two, Jacob Ladum (Jackie until he was an adult, then Jack) was born on October 19, 1924. We three children were similar in several ways: all of us were stubborn, determined and easily angered; each of us had a sense of humor and was reasonably intelligent; we all did well in school. Probably, we all had strong wills and strong personalities. We grew up without a great deal of discipline, unfortunately, and like most children—especially those in odd-numbered families—we squabbled often. But we also played together and got along most of the time.

Shortly after Jackie was born, I developed mastoid infections in both ears and had three operations. My surgeries certainly had a serious and lifelong effect on me, and they probably also had an indirect effect on Jack. While I was in the hospital for a long time, Mother was with me. Jack was fed breast milk from a bottle and was cared for by Grandma Skamser. My Mother always felt that he suffered a sense of neglect as a result of this difficult period. Therefore, when she had the chance, she spoiled him more to make up for it. She felt guilty, too, because she had definitely not wanted a third child. For these reasons, perhaps, Jack turned out to be much more of a problem child than either Alan or I, and challenged both of us all the time.

Alan was a handsome boy, but always spindly and subject to illnesses of various kinds. Like me, he loved to read, and he liked to work with his hands, particularly building the model airplanes that he loved. He read science fiction magazines for years and either suggested I read them, or I asked to read them and I grew up looking everywhere for strange little forms of life from outer space. I've never liked science fiction much since, except for Star Trek in the 80's. Neither of the boys was athletic, although Alan would have tried, had he not been sickly always. This frustrated my poor Dad who really wanted a son who loved athletics as he did.

Jackie was a really cute little boy who may have been hyperactive. He was certainly more active than Alan or I, and at times, he could be almost out of control. Although he was always at his best with other people, Alan and I were always the same, company or not. We grew tired of hearing people rave about Jack, because we knew how naughty and unmanageable he could be at times. Several incidents stand out in my memory. One day when he was six or seven, he got angry at Mother while we were doing dishes, and he went after her with a knife. We grabbed him and no damage was done, but we knew he was serious, and we were all scared. On another occasion, he chased me with a croquet mallet and left several huge dents in the door after I had run through and slammed it behind me—just in time! We lived about two blocks from the Santa Fe Railroad line, and Grandma Roeser's house was a few hundred feet from the railroad trestle used by the Cripple Creek Railroad—we were close to a lot of trains. Whenever a train approached while we were crossing the tracks, Jackie would stand on the tracks until the last possible moment. Everyone screamed at him on these occasions. It's amazing that he survived these tricks, as well as many other silly things.

But he did survive without serious incident and we did have a lot of fun. As members of the Roeser family, we had a lot of special things going for us that many of our friends did not. For one thing, we had two sets of grandparents—the Skamsers, about a mile away (having moved to Colorado Springs in 1920), and the Roesers in Manitou. Christmas was especially nice, since we went to the Roesers' on Christmas Eve and the Skamsers' on Christmas Day, with "Santa Claus" at home on Christmas morning. Another advantage was that our father was a Government employee (highly respected in those days when Government employees were fairly few), with a steady job and, of course, a steady, though certainly not high, income.

These two things became especially important after the depression began in 1932. Because our one grandfather had a shoe repair shop and the other a bakery, and people had to have shoes repaired and buy bread, both of them survived the depression without too much trouble. The depression affected us directly in 1932, when banks all over the country were failing, including the one where my folks lost most of their savings. In other ways, we were not directly affected. But the depression was evident, even to children. Month after month, men by the hundreds, and a very few women, "rode the rails" on trains from one part of the country to another, seeking work. These hobos, as they were known, went from home to home offering to work for some food. Mother always gave them something to eat, and only occasionally had them do some work around the house. We often took clothes or food to a family in the neighborhood, or Christmas trees and gifts, and I clearly remember the haggard look of many of the adults and the shabbiness of their homes. Conversation with anyone was generally about the very hard times most people were experiencing.

We were thankful not to experience any of this personally and I expect most or our neighbors and friends considered us rich. In addition to a steady income, my Dad provided us with a summer home in the mountains at the Fremont Experiment Station, long before summer homes were common. Dad was there a great deal all year, and as soon as school was out, we packed and went up to the Station, usually moving back down on Labor Day—always the day before school started.

Summers on Mt. Manitou were special, and when I think of my childhood, I remember our happy summers there. We were free to roam through the woods, climb on the rocks and play anywhere. We were not strictly limited and I recall no restrictions on how far we could go, but we were told that if we were lost, we should find a stream and follow it downhill which would inevitably get us to town. In any case, I was not adventurous and always too interested in whatever I was doing at home to go far. We had few toys, because moving anything to the Station was difficult. Everything had to be hand-carried up a narrow, hilly trail for a mile, or taken in a very small wagon, about five feet long by two feet wide and deep, drawn by one of the Station's two horses. We played with the materials at hand and a few small toys like small metal cars (filled with paraffin to make them heavier and longer-lasting), jacks, marbles, jackknives and paper dolls. Very few books were available. We couldn't take library books, and we didn't own many. We probably did a lot of typical childhood wailing about "what can I do?" but I don't remember ever being bored. On rainy days we played cards and games.

Our nine months in town were, of course, school days and we walked to school. Columbia grade school was three blocks away, or less, if we cut across the yards in back of us. Columbia had kindergarten and gym in the basement, first through third on the first floor and identical classrooms on the second floor. The kids in the first three grades had all of their studies in the room they were assigned to, but when we got up to the fourth, we moved from room to room for geography, English, history, arithmetic, art and music.

We said the Pledge of Allegiance every morning, but I can't remember if we had a prayer. In 2003, when there was controversy about having the Ten Commandments posted in schools, I couldn't remember whether they were posted at Columbia. I do remember that the picture of the Last Supper was hanging in the hall. I don't know whether it was hung as a famous painting or as a religious statement, but I remember it, because I hadn't learned about Lent and Good Friday, and the title of the picture bothered me terribly. How could this be "the last supper?"

I went through grade school at Columbia, and then went on to North Junior High (perhaps a mile away) which I attended for the 7th grade and half of the 8th grade. Alan attended, and graduated from, Colorado Springs High School, a few blocks from the center of town, and across the street from the Skamsers' house.

There always seemed to be plenty to do when we weren't in school—Girl Scouts for me when I was in the fifth grade, and Boy Scouts for the boys. There were any number of places we could go for Sunday rides and the picnics to which my mother was addicted. The picnics always included a breakfast, often very chilly, on Easter Sunday, after the sunrise service in the Garden of the Gods. My Father was not a picnic person. He went along with them, but spoke from the heart when he said in the midst of one picnic that, "A picnic, at its best, is a dismal failure." This was my feeling too in later years, but like the cards and board games we played whenever we had extra time, picnics just seemed like something one does in life. It took me years to recognize that I really disliked them.

When I was five, we moved to a house on Willamette where we lived from April 1927 until January 1936. It was a lovely house, not a mansion by any means, but a comfortable two-story, three-bedroom house with a front porch, a play room off the kitchen, and sliding doors in the living room. In front, there was a big apple tree, which was great to climb. I remember the three of us climbing the tree and talking about Lindbergh's tremendous solo flight to Paris in 1928.

We enjoyed listening to the radio, which our family purchased about the time of the 1928 election, when Herbert Hoover was elected President. Radio reception was not available on the Mountain, however. No matter what we were doing, we were home at 5:30 p.m. to hear *Little Orphan Annie* and *Jack Armstrong, the All-American Boy*. When I was about twelve, I persuaded Mother to let me stay up to hear *Myrt and Marge* at 9:00 p.m. One of my major disappointments in life was when Wheaties, the sponsor of *Jack Armstrong*, had a contest to find the most three letter words in "Wheaties." I spent days using the unabridged dictionary at the library. To this day, I'm certain I found them all, but no prize was forthcoming. This was even more disheartening than the decoding rings Ovaltine pushed on *Little Orphan Annie*, and which we ordered and waited for patiently, then found disappointing and useless when they arrived.

We found our own entertainment: "work-up" (softball) on the corner lot, the closest thing we had to a baseball diamond; hide-and-go-seek in the long spring dusk; climbing trees; swinging; playing jacks or mumbledly-peg (with jackknives); hopscotch; or jumping rope; playing group games of all kinds in our back yards, and always taking time to sit on the curb to watch the Santa Fe passenger trains go by and count the cars on the freight trains.

Whenever we could, we'd persuade Mother to let us go to the movies and give each of us a dime—twenty five cents after we turned twelve. Since all three of us were tall, we couldn't lie about our ages, as some of our friends did, and pretend we were twelve long after we'd passed it. I loved the Fred Astaire/Ginger Rogers movies, and was so entranced by the Busby Berkeley spectaculars that I was terribly disappointed when I first saw real plays and real nightclubs; what a shame they didn't have all those girls dancing on gigantic typewriter keys! I took piano lessons for about three years (my teacher, by the way, was the widow of a Civil War veteran), then gave it up for a short year of tap and acrobatic dancing—too bad; I was better at the piano!

I loved to read, and walked to the library at least once a week, which meant going by the Skamsers and through downtown. From the time I was ten or so, I often went by myself, sometimes stopping at the dime store which was never filled with many shoppers, for candy or a small purchase. I remember with pleasure my trips to town, finding books of any kind, walking home, and reading as I walked. We were not allowed in the adult library until we were twelve. By then, I felt as though I'd read every book in the children's section. One year we were thrilled when Mother bought a box of books at an auction. There was an old set of the Book of Knowledge encyclopedia, which Jackie read through, and other kinds of books. Mother forbade me to read one of them, presumably because of its sexual connotations. Of course, I began to read that book. But I was soon turned off by the turgid language and descriptions and went no further. I decided then and there that censorship is foolish.

When I was seven, I learned needlework, embroidering dish towels, and when I was about eleven, I was learning Indian beadwork. Grandma Roeser knitted a lot and I found it fascinating, but I did not begin to knit until after we'd moved to Ft. Collins. Because Mother didn't knit, I acquired a book of instructions and taught myself. This so impressed Grandma that, when we went to visit her in Manitou that summer, she sent me to a knit shop to buy yarn and instructions for a sweater. Since then, there has never been a time when I haven't had at least one knitting project in process. I regret not having kept a list of the items I've knitted—literally hundreds, from coats to baby booties. I was much better at coats than booties. I was never able to knit well anything that was small enough for babies.

One thing that greatly affected my life and my development as a person was my hearing loss. From the time I had the mastoid surgery when I was a baby, my hearing was quite seriously impaired and this was a definite disadvantage, both in school and in private. It also resulted in a speech impediment. This was corrected by a speech therapist in 1929 when I was seven or eight. Speech therapy, by the way, was a very new thing. The first testing of speech therapy had taken place in 1927. I had a perpetually draining ear and about 65% hearing. I couldn't use a hearing aid until the transistor type was invented in the 60's or 70's. I never told anyone I had trouble hearing, and most people were not aware of it, but I think now that it made a great difference in my relations with other people, and it may have encouraged me to be something of a loner.

There were technological improvements in those years, but they were being adopted slowly. For example, although refrigerators had been around for some time, we didn't get one until 1934. One invention I remember was the photographic flash bulb which consisted of a bulb with metal inside. It flashed when activated and greatly improved the quality of photography. Our first exposure to it was when Aunt Eunice brought one for one of our Christmases and the bulb itself exploded—a fairly common occurrence—scaring all of us. Eunice was ahead of her time in many ways; she wore two of the first contact lenses ever produced—although she did so in great discomfort! She also skied, long before it was popular, using wood skis clamped to her boots. When she died in 1940, I was given all her personal belongings, including her skis. I still had them when Elton and I moved to the Adirondacks in 1947, but I never tried them.

We saw quite a lot of our grandparents and aunts and uncles, except for my Mother's sister, Eunice, who lived in Philadelphia, and her brother, Dick, in Lincoln, Nebraska. When I was five, and we had our first car (an Essex), we took a ride almost every Sunday and visited one or other of our grandparents. We spent an occasional night or weekend with the Roesers, which I especially liked. They lived in a cute little house on a hill in Manitou and had Nicky, a wonderful German Shepherd. Grandma Roeser was a great cook and always had baked goods from their bakery—day-old, but that didn't bother us. Manitou was fun, with lots of little shops. They were always busy during the summer when the town was full of tourists escaping the heat elsewhere. I believe all three of us sensed more affection from the Roesers than we did from the Skamsers.

The Skamser house was a lovely old residence which was declared an historical site in the '60's. It had three stories with many rooms, some of which they rented out to roomers. Grandma worked very hard, because she did most of the housework herself. We loved to go to the house, except when Mother was socializing, going to a meeting or shopping and we had to go there after school. Although I'm sure Grandma loved us all, she appeared to resent our coming and seemed severe and disapproving. She always gave us a snack of home-made bread with butter and sugar. Because she made bread only once a week and it was dry at its freshest, it was even less appealing when several days old.

We belonged to the First Congregational Church where Alan, Jackie and I were baptized. This was a compromise between the Lutherans and the Catholics, and we attended regularly when we were in town. In the summer we never went to church. Dad sang in the choir and Mother was always active in women's activities. I went to the Methodist church when I was 12 because Alice Petheram, daughter of our good friends, went there; I joined her for their confirmation process. I must say I couldn't see any difference. I always liked church and Sunday school, and somewhere I learned to have a deep and abiding faith in God and in Jesus Christ. But I have no memory of the sacraments or any theology I may have been taught.

Vacations were not as common then as they are now. I remember our family having only two. In the summer of 1933, we took a memorable week-long trip to Carlsbad Caverns in New Mexico. It was a two-day drive in our old Essex, mostly on two-lane dirt roads. We stayed at "cabin courts" where there were communal bathrooms and we had to provide our own linens. Motels as we know them were far in the future. The Caverns were spectacular, especially the exit at dusk of the hundreds of thousands of bats. I don't like caves at all, but this cave is fantastic. Our other vacation was in 1934 when we drove to Lincoln, Nebraska, to spend a few days with my Mother's brother, Dick Skamser, and his family. My Mother always worried that someone would be cold, so the car was full of sweaters and coats even though it was the hottest summer they'd ever had. I believe it was over 100° all the time we were there. There was no air conditioning at the time, and hundreds of people took their pillows to the Capitol lawn to get a little cooler night air.

In 1935, we saw the end of our summers on Mt. Manitou and our subsequent move to Ft. Collins, Colorado, on January 1, 1936. In our last fall in the Springs in 1935, I was 13 and my life was changing in all respects, including a little kissing in the alley with Dwayne Dykstra. My parents' lives were also changing. At about this time, they had the kind of marital problems common to couples in their early forties. Another woman was involved; there were tears, threats, fights and gloom on all sides. My Mother's greatest quality was a natural cheerfulness and sense of humor. She always joked and laughed and played games of every kind, and made it fun to be at home. When this quality deserted her, as it did for a few years, life seemed very depressing. My Dad was transferred to Ft. Collins, because of the closing of the Fremont station, and on a dreary New Year's Day, we drove up to Ft. Collins to live. Aunt Eunice, Mother's sister, was living there at that time, working for the Forest Service. Her presence was a bright spot in our lives.

We lived in Ft. Collins for 2½ years, or at least Mother, Jack and I did. Alan joined us after he finished his senior year in Colorado Springs while living with the Skamsers. Nine months after we moved, Dad was transferred to Custer, South Dakota—I think at his request. My impression, although we were not told this, is that my parents were involved in a trial separation. At 13, I was too much involved in my own adolescence to care about the details unless they affected my immediate well-being, but Dad's transfer affected my life, and I missed him.

I found our move to Ft. Collins very hard and I hated the place at first, beginning a pattern familiar to me now from long experience. I've always hated change and everything about a new place, but I adjust quite rapidly.

Once I've had a little time to settle down, I'm adjusted, and I hate leaving that place as much as I did the one before. It's hardest for everyone to move the first time, and Ft. Collins was a small, unwelcoming farm center, full of retired farmers, conservative middle-class people, and a few associated with the land grant A&M (Agriculture and Mechanical Arts—called Aggies for short) College there. I felt there had never been another new girl in my class in the 8th grade and I felt that I would never get acquainted. I will forever have a soft spot in my heart for the one boy who gave me (and all the others in my class!) my one and only Valentine.

My adjustment then, as since, was made more difficult by my hearing deficiency. I made some embarrassing mistakes by not accurately hearing instructions. Nevertheless, by the time I was out of the 8th grade I'd made a group of friends, especially Betty Stamper who lived about 3 blocks away from us, and we walked to and from school together. Going home, we stopped on a corner midway to talk, then I walked home with her and she walked home with me. It took us a long time to get home! We had great fun together and remained friends until we were in our forties.

We went to all the movies we could, usually at a showing in the late afternoon for which we saved part of our lunch money. We adored Clark Gable, Jimmy Stewart and Tyrone Power, talked on the phone, biked up into the foothills, went on picnics and, of course, went to school. In the summer we swam in the local lake. In the summer of 1937, Mother, Jack and I spent a few interesting weeks in Glenwood Springs. Again, I think this had something to do with my parents' relationship. We spent a lot of time in the hot springs swimming pool, and the rest of the time, I read. Back in Collins, we lived through a serious polio epidemic, we moved into another house, Alan started school at Colorado A & M, Jackie went on to Junior High and I went to High School for my sophomore year.

Since the 9th grade was in the High School, I had two good years there. Ft. Collins had a big, consolidated high school, and it was fun with all those big kids and getting crushes on some of the senior boys. I particularly benefited from the Latin and Spanish I took, from a couple of excellent English teachers, an arts and crafts course and a Social Science course. The teacher of the latter course was very interested in current events, and he made 1937 and 1938 exciting years for us. This period was the beginning of the Nazi Putsch into Austria and Czechoslovakia, and the abdication of King Edward VII in England.

When we were not in school, I went to the Methodist church with Betty, and we belonged to the youth group, Christian Endeavor, and loved the church activities. Once I was adjusted, things were fine for me, though probably difficult for the rest of the family. It was during this period that *Snow White* was released and, for some reason, I was dubbed Dopey after one of the dwarfs, and kept the nickname even after we left Collins—which we did in June, 1938.

The boys went to Colorado Springs to stay with the Roesers and work in the bakery, and Mother and I drove to Custer, where Dad had rented a house for the summer. The house was owned by the Superintendent of Schools, Mr. Lindsey. It was an interesting, pleasant, though somewhat lonesome summer. Everyone (except, perhaps, some of the unattached women in town) was happy to meet Jack's wife and daughter, and I enjoyed being the only child. We drove all over the Hills, Dad taught me to drive, and I went with Mother and Dad to dances in the Community Center and worked on the Gold Discovery Days pageant. The pageant was presented July 27-29 every year and everyone took part. I played the center of the bluebell in the *Dance of the Flowers*—a role without much action and very hard to describe. I met a few of my future classmates, but didn't have much contact. That summer, by the way, there was a tremendous influx of grasshoppers all over South Dakota. They covered every inch of the ground, flew up pants legs, ate everything in sight, including fence posts and clothes hanging on the line, and created a constant hum. They were not pleasant company, but fortunately, they were gone in a month or so.

Towards the end of the summer I rode with a friend of my parents to Ft. Collins, went to a Methodist summer camp for a week with Betty, then stayed with her for a few days. In August, Mother and I drove to Colorado Springs to pick up the boys, then returned to Custer, just in time to move into another house, a funny little fairy-tale-looking house, a mile from town. I started school with Jackie at Custer High where, in the first day in Chemistry class (there should be a trumpet fanfare here), I first met Elton.

Elton

Obviously, I know less about Elton's life as a child than about my own. His was a fairly typical farm life, which meant, among other things, that there were many animals needing to be tended. The Geists had chickens, cows, horses and pigs and one or more dogs and cats. From an early age he had chores to do. First, he collected the eggs, fed the chickens and helped to clean up the coop. They always had a flock of upwards of 100 chickens, so cleaning the coop was a big job, even though he got considerable help from his Dad. His major comment about the chickens was that they were dirty.

Needless to say, the dirt involved was not to his liking. He loved horses, but objected to the work involved in feeding them and the cleaning of the stables. He also helped "slop" the pigs, and as soon as he was old enough, he was given the job of getting the cows into the pasture and back home again. They were brought into the barn every night, milked morning and night, and then put back out to pasture. This was hardest when he lived with his grandparents. Because the cows had grazed in one field so long that there was nothing left to eat, he had to take them to another field a mile or so away. A couple of the older cows, resisting change as much as we do, persisted in going towards their old pasture; each day he had trouble getting them headed in the right direction.

Until the family moved to the Black Hills, Elton rode a horse to and from the small country schools he attended. He didn't start school until he was second grade level, having been taught at home by Grandma Mesick. His first school had twelve pupils. He was the youngest—a cute little blond, blue-eyed kid who escaped the blows used by the teacher to keep order. He was in a couple of other schools, still smaller. It was interesting to note the differences in our early education. He absorbed the lessons of the older kids and probably did not have very much directed at his level, so he gained a lot of knowledge about geography, science, and history, but seemed to have missed some elementary English like grammar and spelling. And he had very little instruction in such special subjects as art and music.

Although he was the only child until he was eight, he had a myriad of Geist cousins and saw them surprisingly often, considering the distances between their homes. One family, the Walls, with children near Elton's age "dropped in" every Sunday for dinner, much to Ethel's annoyance. Twin cousins, children of Nevada Cross, spent one year with Sam and Ethel after their mother died and their father was away, apparently looking for work. They were a couple of years older, but they were company for Elton. He always loved Ramona. She was born on November 21, 1928, but because of the age difference, she was not much company for him.

As mentioned earlier, in February, 1932, Elton and Ramona went to live with the Mesicks and spent a very difficult year and a half. This was probably harder for Elton than for four year old Ramona, because he had to help Granddad with the cows, the milking, and any other work that had to be done. He probably wasn't happy either with the small house, full of Ruth (the Mesicks' daughter) and Bud (her husband) and their children, as well as Ramona and he. They did not see their parents during that time, and for all these reasons, Elton's move to the Custer area was probably not especially difficult for him. It removed him from some of those chores, reunited him with his Mom and Dad and brought him to the Black Hills. He enrolled in the seventh grade in the Custer school system and, although his education had probably not been as thorough as it might have been, he didn't appear to have suffered because of it.

Custer was small, perhaps 1,500 people, but the population was increased considerably during the early thirties by people driven from their farms in the Eastern part of the state by hard times and drought. They moved to the Black Hills where many of them (like the Geists) staked mining claims or simply squatted in the woods. They lived as well as they could from the little they could grow, the few jobs available, and the meat they could hunt. This included some animals not usually considered great eating. The Geists did not join in this. There was wood to keep them warm and they could cook what food they had.

The area was also playing host to the employees of several Civilian Conservation Corps (CCC) camps. The CCC was implemented by President Roosevelt to give young men a way to support themselves and their families and work at something useful. They each received a stipend which they were required to send home. They ate in mess halls and experienced army discipline (administered by a military contingent assigned to the camps) and were given some schooling. There were several camps in forests in the Custer area because there was a great deal of work to do. They cleared the woods, built dams, prepared camp grounds, helped in fighting forest fires, and worked closely with the Forest Service. They left many lasting monuments to a very successful program. Many of the young enrollees were from urban areas, but local boys also enrolled, including four members of the family of Dale Johnson (Elton's brother-in-law), my brother, Alan, and many of our friends.

The Geists lived on French Creek, a mile and a half from town. There were no buses, so the kids had to be driven to school, ride with someone or walk. I believe Elton walked most of the time, although the family did have a '36 Plymouth by the time I knew him. Poor as they were, a car was an absolute necessity.

They were very poor. Sam wasn't able to work at a steady job and although Ethel had no education or training, she did whatever she could, including some practical nursing, some clerking in the dime store and later on teaching in CCC camps. Elton worked throughout high school at what jobs he could find, including work at a gas station, helping with logging and as flagman at a construction site. And he had to take care of the home chores of carrying water, building fires, and all of the other tasks required. Between the three of them they managed, though barely, to keep body and soul together. There was never enough food, and sometimes none, but Ethel managed to keep Elton and Ramona clean and decently dressed.

One thing that must have helped a little was the knowledge that most of those in the area were in the same boat. The people in the Forest Service (including my Dad), some merchants, the manager of a small mining facility and the doctors, banker and dentist were the only ones who seem to have lived at all comfortably. Certainly, the merchants and medical people had a lot of difficulty with unpaid bills. The Geists had a running account at a local store operated by a kind grocer. He carried them for quite awhile and earned their great gratitude. This was a tremendous help but it worried and shamed Sam and Ethel and left Elton with an abiding dread of being in debt.

Elton was a good student and he was well-liked. He was on the first string of the football team for his sophomore, junior and senior years. Somehow, between school, football and all the work he had to do at home, he found time for the Boy Scouts. He became an Eagle Scout. The troop took a trip to Yellowstone one summer—a high spot in the lives of the boys. Custer didn't have the cliques you usually find in a high school, but if there had been, he would have been in THE group. The boys liked him, but so did the girls. He was "cute," smart, well-mannered and a nice guy with a great sense of humor. When he was in high school he acquired the name "Pinky" because of his ruddy complexion and pinkish blonde hair. He didn't like the name, but found it a little better than "Sonny," as he had been called by the family. I thought of him only as Pinky until we'd been married about five years and he finally managed to lose it and become "El," usually misstated as "Al."

On the first day of school everyone met in the gym for directions and instructions. I looked around and found there were several other new girls and I was sure they were all more attractive than I. This was very important since I really wanted to find a boy friend and, like most girls, believed looks were important. But looking back now, I can see that I was really quite an attractive 16 year old—I was tall (5'9"), had a nice figure, shiny brown hair which I always managed well, good skin, nice eyes and I was told I had good legs. I always liked to talk and laugh and I was a smart girl. I expect all the boys thought I was a possible date, including Elton. He was slightly taller than I, well-built, blonde and blue eyed and always clean and well groomed. Certainly a possible boy friend! He was a year ahead of me but we were in the same chemistry class. The first day of his senior year when we met in class, we didn't have any great moment of knowing about the future (Elton always claimed that what he foresaw was "doom"), but we were both quite taken with each other.

Our Courtship

It wasn't until Christmas Eve, 1936 that we got together. There was a special program at the Custer Community Church (Methodist) and I went with my Mom and Dad. The other kids from the Youth Group were going caroling after the program and my friend Dolores said "Pinky will take you home." My parents said okay. I went caroling with the gang and afterwards, Pinky and I took the Rev. Walter Ross out into the country to deliver a Christmas basket. While we waited, Elton kissed me and we were both pretty well hooked from then on. We stayed out until 2:00 a.m., after taking Rev. Ross home. We picked up Elton's close buddy, Dale Johnson, went to Lillian Broyle's for a chat, stopped in the Coffee Shop for a coke and then parked for a bit, doing a little necking in the back seat while Dale sang cowboy songs in the front. When we started to go home the car got stuck in the mud and snow and it took a while for the fellows to push it out. Needless to say, my family was upset at the late hour, but I had a wonderful time.

We both spent the rest of the vacation thinking about each other, but it wasn't until the end of January that we started going together. I immediately broke up with the guy (a geek they would call him now) I'd been dating, Sid Manary; by February, Elton and I were going steady. The school paper that month assigned a theme song to people; ours was *This Can't be Love*. But I guess it was. It even survived a blow when the state championship basketball tournament was held in Phillips. Elton was able to use the family car and take some others to the games, but he didn't ask me to go along. I was so upset I knitted a sweater for myself during that weekend. I realized he didn't have any money and, of course, the others paid for the gas, so I was ready and waiting when he picked me up on Sunday night for the youth group meeting.

Elton graduated in June, worked at a gas station and went to the Civilian Military Training Corps camp in Bismarck, North Dakota, for a month—not so much for the training as for the stipend they paid those who attended. In the fall he continued at the gas station, but Rev. Ross persuaded a missionary friend to lend him $300 and in January he enrolled at South Dakota School of Mines in Rapid City. (I didn't know about this loan, and Elton didn't know the money was a loan, so we were both surprised when the lady wrote us in 1948 and asked us to repay her. Of course, we did.) He lived in the home of some people who provided him with food and shelter in return for help around the house and yard for a few weeks, but Mrs. Schwander was upset with his lack of manners and asked him to leave. Fortunately, Mr. Schwander found a place for him to room and board and paid for the rest of that year. He had very little money but managed to get through the first year.

For Christmas 1939, my family went to Colorado Springs to be with Grandma and Grandpa Skamser and Aunt Eunice, who was very ill with stomach cancer. To our great sorrow, she died in May, 1940. That Christmas I knitted my first sweater for Elton, whom I obviously thought of as a really big man. He was kind enough to wear it once, but it was a sleeveless V-neck that he eventually gave to a 6'4", 250 pound friend—after some alterations to make it smaller!

After Elton graduated, I enjoyed my senior year and "fooling around" with the other girls, including forming a club called the GBWD's. I don't think anyone ever told what the name was, partly because it was a dumb name—"Gee, But We're Dumb." I had my one and only pajama party with the group at my house and it was the event of the year. When there was a major new movie in Rapid City we drove over to see it. The most important one was *Gone With The Wind*. I took part in any school activities I could, like plays and ball games, and helped the family move again—this time from the nice house on the hill that we had moved into in January 1939 to another house across the street. I entertained my friend, Betty Stamper, for a month in the summer of 1940.

I graduated in June, 1940 after a senior skip day with some of the other girls to a ghost town in Wyoming, accompanied by too much wine. My grades should have made me salutatorian of the class, but a rule requiring four years at the school denied me the privilege. It didn't matter much since there was no scholarship or other award attached, but I was pretty angry when the next year they broke the rule for another 2-year student.

Whenever Elton was in Custer, we got together and spent a good bit of time in the football field parking area in back of the high school, up on Big Rock and every other secluded place we could find. There wasn't much to do in Custer and he didn't have any money anyway, so we spent much of our time in the Plymouth. We did have some other activity besides parking. With Mary Kay Bristol, Ray Chard, Mary Ellen Smith, Dale and others we went on hikes, picnics and steak roasts; we went to the movies, and when we had the money and a car (and the 25 cents it cost to buy a gallon of gas), we drove to Hot Springs and swam in the big pool there. In the summer, we swam in Lake Doran and at Hazelrodt, and we sometimes rowed on Sylvan Lake and then coasted our cars down the hill to the main road—a very risky business, but fun. We climbed Harney Peak to see the sunrise at least once every summer. Harney Peak was the highest mountain in the Black Hills.

In July, 1940 Elton again went to CMTC and I spent a good bit of time with a classmate, Dean Gillette. He was a rather low-class guy, but I had quite a crush on him for a while. Elton was pretty unhappy, but by the time I left for my first year of college we were past all of that. I had a job for a while as maid to a working couple, but I was too inexperienced and incapable. They didn't keep me long. In July we had Gold Discovery Day, and this time I was a "Wind" in the *Dance of the Wind and the Rains*.

We had gab fests in the homes of friends and in the drug store. In 1940 we talked a lot about the ongoing war in Europe and the upcoming presidential election and Roosevelt running for an unprecedented third term. That year the draft was initiated, with the guarantee that those drafted immediately would be home in a year. One of the big hit songs was *Goodbye, Dear, I'll be Home in a Year*. We were all sure that eventually America would be in the war.

In September I started my college days at Colorado State A & M in Ft. Collins, and resumed my friendship with Betty, but as an out-of-towner, I now lived in a dorm and made other friends. There were two interesting things about my dorm life: (1) When I started school that fall there were only three girls out of about 200 who smoked; by the end of the year only two others and I did not; I'd tried, but just couldn't finish a cigarette. (2) The other thing is that I got the highest grades among the dorm girls that year. I was majoring in chemistry, thinking I'd like to go into medicine, and I did well. I joined the drama club and enjoyed that. Among other jobs, I was in the choir in *Our Town*, which sang *Blessed be the Tie That Binds* which has ever since made me think of that play. I didn't have (or want) much social life or dates. At homecoming time, Mother, Jack and Pinky came to Ft. Collins and stayed at Betty's. I had thought we might go to the dance, but Pinky didn't bring, or didn't have, suitable clothes, so we just spent the time together. My roommate, Inez Schultz, was from a farm family; she was very naive and provincial—even more so than I—and we had little in common. Nevertheless, she invited me to her home for Thanksgiving.

At Christmas I got a ride to Custer and spent two wonderful weeks enjoying my home, my friends and Custer. And, of course, Elton! Then back for another semester at "Aggies" before beginning the summer of 1941 at home. That year I found a job as a waitress at Tina's. I didn't like it much because I was an outsider to the other waitresses. The job did, however, teach me how to carry two plates at once! Elton was working at various jobs—digging post holes for the phone company (where he worked with my brother, Jack) and as a flagman on a road job. I was very disturbed about our relationship. In those days, "nice girls" didn't have sex before marriage, and although we had no basis of any kind for marriage, except our feelings for each other, I persuaded him that we had to get married. Hence, 1941 was an important year for us.

Back Row Josephine, Jacob Jr. (Jack), and Edmund Roeser
Front Row: Frieda Eugenia and Jacob Roeser, 1918

Jacob Jr. (Jack) and Cora Roeser   Frieda and Jacob Roeser—1948

Clara Ladum Skamser, 1890   Christ Skamser, 1890

The Skamser Family
Back Row: Thelma, Richard, Eunice Carl and Cora.
Front: Clara and Christ

Roeser Family—Summer 1950
Back Row: Alan, Lois (Lui), Betty, Jack, Elton, Doris
Front Row: Great Grandmother Frieda Roeser, Daille,
Cora Roeser, Gregg, Jack Roeser holding Jim Roeser,
Walt Nelson (Lois' son)

Roeser Grandchildren—July 1962
Jim, Gregg holding Craig, Daille, Sally and Carola

Jack and Cora Roeser 50th Anniversary Dec. 29, 1967
Back Row: Harry Kliewir, Carl Skamser, Walt Nelson, Alan Roeser,
Amy Skamser, Jack Roeser, Doris and Elton Geist, Jim Roeser
Middle Row: Husband of Roeser Cousin, Ruth, Cousin Ruth, Lois Roeser,
Jo Kliewer, Phoebe Skamser, Betty Roeser, Carola and Sally Roeser
Front: Lois' Mother, Jack Roeser, Cora Roeser, Craig Roeser

Cora and Jack Roeser—50th
Anniversary

Jack Roeser in Brazil—
Dec. 1969

Geist Family after Grandpa died, 1927
L to R: Irene, Ord, Ella, Tim, Glen, Carrie, Gertie, Earl,
Grandma Geist, Sam, Katie, Persis Nevada and Will (half brother)

Grandma Geist, ca. 1950

Elton, Ramona, Grandmother Mesick,
Henry and Rosa Smith, about 1932

Elton's Father, Sam Geist

Geist House in Custer, 1930's

Panning for gold on French Creek in Black Hills, N.D

Elton's parents, Ethel and Sam Geist, 1943

Doris and Elton with Gregg, 1943

Ethel, Elton and Ramona, 1946

Ethel Geist, 1965

Mt. Manitou Incline Railway, 1962
Doris in scarf, Gregg, Daille, Jack Roeser

Fremont Experimental Station, 1920
Alt. 8,850 feet, reached by the Incline

At Fremont Station, about 1931
Alan, Jack, Doris and Prince

Mother, Alan, Doris and Jack, about 1938

Doris, High School Senior, 1940

Elton, High School Senior, 1939

CHAPTER 3

THE WARTIME YEARS

1941

This was a momentous year in history. World War II (WWII) had been raging in Europe for the past two years. Everyone we knew, and, no doubt, most Americans (except perhaps some Ivy League professors) believed the U.S. would eventually become involved. This was ironic, since many still spoke occasionally of WWI as the "war to end all wars."

Except for the threat of war, the economy was finally looking up, although times were still hard in 1941. The drought was over, the grasshoppers that had infested the state in 1939 and 1940 were gone, and finding employment was a little easier. Armament manufacturing and ship building were picking up all across the country, and quite a few Custer people headed to the West Coast. Every one of our generation living in Custer worked at whatever jobs were available—pumping gas, waiting tables, working in the woods, mines or on road repair crews—and there were a few more jobs available in the Black Hills that summer. We were paid very little—$1.00 a day, or 10 cents an hour was pretty standard—and although prices were low, they were still high for people with little income.

Most people today would consider our homes in 1941 pretty primitive. I knew no one with more than one bathroom until I was well into my twenties. And many who lived outside town, like Elton's family, had no electricity or plumbing. No family had two cars and few kids owned one, but in the Black Hills a car was a necessity and we shared our family cars whenever needed. Looking back now, I think the general mood that summer was pretty upbeat, and I was in love. Our decision to get married changed everything for us, not only that summer but for the next sixty-three years.

Although I think Elton wanted to be married as much as I did, it was I who insisted. It's hard for young people in the early 21st century to understand that when I was young in the 1930's, the entire culture, from ministers, parents and on down, preached "nice girls do not have sex until they are married." Of course this did not mean that nice girls didn't have sex outside marriage. It meant that they sneaked, lied and felt guilty, and in some cases, managed to have abortions. In other cases they had shotgun weddings. For anyone who doesn't know what that is, it was a man marrying a pregnant woman under threat of her father's gun. In our small high school's '39 and '40 classes, there were at least four other couples who certainly had sex, and married right after graduation—lasting marriages in every case. With this built-in indoctrination, I felt that Elton and I really had to get married and it sent us off 40 miles to Newcastle, Wyoming on July 9, 1941, when we both had the afternoon off from our jobs, his as a flagman and mine waiting tables.

We went to Newcastle because South Dakota required a test for syphilis before a marriage license could be issued and, since we both tested negative when we enrolled in college, we thought we could skip that. We found a Methodist minister, and Elton went off to get the license. He also bought a ring at the dime store and asked the local newspaper not to publish the marriage since we intended to keep it secret indefinitely. I did not become a feminist until many years later, but I did notice that the word "obey" was not in our very brief ceremony. We went back to Custer to work, had a few hours at the foot of Big Rock Mountain and went off to our parents' homes and to bed. A few days into our marriage, we drove to Deadwood for their annual "Deadwood Days" celebration, where we were first photographed together as a married couple—in a carnival booth.

Beyond doubt, we were foolish. I was 18, Elton 19 (though we both put 21 on the license). Recently I asked my 30 year-old granddaughter when she had acquired the small tattoo I had just noticed. She said, "When I was 18." I asked her why, and she said, "Because I was 18." This same attitude was certainly a contributing factor to our marriage. We had no money, no home, no education, no careers, and, obviously, no sense. As time went on, it was also apparent that neither of us was in any way mature enough for marriage. We had little thought for the future. It seems to me now that we were more this way at that time than most young people. Perhaps this was because we were sure we would be at war and all the young men would enlist or be called up. In any case, Elton and I certainly had no plans or thoughts for the future when we decided to elope, but we did love each other and were committed to marriage and a lasting commitment.

I've come to believe that people have inner voices, intuition, or whatever you choose to call it, that tells them when they've met the right mate. I've known many who married the day after they met, or decided immediately after meeting that they would marry and it is amazing that most of these marriages work out happily. In our case, I believe I needed Elton's steadfastness, calm, never losing his temper, ambition and easy relationship with anyone; he needed my optimism, cheerfulness, love of fairness and justice. We recognized each other's intelligence and sense of humor, but other qualities were not obvious until later. In any case, despite the many ups and downs ahead, we both believed then, as I believe now, we were meant to be mates.

In 1941, we only knew that we were crazy about each other. But after our little, but momentous, trip to Wyoming, Elton and I went on as we had, living in our respective homes and working. We helped celebrate Custer's annual "Gold Discovery Days." I played the role of Calamity Jane on a float in the parade, and both Elton and Jackie had roles in the Pageant. Elton was working as a flagman on a road project and I worked as a waitress at Tina's until some time in August when it was time to go back to school. Meantime, I'd persuaded my folks to let me transfer to the South Dakota School of Mines (Mines for short) and at about the same time, the Geists decided they would find a house in Rapid City and room and board students. My Mother and I found a room for me at a Mrs. Craig's. The Geists found the house at 23 East St. Joe, rented it and moved in. We began our school year at Mines right after Labor Day.

I was one of only eight coeds, all of whom were pretty much ignored by the male students, but I held my own in all my classes and did very well. I was majoring in organic chemistry and Elton, by that time, in metallurgical engineering. My sex was an advantage in some classes, for instance, physics. It was taught by a non-engineering type whose explanations made good sense to me, but eluded many of the budding engineers. It was certainly not an advantage in others. The professor of calculus, which Elton and I took together, had taught since the school was founded, but had never had a woman student in class—we were sure he'd never had a woman—and I was too much for him. If I moved a chair or disturbed the class in any way, he reprimanded Elton because we always sat together. He seemed to think Elton was responsible for my behavior.

We had not told anyone we were married, and it's hard to tell how long we could have kept it secret—we were not especially discreet. I studied at the Geists' home and when everyone had gone to bed, we made love in the living room. This was pretty obvious to Sam but he said nothing and was relieved when he finally learned we were married. Predictably, I became pregnant and had a miscarriage, and we had to tell. Although at eighteen I was sure I knew everything, I knew absolutely nothing about pregnancy, except that sex caused it and when you got pregnant your periods stopped. When I missed a period around Labor Day, I knew I was pregnant, a conclusion confirmed shortly thereafter when I had a mild case of morning sickness.

I continued to go to school until I began to bleed one day in November. My ignorance kept me from going to a doctor, so it was a few days before I called one and made an appointment. I walked downtown to his office and by the time I got there, I was hemorrhaging and needed help. Fortunately, this happened in the doctor's office. They put me to bed and sent me to the hospital while Elton waited for me in the library until it closed, having no idea what had transpired. I persuaded a nurse to call him at home. He came to see me, then went home and told his folks and called mine in Custer. I suppose he used a "good news/bad news" format—"Doris has had a miscarriage, but it's okay—we're married!" Of course, they all had a little trouble sorting out the good news from the bad. My parents rushed over from Custer to Rapid and we had a long talk. My Mom and Sam thought we should get the marriage annulled; my Dad and Ethel sensibly thought that that wasn't the answer, as it wouldn't have been. We simply would have gotten married again. I was in hospital for several days over Thanksgiving, and then I went to Custer to recuperate and rest before returning to school and deciding how to deal with this new situation.

Like everyone else in the U.S., our lives were severely disrupted on the afternoon of December 7. I was reading when my friend, Mary Kay Bristol, stopped in to tell me that the Japanese had attacked Pearl Harbor. Despite the warring activities of Japan in the Far East for several years, no one anticipated that Japan would propel us into the war. This news changed everything. Our declaration of war with the Axis countries (Germany and Italy) soon followed.

I returned to Rapid and to school and finished the year, as did Elton. My Mother didn't want to publish our wedding news right away. I never knew why, but I really think it was her way of avoiding the truth. Since they had planned to go to Lincoln to Uncle Dick's for Christmas, they went ahead with their plans and I went with them. Elton spent the holiday at Dale's home—our first Christmas "together." We had an interesting trip down to Nebraska. Jack and I sat in the back and sang *Chattanooga Choo Choo*, trying over and over to copy the Glen Miller arrangement, until we got to Sioux City where we had to replace a tire and ran into our first wartime experience. The Government had put a freeze on tires and was rationing gas within a few days. Dad managed to get a used tire and we went on our way. Christmas was pleasant, but I wasn't sorry when the few days were over and we headed back to South Dakota.

1942

Elton and I spent New Year's Eve on a cold bus to Rapid, where I moved into the Geist house in a makeshift room in the basement. I remember Sam telling Granddad Mesick that we were married and he said, "I know," since he knew we were sleeping together (shades of that "nice girls don't have sex without marriage") and in his mind, we were the same as married. He was surprised when he learned the truth.

There were five Mines students staying at the house (seven rooms, a basement and one bath!) along with Sam, Ethel, Ethel's Father, Granddad Mesick, Ramona, Elton and I. Though the program was phasing out, Ethel was still teaching at a CCC camp and staying-over at the camp, about 30 miles away. She'd become very seriously involved with a young man who came back to Rapid with her occasionally, making all of us very uneasy. When the camp closed, she got a job with the Red Cross and, by the next year, a job with the new Ellsworth Air Base, built near Rapid. From about the time they moved to Rapid she'd been pretty much out of it—perhaps somewhat doped up on something—and contributed little to the household, except some cleaning and ironing and her low, but very important, pay. Sam did the cooking, which was pretty basic and consisted of a lot of pancakes, wieners and potatoes. He also did the laundry and Ramona and I helped as much as possible.

Although my Mother had insisted that I be fitted with a diaphragm (no one wanted me to be pregnant again, and my parents were still supporting me), passion triumphed over discretion and I became pregnant about the beginning of April. I suffered more morning sickness than before, partly because of the odor of all those wieners! Elton was beginning to feel he should volunteer for the service. More and more of the fellows were enlisting, including Dale Johnson, who had roomed with the Geists. He enlisted in the Navy and was gone by February. South Dakota, like most of the western states, had trouble filling its draft quota because patriotism led all eligible young men to enlistment, although engineering students could be deferred.

We completed our year at school, and then Elton went to work temporarily for one of the construction companies working on the Air Base. In June he got a job with the Homestake Mining Company in Lead (pronounced "leed"), South Dakota. Lead was a nice little "company town." Hearst owned everything and all employment was connected with the mine in some way. Actually it was our first mining camp. We moved our few belongings to a very small apartment in the Gries Apartments on the main street in Lead and had a "real" life for about three months. Elton was on underground shift work and really liked the experience of working in a mine while I learned to keep house and cook, knitted and read. I spent most of one day watching a fire, a block away, burn down the Hearst Company Store. This was an old-fashioned company store that sold everything from needles, seeds, towels and rakes to cars. Homestake employees charged their purchases, and payment was deducted from their wages, which meant that many of them actually "owed their lives to the company store."

Elton and I enjoyed our brief stay in Lead and we were sorry, though it was probably a good thing for us and the U.S., when the Government ordered all gold mines to be closed for the duration, and all employees, except for skeleton crews, had to be laid off. Elton decided (without consulting me, though I would have agreed) that we should return to Rapid and he should continue his education while we waited for the baby, due about December 15. This time we had a new room in the basement in the house on St. Joe, barely big enough for the bed, a bed with slats that were a little short and fell out with the least provocation. When we sat on its edge, for instance, the noise led to much kidding. The room had just been painted when we arrived and I became very ill, not knowing that paint fumes are bad for pregnant women. I am sure I came very close to losing the baby.

Elton finally enlisted in the Air Force on November 28, 1942. While he was waiting to be called up, he worked as a bellhop at the Harney Hotel, and finished his schoolwork, the first courses of which really crystallized his desire to become a metallurgist.

1943

In December, when the students were gone, we moved upstairs from the basement to the master bedroom. My Dad brought me a nice little tree that I could take to the hospital with me, and I spent most of a month sitting on the bed waiting for the baby, playing solitaire, reading and listening to the radio. *I'm Dreaming of a White Christmas* was new that year and was played constantly. This song always reminds me of those days. I waited all through Christmas, and on January 8, the doctor prescribed huge doses of castor oil and orange juice to start labor. This worked well enough to send me to the hospital, but not to cause continuous labor. I went home again for two more days then back to the hospital and I was finally in labor for 12 hours or more, not making any progress. At 10:00 p.m. an x-ray was taken and the doctor decided I must have a Caesarean. Anyone familiar with today's medical advances for pregnancy would not believe that an x-ray wasn't taken sooner, but this demonstrates the difference in medical procedure in those days. By the way, the total hospital and medical bills were less than $100.

Gregg David was delivered by Caesarean at 2:00 a.m. on January 12 with Elton and my Mother present. Despite the excitement during the previous days, Daddy did very well in his final tests. Ethel had chosen to take a bus tour to California that week to visit her boy friend. I was in pretty bad shape, but happy to have delivered a son. When I was discharged from the hospital about 10 days later, we went to the Geists' house and stayed there until Elton was called up to the Army Air Force on February 22. Gregg and I spent most of the duration of the war with my folks in Custer. Before Elton left, we had a photo taken of the three of us, a reminder for me that we now had a little family of our own. While I lived in Custer, Mother, Dad, Gregg and I occasionally visited the Geists, who were renting rooms to servicemen and their wives, but not boarding them.

When Elton was called up, he was sent to Jefferson Barracks near St. Louis where he took his basic training for more than a month. He was then sent to Superior State Teacher's College in Wisconsin for preliminary flight training. After two months he was sent to the Cadet Training Field in Santa Ana, California. There, the cadets were given extensive tests to determine their fitness as pilots, and it was discovered that Elton had a minor problem of double vision and was "washed out" of the Air Force. Since the Air Force was then part of the Army, he was automatically in the Army and was sent to a re-assignment depot at Fresno, California for about a month.

At this time, the Army, like the Navy, had begun its specialized training program to provide college training for qualified soldiers and Elton was assigned to Stanford University at Palo Alto, where he took a series of tests to determine the type of training he should receive and the level at which he should receive it. He was assigned to City College of New York to take Mechanical Engineering. On August 1, Elton and six other privates, without a leader, were given meal and train tickets, and sent by train across the country to New York City. Here they were assigned to the former Jewish Orphanage on Amsterdam Street.

Since Elton was to be there at least a year, I packed my things and my baby and went to New York in August to be with him. I had first class tickets and berths, but when I changed trains in Chicago, I was put on a 3rd class train, without first class cars. It was a difficult trip, nursing a baby at my seat (in public view!), and there were no dining cars. When I arrived in New York I was shocked to find hundreds of thousands of men in uniform on several levels and I had no idea how and where to find Elton. We had agreed to meet at Penn Station, but at the same time, he didn't know what train I was on. We had to find each other. I had no place to stay, and he had no money and no way to get back to the barracks. In my desperation, I thought of a loudspeaker announcement. I asked a nice black lady to watch my baby and luggage while I located the stationmaster and asked him to make an announcement to tell Elton to meet me at the information desk. Surprisingly, and to our great relief, we found each other, retrieved the baby and bags, and made it uptown to a room Elton had rented until I could find a better place.

After a few days, I moved into another place where I stayed for three months. The house was right on the border of Harlem. Only a few residents lived there when I moved in, because the house had been bought by, or for, blacks, and black people were expected to move in. The house had 12 rooms on each floor, with a bathroom and kitchen to serve each group of six. I was on the seventh floor and the elevator needed an operator, so it wasn't very convenient going out with a buggy, and I often went out for a few minutes to the store without Gregg. The thought of that horrifies me now. The kitchen was alive with cockroaches and we had lots of bedbugs. I kept waking up at night hoping to catch one, but all I ever got were more bites. They never got in the buggy, Gregg's only bed, so he was never bitten. I was somewhat comforted by the possibly untrue story someone told me that cockroaches eat bedbugs.

Our "household goods," a very skimpy collection of the essentials, didn't arrive for a week or more, so Gregg slept in a bureau drawer, and I had only Gregg's spoon and fork with which to cook and eat. I reported to my Mother that "peeling potatoes and cutting up oranges is hard to do" with only those two implements.

By November the management of the house had changed and there were almost no residents left. The manager was black as was the elevator operator who was a young man fresh up from the South. I did not mind the fact that they were black and no one ever gave me any reason to think I wasn't safe with the young man there. I was a little nervous, however, about leaving my room to go to the bathroom or kitchen, especially since I was the only resident on the floor and one of the few in the building. I looked for another place to live and found an older German couple, the Katzensteiners, who had a large flat on 136th St. and wanted to rent out a room. Next to my room was another empty one and a bathroom and I was permitted to use her kitchen. Mrs. Katzensteiner and her husband owned an auto repair shop and couldn't get help, so both were gone most of the day and night and I felt quite comfortable and safer than I had in the other place. We lived there until June 1943.

New York was fascinating to me and at first I wrote to my folks that I really loved it, but I was soon complaining about all the foreign languages I heard and the many people, whether black, white or foreign. My blond baby got a lot of attention whenever we went out since many people were Italian, Hispanic or black. Early on, I had to get the rest of Gregg's baby shots, so I called the City Health Department to learn the location of the nearest clinic. Because of my unfamiliar Western accent, or perhaps because I mentioned South Dakota, the operator apparently thought me to be black and directed me to a clinic in the heart of Harlem. From the time I left the bus, walked to the clinic and returned to the bus, the only white face I saw was that of the doctor. It seemed very strange to me, but I certainly was not afraid.

I found the New York accent most interesting (e.g., Long Guyland, for Long Island, bottull for bottle), also the wax-covered paper "bottles," instead of glass, the strange baby buggies (not collapsible), all the different foods available in the shops and the soft water—wonderful, when accustomed to it, after the terribly hard water in Custer. Elton found the great transportation system (cabs, subway and buses) impressive, and at that time they were not expensive. We had to live with very little money. I was given most of Elton's pay for my allotment, and he received $22 a month. My allotment was about $90. My first room cost $6.00 a week including cleaning service.

The war was present in many ways—in the news, the letters from our friends and relatives in the service, and in the thousands of servicemen we saw wherever we went. I think Elton and his classmates felt rather left out of it, though they worked hard and expected to use their education in the war effort when their year of study was completed.

Looking back on that year from today's perspective, the early 2000's culture, it occurs to me that, in those days, mothers did not go to work but stayed at home and took care of their babies. It would have been almost impossible for me to go to work and care for Gregg, but perhaps I could have helped the Katzensteiners and at least paid for my room. They ran a garage and were almost never home since it was really hard to get help. I probably could have taken Gregg there and helped with a variety of routine tasks, learning something, helping them and still taking care of Gregg; the possibility didn't even occur to me, or to Elton, or, apparently, to the Katzensteiners.

Gregg and I went out for walks, and I carried him on the subway or bus to see the city. I think that was how he learned to love cities, even though he was only eighteen months old when we left. On weekends, Elton and I toured the city when we had someone to watch Gregg (at a cost of $2.00 for the evening). We went to Broadway shows—servicemen could get free tickets to anything they wanted to see. The first show we saw was *A Connecticut Yankee in King Arthur's Court* which disappointed me because the stage didn't look like the one in the Busby Berkeley movies. The one that impressed me most was *Othello,*with Paul Robeson.

One of the sitters we had was an elderly lady, Mrs. Pusinelli. She was exactly the same age as Elton's grandmother, Grandma Geist, who had been a farm wife, had had 13 children, 60 grandchildren and probably 10 or more great grandchildren at that time. We found Mrs. Pusinelli's life to be fascinatingly different. She had lived all her life in the city, had had only one son who was then about 45 years old, and one grandchild about 5 years of age.

Elton was home for only two hours each evening and from Saturday noon to Sunday evening, but we made the most of it. I think I should have been bored, but it was a lot of work to take care of Gregg, wash everything by hand and hang it on indoor drying racks, cook with inadequate supplies and utensils and do the shopping. I read the *Daily News* and books from a nearby library; I listened to the radio, knitted and wrote letters. One pleasant event was a train trip to New Haven to spend the weekend with Elton's cousin, Glenna Cross, her husband and baby. Another was the arrival of Jim Parsons, a former classmate from Custer High, and one of the Geists' former boarders in Rapid. Jim had received his BS in chemistry and had been hired to work in New York City on the early development of the atomic bomb—the very hush-hush Manhattan Project. He rented the other vacant bedroom from Mrs. Katzensteiner and lived there for a few weeks.

1944

In November, 1943, Sam, Elton's Dad, became quite ill and Ethel contacted us to come home. We made arrangements with the Red Cross and took the train there and back. When we got there, we found Sam improved and we had a lovely one-week vacation. We were contacted again on the first of June, 1944 for the same reason. By that time, I was pregnant again and due in November. Since Elton's assignment at CCNY would be completed in August, we decided that I should remain in South Dakota once we got there. We packed up hurriedly and had another train trip to Rapid. While on the train, we received a wire from Ethel with the very sad news that Sam had died. It was June 6, D-Day, when the Allied invasion of Europe began.

We were in Rapid for the funeral, which was attended by many members of the Geist family from the eastern part of South Dakota. Sam was buried in Custer, but after the war, his body was moved to the National Cemetery

in Sturgis. Elton returned to New York the day after the funeral and I took
Gregg back to Custer.

As it turned out, we were there for nearly a year, living for the latest news
of the war. Jackie was in England and Alan in basic training with the Air
Force. I was also anxiously waiting for the daily letters from Elton, enjoying
my new baby and seeing Gregg grow from one and a half to two and a half.
Again, I could have gone to work at least part time, helped our finances and
contributed to the economy, but no one even suggested it. This seems strange
now, looking back on the war effort and realizing how many women went
to work in war industries. Many men and women left the Custer area to go
where there were jobs in these industries. There were no such opportunities
in the Black Hills, except for the small mica plant. Heat resistant mica was
plentiful in the Hills, and before the age of plastics, large pieces were used in
place of glass in some instruments. Sorting it employed much of the available
labor force in the Hills during the war.

Mother and I spent a lot of time together, and had fun, coping with
wartime scarcities and rationing. Several things were rationed, including
gas, meat, butter, sugar and shoes, with a certain number of ration stamps
apportioned to each person. We tried to make butter, soap and sauerkraut,
with pretty poor results, and I did a lot of sewing—for the children and for
me. I made over from hand-me-downs most of the children's clothes, including
a snowsuit for Gregg from someone's old bathrobe and a darling dress for
Dale from a man's white shirt, among other things.

Without a husband or close friends, I decided in the fall that I would start
a bridge group, so I got together seven other women. Only one of the women
was married to a man who was not in the service; one was a new war widow;
and one was married to a flyer missing in action. We all commiserated with
each other, and the get-togethers brightened the year for all of us. During
this year, Mother and I got along beautifully. She gave a shower for me before
Dale Christine was born on November 17, 1944. It was the only shower I
ever had.

During the year we drove to Rapid to see the doctor and visit the Geists
from time to time. On one of these visits I was told that I could have a normal
delivery only if the baby had a very small head. Since big heads (pun not
intended) were the rule in both our families, another Caesarean was planned.
We also decided I should have a tubal ligation, but to have this, I had to have
written permission from my husband! This was another thing which has really
offended my later-life feminism but which I accepted then without question.
The problem was that Elton was out in the field in Jackson, Mississippi, where

he had been sent for ordnance training, and correspondence was difficult. As it turned out, his letter arrived on November 16, two days after the scheduled delivery date. Due to a bad snowstorm on that day, my schedule had to be moved back, and the letter was on time. Elton, however, didn't know Dale was born, until two days later.

During that year in Custer, we tried to keep up with the national news, including Franklin Roosevelt's election to an unprecedented fourth term in November 1944, with Harry Truman as Vice President, and then Roosevelt's death on April 12, 1945 and the end of the war in Europe. There were celebrations everywhere on VE day, but west of the Mississippi, we had always been more aware of the war in the Pacific and this continued. In fact, Elton's outfit was training for the invasion of Japan. Although we were always concerned about the war, we were not reminded of it constantly as we are in the 21st century. We could get radio reception only after dark and read the Rapid City Daily Journal. Certainly, I felt much less aware of the war in Custer than I had in New York City.

Elton was home on furlough during the first two weeks in December, and we spent most of that time in Rapid. He went from there to Camp Chaffee, Arkansas, where he spent a lonely Christmas, while we spent a lonely one in Custer. But at least I had the pleasure of the company of our children.

1945

In January Elton was transferred to Camp Gerber, Oklahoma, for a month or so and was then sent to still another training school in Atlanta, Georgia. In May he was reassigned to the 3613th Ordnance Squadron in Camp Bowie, near Brownwood, Texas, and the children and I joined him. We rode the bus to Colorado Springs to visit the relatives, and then took the train to Ft. Worth, and another bus to Brownwood—a hot, dreary little town on the plains.

We had a one-room, up-stairs apartment in a leaky motel-type building with a shower and toilet on the ground floor. The leaks didn't bother us because it was sunny, dry and hot (over 100°F) the entire month we were there. The mosquitoes, however, did bother poor little Dale, who was being rapidly destroyed before we discovered oil of citronella and saved her. Elton's buddy, Ev Haselwood, was there with his wife, Merla, and a little boy, Bobby, who was Gregg's age, so we had a pretty good time, despite the quarters, the heat and mosquitoes.

When July came, the outfit was transferred to Camp Hood for a field trip. Since Elton was due for a furlough afterwards, the children and I started back to Custer. We waited a few days in Colorado Springs with Grandma Skamser for Elton to arrive, but his furlough was postponed and we took the train back to Custer. There was so much rail traffic in those war years that every possible piece of equipment was called into service, and every car was full to overflowing. I sat with both children in one seat all night. In Custer, we saw my brother, Alan, home on furlough from the Air Force for the first time in three years. Jack was in Europe at the time. He had been in England earlier and in the invasion after June 6 for nearly a year.

Toward the end of July, Elton's furlough came through and he came to Custer. While there, we had Gregg and Dale baptized in the Custer Community Church. I planned to go with Elton to his next camp, taking Gregg and leaving Dale with my mother. Mother, however, was in Colorado with Grandma Skamser (who died later that fall after being ill most of the summer). Elton had been transferred to Camp Breckenridge, Kentucky, so when we left for Kentucky, we took Dale to Ramona and Ethel. When Mother returned, she took Dale back to Custer with her. By the time I returned, I seemed a stranger to her as she had been left with three strangers over the course of two months. She was very insecure for a long time.

We left Rapid for Kentucky on August 5, the day the U.S. dropped the atomic bomb on Hiroshima, a turning point in world history. I was demoralized by the event and spent the next several years believing my children would not live to adulthood, and doubting God's existence. Nevertheless, within a week after our arrival in Kentucky, we all realized that the war was over and that, at least, made everyone happy.

We found a room in the tiny backwoods town of Corydon and stayed there for a week before moving to Henderson for the rest of our stay. In Henderson we had one of the many bedrooms in a ramshackle house full of Army wives and children. The Hazelwoods were there too, so again we had company. And they had a car! The Squadron had been sent to Breckenridge as its last stop before being shipped off for the invasion of Japan, and since that was not going to happen, the men remained there until they left for discharge or other positions. Most of our free time was spent speculating when the guys would be discharged. There was a point system for discharge, including marriage and the number of children, so Elton was pretty high on the list. He was discharged on November 28, 1945, three years after he enlisted. This was a red-letter day for him and for us.

Because my mother needed to be with my Grandmother, I had taken Gregg back to Custer on October 1. I took the train from Evansville, Indiana, and changed in Chicago at a station that was a madhouse. The country had been on Daylight Saving Time throughout the war and went off DST that day. All schedules and plans were in turmoil. We finally arrived in Custer late that evening and were reunited with my baby girl.

We spent the next two months waiting for Daddy to come home, but in the meantime, I had the best birthday gift ever—two boxes of laundry soap! Many of the things that weren't rationed were very scarce during the war, including all rubber products, good quality yard goods or clothes and needles and pins. When sewing, we were very careful not to misplace a needle. One of the scarcest and most important things was soap. Custer's water was very hard and we had only hand soap for washing diapers (no disposables in those days), children's clothes and household laundry. No softener or other product really took the place of soap and, when Elton sent me a box from the Post Exchange and Mother sent me a box from Colorado Springs, I was very happy. Incidentally, these were soap flakes, not detergents, which were not produced until the late 1940's.

Mother was in Colorado Springs most of October. Her mother died on my birthday of ulcerated varicose veins and kidney failure. Carl stayed on in the house and eventually he, mother and Aunt Phoebe agreed on the disposition of Grandma's belongings. It was a difficult time for Mother.

By the time Elton reached home after his discharge, I'd been in Rapid and had located and rented a small basement apartment for us at 300 West Boulevard. I met him at the station and we had a happy reunion. The war was over, Elton was home, we were together and the only thing that cast a cloud over our reunion was the question of how we would live in the future. Elton worried about how he was going to support his family and was disturbed about the rental commitment. He was sure that things would return to the way they were pre-war and jobs would be scarce, especially with all the returning servicemen. We didn't recognize what changes the war had made in the economy and the effect it had on various government actions. One of the most important was the enactment of the GI Bill by Congress in the fall of 1944. This made it possible for Elton and millions of others to go back to college. We knew that if he were to go back to school he would get a stipend, but this would not be until September, almost nine months away. No one realized that we were about to enter a period when times would get better and better. With pent-up demand for all kinds of consumer products, employment and money in many hands, few would have to worry about jobs for a long time. Although we found it hard to realize that the war was over and that the depression was behind us, we were off to a fresh start.

CHAPTER 4

AFTER THE WAR—ON OUR WAY

1946

Elton was surprised but pleased that he was able to get a job at the Air Base and go to work by the end of the year as a mechanic in the motor pool. Although he was never very handy at manual labor of any kind, despite having done it all his life, he was very good at thinking things through and organizing. He was later appointed to design a maintenance program.

Our lives were pretty rocky those first two or three months. Dad had been transferred back to Ft. Collins and he and Mother moved after spending Christmas with us. Elton and I had different expectations of what life would be like when he got out of the service. He expected a quiet place to put his feet up and read, with well-behaved and disciplined children, no one to boss him, and a responsive wife; I expected help with the children and more companionship. Meantime, the children—Gregg now nearly three, and Dale one—had their lives disrupted. There were no more doting Roeser grandparents, a new place to live and a man in the house who expected them to do as they were told (certainly Gregg). The Geists, whose house was only two blocks from us, rather expected Elton to take Sam's place and help run things. Gradually, we all became accustomed to each other and learned to get along. The children learned to be more obedient, and although it was nice to be together again, we had some difficult times.

By February 1946, housing became a serious issue. Our rent was taking nearly half of Elton's pay, and the house Ethel had rented since 1941 was about to be sold from under them. Our housing was bad in many ways. The apartment I had rented was in the basement, very small, with one bedroom, and a bath shared with another couple. There was no heat except from the burners on the gas stove, the fumes from which were most objectionable. After much cogitation it was decided that a house should be built for Ethel with an apartment for us. Granddad Mesick and Elton, who would be able to take plenty of time off from his Government job, would work on it until he had to return to school in September.

Our first step was to buy a lot in North Rapid with the help of Elton's veteran status. I should mention that the deed specified that this lot could never be sold to a Negro or an Indian. The bank told us that this stipulation could not be enforced, but even at that time, it bothered us. The next thing was to find suitable houses for Elton's family (Ethel, Mona, a high school senior, Granddad and Dale Johnson) and for us. We found rental houses for the two families. Both were small and unsatisfactory, theirs without sewer, and ours without water or sewer—and both houses, by the way, were within the city limits. We only had water outside the house, and it had to be carried in from the back porch. The toilet was down a path in the back. It was scarcely my idea of comfort, but I, at least, didn't have to run to the toilet every five minutes, and Gregg used a pot inside the house. Our house, however, was only about a block from the new housing site, so that was convenient.

One of the memories of our short stay in that house was Gregg's tendency to wander around outside naked. I'd put him to bed for a nap, tend to my laundry or dishes, and before I knew it, he'd undress himself and be gone. Even though he was just over three, he never got lost and always knew where he was and how to get back, although, of course, I chased after him. In those days, seeing a little naked boy walking down the street alone must have been shocking to the neighbors. I'm sure I was held in contempt. It didn't take me long to give up trying to get him to nap. Another memory is the disdain shown by a friend I'd made in Custer. She came to visit us and obviously felt that associating with people who lived as we did was beneath her. I missed her company, which I'd enjoyed, but then, as now, I had no use for someone with such an attitude.

Before work started on the new house, Elton, Granddad, Dale and my visiting brother, Jack, went to Custer to tear down the old house and bring whatever was left of it for use as rough lumber for the new house. Next, the basement was dug and the foundation poured. From then on Elton and Granddad did most of the work. The new house was completed sufficiently for Ethel and her group to move in by June 1; we moved in on July 1. At that time, the house was little more than a shell, and there was no bathroom yet. They placed the toilet directly on the sewer pipe until they got the fixtures in and cobbled up a shower. All of us spent our spare time working on the house, but after trying for two weeks to keep the children out of Granddad's way, I took them to Ft. Collins to visit my parents. Dale Johnson was still living with the Geists until some time that summer when he asked Ramona to marry him—rather to our surprise, since we hadn't realized there was anything between them. Ramona told Dale she didn't want to get married for a year, so he decided to go to California, live with his older half-sister, and go to business school.

When the children and I returned to Rapid City around the first of August, I took over the washing, ironing, canning and cooking for all of us and worked on the house between times. During those two months, I worked as hard as Elton had for months; every spare minute was spent on the house. Our apartment (living room, bedroom and kitchen which eventually became the porch) was completed by October, but it was two years before the rest of the house was finished. We all shared one bathroom and we put the four of us in one bedroom with two rollaway trundle beds that fitted under our double bed during the day. We lived there for a year, and after their marriage in August, 1947, Mona and Dale lived there for three years. Finally, in 1960, the partition between the living rooms was torn down and the house was made into a full house for Ethel and Granddad.

Elton returned to Mines that fall for his last year after quitting his job at the Base. When he told the officer in charge he was quitting, the officer said, "You can't quit. I need you!" Elton was delighted to say, "Yes, I am," because he had hated every officer and every minute having to obey orders while he was in the Army. Nevertheless he was a good, hard-working and intelligent employee. The reaction of this employer was to be repeated in the future.

Elton did quit, and thanks to the GI Bill, he was able to go back to school for a comparatively easy scholastic year. The returning veterans all felt a little intimidated by school and feared that they would do poorly. Instead, they found that their discipline and determination made such a difference that the younger kids, fresh out of high school, couldn't begin to compete with them. There were many married students with children and we enjoyed socializing with a few of them and going to their parties. It was a congenial and happy bunch of people. Elton worked part of that year at the Harney Hotel as a bellhop. I helped him occasionally with the janitorial work that was part of his job and had an important learning (ah-ha) experience when I was cleaning a restroom one night. Some women came in, looked around to see if they were alone and decided they were when one of them said, "Oh, it's only the girl!" Ever since then I have viewed help of any kind with the respect any human being deserves. I had another important experience when Elton got an F at school because he'd misspelled "separate" twice in a paper—a paper I had typed and edited. This was especially poignant, because I'd always been insufferable about what a wonderful speller I was. I am an excellent speller, but I learned then not to believe I was perfect.

It is important to mention here that while Elton had always expected and was determined to finish college, it was a great joy for us and all veterans that Congress had passed the GI Bill of Rights in 1944. This provided support for school, job hunting and other aspects of returning to civilian life. It made it possible for many veterans who had never expected to get a higher education to do so. The GI Bill allowed a stipend of $105 a month for a married veteran ($75 for single). This was not much for a family of four, but with free rent and Elton earning a little here and there, it allowed him to go to school full time and graduate the following spring with a B.S. in Metallurgical Engineering. When the National Lead Company hired him for $225 a month plus overtime, we felt richer than ever before. For the first six years of our marriage, our total income had been a little over $6,500.

During that year in Rapid, we didn't have a car, but the Geists' 1936 Plymouth was more or less our car, as long as Ethel could use it when she needed it, which wasn't often—mostly to buy groceries. She got rides to work at the Air Base about 30 miles east of Rapid. The Plymouth was the car the Geists owned when Elton and I started dating. When we were trying out a new Cadillac in 2002, I said to Elton, "This is a little different from the car we courted in," and when the salesman learned that that car was a 1936 Plymouth, he said, "You should have kept it. It would be really valuable today." I spent days chuckling about the many moves we've made and what they would have been like with that car in tow, especially in view of the fact that it was actually a wreck the last couple of years we drove it. The driver's seat was loose and if you didn't balance correctly, you fell over backwards; the windshield was smashed, the front passenger seat was also tipsy and I had to reach over to hold whichever child was in that seat (no seat belts at that time) and the driver's window wouldn't close. Luckily, most of our driving was to the grocery store or a movie. We also began taking the children to the Methodist Church for Sunday school, though I don't remember ever going to church ourselves except on Easter Sunday.

Our Christmas gifts in 1946 reflected our comparative poverty. I had reknitted an old sweater that had belonged to my cousin, Mary Jane, into one for Elton (one that fitted); he had bought me a pair of every-day shoes, which I desperately needed. Alan and Jack were home from the service and back in school—Alan at Colorado A&M and Jack at Colorado U. They drove up from Ft. Collins and took us home for the holidays, and the whole family had a marvelous time. One of the most pleasant memories of that visit is a record someone bought for Gregg for my folk's 78-rpm record player. We played it over and over and learned the words "I'm Genie the record, that's who I am, it's true I am the record. I can make you smile and make you laugh as I spin around on your phonograph." We all loved it, especially Gregg, who turned out to be a great music-lover and had had very little music in his life so far. We took the bus back to Rapid and, because of Uncle Carl's $10 gift, we were spared having to borrow the fare from my folks.

Elton graduated on June 6, 1947, and the following day he took the train east to Tahawus, New York, where he started working as a metallurgist for National Lead's titanium plant with wages of $292.50 per week. Tahawus was deep in the Adirondacks, thirty miles from the nearest drug store, or other shops, and surrounded by woods. It was a far cry from our previous home in New York City. The company was building new houses, one of which was planned for us, but they would not be ready for occupation until November (in June they thought the houses would be ready in August). Since Tahawus was strictly a company town, there was no place for us to live until the houses were ready. Gregg, Dale and I stayed in Rapid City and Elton lived in the company staff house until we were able to join him.

By July 10, I had packed all our things and vacated the Geist apartment. The children and I then left for Ft. Collins to spend a month with my folks. While we were there I took our very meager savings and went to Montgomery Ward in Denver to order beds and kitchen chairs to be delivered by the nearest Ward center in Boston to this new, small, unknown town in New York. Credit cards did not yet exist, so I was obliged to use just about all our saved cash. I was pleased with the purchases then, but the order was never delivered. Predictably, no one in the Boston store could figure out why we didn't get the order. We did, eventually, get a refund; in fact, we got two checks! But this was many months after much correspondence and the purchase of other beds and chairs.

While we were still waiting for the house in Tahawus, Ramona and Dale Johnson were married in Rapid in a small church wedding on August 16, and they moved into our apartment. The children and I returned to Rapid for the wedding and stayed with Ethel until we left for New York late in September. While Mona and Dale were on their honeymoon, I had word that my brother, Jack, had been married on August 25, to Betty Gaskill, an ex-army nurse from Omaha, who also went to Colorado U. They had known each other only a short time and none of us had met Betty at the time. I did meet her when she and Jack were in Custer on their "honeymoon." Actually, they were there because Jack was serving as best man at the wedding of one of my classmates, Mary Kay Bristol. After their weddings, Dale, Jack and Betty went back to college on the GI bill.

By September, our house in Tahawus was still not finished, and Elton found out that the regular bus service into Tahawus was to be terminated by September 30. Since he didn't have a car and no way to pick us up elsewhere, we had to use that bus. Elton found a lakeside hunting cabin in Newcomb to rent for us until the house was finished, and arranged rides to work with a fellow employee who lived in Newcomb. The kids and I took the train to Albany, spent the night there and then took the last bus into Tahawus. Elton joined us there, to our great pleasure, and Dale exclaimed, "Dere's my Pinky!" Elton was happy that she was pleased to see him but somewhat taken aback. He had been trying for years to get away from the "Pinky" nickname, and had finally found a place where no one knew him as other than "El." I stopped calling him Pinky with great difficulty, but from that point forward, he was El or Al.

We four took the bus into Newcomb, about twenty miles from Tahawus. Newcomb had the reputation of being the longest one-street town in the U.S. without cross streets, and had houses for the population of about 1,000 strung out all along the very long street. Although the area seemed, and certainly was, isolated, the Town of Newcomb actually included the Tahawus Tract, a large area that, in the early 1800's, had been discovered to have deposits of iron ore. The ore had been mined between 1827 and 1857 as the best steel-producing iron ore discovered in the country up to that time. The difficulties of mining and shipping the ore in this isolated area, as well as the presence of titanium dioxide, forced the mine's closure in 1857 and the land had reverted to wilderness. However, the titanium had become an asset by 1940 and National Lead Industries had begun to mine and produce iron and titanium. It continued to do so until 1989 when the area again returned to wilderness; it is now part of a conservation area.

When we arrived, National Lead had a mine, several big mills for the many stages of ore treatment, all of the necessary auxiliary buildings, a connecting railroad and a town of company houses for, perhaps, 1,000 employees and families. Until the house was ready, Elton was riding to work with Ken Keating, another new engineer who lived nearby, and the Keatings and our landlord were very helpful in getting us to grocery stores and finding the things we needed.

It was lovely seeing Elton again after four months and to be together. He was thrilled to be working as an engineer and actually making a living wage, even though we would be roughing it in our temporary housing. The cabin was one room, with an outhouse a block away (outhouses kept popping up in our lives), a kerosene stove and discarded furniture. Water had to be carried from the landlord's house or taken from the lake and heated on the kerosene stove for laundry and dishes. The cabin looked as if it had not been thoroughly cleaned in years, if ever, so I was pretty busy making it livable. But it was in a beautiful setting on the lake, especially during that autumn season which we especially enjoyed because we had never been in a wooded northeastern state in the autumn.

Meanwhile, completion of the house in town was moving slowly and we worried about what we would do when the hunting season began and our cabin would be needed for hunters. As it turned out, the company let us move in before the house was completely finished, in mid-November. The company houses ranged from very nice and modern for the highest-ranking employees—on what everyone called Snob Hill—to smaller houses, apartment houses and six-plex side-by-sides. We had the end of a six-house building, two bedrooms, a nice living room, dining room, kitchen, a bathroom (which was most welcome), but almost no furniture. All walls were painted "mining company yellow" which seemed to be the color used in every company house we ever lived in. I had bought an old couch and matching chair from my folks, but we were without our beds from Ward's. Elton had to go to a nearby town with someone and buy twin beds for the children, a bed for us and kitchen chairs. He built a table and bookcases.

The children had very few toys, but blocks of wood left from the house construction. We had very little china, silver, pillows and bedding and our one and only appliance was a toaster. We didn't have a refrigerator for more than a year, and kept food cold on the windowsill. But we got an icebox from someone, and ice was delivered in July and August. In winter we put icicles in the box to keep food fresh, but we went to the store nearly every day. Frozen food was still in the future. Without a washing machine, I washed clothes by hand in a tub and hung them on a pulley line from the back door to a tree up the slope in the back. Or I hung them in the dining room, which had no furniture until we bought a dinette set from someone a year or more after we moved in. I was very happy when our next-door neighbors gave us their wringer/washer when they bought a new one. I was also happy to have a new refrigerator at last.

We suffered from the cold that first winter and didn't get any heat at all from the radiators during the day, despite the fact that maintenance couldn't find anything wrong with the furnace, located in the basement of the six-plex opposite us. They eventually found that the one thermostat for the whole building was in the apartment at the other end and the tenants there carefully turned down the thermostat when they left for work each morning, thinking it was for only their apartment. This was difficult for those of us with children running in and out. The one appliance provided by the company was an electric stove and, to get a little warmth, we turned on its burners.

As a company town, Tahawus had no stores or business establishments, except for a small commissary where we bought our groceries and a few other necessities. The YMCA was just completing a building that provided a bowling alley, auditorium and meeting rooms. These were also used for church services and an occasional movie. The church services in the "Y" consisted of a very large group of Catholics (there were many French Canadians in the town) and a very small group of faithful Protestants who shared, some of the time, a female Methodist missionary pastor from Newcomb. I taught Sunday school most of the time we were there.

There was a small library next to the post office. We read every book in the library and were happy to have our subscriptions to *Time* and *The Saturday Evening Post*. The Syracuse newspaper was delivered daily. Radio reception was very poor, so we spent our evenings reading after the children were finally in bed. I spent a lot of time knitting and sewing. I borrowed a sewing machine from someone for a month and later someone sold me a treadle machine (operated by a foot treadle, not a motor), and I loved it. I made all of Dale's clothes, most of my own and made some tailoring attempts for Gregg and even Elton. My material, yarn, needles and everything else came from Sears or Ward's catalogs.

It will be unbelievable to anyone living in the 21st century that the only phone service was at the company office and the "guard house". The guardhouse was not a military guardhouse, but was used for directions and information. Our house was the last one in town and we had to walk a mile or more to the commissary and post office. Since the house was at the top of a quite steep hill, going down wasn't bad, but walking home was strenuous. I pulled the children in a wagon or sled to the post office or the store, but I encouraged them to walk home whenever I could. And yes, throughout most of the winter there was snow—a lot of it.

That part of New York is lovely, wooded country, but as a native of Colorado and the Black Hills, the density of the woods and the lack of sunshine were depressing, except in the autumn. In those days, people did not move as much as they do today and most (with the exception of the engineers) came from nearby and had no comprehension of what the west was like. But most of the people were friendly and neighborly, and the Donahues across the street had a boy exactly the same age as Gregg, while another neighbor had a daughter almost exactly Dale's age. There was a lot of informal entertaining and visiting, and we enjoyed that. We spent our Christmas alone, with toys and gifts from the catalogs. We cut our own tree in the woods and decorated it with paper wreaths and strings of popcorn and cranberries.

1948

Gregg and Michael Donahue were five in January 1948, and were allowed to begin kindergarten. Gregg went on to the first grade in September, since the teacher thought he was ready, while Michael went back to kindergarten. Many years later, when he was in his thirties, Gregg and I concluded that he was dyslexic, a disability that wasn't known until he was out of school. Although he was exceedingly bright and had an excellent memory, Gregg had trouble learning to read and write. Had he started school later he might have been better off, but who knows.

I should probably mention here that we had an interesting medical situation in Tahawus. The company doctor lived in Newcomb and was in Tahawus three days each week, when he would call on or see anyone. Between those days, one had to go to Newcomb to see him. Naturally, when our children were sick, it was on the evening of the day he had been in town. Only once in the two years we were there did we get someone to take us to Newcomb—when we thought, mistakenly, that Gregg had taken a lot of aspirin. Amazingly, the children were always well by the next time the doctor came to town. This was another important lesson and, in the future, it saved many pointless trips to a doctor.

We longed for a car, but it wasn't until the summer of 1949 that we had enough money to buy one. Meantime, we entertained ourselves at home. In the spring, we tapped some maples and learned what a job it is to make syrup; in the summer, we picked berries, day after day. The area around the mine and company plants had been pretty well cleared off, leaving many shrubs and berry bushes, especially raspberries. The children and I spent days picking, then I cleaned, sorted, canned, made raspberry concentrate and jam and we ate as many as we wanted. Gregg and I detested picking berries, but Dale liked it and it was kind of fun picking berries together, usually with other people. There was little else to do without a car. We also went on picnics and swam in the headwaters of the Hudson and occasionally someone invited us to go along to one of the many lakes in the area.

In June 1948, Ethel and Granddad came for a rather unhappy visit. Instead of waiting until Elton was able to take a vacation, they came a week early, so they saw little of him. A friend was able to take them on some short trips around the countryside. Later that summer, Elton and I took the kids by bus to New York City for a three-day vacation. The most memorable parts were when Elton carried three and a half year old Dale to the top of the Statue of Liberty, and then seeing, for the first time, televisions in shop windows.

In October, my parents drove from Colorado and we had a great time with them. We really enjoyed our first tour of the area—Ft. Ticonderoga, the Saratoga battlefield, AuSable Chasm, and, on a trip to Montreal, a little of Quebec Province, Vermont and Lake Champlain. We also got to Glens Falls to do some shopping, which was wonderful after so much shop-deprivation and catalog-shopping. Elton and Dad drove to Hanover, New Hampshire, to see their first Ivy League football game between Dartmouth and Yale. One of the major topics of conversation with my folks was the upcoming marriage (the day after Thanksgiving) of Alan and Lois Landblom (Lui). My folks thought it a terrible union, since she was four years older than Alan, had been married twice, had a seven year old son, Walter, and was unable to have more children. Her first husband died before Walt was born, and the second marriage ended early in divorce. Obviously, she was not the best candidate for Alan's wife, but I was really astonished to find that the major objection of my folks was that she was ugly—both of my parents were obsessed with good looks.

Immediately after my parents had left for home, Ethel came to stay through Christmas. She was a rather difficult guest, and didn't really want us to do much, either with her or without her. She did, however, serve as a reluctant baby sitter, and we were able to go to a few parties during the holiday.

1949

Just after the New Year, Elton's job changed a couple of times, most of his work so far having been in the sinter plant. He was now on shift work as one of three foremen in the flotation plant. He adapted to shifts without problem and, although this was the shift he liked best, I didn't like the swing shift (4:00 p.m. to midnight) because of the long evenings alone. Graveyard shift was no problem for Elton, since he was able to sleep any time, no matter what was going on. In June, he had a serious infection caused by a bad tooth. The doctor thought he might have a heart problem, which concerned Elton deeply, considering his father's death. But once the tooth was out, he recovered quickly.

About the time his infection cleared up, he went to Albany and paid $150 for our first car, a 1940 Chevy. It might have been a brand-new Cadillac as far as we were concerned. We could finally go somewhere on our own. Now that we had a car, we felt we could solve our next problem. National Lead was eliminating the shift foremen's jobs and it was possible that Elton would lose his job. As it turned out, he was the only one of the three to be retained, but he was sure he would be out of a job soon, so we borrowed a typewriter and I began writing some sixty letters to potential employers. This was the summer of 1949 when there was a downturn in business. Elton got rejections from all but one and we drove to New York City for an interview. One offer received in September was for Assistant Mill Superintendent at Telluride Mines in Telluride, Colorado. The company mined gold, silver, copper, zinc and lead (which usually occur together), so it would be an interesting production change, a step-up in rank and more money—$350 a month. This sounded good, especially since the job was in Colorado and I always wanted to return there.

Elton gave notice; we spent two weeks packing and hired a moving company. We had saved all year for the car and had very little money left, but South Dakota had just passed a bill giving a bonus of $300 to every veteran and we agreed to borrow some money for the movers from Ethel to be repaid with the bonus. We left Tahawus with regrets. We had made many friends, including Jay and Florence Poll, Bill and Lorraine Aubrey, Bob and Gert Kingman and the Donohues, and we had grown to love the country and beautiful woods, particularly on that autumn day, October 1. But we were looking forward to the mountains and a new job.

The only 4-lane interstate in existence at that time was the Pennsylvania Turnpike, which had opened only recently, but it was not our route. Our trip to Colorado was on two-lane roads, through many small towns and picturesque country. We drove through the picture-book apple country of upstate New York, and had a late-night drive through Cleveland, with an overnight stay in Elyria. We made a stop in Iowa at our Custer pastor's new home and spent a few days in Rapid City with the family. Mona and Dale now had a one-year old baby girl, Nancy Jo, who was born on August 31, 1948. We enjoyed our reunion.

We drove on to Colorado Springs where Dad had just been transferred from Ft. Collins. I had been telling the children for weeks how beautiful the mountains were in Colorado and when we crossed the eastern Wyoming/ Colorado border, with nothing but dry plains in sight, Dale burst into tears. "This can't be Colorado!" she cried. Telluride was still a few days off for the children and me, but things improved when we finally arrived.

Elton left us in Colorado Springs and drove on to Telluride where he received one of the major shocks of his life. Without a job and with almost no money, the family in Colorado Springs and our furniture about to arrive, he was told in the company office that the man who had hired him had been fired and that there was no reason for him to hang around Telluride. Since Elton had no place to go and had to wait for the mover and no idea where to unload, he hung around anyway until the workday was over and the new boss came in from the mine. To Elton's great relief he was told that he was indeed hired, and that they had a house for him. Thank God! An interesting postscript to this is that the office manager who told him to leave was, apparently, stealing gold from the product placed in the safe. She wanted Elton gone because she was afraid someone who knew something about mine production would catch her. She was, in fact, eventually caught and fired, partly because of information supplied by Elton.

The furniture arrived the next day with the van driver sweating blood over the mountain roads. He felt he had had all the mountains he wanted in Tahawus, but Telluride was quite different. It's about 8,000 feet high, located in a small, deep valley at the foot of Mt. Sneffels, one of Colorado's 14,000 foot high mountains, with other mountains on every side of the valley and just one very narrow two-lane road to the outside, with occasional wider spots where one could turn out and allow cars from the other direction to pass. The van driver told Elton that he was relieved he was going back by way of the Million Dollar Highway out of Ouray. We've always wondered what he might have said as he drove over it. It was, and is, a frightening highway with sharp drop-offs and narrow curves. It was built in the early 1900's and earned its name from its construction cost. It was said to have cost a million dollars per mile.

We were anxious to get to Telluride, not only to be together but because Telluride itself had an interesting history—though not as long as that of Tahawus. In the 1870's, after the gold strikes in California and the other western states, the gold seekers invaded all parts of Colorado where precious metals are common but hard to find and to mine. The town of Telluride and its mines operated from the 1870's. The mines were notable because some of the early workers' strikes took place there, and one of these, in 1903, was especially bloody and destructive. At the time we arrived, Telluride Mines, Inc. had been successfully operating the mine and plant for some time, but I believe there was little mining done there before WWII. I am sure the mines are now closed and have been replaced with ski slopes.

The roads into Telluride that the driver of the moving van had been sweating about did not discourage us; all the roads in that area were the same and there was no airport at that time. Mountains surrounded the town, and after the sun came up in winter, it promptly went behind another mountain.

The kids and I finally made plans to join Elton. Mother and Dad drove us to the first stop on the west side of Monarch Pass where Elton would meet us. On the way, a hose in Dad's new car came loose and a small fire started under the hood. This meant a two-hour stop in Salida, while Elton waited, and we had no way to call him (no cell phones then). Poor little Dale had suffered enough and this was too much. "I'll never see my Daddy again!" she wailed. We were all happy when we met and the four of us started for Telluride.

Our house had been built as a solid stone retort house for a mill which had later burned down. It was about two miles from town, between Telluride and the present mill, and in the middle of a flat area, of about 2 acres; there was a cliff behind, and a garage that threatened to collapse if touched. The house had no windows, so windows had to be cut through the stone. An interior plywood wall was built and fitted with regular windows. There was a window in the children's room with a stone wall on the other side. No two windows were the same size. There were four rooms and a bath; the living room/dining room had a space heater in front and, next to it, a roomy kitchen. Two outside doors opened in front to a long wooden slat porch—one door led into the kitchen, and the other, right next to it, led into the living room. In front of the house were a tiny yard and a wall between the yard and the one-lane road to the mill. On the other side of the road were narrow gauge railroad tracks. We could see the mill's tailings pond, the mill building within a short distance, and the falls that provided our water.

The range in the kitchen burned wood and coal. The only warmth in that very cold location came from the range and the space heater. The stone walls assured that the back of the house would never get warm in winter. Cooking was a problem, and we had nothing hot to eat for several days because I was used to cooking on an electric range and at that altitude, everything required longer cooking times. Except for the refrigerator and washing machine, we had no electric appliances. We didn't even have an electric coffee pot. For my birthday, Mother gave us a pressure cooker that was a real godsend. A microwave would have been wonderful! Washing clothes was kind of fun until the winter snows began. Elton put up a clothesline and I hung things out. I didn't wear a coat and was comfortable in the sun, but the clothes froze on the line immediately and dried very fast.

We discovered that living at that high altitude had some other interesting effects. Alcohol affects the body much quicker and eating more food does not necessarily result in weight gain. I should also mention that there was no television reception at that time and we could get radio reception only after sundown. We got our news from the *Denver Post* and missed a lot of the McCarthy hearings, most of the Korean War and the problems of General MacArthur and President Truman.

Gregg was already more than a month into the second grade so we enrolled him immediately. He took a bus to school, and carried lunch, which he never ate. I toyed with the idea of sending him off without lunch, but I didn't want to be talked about. The teachers were decidedly second-rate. They were college graduates, but none of them had any training in education. There were two retarded girls in the class who talked all the time, and altogether, Gregg's two years there were not very productive.

Since I was a native Coloradoan, I had expected people to be friendly, but I'd forgotten that we came to town in a car with New York plates. In those days, long before skiing was possible or popular, people from the east were not really welcome in what was a very parochial town. Most of the people had lived there all their lives; their parents had come in the 1880's after gold was discovered. We made friends with a few at the mine, and a few who went to the small mission church that was without a permanent minister most of the time we were there. I became co-leader of a Girl Scout troop and, in some way that I don't remember, I joined a bridge club. Elton had a hard time getting into things, partly because his immediate boss was not too happy with an assistant who knew more about milling than he did. Nonetheless, it was a wonderful area for sightseeing which we did every weekend. That is, we did it after replacing the tires, which had almost disintegrated shortly after we arrived. We still don't know how we had come clear across the country and through the mountains without flat tires. Actually, once the snow began, we put on chains and drove with them until spring.

Before the snow arrived we had a frightening experience one day when Gregg, seven, and Dale five, were playing outside with two neighbor children down the road and failed to come home on time. It turns dark quickly at that location, and when the sun goes down it gets very cold. We couldn't find them and called the police, the volunteer fire department and the Boy Scouts. Someone found the four of them about 8 o'clock in an empty cabin up the side of the mountain behind our house. They were perfectly safe, had built a fire in the stove (if that's perfectly safe) and found some peanuts. They felt they were having a real adventure. We didn't call it that.

Ethel arrived the weekend after Thanksgiving, and we drove to the Springs the following weekend, where she got the bus to Rapid. We visited my folks before leaving the children with them for the weekend, and Elton and I went to Boulder for a night with my brothers and their new wives. Jack and Betty's baby, James Vincent, had been born on August 8, 1949. On our way to Boulder, we stopped in Denver for a wonderful shopping spree. Our major purchase was a combination radio and record player and three 33 1/3-speed records of *South Pacific*, *The Nutcracker Suite* and a great collection of Gilbert and Sullivan *Patter Songs*. With radio reception only at night, and no other records, we learned those three by heart very quickly.

1950

Mother and Dad spent Christmas with us and arrived about the same time that Elton returned from an interesting truck trip to Salt Lake City. He and a driver had taken a very valuable load of gold to the smelter there with waste from the gold refinery.

In March 1950, Mother got word that she had to have a mastectomy and it was agreed that I would go to the Springs for a few days when she got out of the hospital. Elton had to make another trip to Salt Lake City, so he flew from the Springs, and the children and I stayed to help Mother. I was precious little help with two little kids running around and a really bad flu which knocked me out for a couple of days. We got back to Telluride just in time for one of the coldest Easters I have ever experienced.

People liked visiting us in Telluride because it was so picturesque and different, but, as yet, there was no skiing. Jack, Betty and Jim came in February for a few days, and then Ethel was back for a week. In May, Ramona, Dale and Nancy arrived to spend the summer. Dale was studying mining engineering at South Dakota Mines and had a summer job at Telluride. It was fun having them there, although our Dale might not have agreed. She was nearly five and had trouble getting along with two-year old Nancy who was at a biting stage. Dale Christine was thrilled one day when "Nancy didn't bite me once!" While they were there, we went on picnics and hikes; we went fishing, too, and had a lot of fun. We all went on a two-day trip to Mesa Verde, and in August, Elton and I took the children, left the Johnsons, and went to Colorado Springs for a few days vacation and a Roeser reunion. Jack had gotten his law degree from CU in June, and he, Betty and Jimmy were living temporarily with my folks. Alan, Lui and Walt came down from Boulder for the weekend.

In the fall of 1950, we acquired a dog whose mother was a Collie and whose father was thought to be a coyote. We all loved Bobbie, until he got distemper and was very sick for several weeks. He was about over it before we finally got him to a veterinarian—not easy since we had to go all the way to Montrose. He did recover to give us some interesting experiences. One day he dragged a deer head from somewhere to decorate our front yard. After it was put in the garbage can it magically reappeared in the yard. Was it some sort of trophy? One day he ran into a skunk. This was a great experience for him as well as for us.

Also in the fall of 1950, Dale turned six. There was no kindergarten in Telluride, and she had to have had her 6th birthday by October 1 in order to start first grade, so she couldn't start. She was ready and really wanted to go to school, but she was good company for me in the interim.

We spent Christmas 1950 in Rapid City. While we were there, Elton, with his Mother's assistance and without my even looking at it, bought another car, a 1946 Chevy. Returning to the Springs on January 30, to spend New Year's Eve with my family, the car developed major problems and we went into the town of Bushnell, Nebraska to see if it could be repaired. Surprisingly, there was someone who was able to replace the piston rings and repair the ignition system, and there was a small motel where we spent the night. We got back on the road by nightfall on the 31st. I was very angry, mainly because the car had been purchased with Ethel's input and not mine. For this reason, the name "Bushnell" was a dirty word in our family for years. As I recall, we reached Colorado Springs in time for New Year's Day.

1951

We had two memorable events in the spring of 1951. One was a fire in the house, which began when I put too many cardboard cartons in the space heater in the living room. The plywood wall where the stovepipe was attached got too hot and began to blaze. The fire covered a good bit of the wall before I realized it was burning, and Dale was thoroughly frightened. I was too, but I got the fire extinguisher, hurriedly read the instructions (which I should have known by heart) and put out the fire before it did too much damage. I was happy I was able to react as quickly as I did, but Dale was really upset. The other notable event was waking up one morning to a chorus of sheep ba-a-a-ing loudly—an army of wool surrounded the house. They were being driven to high mountains for the summer. We'd seen a lot of sheep since coming into the San Juan Mountains, but nothing quite like this.

The most important event of that spring of 1951 was Elton's decision to look for another job. We loved the Telluride area and never again were we able to spend as much time with the children, but Elton's work situation was not entirely happy, mainly because of the proprietary attitudes of his boss and others. He was not making a lot of money and had not had any raises even though the economy was beginning to boom. Elton thought he could do better somewhere else. We sent out many letters and, unlike two years earlier, he got several offers. He was interested at first in jobs in Chile, which would have been interesting, and in Idaho, but he finally decided to get in on the hot, new taconite business on the Iron Range in Minnesota. He had offers from all four of the iron mining companies to whom he had written—Erie (Pickands Mather), Cleveland Cliffs, U.S. Steel and the M.A. Hanna Company.

He arranged for a meeting with Dmitri (Dee) Vedensky, Vice President of M.A. Hanna, in Denver on the day after Easter, which made for a very interesting weekend. Mother, Dad, Alan and Walt came to Telluride for Easter, and we all left Sunday morning to drive back to the Springs, so that Elton, the children and I could go to Denver on Monday. Elton took the children and me to visit his cousin, Irene Wall Cowgill, while he met with Vedensky. We had a terrible snowstorm, and Elton was snowbound in downtown Denver, while we were snowbound in Littleton until Tuesday night. Vedensky did arrive, however, and Elton had a long and promising discussion with him.

We returned home after another memorable trip. As we went over the top of Monarch Pass, we ran into several cars that had gone off the road into the deep snow and we followed them, just as Dale lost a baby tooth and began crying. Things were cleared out fairly quickly and we got home to the coldest house I've ever experienced. Nevertheless, we were looking forward to a new job and a new location, and once the definite offer came in for the job at the Groveland Pilot Plant, we began getting ready for the move. The pilot plant was being built near Iron Mountain, Michigan, and Elton would be at the Hanna Research Lab in Hibbing, Minnesota for his initial indoctrination, which was to begin at the end of May.

We had no idea where we would live and thought we would have to put our things in storage. I washed everything the day the moving van was to come, assuming I'd have time to get the laundry dry before the van arrived. But the driver came early and it rained (not common there in May) and I tried all day to dry the linens, blankets and clothes in the kitchen with a roaring fire in the stove. I was most unhappy and complained all day. Elton said I blamed him for the rain, and I might have. I was ready to blame anyone. When we finally finished packing and were ready to go, I called my mother to tell her that we were on our way and how awful the day had been, she just said, "And I'll bet you got your period too!" Of course I did.

We drove away down the mountains, sorrowfully, in spite of the fact that we had never felt very welcome in Telluride, and we were looking forward to a new job and more pay. I will always miss Colorado's mountains, particularly the San Juans in the southwest corner of the state. We still believe it to be the most beautiful area in the United States.

CHAPTER 5

OUR YEARS WITH HANNA—PART I

1951-1957

Leaving Telluride in the middle of May, 1951, we looked forward to our new life and our trip to Minnesota. We stopped first in Colorado Springs for a few days, and then went on to Denver to see Jack. He was working there as an adjuster for an insurance company while studying for his bar exam—which he passed later that year. He and Betty had a new baby, Sally Beth, who was born on February 21, and we spent a day visiting them and 18 month old Jimmy. From there we went to Rapid City for a day or two. Dale Johnson was about to graduate and had taken a job with Climax Molybdenum in Climax, Colorado. Although we did not see them on this trip, Alan and Lui were also making a new start. Alan was about to receive his M.A. in mechanical engineering from CU and was to begin working for Boeing in Seattle.

On arriving in Hibbing on May 27, Elton reported to the lab for assignment and we had two shocks. First, we found that Hanna paid at the end of the month, so he would not have any pay until June 30. This was difficult, because we had borrowed on our life insurance to pay for the move and had NO extra cash and certainly no reserves. The second shock was that no consideration had been given to housing for us. We were on our own. There was almost no available housing in Hibbing, but luckily, we were able to rent a house for the summer from the high school swimming teacher, Paul Lukens. As it would not be available for a week, we had to stay in a motel until Paul and his family left for the summer. After Elton put a new roof on it, paid for by Lukens, we were able to store our furniture in their garage. We decided to use our own mattress in the master bedroom because it was vastly better than the one there.

Hibbing was an interesting town in many ways, but it certainly lacked scenic beauty, and was cold and unwelcoming. It was cold in every way. The Lukens had used up the last lump of coal and stick of wood before they departed, so there would be no heat in the house unless we were to buy some fuel. Since we had not expected to live for a month without income, and would be living on change from the kids' piggy banks before June was over, fuel was out of the question. That left only the heat we could get from the gas stove in the kitchen. Luckily, gas and electricity were included in our rent.

Elton's job was as a metallurgist in the research lab under Les Bechaud who was in charge until 1952. Hanna was building a pilot plant that summer at the Groveland mine, 20 miles from Iron Mountain, Michigan, and Elton was hired to help run it. At just about the last minute, he was told he would be in charge of the operation—a real thrill. Meantime, he spent most of August at the company's property in Iron Mountain, Missouri, where he worked with Floyd Lee and John Reed who became life-long friends.

The kids and I spent the summer in Hibbing where I rented a sewing machine and made a school wardrobe for Dale. The kids went to the park and to a summer Bible school and entertained themselves. In our eagerness to find a place to live, we had unthinkingly agreed that renting the house was contingent upon letting the Lukens' daughter, Sally, stay in the upstairs bedroom in August while she got ready for her October wedding. This was not an attractive arrangement. Sally, of course, felt at home in the house, while we felt it was our home. Although we had no real falling out, I was unhappy about the situation. We also had trouble with the dog, Bobbie, who bit a neighbor in July. It wasn't a bad bite, but even so, we were lucky to avoid being sued or having the dog put to sleep. Sally didn't help at all. If she woke up and thought he needed to go out, she would let him go without a leash.

We had another unpleasant experience at a carnival where the kids were on a ride. They were caught in a car high above the ground for an hour or so. While not a serious event, it was nonetheless frightening. I spent the summer without any contact with the lab people; two neighbors did come to visit—neither of whom had suffered from dog bite.

All in all, we were happy when the time came to leave Hibbing and move to the Groveland plant in Michigan. We drove down on Labor Day and liked the Upper Peninsula from the first, especially when we drove by the pilot plant and Elton saw it. He loved his new baby at first sight. We weren't so sure about our house, however. This farmhouse was on land Hanna had bought for its underlying iron ore. It had a kitchen larger than the living room, dining room and two bedrooms combined, three nice bedrooms upstairs with a narrow staircase, an ancient coal-electric range and a horde of mice in the basement. Gregg was assigned one of the upstairs bed rooms because it was impossible to navigate the narrow staircase with a full-size mattress or spring. Outside there was a huge and very modern barn which we used as our garage. The house was clean and freshly painted and it was nice to be in the country.

This was my first (and last) experience on a farm and, during that first week, I was more nervous at night than I had ever been in New York City. On our third day, Elton had to leave for Missouri for most of September. We kept ourselves occupied some of the time by setting traps for the mice, catching more than 30—on one occasion catching two in one trap. Gregg, at eight, was less squeamish than I and emptied the traps for me. I was very glad to get rid of the mice. It was disconcerting to find mice dung everywhere and to have them running wild in the living room.

The first day we were there, we registered the kids for school in Felch. Felch was, and may still be, a very small, isolated, ingrown community of Swede-Finns. These were the children of Swedes who had emigrated to a part of Finland and then to the U.S. Their children were not unfriendly, but poor little Dale had a rough time during her first, eagerly-awaited year in school. This was mainly because she wore cute and up-to-date clothes, instead of the old-fashioned long dresses and long stockings the other girls wore. Gregg adjusted to his third school more easily and he was very protective of Dale on the bus and at school. They were soon ardent Felch fans and their lives centered around school, except when school was out and they spent most of their time working on their Peter Pan project.

This was an offshoot of Gregg's passionate love of movies. He'd seen his first movie in Evansville when he was three, and particularly loved the Disney movies, which he read about, heard about on the radio, talked about and completely memorized. When he found that cartoons were made by having picture after picture with very slight differences he decided he, with Dale's willing help, would make Peter Pan. He drew and colored hundreds of pictures in a little building on the property, his studio. This was a huge project which, fortunately, never advanced to the point where he had to figure out how to put the pictures together into a moving picture.

Iron Mountain was our shopping center and we went there to the movies, church, doctor and dentist. The people in Iron Mountain and the whole area were very friendly, partly because the area had been depressed since Ford had stopped building wooden auto bodies there some time before, and the people were thrilled with any new business. Since we were 20 miles out of town, we did not become very well acquainted, but the wives of the employees of the pilot plant were friendly and we had many vendors visiting and taking us to dinner, as well as Dee Vedensky from Cleveland and Les Bechaud from the Hibbing Lab. It was a big thrill for Elton when George Humphrey, then Hanna's CEO and later Eisenhower's Secretary of the Treasury, came to visit the plant.

We were asked to one big cocktail party and dinner in town before Christmas and met many of the local business people. Oddly enough, that party was responsible for our becoming Presbyterians. We'd gone previously to Presbyterian, Congregational or Methodist churches, more or less at random, and, when we did go to church in Iron Mountain, we went to the Methodist Church. But the Sunday after the party I went to church and heard a long sermon on the evils of liquor. We'd had a wonderful evening and I didn't believe we'd done anything wrong, so I swore off the Methodist church—not liquor—and we became Presbyterians.

Elton was really happy running his first plant and although he put in upwards of eighty hours a week, he loved it and was home often enough. He came for all his meals, since the plant was close, so I didn't mind his working long hours. We finally bought a sewing machine and I spent many happy hours sewing.

Mother and Dad visited us in October and we saw, and nearly froze at, our first Green Bay Packer game which was held in the high school bleachers that they were then using as a stadium. We also took an overnight trip to the Soo (Sault Ste. Marie). The Roesers had no more than left than Granddad Mesick arrived to spend about two months. Ethel came for Christmas and they returned to Rapid City together.

In May, 1952, the operation of the pilot plant was completed and the plant was closed. We thought, at the time, a large operating plant would be constructed very soon, using the results obtained from the pilot plant, so when Elton was returned to Hibbing in June, we felt it would be a temporary assignment. It was a month or two before we realized we were there for good. Because we had been expecting to return soon to Iron Mountain, we moved to an apartment in Hibbing, leaving behind my plants, jars and other household items, as well as Bobbie, our collie. He stayed with the Ole Olsens who moved into our farm house. We saw Bobbie just once after that in the spring of 1953 when we took a trip from Hibbing to Groveland. Eventually he had to be shot because he was hurt in an accident.

We lived in Hibbing from July 1952 to June 1956 and were happy to leave when we finally did because we didn't like it even though it was an interesting place. Hibbing was the biggest town (maybe 30,000) on the Mesabi Iron Range which is one of a dozen or so iron ranges occurring in Minnesota, Michigan, Wisconsin and Ontario containing vast quantities of ore, mostly iron. The Mesabi was the richest developed iron ore deposit in the world and had supplied most of the iron used in the country from the time it was first developed around 1880 until well into the 1950's. By the fifties, most of the direct shipping ore (which could go to the blast furnaces with little or no treatment) had been mined and shipped and the major iron mining companies were looking for ways to treat the harder taconite ore to make it usable as blast furnace feed. This was the reason Elton's application for a job, as an experienced metallurgist, had been well-received, and development of ore treatment facilities was the major work of the Hanna Research Lab and the work of the Groveland Pilot Plant.

The population of the Mesabi Range and a couple of adjacent ranges was probably about 200,000 scattered in a fifty-mile radius of Hibbing. The population was largely foreign born or first-generation American. They were Swedes, Finns, Italians, Greeks and Yugoslavians of all kinds, for example, Croatians, Serbs, Slovaks and others. There were some Jews, but no blacks or Orientals. Everyone was asked by a new acquaintance what his/her nationality was, what church he/she attended and what the husband's job might be (not what the wife's job might be since she was supposed to be in the kitchen). This was a great help in dropping people in their proper slots. Hibbing life was very stratified socially. At the top were the Caucasian mining company executives, mostly Episcopalian or Presbyterian; next were the middle managers, mostly Swedes or Finns who were often Lutheran; this ranged all the way down to the Slovaks and Croatians, always Catholic or Orthodox. Since the Hanna Lab was not part of an executive office or production operation, people in the Lab didn't fit into any category. This meant that we were accepted even less than we would have been in any case.

The people were not friendly to newcomers. I was told once by a fellow Sunday school teacher that they didn't like veterans, college graduates, or people from other places. They were inordinately proud of Hibbing—even though it was miserably cold, had little scenic beauty and its culture was limited to hunting and fishing. Economically, however, it was very well-off. Everyone worked and made relatively high wages. The mining companies picked up the tab for any special expenses, including medical clinics, the excellent city library, all books and supplies for the schools and even a swimming pool in the high school.

The town itself had been totally moved from its original location because it was on ore which was later mined from the "Hull Rust Pit, the Largest Iron

Ore Open Pit in the World." While we lived there we often saw houses, some quite large, being moved from one area to another. They were often purchased for small amounts and put on new foundations in the town.

Like most of the U.S. at that time, life was fairly regimented. Almost everyone went to church on Sunday; on Monday the housewives did the washing; they ironed on Tuesday; had church circles and club meetings on Wednesday; cleaned on Thursday and/or Friday, and baked, shopped and got ready for church on Saturdays. This now sounds terribly regimented, but it wasn't required that we keep this schedule. Everyone just did it. Women ALWAYS wore a hat and gloves when they went out, even on the hottest days. There were always a few hot days every year and people were fond of saying, "If summer is on Sunday, we go on a picnic," or "Hibbing has two seasons, winter and poor sledding." Many of the residents of all the iron range towns had summer cottages on one of the many lakes, and for those of us who did not, spending a day at someone's lake cottage was a big summer treat. The churches were very important to most people and we joined the Presbyterian Church. I became active in Sunday school and the Women's Association, we joined a couples' club and we finally became acquainted, but it wasn't easy.

Although we did make many friends, I disliked Hibbing because people were not accepted for themselves and the natives were very full of their own importance. I think they were smug about their product—the iron ore—being absolutely essential to the U.S. and the world. They expanded this to mean that they, too, were essential to the world.

When we moved to Hibbing from Felch, our apartment was in the Belmont Apartments near the Hibbing High School—a magnificent school with a swimming pool, way ahead of its time, thanks to iron mining money. We lived in the Belmont for about three months. It was relatively expensive for that time ($105/month) and had only one bedroom and a Murphy bed (pulled down from a closet). We were on the third floor, so we did a lot of walking up and down. I hadn't realized until then that kids never walk if they can run, but apparently the neighbors didn't mind and were surprisingly nice about it. We entertained Ethel for a brief visit while we were there and enjoyed listening to the Presidential national conventions on the radio. This was something we had never been able to do because this was the first time we had good reception all day long.

Elton took his first real business trip for Hanna that summer, going to Detroit where he met and worked with Alan English for the first time. He ran out of money very quickly and had to ask me to wire him some. This was an interesting maneuver because they had misspelled his name on the register as "Ehon Gust." They couldn't find anyone by that name to come and collect the money I'd sent to Elton Geist until I insisted they try to get it straight. They finally did. But from that time on, he arranged his finances directly with the company.

In September there was an outbreak of polio and the schools were closed for a while. When they re-opened, we were scared when Dale was sent home with a bad cough, apparently from allergies, we decided later. But the epidemic was real and it was serious. A number of children in town were hospitalized, disabled or died. Luckily, our kids did not contract the disease and, within two years, the Salk vaccine was developed and vaccination was made mandatory by the schools, much to everyone's relief.

It soon became obvious that nothing was going to be done about building a plant at Groveland, that Elton would continue at the lab and we were going to have to find another place to live. There was not much available, but we finally found an apartment—the ground floor and basement of a house on Second Avenue. It had a lovely kitchen, but the living room and two bedrooms were painted in dark and unpleasant reds, violets and greens. There was also a room in the basement which became Gregg's bedroom. The house was close to downtown, to the schools and church and to neighbors who pointedly ignored us. We had several confrontations with the owner, Mr. Bloomberg, who wanted to raise the rent. But rent controls were still in effect from war time regulations, and when the rent control officer came to check whether we were paying enough, I had to keep him waiting at the front door until I found the screwdriver we needed to turn the latch. We did not have a rent increase. Granddad Mesick visited us that winter and again spent Christmas with us, but Ethel did not.

1953

In January we went on a shopping trip to Duluth where Elton bought me a lovely aqua wool winter coat—the first new coat I'd had in years. But except for that trip, we were pretty much housebound all winter. In January, our car conked out and we had no transportation. We ordered a **new** Chevy, but there was such a huge demand for new cars, it would be April before it was delivered. This new car seemed every bit as wonderful to us as our first car. During the winter, Elton was gone a good bit on a research project in Crosby, Minnesota. Fortunately, we were within two blocks of the Red Owl where I bought our groceries and close to downtown for other things. Nevertheless, it was a long, cold, lonely winter for me. During the year, both kids had chicken pox and measles.

Les Bechaud left Hanna in January and we gave a farewell party for him and his wife with the Lab personnel—the first time they had ever gotten together. I bought a beautiful dress for the party—red taffeta with a little rhinestone trim. It was about the prettiest dress I ever owned. The party was a good one, and it led to friendships and sociability with the other Lab employees. Elton was put in charge of the Lab temporarily, and in June he decided to accept the job on a permanent basis.

We thought this would give us the opportunity to have the Bechaud's company house, but it took some politicking on Elton's part and offers by Dick Whitney, Hanna's top man, of a couple of other miserable company houses before it was agreed that we could have the house on First Avenue. We moved in July, 1953, and loved the house, a fairly old center hall Colonial two-story with three bedrooms, one bath and large, light rooms, as well as a nice, though unkempt yard. Though we had too little furniture for it, we enjoyed being able to buy some nice furniture during the three years we were there. We were happy that we could finally acquire an automatic washer and a DRYER—the most wonderful invention in the world for those who live in cold, snowy country. I was thrilled, too, when Elton bought me a sterling silver service the Christmas of 1953.

Very soon after we moved into the house in 1953, we took a vacation trip to Yellowstone. The kids and I had our first plane trip. I had a hat for the occasion; we had food served; and it was a very civilized journey, unlike most plane trips since 2000. We went to Colorado Springs for a few days with the Roesers, then they drove us to Climax where Dale and Mona Johnson lived, and we drove with the Johnsons to Rapid City. Elton had driven from Hibbing and we took off the next day with Ethel for Yellowstone and the Tetons. It was a thrilling and exciting experience, especially for the kids. After a stop in Miles City, Montana to visit Elton's Clark cousins (children of Persis Geist), we returned Ethel to Rapid and drove back to Hibbing.

Although the kids should have been in the same school, Dale was enrolled in the Cobb-Cook school (a few blocks away from us) where she went for the third and fourth grades, at which time they opened the new Greenhaven School near us. Gregg was bused to the old Lincoln School in North Hibbing for the 6th grade, which was taught by Sulo Lundgren, a wonderful teacher who appreciated Gregg's tendency to get absorbed in, and learn everything about, one subject, ignoring all others until he was obliged to pay attention. For the next two years he bussed to Junior High in the High School. Dale walked to school and came home for lunch. The Hibbing schools had released time for church participation every Wednesday and I undertook teaching, inadequately, in our church's school. At the time, I thought released time was a good idea and didn't appreciate until later its inappropriateness (and "Political Incorrectness").

In October, 1953, Granddad Mesick had a serious heart attack. He was in hospital for several days and it was decided that he would come to live with us, more or less for good. This was another of our life's decisions made by Elton and his mother, and it took me a long time to get over my anger. I didn't mind having him with us, I just didn't like being by-passed and having his mother make the decisions I should have made. To get Granddad, Elton and I made a hard, two-day trip to Rapid and back. Ethel spent that Christmas with us, and by April, Granddad seemed his usual self and insisted on returning to Rapid.

1954

This year of 1954 was marked by several important events. Though our first new car was less than a year old, we bought another, a green Buick sedan. In June, I acquired a Springer Spaniel puppy whom we named Duke. He was a timid, loving dog, who became pretty neurotic after some hectic years. Duke was a one-man (me) dog, who still loved everyone else. We borrowed a used piano from the Bob Brandts, and the kids began music lessons. I'd made up my mind I wouldn't nag them about practicing, so Gregg didn't; Dale was always responsible and obedient—she practiced diligently. Gregg was the despair of his teacher, Miss Freimuth, who wanted to stop his lessons if he did not practice, but she kept coming until we moved away. Gregg really loved music and was quite talented, but he couldn't read music (probably because of his undiagnosed dyslexia), and the teacher frowned on memorization.

Another interesting event was a visit to Hinkley, Minnesota, when my mother was visiting us. They were having a 60th year celebration of the great Hinkley fire which my grandparents had escaped when Mother was three months old. We had thought someone would be interested in one of its older survivors, but the few people we spoke to thought it didn't count unless you'd returned to Hinkley and grown up there. Both Mother and Dad visited us later that fall and, as usual, we had a good time and did a lot of touring, including a weekend in Minneapolis and a Big-Ten football game. As I recall, Minnesota played Michigan and Michigan won.

We took our next real vacation trip that winter of 1954, going to Lincoln to Dick and Phoebe Skamser for Christmas. We had a pleasant two or three days there, spoiled for Elton because they refused to open gifts until their notoriously tardy daughter, Wilma, and family arrived, and our kids had to wait too. One memorable moment was an interesting commentary on Elton's progress in the working world when he commented on having reached the $10,000 a year mark. Both Dick, a postman, and Dad, a forester, were amazed as neither of them had ever gotten near that pay rate. I must say it still seemed pretty wonderful to us, too, to have enough money, finally, for a very comfortable life.

On leaving Lincoln, we headed through Missouri and Arkansas to Louisiana and New Orleans. We hadn't driven in any big towns ever, so it wasn't easy for either of us, but we enjoyed being in a city. We loved the automatic car wash—the first we'd ever seen—and the Hoagie sandwiches (now usually called Subs). While it had nothing to do with our trip, I might mention that 1954 was the year transistor radios came on the market.

Our stay in New Orleans was great, but it was cut short by the rising hotel prices for the New Year's Sugar Bowl game. We took off for the Gulf Coast where we spent a few days in the pleasant summer weather. We stayed at a motel in Pass Christian, Mississippi, a dry state, and were astonished to find a bar openly operating at the motel. Since it was against the law anyway, there were no closing hours, and apparently all of this was made possible by simply paying off the sheriff. We went as far east as Pensacola where it was too cold for swimming, but where the water was warmer than in the Minnesota lakes in the summer, and then drove through Alabama and back into Tennessee, and north to Hibbing. Surprisingly, considering the fact that the kids spent most of the trip reading comic books, they enjoyed the sights and retained clear memories of what they saw, including the obviously wretched conditions of the black population.

1955

Back home in January 1955, the kids returned to school. Both of them were in the Scouts but didn't go very far. Gregg didn't like it much and hated the one week of camp he attended. I became a Brownie leader and went along with the girls when they "flew up," but I'm not much of a Scout leader and didn't inspire Dale to go much further.

The winter of 1954-55 was the first year of television in our lives. I should note that wherever television became available, there was a certain amount of intellectual snobbery exhibited by many people and everyone didn't get TV. We felt somewhat the same way, but after resisting for several months, we succumbed in March, 1955 and spent several months in the familiar condition of doing everything with our eyes turned to the TV. This was a boon for me, because by this time, Elton was spending a great deal of time traveling, more each year, and the evenings were much less lonely after the advent of TV. It was also a boon to Granddad Mesick who spent two months with us that spring. He had never seen TV and he watched everything, even sports with which he was totally unfamiliar. For this visit, we picked him up and took him back to Minneapolis where he connected with the bus.

By this time we'd become acquainted in Hibbing. I'd started a bridge club; we joined the 66 Club at church (when our combined ages reached 66 we were supposed to drop out; Elton and I were pretty sure we'd never reach that advanced age). We also joined the Cosmopolitan Club, a dance club, which was a lot of fun. We had met and become friends with several couples whom we thoroughly enjoyed—the Bob Hawkinsons (Lois was my co-leader for the Scouts), the Merlyn Woodles, the Jim Greenaways, the Jim Youngs and others—so Hibbing was much more pleasant for me and I kept busy. I was still knitting, as always, and sewing most of Dale's and my clothes, and in the summer of 1955 we started golfing. That summer was reasonably warm, so we played golf often at the municipal course, since Elton's application for membership in the Hibbing Country Club had been rejected. I gave Elton a slide camera for Christmas 1955, and we took pictures of everything for years.

The Roeser family had a reunion in the summer of 1955, the last one before Grandma Roeser died. We drove to the Springs for that affair. Jack and Betty had a third child, Carola Zoe, on July 3. The Johnsons had also had another girl and now there were three—Nancy, Vicki Virginia born on August 14, 1952, and Elizabeth Elaine (always Liz), born on April 15, 1955. The two younger girls were born in Climax, which they later kidded about. We did not see the Johnsons when we visited Colorado, but later we met them in Rapid and spent time in Custer where we went to see the Gold Discovery Days pageant. We also saw our very first McDonald's. These were the only vacations we took that year, although Elton traveled a lot, spending time in Cleveland at Hanna's home office; in San Francisco, where design of the Groveland plant had begun; in Riddle, Oregon where a nickel smelting plant was starting up, and in various other places, checking out various plants and processes.

For a year or two, Gregg had been very close to Joe Arko and Lance Bredvold and they did everything together. In the school year beginning in September 1955, they decided they would have a dinner party every Thursday, first in one home and then another. Of course they tried to top each other, and all the families enjoyed the formal dinners when the boys were at our respective homes. Gregg, by the way, told me one day that he wished I were like Lance's mother, who played all kinds of games with them. I don't like games and always avoid them, but when I mentioned this to Lance's mother, she laughed and said, "Lance said he wished I were like you and would kid and laugh with them."

Lance and Gregg took a morning paper route that winter, and with Lance's family on an extended vacation in January, Gregg did it alone. The route started eight blocks from our house and was a long route. January in Hibbing is COLD, and Gregg developed a serious sinus infection and was a very sick boy in February.

Meantime, Dale was busy with many friends, particularly Susan Hawkinson, who was also born on November 17, 1944. They were both in the Junior Choir at church and in the scout troop. I still read to Dale and Gregg before they went to bed, and might have kept it up even longer, but the last book I read aloud was *The Swiss Family Robinson* which I continually interrupted with comments on the idiocy of the book, and they decided to retire me as reader.

At some point during that time Dale changed the spelling of her name. She didn't like Dale because teachers put her in boys' gym classes, but she didn't want to be called Christine. I met a woman whose name was Beauradaille who was called Daille and I suggested to our Dale that she might want to change her name. She thought that was a great idea and from 1956 on she has been Daille. Oddly enough, everyone seems to know how to pronounce Braille, but many have had trouble pronouncing and spelling her new name.

Ethel drove east to visit us that spring and no sooner had she left than my folks drove in. Meantime, Elton had been asked to spend the summer at the Riddle, Oregon plant, so we decided that the kids and I would join him when school was out. We packed the car and loaded the four of us and Duke in the car for the three-day trip. Duke was a poor traveler; apparently, he always thought he was on the way to the vet. He stood all day long, drooling on patient Gregg's knees. Despite this, it was an interesting trip. We saw country we hadn't seen before, and haven't seen again since. We drove straight across Minnesota, North Dakota, Montana and Idaho and down the Columbia River. We were excited seeing the Coeur d'Alene district of Idaho, the huge firs of the northwest and the waterfalls on the river and will never forget our first glimpse of Mt. Hood in the sunset.

Our summer was spent in a house sublet by a teacher who specified only that we keep up his garden and his rose bushes. It was a lot of work but we had luscious strawberries, raspberries and vegetables all summer and roses in the house. Gregg was supposed to do all the things one is supposed to do to roses (not worth the effort in my opinion), but he was going through a typical, indolent, 13-year old period, and I did a lot of it. Elton was very busy helping to get the nickel smelter project perfected so that the production of nickel could be profitable, but we still managed to do a lot of touring, most notably to Crater Lake (a magnificent sight), the Rose Festival in Portland and the Oregon coast. We loved the coast at Bandon, the wild trip down the "Seven Devils Highway" and the seal rocks. During the week, the kids and I swam in Cow Creek, which is more beautiful than it sounds; went shopping in Roseburg and had a great time. The people were wonderfully friendly, thanks mainly to Jeanne Coleman, the manager's wife, and altogether, we were not the least bit sorry in August to find that Elton was going to stay on and we would move there from Hibbing.

In order to do this, we found a house in Myrtle Creek, some 20 miles from Riddle, and drove to Colorado Springs after putting our few belongings in storage and Duke into a kennel in Grant's Pass. He was, apparently, prescient; he'd known he was on his way to the vet's on the way west! We headed east through northern California, hot and dusty Nevada and Utah. We left the kids and our '56 blue Buick with my folks, and Elton and I flew back to Hibbing to pack, find a mover, straighten our affairs and say goodbye.

After we got back to the Springs and picked up the kids and the car, we spent a night in Leadville with Mona and Dale. It was a sleepless night for me because they had just bought a house and moved in that week. It was so run-down and miserably built that we were sick about them living in it. They eventually did some fixing up, but never hired anyone to help them and it wasn't much better when they finally moved to a better house a few years later.

When we left Mona and Dale, we took off on a comprehensive sight-seeing trip which was marvelous, even though we took less time than we should have for all of it. The kids always kidded later about seeing the Grand Canyon with the engine running, but it wasn't quite that bad. We saw Santa Fe, the Painted Desert, the Grand Canyon, Las Vegas, Death Valley, Yosemite, the capital at Sacramento, the redwoods and finally headed up the coast to Myrtle Creek. Most memorable was the trip across Death Valley on an August afternoon. It was unbelievably hot in those pre-air-conditioned automobile days. We were all quite sure we'd die of heat prostration.

We were happy to be able to stay in the Hanna guest house in Myrtle Creek for a few days while we were getting settled in our house. Elton had left town for San Francisco an hour before the moving van arrived. His ability to schedule his departures, seemingly on-call, was a real skill. The house itself was very nice, with a lovely yard, and I loved it and everything about our next nine months there, except the unsettled situation with Elton's job. We had barely settled and had the kids in school when Elton was assigned to the San Francisco office of Bechtel to supervise the designs for the Groveland plant to be built in Michigan. This meant that he commuted, driving to Medford on Mondays, flying from there and back again on Saturdays. Fortunately, he now had a company car, so I didn't have to drive him back and forth to Medford as a rule. Driving was difficult in this area in the winter. It was always foggy at night and patches of ice would crop up when least expected.

Although Elton was gone most of the time, we were all used to it and, by this time, Daille and Gregg were great company; we had fun just talking. I finally got the piano I'd wanted and I spent time playing it, playing bridge, sewing, entertaining and enjoying the great weather. Myrtle Creek was far enough inland that it didn't get the rain and fog suffered by the coast. We had one spell when it got below freezing and they closed the schools—astonishing after living in Hibbing where they never closed the schools, even at 40° below zero. Other things about the area were also astonishing to me, for instance, the lack of interest in nationality. When I asked an Oregonian where his folks were from, he'd say "We-e-l-l-l, my folks were from Broken Bow, Oklahoma." There was also an amazing number of families made up of "my kids, his kids and our kids." People were very casual in dress and habits. We did the laundry when we felt like it and only wore hats when it was necessary. After Hibbing's rigidity, this was pleasant.

But it was a rough year for 12 year old Daille. She had hated leaving her friends in Hibbing and she was in the throes of early adolescence. Gregg, on the other hand, seemed to get along all right in his year there and did well in school. He played the trombone in the band and Daille started the flute while she was there.

We had plenty of company during the early months of 1957. Elton's mother flew out for a visit after Christmas, and my dad, who retired that spring, drove out with Mother for a couple of weeks. We drove to Seattle in the fall to visit Alan and Lui and they drove down from Seattle with Walt for a weekend in January. We also found that my cousin, Richard Skamser, was living in Roseburg with his wife and three daughters and we visited them a couple of times. Their marriage was rather typical of many marriages in those days. Richard had gone out with Rosemary, she became pregnant and, since she was Catholic, she had to get married (THAT is a shotgun wedding!). They had nothing in common and were eventually divorced.

One weekend that winter, Elton and I went to San Francisco for four days. This was our very first trip alone together and we had a wonderful time. Among other things, we had dinner with Frank and Kathryn Madison whom I met for the first time. In March, we flew again to San Francisco for a weekend, but this time with the kids. A Bechtel friend of Elton's, Ray Russell, had rented an elegant suite for us at the Huntington, and we enjoyed much more elegant meals at the best places, and trips to the major sights of the city. We all went home loving every bit of San Francisco and decided we would go there for the summer—hoping we would have a more definite location in the works by the time school started.

As soon as school was out, we put most of our belongings in storage and shipped off poor 'Dukie' dog to Rapid City to spend the summer with Ethel. Elton had sub-let an apartment in San Mateo for the summer from a Bechtel employee. We spent three weeks there before they decided that they wanted the apartment back, and we had to be out by July 1. There we were—no furniture, no house, no place to go, and, of course, no Elton—he was out of town). It was a discouraging moment. I went house-hunting, without success, until a realtor told me she knew of a house whose owners had wanted to lease it for the summer, but they'd taken it off the market because they were leaving the next day. We rushed out to the place and I all but offered them one of the kids as collateral and they finally decided we could have it—if we would care for their hamster for the summer. I would have promised to sleep with it if necessary, so of course we said, yes. The next day when we started moving in, we found the hamster dead! I dreaded writing to tell the owners, but they didn't sound too upset when they responded.

The house was an extremely modern one in a development of others like it on what we called Eichler Mesa (Eichler was the developer). It was not a house or an area I'd have chosen to own or live in, but we were delighted to have it for the time being. I had the use of a dishwasher for the first time. What was to become of us by the end of August, and where would the kids go to school remained the unanswered questions; they were the cause of my having a painful and persistent stiff neck. Nonetheless, we took advantage of being near San Francisco and spent as much time in the city as possible. One day we saw *Around the World in 80 Days* which enchanted all of us, especially Gregg, and Elton and I went to *My Fair Lady*, the play, with Abe Dor, a fascinating Bechtel engineer. We spent a weekend in a summer home on the coast with Don Johnson and his family. Don was Dale Johnson's brother and one of my high school classmates. The weekend was memorable, not only because we had a good time and a good visit, but also because Elton used the weekend to stop smoking. The kids and I spent one hilarious day with Kathryn Madison at their home in Palo Alto, joined in the evening by Frank and Elton.

But the most important event of the two months in San Mateo was a brief trip down to San Diego, Palomar and Juarez, and then back for a wonderful, unforgettable day at Disneyland which had been opened only a few months before. This was a high point in the life of our Disney fanatic, Gregg, and a revelation to Elton and me. We had grown up with carnivals and amusement parks, which were not at all like Disneyland. Now everyone is used to the neat, clean, attractive lay-out of theme parks, but Disney created a completely new entertainment form which entranced us. On that same trip, we picked up Ethel at Riverside where she had been for a conference, and took her to Disneyland for a day before returning to San Mateo.

On August 12, 1957, Hanna announced that they were going to begin construction of the pelletizing plant at Groveland and Elton was to be superintendent! We finally had an answer to where we were going and what Elton would be doing in the future. Our 15 months on the West Coast had taken us to many places we'd never seen before, given us priceless memories and certainly expanded our horizons. Now, though, we were happy to know we would be reunited with Duke and our furniture; we would be back in Iron Mountain and the kids would go back to school. Most importantly, Elton would have the job he had looked forward to for five years.

CHAPTER 6

OUR YEARS WITH HANNA—PART II

1957-1961

At the end of August 1957, we packed up again, and for the second time, headed east on a very hot trip through Nevada and Utah, with the mandatory stops in Leadville, Colorado Springs and Rapid City. It was especially important for us to stop in Rapid to pick up Duke, who was as pleased to see us as we were to see him. When we got to Iron Mountain, we stayed in the home of Les Larsen (one of the employees in the pilot plant) until our furniture arrived, then we settled into a rented house, which was the first (and worst) of the three homes we had in Iron Mountain. This was a three-bedroom house with every room painted some ghastly color but with a decent kitchen and roomy dining room. The basement was so full of junk we had to hire someone to clean it out, but all in all, it wasn't a bad home for the year we were there. Mrs. Roach, the landlady, left lots of African violets, which I loved, and kept from then on.

The children enrolled in Iron Mountain High School for Gregg and Junior High for Daille. Both spent a rather unhappy year getting acquainted and making friends. Gregg especially had problems, and I now believe it was because the other boys recognized that he was gay. We were ignorant of this, however, and knew no reason why he wasn't liked. Gregg never gave any sign of being unhappy. He had the marvelous capability of getting immersed in something else that enabled him to forget about the present. Both Gregg and Daille got hooked on *The American Band Stand* on TV, with Dick Clark hosting the show, and they rather liked Elvis Presley who began to be a hit in 1954 and horrified most older people.

Elton, on the other hand, was really happy. His job was General Superintendent of Open Pit Operations of the Michigan District. This included his supervision of Groveland and the Moose Mountain property near Capreol, Ontario, (about 300 miles north of Iron Mountain). A concentrator was being built at Moose Mountain and concentrator and pellet plants were being built at Groveland to process the ore from the mines. A pellet plant was built later at Moose Mountain. These were the first two of the six pellet plants Hanna was to build in the next nine years, all of which Elton supervised. Pelletizing had been found to be the most effective process for treating taconite ore, which was mined, crushed, ground and separated by flotation and magnetism and then rolled into pellets which were heat hardened and shipped to blast furnaces where they were fed directly into the furnaces. Reserve Mining opened the first pellet plant in Minnesota in 1955. There were only a few others in operation by 1959 when Groveland opened.

Unlike the production of direct shipping ore, pelletizing was extremely capital intensive. It involved huge and complex buildings and equipment. When Groveland was being built, George Humphrey, former CEO of Hanna, came to visit. When he saw the enormous layout, he promptly fired Elton for designing and promoting such an expensive project with no revenue. Elton began to pack up his office, but the acting CEO came in and told him to stay. This didn't keep him from worrying about his job until the plant was in operation, hugely successful and profitable. He didn't tell me until forty years later that he had been fired!

Unfortunately, pelletizing was also very energy intensive, and when international oil prices doubled in 1973, the pellet boom began to collapse. In 1957, however, there was joy and optimism in the Upper Peninsula and everyone involved in the pelletizing project was welcomed with open arms by the friendly residents of the UP, especially in Iron Mountain.

As the manager of this big new plant, which would provide some 300 jobs upon completion, in addition to plenty of jobs during construction and business for all kinds of auxiliary goods and services, Elton was very warmly received by the people in Iron Mountain. I was too, but I was so naive it took me a long time to realize how important we were, and the perks we had because of his position. We had many friends too, some of whom were friends only as long as Elton had his job. One night in November 1957, when Elton was gone, I was asked to dinner with Albee and Thelma Flodin and Bun and Helen Reeves and was asked to sit next to Albee Flodin. I really didn't realize until later that the Flodins were, so to speak, the rulers of Iron Mountain. I should have been highly honored, but I was not class-conscious enough to realize it. But I did enjoy the dinner and the company!

Another example of my lack of awareness: I was asked to join the Tuesday Study Club. I heard about the Study Clubs soon after we moved there and I knew this was something I would love to be involved in. There were three of them, made up of women who met every other week to study an agreed-upon subject. When I found that membership was by invitation only I was sure I would not be asked. I was asked to join all three. I chose the Tuesday Club and loved my time in it. In the next few years, I presented several reports on which I worked very hard. I think they were good reports and doing them certainly encouraged me to go back to college later.

During our first few months in Iron Mountain, the plant was still in the design stage, even after construction had begun, and Elton spent a lot of time in San Francisco and Cleveland. On one of his trips to the west coast his return flight took off about the same time as two others, which collided over the Grand Canyon; all passengers were killed. I was very worried about the possibility that Elton's plane might have been one of them, but he arrived home safely.

In November Elton had a great opportunity to go to Europe, the first of many during the coming years. He went primarily to Sweden and Norway to visit iron-sintering plants, but he spent a day or two in London as well. He brought us all such lovely gifts and wrote such interesting cards and letters, we all enjoyed the trip vicariously—though we all would rather have gone along.

Elton spent considerable time at Moose Mountain and I drove up with him several times. It was always fun going to Capreol (the town near the mine) and I enjoyed visiting Sudbury. Elton soon got acquainted with Cassio's Motor Lodge in Sudbury, run then and until 2002 by the Cassio family and he began a friendship with the Cassios and their children that still continues. When my folks visited us in 1959, we took them to Capreol and spent one lovely weekend in Depot Harbor, Ontario, on Lake Huron.

Iron Mountain was a real party town, with frequent cocktail parties and dinners, and we were invited to everything. A lot of it was centered on the Chippewa Club which can be described as a country club without golf course or pool and which Elton eventually served as President and I as President of the Women's Association. Almost every night during weekends and the holiday season, there was at least one big cocktail party and dinner, and we even went to an open house held every Christmas morning at Dr. Huron's home. Our high school children loved this, as did my parents who were in

Iron Mountain for our first Christmas. During the years we were there we entertained too, and made our open house every December 26 a big affair, with more than ninety guests one year.

Iron Mountain was not only a party town, but also a church town. We joined the Presbyterian Church immediately, and while we were there a new church was built, with Elton heading up the fund-raising. The town was pretty much split in half with the Catholic Italians in the north end of town and the Protestant Swedes, old-line Americans and others in the south end. Of course the high school girls were always dating boys from the other group, getting pregnant and having to get married. A major topic of conversation was always which kids were involved? In those days, living-together, or having a child "out of wedlock" was not to be countenanced.

1958

In February 1958, we went to the AIME (American Institute of Mining and Metallurgical Engineers) convention in New York with the Reeves and the Flodins. New York was having one of its worst snowstorms but we had a limousine, so it was no problem! The trip was exciting and wonderful for me—my first national convention, flying to Chicago on the Lake Shore company plane, taking the train to New York and riding in a compartment. How luxurious that would have been in 1943-44 when I had to travel coach with one or two children on my lap. We stayed in the Plaza and saw the hit show of the season, *The Music Man*. What a special trip!

John and Marvel Greenly moved to Iron Mountain in the spring of 1958. John went to work for Lake Shore Engineering, Bun Reeve's company. We began to do almost everything together, and soon had a group of 6 or 8 couples who were together at all the events and parties, golfed and played bridge, spent holidays and other good times together. The Greenlys, Buck and Jane Miller, Jim and Florence Clark, Lorn and Magee Johnson and various others came and went from time to time. This was the only period when we had a compatible group of friends who were in the same age range as we, though our children were older than theirs. We also spent a lot of time with the older Reeves, who became good friends.

Meantime, in the spring of 1958, we were anticipating a move into a better house. Until then, and many years afterwards, mining companies provided housing for the top management of its properties, so Hanna decided in 1958 to buy a house for us to live in until six new houses were built for the top Groveland people. The house was purchased from a family named Cohodes. It was across town, on the east side of Iron Mountain and it was an interesting old place with some very nice features. The kitchen was updated for us, with a dishwasher and disposal—our first. The things I remember most about that house were the Christmas decorations. We had four equal side-by-side windows in front, and Gregg decided to cut large red Old English letters, N O E L, and put one in each window. Unfortunately, he never got past the N and the O. This struck me as particularly funny since the previous owners were Jewish. Even though our windows said "N O" we had a wonderful Christmas celebration. And we had a much nicer house in which to spend the holidays than we ever had before.

Prior to moving into that house in August 1958, we took the kids on a memorable, combined sight-seeing and shopping trip to Chicago, then to Dearborn Village, Niagara Falls and, on our way back, Mackinac Island. On the way to Chicago we saw the Milwaukee Braves play in our first major league baseball games. Elton and I saw them play again that October when we went to a World Series game between the Braves and the Yankees. The Braves won and the day was made for all of us Braves fans who supported the American League but were very much anti-Yankees. Iron Mountain, and the whole Upper Peninsula were much more attuned to Wisconsin than to lower Michigan. The Braves were their baseball team and the Green Bay Packers were their football team. When there was a Packers game in Green Bay, most of Iron Mountain's population was in Green Bay.

1959-1960

We spent a year in the Cohodes house, with Granddad there for most of the winter. He and Ethel flew in to visit us in the fall of 1958, and Granddad stayed after Ethel left, rather unhappily. With two teen-agers in the house, Elton mostly at the Groveland plant which was rapidly being completed, and my involvement in all sorts of things, there was far too much coming and going to suit Granddad. Added to this, our active (and noisy) social life and drinking caused Granddad to feel left out, abused and disapproving. He was most anxious to return to Rapid and finally did so in the spring of 1959. We took him to Minneapolis and he flew from there to Rapid. This was the last time we were to see him, for he died suddenly the following November. My Grandmother Roeser had died in April 1959, so for the first time, we had no grandparents and our children had no great-grandparents.

One happy and unusual event occurred when we were in that house. Elton was the best man at a wedding, his one and only shot at this job. It was the wedding of Raman Rao, a Bechtel engineer with whom Elton had worked in Riddle, and who was now working on Groveland. Raman became acquainted with Roxanne Reeve, and their whirlwind courtship ended in a wedding in June. Raman was from India and Bun Reeve was dubious about his background so he made some in-depth inquiries before he would go ahead with the wedding. Unbeknownst to Bun, Raman came from an important family, and they were equally concerned about the wedding, so at the same time Bun was checking on them, they sent someone to check out Bun! Raman was (and is) a high-class guy and one of our dearest friends. Because he had no family in the States, he asked Elton to be his best man.

Elton was either at the mine or traveling that summer of 1959. I spent a lot of time at the country club golf course and a lot of time looking for Duke. He would disappear every time he got outside, and usually the dogcatcher got him and I had to go and bail him out. We could not train him to stay at home, and he wouldn't get used to a leash, so by spring of 1960, we decided we had to put him to sleep—a very sad moment.

While the new house was being built we went to Green Bay to buy furniture, carpets and drapes, and worked with a decorator for the first time. We moved into the new company house in August. That year I turned 37 and, in my usual habit of making lists of everything, I calculated that this was my 37th move! But at least we had gradually moved upward, and this house was a beautiful center hall Colonial, with a big yard, which was landscaped by company employees. Except for the piano, we had all new living room furniture. The carpet and drapes for the living room and the rest of the house made our older furniture in the other rooms look good. I really felt we had reached the top until one day some friends and I were talking about some of our problems, and it turned out that the major problems experienced by this group were 1) cleaning women, 2) losing their diamond rings 3) keeping their silver plate polished and 4) storing their furs. I realized then that my climb wasn't over yet but my problems were minimal—I had no cleaning woman, no diamonds, no silver plate and no furs! I should add that I did have furs before the year was over. Elton gave me a lovely silver fox stole for Christmas.

We had a lot of out-of-town company, even though Iron Mountain is not exactly on the way to anywhere. Dale and Ramona and their girls came to see us in the summer of 1959 and Ethel came back for a visit after Granddad's funeral in November 1959 in Gettysburg, South Dakota. We hired a small plane to fly us from Green Bay to and from Gettysburg for the funeral. Elton had often told me of his childhood memory of the beautiful trees in the Gettysburg cemetery. Having lived now in wooded country, we were both amused at those poor struggling little trees, although they looked pretty nice on the South Dakota prairie. Also in the spring of 1960 my folks were in Iron Mountain, and Alan visited during a business trip in June.

In the spring of 1960, the U.S. Census was taken and I thought it would be fun to go from house to house to get information, so I applied for a job. We had to take a test to be accepted, which was okay with me, but I got a perfect score (unusual, I was told) so they felt I should be promoted, even before I began, from census taker to Inspector. I was disappointed, but this was fun too, because I became acquainted with the census takers and enjoyed learning a great deal more about the people in Iron Mountain. At about the same time, Elton took his second trip to Europe. I was terribly disappointed, but since he was going with a group of Dravo Engineering employees, it would have been awkward for me to go along. Working on the census gave me something else to think about while he was gone.

We made up somewhat for not going to Europe by taking one of the best family trips ever in our new Mercury in June 1960, with Ethel accompanying us. This was part of our graduation gift for Gregg. We drove to Washington, D.C. by way of Chicago, Pittsburgh and Gettysburg and spent four days sightseeing in the capital. We then spent a couple of wonderful days at Fredericksburg, seeing battlefields of the Civil War, which was my major interest at that point in my life. We went on to Williamsburg, then the Great Smokies, where we had to have an emergency stop to find a doctor for Gregg, who had suffered a severe sinus infection, and a dentist for me and an abscessed tooth. When we had both been doctored up and felt better, we went on to Nashville and through Indiana to Chicago.

In Chicago, we decided to see a movie and chose one about which we had heard nothing, *Psycho*. It was a frightening murder mystery from which we have never fully recovered. That night, after insisting on rooms with two bedrooms throughout our trip, we happily took one bedroom and would not, under any circumstances, have stayed in a motel called "Bates," like the one in the movie. Having lived safely through the night, the next day we went on to visit Ethel's birthplace in Princeton, Wisconsin, then back to Iron Mountain. Daille accompanied Ethel on the train home to Rapid and stayed with her for about a month. At the end of June, we drove out for the Mines alumni reunion and picked up Daille in Rapid.

Elton traveled during 1960, as he had all of our years in Iron Mountain, but this time we traveled a lot together. In the fall, we went to Las Vegas to the Mining Congress, which was a memorable trip. It was our first time in Vegas. Neither of us liked to gamble, but it was, even in those days, amazing, fun and exciting. We saw friends from all over; some great shows and had a wonderful time. We also had a wonderful time in the spring of 1961 when we went to Quebec City to the Canadian Institute of Mining convention. We took the train, stayed in the Chateau Frontenac, and spent a day in Montreal on the way home.

The Presidential election of 1960 was a high point of that year, and Kennedy's win over Nixon was a low point in my life. Not only was I a confirmed Republican, but I was really uneasy about a Catholic president. My unease was pretty common, since those of us who had not grown up in Catholic homes or communities worried a lot about Vatican influence. I must admit that at that time I also had a built-in dislike of the Irish and the Ivy League for some reason. None of these fears were justified, of course, though I would not readily admit that JFK was a very good President. But his election was the end of the fifties and the zeitgeist of that period.

The 1950's were considered later to be a period in which the spirit of the times was a dull, routine and predictable, home-style life. In many ways, that was true, at least in the Upper Peninsula. There were many major changes in the fifties, some of which became major issues later, but we were quite removed from them—for instance, the growing civil rights movement. There were no blacks, Orientals or Indians in Iron Mountain, so race was not an issue, except in a rare case when it became personal as it was when the daughter of friends, Wendell and Syrie Haben, married a black man. It was a very brief marriage.

While we were very much aware of the cold war, we weren't really affected by it. The great news of the Russian Sputnik circling the earth in 1957 thrilled everyone and spurred most schools to demand more work in mathematics, but generally we ignored the Soviet threat. In some parts of the States bomb shelters were built, and we joked about doing it, but as far as I know there were none in our area. Looking back on this period makes me realize how radically life has changed since then.

Other events included the development of fast food restaurants. Geographically, the United States became larger when both Alaska and Hawaii were admitted to the Union in 1959, and the Great Lakes were made accessible to international shipping when the St. Lawrence Seaway was opened. One of the changes was comparatively minor, but seemed important at the time. The replacement of telephone operators with the dial phone was the first of many innovations affecting the use of the telephone. The first dial phones and long distance dialing were installed in 1960 in a few towns, Iron Mountain being one of them. No one had problems coping with the change because of the extensive advance publicity and the provision of adequate user instruction. I must say, however, that having a live telephone operator connecting one's calls had been rather comforting.

While world and local events transpired in the late fifties, Elton and I were busy with our individual and joint activities, Gregg and Daille were busy with school, friends and work. When we moved into the new Hanna house, we also moved to Kingsford, Iron Mountain's twin city. There was no physical separation between the two towns, but each had its own government and, unfortunately, school systems. Daille reluctantly transferred to Kingsford. Because Gregg was about to commence his senior year when we moved, we felt it was unfair to ask him to change schools again, and we bought a used car for him and he drove to school. It's hard to believe, after we'd lived without a car for so long, we now owned two and had the use of a company car. Gregg's car was in great shape when we bought it, but it was pretty banged-up by the end of the year. He enjoyed banging it up, I think.

After his first year in Iron Mountain, Gregg seemed to enjoy school more. He played the trombone in the school band and had a major part in the senior play. When he was a junior, Gregg and Ray Ganga became close friends. Ray was a local boy, a football star and a popular guy, which I'm sure made Gregg more acceptable to the other students. He was a good student when he wanted to be, very bright with an amazing memory, except in math. When Gregg was in the fifth grade I worked with him night after night, helping with his multiplication tables, which he never really mastered. To the end of his life, he did not know the answer to 8 times 7. Gregg was always a slow reader, no doubt due to dyslexia. He was a practiced procrastinator, but somehow he got good grades and graduated in June 1960, in the top 10% of his class. Throughout the last two years in high school he worked at Colenso's clothing store.

Gregg didn't know what kind of career he wanted and the only thing we noticed that indicated any tendency on his part was his terrific eye for architecture, so in the fall of 1960, we had him enroll at Michigan Technological College in Houghton in engineering as a basis for architecture. Since we had always lived in small towns, Elton and I were woefully ignorant of the many hundreds of possible career choices young people could make, but after we'd lived in Cleveland for a few years, I realized how limited our backgrounds had been. For instance, we had no idea of the field of advertising design, which Gregg eventually found and excelled in.

Meantime, he spent an unhappy year in the isolated and patriarchal town of Houghton, the home of Michigan Tech, where the students were mostly males whose interests were very masculine—fishing, hunting and sports. Gregg loved drama, art, music and cities. His experience at Tech wasn't made happier when he was hit by a car in January and fell on the street. Cinders became embedded in his face, and they had to be surgically removed the next summer. He was in the hospital in Houghton for a week and we weren't even notified! When he decided on his own to transfer to the University of Michigan in Ann Arbor for his second year, I was not sorry. And he loved it immediately.

Gregg's plastic surgery was his second surgery in Iron Mountain. In 1958 he had surgery on his nose to straighten the deviated septum. This helped a little to alleviate the sinus trouble from which he suffered all the time we were in Iron Mountain and thereafter. We learned in 1960 that Daille had a thyroid deficiency and she began taking medication, which made a big difference in her well-being. She had been a lethargic baby, though obviously not retarded, and had physiological problems with all her bodily functions so it was good news that this could all be corrected. She also had her teeth straightened and we made regular trips to an orthodontist in Green Bay for a couple of years.

After we moved to our new home, Daille kept busy at Kingsford High where she spent her freshman and sophomore years and half of her junior year. She was always a good student and responsible in anything she was asked to do. She complained, with justice, that if she got a B, we scolded her for not getting all A's, while Gregg was complimented if he got one A. Daille made friends with a group of girls, one of whom, Dee Aldrich, was one of her bridesmaids and a life-long friend. Daille played a flute and worked hard to become first chair in the band, which she didn't quite make. She also joined Job's Daughters, and Gregg was an unenthusiastic member of DeMolay, both Masonic groups.

Because of her late start in school, Daille was probably the oldest in her class and, unfortunately, she matured early, and was ready to date before most of the kids. At the same time, she was pretty fussy about whom she liked and that was fine with us. When she occasionally bemoaned the fact that so and so had a boy friend and I'd ask her if she would go out with him, she would say, "Absolutely not!" Throughout high school she always had a date for any important prom or dance, but didn't have any steady boy friends.

Daille worked in the summer between her second and third year in high school as a waitress at Myke's, and that fall she got a part-time job at the library in Iron Mountain. She was a good kid and we had no problems with her. Our major arguments were about clothes, which she loved. I had always made most of her clothes, but she never ceased to want something more, and finally, in her junior year, we put her on a clothing allowance. She became a good money manager and was much less eager to have expensive items. She suddenly decided that it was better for me to make something for her if it was cheaper than the ready-made product.

Daille turned 16 when she was a junior and was happy that she was finally permitted to drive. Gregg, surprisingly, hadn't cared much whether or not he got a driving license when he turned 16. We finally pressed him take the test. Daille was wild to get her license, and I think she was at the police station to take her test at 9:00 a.m. on the day she turned 16. It was convenient when we took our trip to Quebec and left her with a sitter who could not drive at night and Daille was able to drive her home.

Gregg and Daille were as active in the church as we were. We were very fond of the Presbyterian minister, Paul Sobel, of a converted Jewish family. His wife was a wonderful Christian who was Jewish but had grown up in Chicago with no religious experience. Her mother had been a reclusive, impoverished, illiterate immigrant, deserted by her husband, and Ruth grew up on her own. She knew more than anyone else I've ever met about the seamy side of life. Paul converted her when he was a street minister in Chicago and she became an enthusiastic and dedicated Christian. Ruth was, of course, ignorant of small-town culture and the way things were run in churches, and told hilarious stories about learning to fit in. She was really a wonderful person and I loved her and Paul.

Alan stopped in again on his way home from a business trip in May 1961. In June, Jack and his family also visited us for a week with their brand new baby, Craig Alan, who was born on June 3, 1961. They arrived a day earlier than planned and, although I am always ready for company at the expected time, I was unprepared for their early arrival. I had no beds ready, no food in the house, and it took me a day or two to get organized. This was especially annoying since it was probably the only time in his entire life that Jack was early for anything. When Mother and Dad were there in the fall of 1961, we toured the U.P. and Ontario with them.

By fall of 1961, we were thoroughly entrenched in Iron Mountain. We knew and were popular with all the civic leaders. We had also formed an integrated and happy work force at Groveland by entertaining all of the supervising force from foremen on up and by making sure that newcomers to town were introduced. Many of them were transferred from Hibbing, including Wendell Haben, Don Draves and George Kotonias, who had worked in the lab. Elton was an excellent boss who earned loyalty and respect from every employee. We had a beautiful house, good friends and a full life and I would gladly have stayed there. It was a terrible shock to me when Elton came home from a trip to San Francisco in mid-December and told me we would be moving to Cleveland, where he would be Manager of Taconite Operations.

Although I think he also hated to leave Iron Mountain, he was thrilled to be moving to company headquarters. He had always hoped to be president of a major corporation and this seemed like a door opening to that goal. The future turned out to be somewhat different than he'd hoped, but meantime, we had to make the move and give the news to family, friends and employees. This move made very little difference to Gregg who was happily adjusting to the University, but Daille was nearly as unhappy as I, and all the people we knew expressed regret. We spent Christmas with Ethel and attended many parties as usual, but with the addition of champagne at every party to drown our sorrow. By New Year's Day, Iron Mountain had no more champagne, and shortly thereafter, no more Geists.

On January 2, 1962, Elton, Daille and I drove to Cleveland to look for a house. Although we spent another two weeks in Iron Mountain packing and saying goodbye, essentially our lovely years there were over.

CHAPTER 7

OUR YEARS WITH HANNA—PART III
CLEVELAND AND HIBBING AGAIN

1962

After we vacated our house on January 22, we spent the very cold night at the Chippewa Club, then loaded the plants and the rest of our belongings and drove to the Lower Peninsula where we spent a night in Jackson. The next morning we stopped to visit Gregg in Ann Arbor (our first time there) and drove on to Cleveland. We exited the Turnpike at North Olmsted and approached the city on Lorain Avenue—certainly not the most encouraging view of the city—and spent the night at a motel on East 30th and Superior. The next day we began hunting for a place to live.

Driving in a city was a new and unwelcome experience for me, and I got a serious indoctrination in the three days Daille and I were house-hunting. Elton, predictably, flew off somewhere on business and she and I were left with Want Ads, city maps and a car. We looked first on the east side, then drove across the south side of the city, past miles and miles of depressing developments of small look-alike houses to the west side and more of the same.

The housing we'd seen in the area was depressing enough, but we were also introduced to the Cleveland culture by two events. First, I was turned off by the comments of the real estate agents who introduced us for the first time to the East/West dichotomy in Cleveland. Those on the East Side said, "Oh you don't want to live on the West Side and drive into the sun morning and night," and those on the West Side said, "You don't want to live on the East Side with all those Negroes and Jews." My reaction was to avoid the West Side and the bigotry there. The other event was a conversational comment by Daille about the wonderful exploit of Alan Sheppard the day before, going into space for the first time, and she said "What do you think of what Sheppard did?" and we got a blast about how tired Clevelanders were of the Sheppard murder. This had happened eight years earlier and was a really big deal in Cleveland, but we hardly knew what she was talking about. Neither of these comments made us more eager to move to Cleveland, but unfortunately, we had no choice.

Daille and I had dinner at Stouffer's and went to a movie downtown the first night, then had dinner with Phil and Lu Dettmer the second night. On the third day, Elton arrived and we went house-hunting together. We had checked with the Chamber of Commerce about the schools in the area and found that Shaker and Lakewood rated best in every way, but Daille began to question going into a big school as a stranger. It turned out that this had to be a secondary consideration. Because we didn't know what we'd want in a year or two, we preferred to rent, but rental housing was very scarce. We had located two possibilities which El turned down, one an upstairs flat in a Shaker duplex, and the other a house in Orange. We were getting pretty discouraged until a Lakewood realtor told us about a house which was one of ten built to sell by a developer in Westlake. Five of them were still unsold after two years on the market and he had decided that day to rent them. Cleveland, like every U.S. city in that period, was full of middle managers being transferred by their companies every other year. They needed housing for only a couple of years until the next move. These nice, roomy houses—two story, five bedrooms, two baths, fireplace and full basement—were all rented that day, one of them to us.

The next day, Daille and I drove back to Iron Mountain and packed. When Elton arrived and we'd lived through several good-bye parties, we drove back to Westlake, arriving on January 23, 1962.

The house was not in the city at all, but on the western edge of Westlake, adjacent to farmland. In fact, these houses were built on part of a grape orchard, the rest of which backed up on our property. For Elton, traveling to the office downtown (about 15 miles), it meant either an undependable and slow Greyhound bus, a ride into the Rapid Transit stop at West Park, or ride downtown with a neighbor. I had thought that the one advantage of moving to a city was access to a city's attractions, not living miles away, and since I continued to be angry about moving, that was just salt in the wound. We were back to one car, because a promotion to the home office eliminates the field's fringe benefits of car, company house and yard man, and we were paying rent again for the first time in years. Elton had a raise, of course, but it didn't begin to cover our increased expenses.

Most of the time, he didn't have to worry about the commute. He spent most of his time that year away from Cleveland. His job was to take charge of Hanna's new operations, which included a new plant and pelletizer in Labrador, and a new pellet plant at Groveland, which meant extra time in San Francisco and Pittsburgh with engineering firms. I felt like one of my neighbors who said she only saw her husband when she took clean shirts to the airport. We new residents spent a lot of time taking our husbands to and from planes.

As for Daille, our search for the best schools proved fruitless. Westlake had been rated poorest in many ways, but it turned out to be a pretty good school—certainly better than Kingsford. For one thing, she had writing assignments for the first time ever. She found it hard to move in the middle of her junior year and had a miserable cold for a couple of weeks—always her reaction to change. But she enrolled in the Westlake High School, plunged into the scholastic end of school with zeal and thrilled us all the next year by being Valedictorian of her class, barely beating out a Westlake native. One of her major hurdles in the move was getting her driver's license. The parallel parking kept her from getting it until her third test. She was furious when the examiner told her he hoped she could cook better than she could park. At school she made some friends and had enough dates to keep her spirits up, and since Elton was out of town most of the time, she and I took advantage of plays, ballets, opera, and other events in Cleveland and had a nice time together.

Our neighbors turned out to be really compatible. They were all from out of town and similar in job level, education and age. We spent the whole winter of 1962-63 celebrating 40th birthdays (including mine). Our next door neighbors, Virginia (four days younger than I) and Perry Arnot, from Tulsa, became special friends. There were also many Hanna people on the west side. We found ourselves living in the same town again with the Carlsons and Rossers from Oregon, the Carl Andersons from Michigan and the Jim Youngs (of Pickands Mather) from Hibbing. Vince Vellella, who had worked in the Hanna Lab, introduced us to several couples with whom we became friends, and Alan English, who had been Elton's good friend for many years, lived in Cleveland Heights with his family.

I was asked to join the Hanna ladies bridge club and I joined the League of Women Voters as soon as I could. I'd belonged in Hibbing for just a few months before we moved away and had wanted to be in the League again ever since. My membership in P.E.O., which I'd joined in Iron Mountain, primarily because Jane Miller had introduced me, gave me the opportunity to visit other chapters. I joined Chapter AE before summer. We also joined a nearby Congregational Church, but it was months before we were greeted by any of the other members. We found it hard to greet them because they didn't look at us.

We were concerned about Gregg during the first few months we were in Cleveland. He was pretty discouraged because he didn't really know what he wanted to do with his life. Because we were relatively close to Ann Arbor, he spent breaks and weekends with us, mostly worrying about what to do. He didn't want to go into architecture, which he had signed up for because he didn't like the plumbing, electrical wiring and all of the technical part of the profession, yet he didn't know what he would like. He had found in a required life drawing class that he definitely had art talent, and we all thought that was great, but we had no idea how to make a career of it until after I went with Daille to a school presentation on possible career choices. She and I decided to hear what an advertising executive had to say about his profession. Listening to him, I thought this sounded like something Gregg might like. I called the man later and asked if he'd consider talking to Gregg about his profession. He agreed, and told me to have Gregg bring some of his work. Gregg spent an exciting afternoon with him and decided then and there to switch his major to advertising design. He never regretted his decision and told me often later that he sometimes felt guilty taking pay for something that was so much fun.

Gregg was not the only one who made a major change in his life—I did too. With Elton suggesting and encouraging me, I decided to go back to college. It had never occurred to me that this was even possible. Like most people at that time, I thought college was behind me when I got married. Elton told me that since there were several colleges quite close, I should go back and get a degree. I'd met a lot of women in the years since my sophomore year at Mines who were active in the American Association of University Women. It was especially galling to me that these women (much dumber than I) looked down their noses at me because I hadn't graduated from college. My reading had tended to scholarly subjects and I'd relished preparing the reports for the Tuesday Study Club, so I was really thrilled at the thought of going back to school once I had made the decision—but I was nervous too.

I chose Western Reserve University because I could get there by rapid from the nearest station. I interviewed and took the necessary tests. Surprisingly, all of my college credits were accepted except Mineralogy, which oddly enough was identical to a course in the WRU catalog. I had intended just to get some further education, but I was required to be in a degree program, so I signed up to work for a B.A. Starting school in September, 1962, I entered a whole new world. At that time, few women were attending college. Most were busy being housewives, but I did find several who were doing the same as I. It was a pleasant surprise, by the way, to discover that I was not dumber than the younger students, but had somehow learned quite a lot in my twenty years out of school. The first year was difficult because it took an hour and a half to get to school by car and/or rapid and I had trouble learning to study again. But Gregg and Daille were enthusiastic about my going to school, and Daille and I helped each other with homework. Although most of the adults we knew, including my mother, thought my going to school was ridiculous, my fellow students, even the young ones, thought it was great and it was fun sharing our scholastic experiences and skills.

When the summer of 1962 arrived, Elton insisted that Gregg get a job on his own. He tried, but without success. He probably applied for more jobs than any other ten kids his age put together. After an abortive attempt at encyclopedia sales, he spent a month or two picking berries at the grape and berry orchard abutting our back yard. It was hard work with very little pay, and it certainly was not a pleasant way to spend the summer. But was it a character-building experience? We hoped so. At least he learned something about the value of money. When I suggested he buy a hat to protect himself from the sun, he felt it would cut into his profit too much.

Elton took a week's vacation in August and we drove to Colorado. We had a lovely week visiting the Roesers and being tourists, including a ride up the Incline and a hike to the old abandoned Forestry Experimental Station. When Elton left to return to work, the three of us drove to Leadville to visit the Johnsons. We then went to Rapid City and on to Iron Mountain where Elton joined us for a round of parties and fun. Then it was home to Cleveland and work and school for all of us. In Daille's case, work meant playing the piano at a ballet school, and school meant hard work in her senior year with an eye toward college.

December, 1962 was a memorable month. On December 6, three of my new neighbors played bridge at my house and Marilyn Klusmeier, whose husband worked for Dow Chemical, brought me a box of a wonderful new wrap—Saran. This was almost as memorable as the snow we had that night. We had never experienced a worse snow storm. On the same day, the Cleveland newspapers went on strike and we couldn't even read about the storm. We couldn't shovel it either. We had no garages, but we did have long driveways. All the men on the block were out of town on business, as usual, so we spent a miserable week-end, trying to get our cars out. The men dragged in from the airport by cab, one by one. The snow lingered for a couple of months, but the men were off on business again next Monday.

It was about this time that Hanna announced a new slate of officers, including Bob Anderson as Vice President. This appointment, in effect, put a stop to Elton's hope of moving far ahead in the company. As it turned out, Hanna's choice of Anderson was a terrible mistake. He would summarily fire or publicly humiliate many Hanna employees; others he would degrade by moving inferiors over them. He ran the company into the ground with poor management and, by the turn of the century, Hanna was no more. Sadly, when ex-employees heard in 2001 that he had Alzheimer's, their first reaction was that of joy. In any case, Anderson's advancement was a real blow to Elton and, together with my resentment and anger about moving, some very difficult years followed.

In the meantime, Gregg came home for Christmas with mononucleosis and spent his vacation recovering, except for two days that we spent in Pittsburgh renewing a close family relationship with Frank and Kathryn Madison. They now lived on a farm near there. It was a wild, drunken weekend, but fun and exciting, as were all our visits to our drinking friends in Pittsburgh—probably a fitting end to a wild year. It was so much fun that we revisited the Madisons after Christmas the next year.

1963

The cold weather and snow we'd had in December continued into 1963, and Cleveland had a record cold day of -17°F in January. We were convinced that we'd moved to a banana belt since we'd never lived anywhere except Oregon with a record low to equal it. Everything in town was cancelled that day, and although I went to school, most students were absent. I knew that the scheduled meeting of the Hanna ladies bridge club, with all those ex-Hibbingites, wouldn't be cancelled, and it wasn't. Like me, they all wondered why everyone thought it was cold.

Daille and I drove to Athens in March to look at Ohio University, then to Marietta to look at Marietta College. Elton and I felt strongly that the kids should go to state schools which had much lower tuition than private schools, and Daille liked the looks of Ohio U. However, because she received an honors scholarship for one half tuition at Marietta, that's the school she picked. She did not want to go to a big college for several reasons, one being the increased competition from thousands of others.

During spring break at Easter, we took the kids and spent four days going to Tahawus. This was the first time, and as it turned out, the only time, the kids and I had been back there since we left in 1949. We made the effort to go because the whole town was being moved to allow National Lead to get to the ore below. The trip was rushed because the three colleges had different spring breaks, but it was a thrill, nonetheless, to see our old home and our old friends. Back home in Cleveland, we saw other old friends fairly often. When the Greenlys or others from Iron Mountain came to Cleveland on business, they often stayed with us.

We had an eighteen-month lease on our Westlake house and we were due to move out in June, 1963. We had decided to try apartment living next, so I began in May to look for apartments. There was not a large selection, and we finally settled on one that satisfied most of our requirements, the major one being three bedrooms, but which was as far east from Cleveland as Westlake was west. People simply didn't move from the west to the east, but we did, and on June 15 we moved to Beachwood. Our friends on the west side said "You CAN'T live on the east side!" and our friends on the east side later said "You lived on the West Side!" We found that there were advantages to both sides and have never quite understood these still prevalent attitudes.

Before we moved, Ethel came for Daille's graduation from Westlake High on an unusually hot June 6, 1963. The weather turned cold the next day, but we took Ethel to see Niagara Falls and some of the St. Lawrence. We returned for a frenzied week, getting Gregg off to Groveland for a summer job (this time arranged by his dad), getting my two final exams out of the way and packing and moving. We had furniture and appliances for an eight-room house with a basement and were moving into five rooms, already containing the necessary appliances and with only a closet for storage. To this day I wonder whatever happened to this or that piece of furniture or decorative item. I gave things away, sold what I could, stored carpets and some of the appliances, and put out a lot for the garbage man.

Once settled, Daille enjoyed a lot of time in the pool and had her hair cut and permed. This was the last permanent she ever had because it made her hair a mess. At this time, the beehive hair-do was going out and long straight hair was coming in. Daille's hair fitted the new style perfectly. When her perm grew out, her always gorgeous, straight blonde hair was the envy of other college coeds.

On one of Elton's trips to Labrador that summer of 1963, Daille and I drove with him to Montreal and then came home without him. We'd turned down our only opportunity to see Labrador! We didn't think we'd enjoy it much and I can't say I've ever regretted our decision. We were rear-ended, however, in a little town in New Hampshire, and were pretty sore for a day or two. We were lucky we had no lasting ill effects for I had foolishly signed off on any claims. Later in the summer, we drove to Iron Mountain for a couple of weeks and brought Gregg home to prepare for his junior year at Michigan.

We spent a lot of time and energy that summer getting Daille's college wardrobe ready. Girls were then wearing a profusion of skirts, dresses, pants and sweaters, all of which became jeans and tee shirts a few years later. In September, Gregg came for a weekend and we drove Daille to Marietta. She liked school, as always, but wasn't very happy with her dormitory. She had two roommates, never a good arrangement. But she pledged a sorority, Tri Sigma, had plenty of dates and seemed to enjoy herself.

With Daille gone, we were left with an empty nest. It was hard for both of us to see our baby leave, but Elton dealt with this personal trauma as he dealt with all of them. He left. He made sure he was out of town on business rather than arranging to stay home and comfort me. I started my second year at Reserve, and had French and English literature to study. I stayed busy, as always. It took a little getting used to, but I liked apartment living. There was much less housework, and no outdoor work. Transportation was a little easier for Elton, with a rapid stop less than a mile away and there was good shopping nearby. I'd joined the South Euclid-Lyndhurst League as soon as we moved, and immediately got a League job of some sort and worked on various studies. I stayed in the same P.E.O. chapter and went to meetings in Bay Village and other points west; it was always a long drive. I also stayed in the west side Hanna ladies bridge club through the spring of 1964. One day, in the middle of a game, I suddenly realized that I really disliked bridge, I didn't like cards and I didn't like games. It certainly took me a long time to realize this—I'd played cards and games my whole life! I gradually withdrew from bridge clubs, but did participate in different clubs during the next few years.

October found us in Las Vegas for the Mining Congress. It was not nearly as much fun as our first trip had been, but I enjoyed having a few days with Elton. Shortly after our return to Cleveland, my folks drove east to visit us and we had a wonderful time with them. We did a lot of sight-seeing, including the apple festival in Amish country and the Football Hall of Fame. Dad, Mother and I drove to Marietta on an overnight trip to see Daille, and with Elton along, we went to Ann Arbor for a football game and a visit with Gregg. He spent the day with us, despite the fact that he was quite ill. Soon after our departure, he went into the hospital for a week with an infection caused by cold sores.

Like the rest of the country, we had our Thanksgiving sadly disrupted by President Kennedy's assassination. We were not Kennedy supporters and I had wept bitterly when he won the election, but we found his assassination shocking. Daille arrived home the day after the assassination when Marietta closed until after Thanksgiving, and Gregg arrived the next day. Because Alan English was out of town, we had Evelyn and their boys for Thanksgiving dinner and, with the rest of the nation, spent the weekend watching television and the events following the assassination. The mood throughout the country was somber and remained so for months.

1964

After a quiet Christmas at home, Gregg spent most of the Christmas vacation of 1963 with a friend in Florida. Both kids went back to school in January until summer, with visits home from time to time. Because we were spending so much money repairing the Mercury we'd acquired in Iron Mountain, we bought a new blue Buick Skylark in the spring. It was a sporty car, and I grew to love it. Ethel came to visit us for a couple of weeks, and while she was here, Daille borrowed her car one day; she had an accident and we were again spending money on car repairs! Ethel had hesitated to drive, but Elton had told her that one of the kids might be able to drive home with her. To Ethel, "might" meant "will", so she was counting on it. She was not very happy when she discovered that, with both of them working, neither Gregg nor Daille could go. Elton, therefore, drove to Chicago with her and she drove home alone from there.

Daille had a job nearby at a Manners restaurant. It was one of a local chain of hamburger joints, a sort of precursor to McDonalds and other fast food chains. Gregg had a real opportunity to start his career in Detroit. He was one of a select group chosen to work on a special training program at the Campbell-Ewald advertising agency. Although Daille went with me to baseball games and other events, both children were becoming pretty independent of their parents. This was a good thing, because we were at the beginning of a near-split in our marriage and were glad the kids weren't involved.

As I remarked about our wedding, not only did we lack home, career, future, money, etc., we were both immature and lacked the experience or information to deal with emotional problems. This was bound to affect our lives at some point, and this year its effect was almost fatal to our marriage. Our immaturity was evident by our reaction to problems or emotional stress. Faced with a problem, I would look for sympathy and understanding; Elton would devote himself to work, leave town, or go out with the fellows until all hours. I would then get mad and he would react by staying away or going away again. On the other hand, if he had a problem, he would barely mention it, although he too needed sympathy and understanding which I didn't give him. It wasn't until 1964 that I recognized this vicious circle.

This year had not started well. We both were suffering some serious flu-like symptoms, and we had a difficult January. It was only the beginning of a really difficult year. We were not on very good terms throughout the winter, and by spring Elton had told me by his body language, his obvious lack of affection and unexplained and increasingly frequent periods of sweating that something was seriously wrong. This all happened gradually and I eventually realized that it had begun the first winter we were in Cleveland. I should have known much earlier that something had gone very wrong. I suppose I had never doubted Elton's complete commitment to me, so whatever was troubling him, I did not suspect another woman.

In June 1964, the doctor found a lump in my breast. He must have believed it to be benign (which it was) because he waited two weeks to remove it. Meantime, we drove to Iron Mountain for Ruth Reeves' wedding. We stayed with the Greenlys and, since Elton left the morning after the wedding to return to Cleveland "on business," John drove back with me a few days later on his way to a business meeting. I went into the hospital and was dismissed in time for the July 4 weekend with both kids home. About the middle of the month I flew to Colorado for a visit. I was with my folks for two nice weeks. At dinner one evening with Jack and Betty, I met a friend of Jack's. It was obvious that I turned him on—a very pleasant experience at that point. I then visited Dale and Mona for a few days. They drove to Rapid with their kids; I went with them and flew home from there.

On that trip I thought a lot about my relationship with Elton. We were having serious problems, and I thought they might be partly due to his age. I knew that whatever the cause, and whatever difficulties I had had with him as a husband, I had contributed to them. Since moving to Cleveland, I had been pretty unpleasant to live with because I had been so unhappy about the move. And I had been unpleasant about his continual absence from home. I had not been very sympathetic about his disappointment with Hanna's politics and promotions either. I decided right then that, whether or not he showed any love for me, or whether or not he traveled all the time, I still loved him and I would make every effort to control my temper and be a pleasant wife. When I got home, I really turned over a new leaf. I didn't lose my temper or bitch at him—I was nice.

I believe Elton, too, had done some thinking about our lives and he was bracing to tell me about his girlfriend. He started by telling me the night I got back from Colorado that he no longer loved me. This was devastating, but in view of my decision, I was as sweet as I could be and we had a reasonably pleasant few weeks. Then, on the way home after taking Daille back to school for her sophomore year, we had a nice dinner and several drinks and he told me that he was involved with another woman. He wouldn't tell me who she was and he didn't ask for a divorce.

Words cannot describe how shocked and hurt I was. The next few days were really awful. I slept little, cried a lot and had a hard time getting back to school or getting ready for a trip we'd planned to New York for a mining conference. Elton apparently didn't want a divorce, and I certainly didn't want one. I'd always declared that if my husband were unfaithful, he would have to leave, but I couldn't bear to think of that possibility. I loved him. I'd never loved anyone else and had no interest in having another man. Because I was personally very insecure, I couldn't imagine that any other man would want me. From a practical standpoint, I had no marketable skills and would need to be financially dependent on him. We were doing all right on our income, but we did not own a house, had little money saved, and with two kids in college as well as myself, we would not have enough money to support two homes.

I'm sure the financial problems were equally important to him, but he hated the idea of divorce. He knew it would affect his relationship with the kids who were much closer to me than they were to him, and I think he had a lot of affection for me and needed me in many ways. We spent some close and affectionate time together and he didn't ask for a divorce, but neither did he promise to give up his girlfriend. I'm sure he felt it was much better to continue to have his cake and eat it too. Who wouldn't? I was unhappy, but nothing much had changed, except that I was even more insecure and uncertain about what Elton was doing at any time. I could only wonder what would happen to us.

We went to New York for a week in September to attend the International Minerals Conference where Elton presented a paper. We saw some shows and the World Fair. It should have been a great week, but I did not enjoy it much. Alan and Lui came to Cleveland for a few days. We pretended everything was fine and carried on as usual, with nothing settled about our future. Then in November, we found that things were even more unsettled than we could have imagined. Elton was shocked to learn that he was being sent to Hibbing to manage the construction of two plants in trouble, working under the district superintendent. We were both miserable about this. No matter what he was told, it was a demotion for him. I, on the other hand, had adjusted to city living, believing we were in Cleveland for good and I really wanted to get my degree. We both hated Hibbing and had thought it was one place to which we would never have to return.

1965

That winter was a very unhappy one. We were back to being strangers, and had no idea what lay ahead. Elton hated moving. He did it alone because he hoped it would be a temporary job. He had set the condition with Hanna that I wouldn't move until June, which was all right with me since I also hoped the job would be temporary. He left on January 2, worked very hard, did a tremendous job, creating order out of chaos on the job, and stayed in Hibbing. He called nearly every day, but came to Cleveland only about one weekend a month. I worried, of course, that he was spending much more time with his girl friend. He certainly was seeing her.

All through spring our condition was uncertain. The big question was whether we would stay married. Would Elton get sent back to Cleveland? Would he get a house in Hibbing? Should Daille and I go on the European tour we'd planned and saved for? Should I go to summer school and get my degree? Should we give up the apartment? And how would we resolve all the minor problems hinging on the bigger ones? I spent my time wondering how all these questions would be answered, studying and being with my friends, and sewing clothes for the European trip that may take place.

As the time for Gregg's graduation rolled around, everything else took a back seat. The graduation was on May 1, and my folks arrived for a visit a couple of weeks earlier. Dad had shingles and he was miserable; I was miserable too, and they didn't know why. It was not a happy visit, but Gregg's graduation day was a great day. Elton came home for the graduation, and Alan was with us for the weekend, which greatly pleased me. We all drove to Ann Arbor in two cars, then brought Gregg home for the weekend. The next Monday he started work for J. Walter Thompson in Detroit.

One of our problems was resolved when Daille arrived home for Gregg's graduation, enthusiastic about her new boy friend, Tom Pettit. She no longer wanted to go to Europe; she wanted to go to summer school at Ohio U. with Tom. When her year in Marietta was finished, I brought her home and she got ready for summer school. Tom drove in to pick her up after visiting his folks at their summer home in Syracuse, Indiana. He seemed to me to be a good guy, and Daille was certainly much enamored. When I watched them walk together to his car, I knew they were going to get married eventually.

By this time it had become obvious that Elton was not going to be transferred back to Cleveland soon, and I was going to have to move back to Hibbing—as long as we were still together. I had decided to go to summer school and get the degree. I gave notice on the apartment, arranged for the mover and storage, and did the million and one things that needed to be finalized. I finished my finals, enrolled for the summer quarter and arranged for my lodging until the sessions were over. The day Daille left, everything was done and I caught a plane for Iron Mountain where Elton had arranged to spend a week with me. I arrived there in a state of exhaustion and near a nervous breakdown. Although he gave me the good news that his affair was over, he told me he had to go back to Hibbing in two days. I cried all night, prompting him to suggest that I see Dr. Harshman when I got back to Cleveland. I spent a week in Iron Mountain, and then returned to Cleveland to move in with my friend, Elna Molnar, in Rocky River. When she left on a trip, I moved in with Sara and Jim Young in Chagrin Falls. After two weeks there, I went to the Commodore Hotel on campus. It was neither elegant nor clean, but it was close to classes. In the interim, I saw Dr. Harshman. When I told him about all the confusion in our lives and my responsibilities and concerns, he asked me, "What does Elton expect of you?" It was a very good question. Of course, I recovered!

Between the two summer terms, I met Elton in Chicago and we flew to Rapid City for my 25th reunion at Custer High School. We had a nice trip and got along very well.

Daille spent a week with me toward the end of August before going to Madison to finish her schooling at the University of Wisconsin. While she enjoyed her time at Marietta where she met Tom, she decided that now she wanted a bigger school and a less rigid and freer atmosphere. She chose Wisconsin partly because it was closer to us than some other possible choices, and partly because it was reasonably close to Parsons College in Fairfield, Iowa, where Tom was now studying. One day while she was in Cleveland, both Tom and Elton were there. Elton, as a father, was convinced that Tom was quite unsuitable as a husband for his only daughter and it was not a happy meeting. During that same week, we treated Gregg and Daille to a trip to New York for a couple of days so that they could visit the World Fair.

Elton came back for my graduation—a red letter day. It took 25 years, but I had a B.A. We had a lovely dinner and a good evening, but the next day was a real let-down. We loaded the rented trailer with all the things I'd spent a week collecting from the various places I'd left them, packed Daille's belongings, and started out for Hibbing. We went first to Madison to drop off Daille's things, and then drove on to Hibbing the next day. It was a miserable trip. I cried off and on along the way, thinking about living in Hibbing again. I found the town unchanged. It remained isolated, unwelcoming, ugly, cold and smug. But once I got into the house Hanna had rented, I decided that further protest was pointless; I might as well adjust to being there. So I did.

The rented house was quite nice and I figured it would be fine after I had done a little redecorating. But before that could begin, we had to experience a flooded basement two days after our arrival. The water ruined our suitcases and some boxes that we'd stored down there. The man who came to clean the drains said, "I'll bet you're glad to be out of Cleveland and back here." I really let the poor guy have it!

Now I could begin the redecorating. Hanna came and painted the house inside—and it needed it. I bought shelves and bricks to make bookcases. With the addition of throw rugs and other odds and ends, it became quite livable in a couple of weeks.

Elton was home a good bit of the time, which was a nice change, and we did have friends—the Hawkinsons and Dick and Gini Smith in Hibbing, Leon and Marie Keller in Virginia (Hibbing's neighboring city) and others whom we'd known previously. People were, indeed, now friendlier, as I'd been told they would be. In the spring, Len and Dora Carlson had thrown a party of Hanna people as a send-off for our being back in Hibbing. It was a horrible party, more like a wake than a celebration, and I retired to the bedroom every few minutes to cry a little. Luckily, Gregg was at the party with us and he would join me in the bedroom and sympathize and I would rejoin the guests for a while. Dora told me that night that though I hadn't liked Hibbing before, I'd like it now because Elton would be "somebody"—a poor recommendation for a town, and I added it to the list of things I didn't like about Hibbing. But it was true. We had invitations for all kinds of functions and to places we'd never been invited before, including the Country Club which hadn't accepted our membership application in the fifties.

We had been in town only three weeks when we left to drive to Rapid City for a few days vacation. We flew from there to Colorado Springs where we found that Jack was running for office as County Judge. He was elected in November and remained a judge until he retired in 1984. From the Springs, we went to Las Vegas for the Mining Congress, and from there, to San Francisco for a week in the gorgeous apartment the Hanna guys had rented.

Changes in our personal lives had been more important to us this year than changes in American culture, but The Topless Bar was introduced!

Elton took me to one of these in San Francisco. Many people, certainly most women, found it scandalous that barmaids wore no tops. I agreed, but it was a revelation to me when I saw the contempt with which the girls looked upon their customers.

Our vacation in San Francisco didn't last. After just a few days, Bob Anderson called and insisted Elton return to Hibbing. I was simply furious. I stayed a few days, spent a night with Roxanne Rao, and then flew to Rapid. Once there, I drove back to Hibbing, accompanied by Ethel, for what was to be a long stay. She was retired now; she didn't have to go back to work, and she didn't go home until after Christmas. She was hard to live with, because she never ever said anything nice or complimentary; she complained a great deal about her illnesses; she didn't like all the company we had; and she didn't want to go with us when we received invitations. She did enjoy going out to dinner, however, when a vendor invited us. At least Ethel didn't bother others with her problems—just us.

Gregg wasn't able to get enough time off from work in Detroit to come for Christmas—it was our first without him. Some time during that year he called to tell us he had been rated 4-F in the draft for the raging Vietnam War. We were shocked and astonished and didn't realize until later that he had probably admitted to being gay and was rejected for that reason.

Daille, who was enjoying the freedom of the University of Wisconsin, came "home" for Christmas (her first time in our house) and Tom came, too. His father was head of the languages department at Marietta College and he and his wife were on a Fulbright fellowship in Colombia, so we asked Tom to join us. On his first night with us, Tom made a couple of unfortunate remarks which really turned Ethel off. She was mad at him and wouldn't speak to him the whole time they were together. Tom didn't mind too much and he and Daille had a good time snowmobiling, spending time with Susan Hawkinson and just being together. We had several parties, and despite the cold weather and Ethel's cold shoulder, it was a pleasant holiday, even without Gregg. After Christmas, Ethel flew back to Rapid and the four of us drove to Iron Mountain to spend New Year's Eve with our friends. Our plans were to go to Green Bay for a big Packers game, with Tom and Daille going on to Madison and back to school from there. Tom was thrilled at the idea of going to a major league football championship game, but the weather didn't cooperate. It became so icy that we went back to Iron Mountain and Tom and Daille struggled back to Madison. Poor Tom didn't get to an NFL game until 2000 in Cleveland, when he left after the half because the weather was so bad!

1966

Back in Hibbing after New Year's Day, we returned to our busy routines. As might be expected, I had become as active as possible when we moved. We became involved in the church and I rejoined the League of Women Voters, joined a local chapter of the P.E.O. and went to, and gave, many luncheons and bridge parties; I felt I couldn't quit bridge at this point. I enrolled in a Social Science course at the Junior College so I could keep up with my studies. I also joined the American Association of University Women, now that I was a college graduate. I was amused, after wanting to belong to this prestigious organization for years, when Daille went with me to a meeting and was thoroughly disgusted. The subjects of discussion were the non-academic, very housewifely topics of carpet cleaning, home decorating and cooking.

I drove Daille back to school in January and after her spring break in April. She wanted a job in the summer and Elton arranged for her employment at the construction company working on the Hanna plants. She made quite a lot of money and I suggested she spend some of it on contact lenses. I knew she had wanted them ever since high school when she found she needed glasses. At that time, they were much more expensive than glasses and her Dad always told her he would not spend all that money for vanity. Daille knew Tom felt the same way, but she agreed with me that now was a good idea to get them; and that's what she did. Interestingly, after she married Tom, they found that her contacts needed replacing much less often than his glasses, so they were actually less expensive.

Before Daille came to Hibbing for the summer and went to work, Elton decided, with my complete agreement, that he was going to make a big change in our lives. Since learning that he was being transferred to Hibbing, he had begun to realize that there was no possibility of his ever gaining a top position with Hanna and he should look for another job. The events of the year confirmed this view. He'd been demoted; he now had two people over him who should have been answering to him; and in December, Hanna announced Floyd Lee's promotion to a vice presidency in Cleveland, Elton answering to him too. This was a major blow, since Floyd had been Elton's assistant at Groveland. And although he'd rescued the two plants from disaster, he got no real credit for it. As the year advanced, he came closer and closer to terminating his employment with Hanna. He handed in his resignation on June 1, 1966.

Our "wedding portrait" taken in a Deadwood carnival
booth a few days after our July 9, 1941 marriage

Elton and Doris,
Rapid City, 1942

Doris, Elton and Gregg,
Rapid City, 1944

House built by Elton and Grandpa
Mesick in Rapid City, 1947

The six-plex, Tahawus, NY, 1947

Our house in Telluride (the former retort building), 1949-1951
(photographed in 1996)

The farmhouse, Groveland, MI, 1951

Elton, Groveland, 1951

Elton, the superintendent!

Elton at play, Sinaloa Club,
San Francisco, 1956

Superintendent, Hibbing Research Lab, 1953

Christmas morning, 1959 at Dr. Huron's,
Iron Mountain

Christmas, 1960

Geist House, Iron Mtn.
1959-1962

CHAPTER 8

BIRTH OF MINERAL SERVICES, INCORPORATED (MSI)

1966

From the time Elton had been transferred to Hibbing, his friends in the industry knew he was unhappy and he talked about leaving Hanna and getting a job with another company. In the fall of 1965 his friend John Riede suggested that Elton start his own small company and he offered to help. John was tremendously successful with Ramsay Engineering, his own small electronics company, so he knew something about starting a company. Starting a mining company or building a big lab would have been next to impossible because of the large capital requirement, but John and Roy Bierman, his Assistant Manager, suggested that a company that sold (actually brokered) raw material resources for the steel industry—bentonite, limestone and dolomite—could be a possibility. Bentonite is clay, used in making iron ore pellets, and because of its water absorbing characteristics it has many other applications, for instance kitty litter. Limestone and dolomite were used in making steel.

Riede and several Ramsay employees had already written the Articles of Incorporation for such a company, and named it Raw Materials, Inc. The company was incorporated on February 4, 1965 with Bierman as president. Meantime, Riede had met with people in Greece and Yugoslavia about bentonite supplies and sales and made contact with commodity traders in Paris. On several occasions, during late 1965, and early 1966, Riede, Bierman and Gordon Smith (another Ramsay participant) met with Elton and discussed ways in which Elton could fit into this operation. Should there be another company? Should he work with Roy? It was finally decided that Elton would become President of Raw Materials with stock options he could exercise that would make him majority stockholder within two years with at least 51% of the stock.

The problem then was how to put the company together and how to finance it. Riede suggested people who might be interested in owning stock and buying ten-year debentures and suggested that Elton meet with them and discuss his leaving Hanna. In late February, Elton and I spent a weekend in White Bear Lake with John and his wife, Doris, and others joined us. Jack Kringle and Jim Townsend were there, along with Bierman and Smith, and a plan was drawn up outlining the company's purpose and organization. It was agreed that Elton would leave Hanna and become President of RMI at $25,000 per year (his current Hanna salary). It was decided to put together a team to sell stock and raise at least $400,000. It was also decided to change the name of the company to Mineral Services, Inc. (MSI) and to locate in Cleveland.

I was happy about the plans because I knew how frustrated Elton had been about his status with Hanna. I was also happy about going back to Cleveland, since I wanted to continue school, had made some friends and knew and liked the city. Although I knew next to nothing about finances or running a business, I had confidence in Elton and felt he would be successful in his own business. He was comfortable in Cleveland, and also thought (mistakenly, as it turned out) that he could do business with the major mining companies in Cleveland.

From February until June 1, Elton continued with Hanna and the Butler and National Steel plants. At the same time, he created a business plan and lined up potential stockholders. On June 1, he submitted his resignation to Bob Anderson, who said that Elton absolutely could not leave Hanna—even though Bob had been doing his level best for two years to encourage Elton to do just that. The reaction among townspeople and industry folks was mixed, but predictable; some cut us off and others wished us the best of luck. We had a strange month or two, although we celebrated our 25th anniversary on July 9, with dinner in Grand Rapids (Minnesota). Daille was in town after completing her junior year at Wisconsin and was seriously thinking about marrying Tom. She was working for the Bechtel consulting team and held the fort at home while we were gone in August on our first MSI European business trip.

We decided to move about Labor Day. This would give us time for the first order of business, a trip to Greece and Yugoslavia to look into and arrange the purchase of bentonite previously researched by the company, then to Sweden to make sales contacts. Plans were made to leave on July 22. I was delighted to be going to Europe at last. We arranged for passports, made travel reservations, went to Minneapolis to do some shopping and met the Greenlys who were soon to become stockholders.

This was a very important business trip and many serious negotiations took place. I have limited this history, however, to mostly non-business content that was most interesting. The trip was interesting, however, from any standpoint. First, just before we were to leave, a major airline strike was called; all U.S. airline employees were out. We arranged to take a train to Chicago and then fly Air France from Toronto. It was exciting to be riding on a train and taking an overseas flight. I was thrilled to see the southern coasts of Ireland, England and the red roofs of France as we approached Orly. In Paris we met George Kauders, son of one of the commodities traders with whom the Riede group had been in contact. He turned out to be charming, intelligent and a good leader for two amateurs. We spent the day at Orly, trying to resolve our reservation problems. The three of us were able to take off for Athens late in the afternoon, arriving there at dusk. The sun was setting, the Parthenon lights had been turned on and all along the road to the city were outdoor restaurants with people singing, laughing and having fun. It was a perfect introduction to Greece and to Europe.

We stayed at the Hilton on top of a hill overlooking Athens and enjoyed breakfast on our balcony, overlooking that fabulous city. The first day we toured the Parthenon and the Agora and many other ruins. I had done my homework, so it was especially interesting to me. My only complaint was my sore feet. I had foolishly worn new shoes all day. The second day, while the men worked, I toured the city, went to the museum and did some shopping. We had cocktails at the gorgeous home of Mr. Eliopoules, one of the people with whom we hoped to work, and later went on to dinner at his club.

On the third day we took a boat from Piraeus to the Island of Milos where the bentonite deposit was located. We arrived at another island near the eastern coast of Milos at about 10 p.m. George, who spoke no Greek, struggled to make the crew understand, that we wanted to land on the east side of Milos, whereas the boat was going around the island to the city on the northwest side. It developed that we could get a small fishing (motor) boat, maybe 15 feet long, with a crew of two or three, and go directly to the mine port. This we agreed to do. So there we were, out in the middle of the sea, no land in sight, no lights, for an hour or two with a crew with whom we could not communicate. When we pulled into the dock at the mine and landed, it was a great relief. It was dark and isolated, but we were escorted to a guesthouse where we thankfully went to bed.

While the men discussed business for a day or two, I read, walked and swam in the Aegean but did not spend much time at the very rocky beach. We were given a tour to an ancient location where they had found many artifacts and where the Venus de Milo may have been found. On the third day we were driven across the very picturesque island and took a boat back to Piraeus (from the port city on the northwest) and into Athens where we spent the afternoon and night, this time at the Palace Hotel on the corner of Constitution Square.

In the afternoon, we went to the airport after first taking a cab to the Parthenon and telling the cab driver we'd be right back. Elton had ruined a film while changing it in his new camera and we'd lost all the pictures we'd taken the first day. We replaced them quickly, and were not surprised that the cab driver was shaking his head about the Americans who toured the Parthenon in a total of five minutes.

With George, we took a small plane to Belgrade. We landed in Dubrovnik to refuel. As we were about to take off again the engine on the right wing caught fire. While the memory of that scene still amuses me, it never ceased to embarrass Elton. Sitting on the left looking out the other window, I saw nothing until I turned to speak and saw Elton and George at the front of the plane by the door, ready to leap while flames enveloped the engine outside the other window. So much for "women first" and husbandly protectiveness! We all got out safely and with the fire extinguished, we continued on the same plane. Nervous but without further incident, we arrived in Belgrade an hour or so later.

Our arrival in Belgrade was interesting but disturbing. Yugoslavia was a communist country, united under Tito—also disturbing. The city was in almost complete darkness. We found out later that working hours were from 6:00 a.m. to 2:00 p.m. with a brief breakfast break, so 11:00 p.m. is the depth of night. At the hotel there was only a room clerk, who caused us to relinquish our passports at the desk. We had been unaware of this practice, and were quite worried.

In the morning, while the guys tried to contact the person we were supposed to meet, I walked around the city, noticed the shabbily dressed people, the scarcity of cars and the paucity of goods in the store windows. We collected our passports at the hotel and were ready to drive to Petrovac (about 300 miles from the Adriatic coast), in a 1950 Ford sedan, with Vojin Krtolica, the Director General of Hempro, the bentonite producing company. The Director General spoke Serbo-Croatian and German, George spoke German and English and the driver spoke only Serbo-Croatian, so conversation was limited, but the scenery was fascinating. This was 1966, and our big fancy car (!) attracted attention all along the road, whose traffic was mostly donkeys and pedestrians. We saw many monuments of Tito; yet historic monuments pre-dating his regime were not pointed out to us. Roads were mountainous and poor and we observed people along the way working in the most primitive ways. Speaking of "primitive", this trip was my first exposure to what Gregg later called, s . . . à la Turk, a toilet consisting of two footprints and a hole between. We spent the night at an inn, which, like everywhere else, had no toilet paper or Kleenex—thank goodness I had quite a lot. Linens on the beds were clean, but a real mixture of style and material.

It took almost two days to reach Petrovac where we checked into the Hotel Oliva. The tourists in this town were mostly Germans or Hungarians, so not much English was spoken. Elton and George were tied up for three days in rather futile and frustrating negotiations while I read, spent time on the beach, and shopped. About the only thing I bought was a carved wooden plate at a fair. I had no local money but they were thrilled with an American dollar. Our meals were elegant and beautifully served. One night we had dinner with the Lazlos, an Hungarian couple whose only English word was neeagahra (Niagara). They were nice people, but conversation failed to flow easily. We were also invited to a banquet in the Montenegran Mountains, with lots of speeches in Serbo-Croatian. Altogether, it was a great experience and we left with tentative agreements and a bag of bentonite, which caused trouble at every passport check from there on.

We drove north to Dubrovnik along the beautiful Adriatic Sea coast, mountains on one side and sea and picturesque islands on the other. It was certainly some of the most beautiful landscape in the world. From Dubrovnik we flew to Zürich with a layover in Venice, where we spent a couple of lovely hours. We rode on a gondola, visited St. Mark's, saw the pigeons, went into a museum or two and ate some of their wonderful ice cream. Late in the afternoon we returned to the airport and flew over the Alps to Zürich. There we met Mr. & Mrs. Kauders, George's father and stepmother, and Eric and Lilly Nettel, the traders from Paris. After a lovely and leisurely two days, George took us to the airport and reluctantly left us there for our departure to Sweden. He had been our tour guide all the way from Paris. He had organized everything, and he obviously felt we would never be able to survive without his ministrations.

We reached Stockholm without problems and checked into a very large and expensive room at the Grand Hotel. We spent five days there—at least I did. On the second day, Elton flew north to Kiruna for three days of meetings with LKAB, a steel producer, and I moved into a smaller room to save money. It was cold in Stockholm on August 11, and because I had nothing warm to wear I shopped. I bought a handsome blue knitted suit and other things. Communication was much easier here because the language is closer to English, but I did have a little trouble making myself understood when I needed sanitary napkins! I took a tour or two and met some other Americans and, of course, I read. I brought with me enough books that I seldom ran out of reading material. When Elton returned from Kiruna, which was even colder than Stockholm, he had a bad cold and had to stay in another tiny room (both of them really tiny) and I went back and forth all night to make sure he was okay. The next day we took the train to Sala for more meetings. We drove back with one of Elton's contacts on roads that were already marked for left-hand driving, which was to begin the following weekend.

Stockholm and what I saw of the country was interesting and picturesque but some anti-U.S. feeling existed because of the Vietnam War. Since I had never heard anything good about Sweden from my Norwegian grandparents and mother, I was not as affected by the anti-American sentiment as I might have been.

I was really looking forward to our next stop, Paris. We had a weekend at the Celtic Hotel, the first day of which Elton stayed in the hotel because he was still suffering the effects of his cold. I walked down the Avenue des Champs Elysée (one block from the hotel) to the Louvre. What a thrill to see all those beautiful, and famous, paintings and sculptures. I had a lovely day, took a cab back to the Hotel and ended the day with a fine dinner there, with wonderful Crêpes Suzette for dessert. The next day we took a bus trip to Versailles.

In later years Gregg would say that Paris is wonderful except for the Parisians. I rather agree with him after the trouble I had trying to make a cab driver understand "Celtic". But I agreed then and still do that Paris is wonderful. I told George Kauders later that Paris is truly elegant and he said, "élégant is a French word." On this, my first visit, we found few people in Paris since most Europeans take their vacations in August.

On Monday, Elton had one final visit with the Kauders, who lived in Paris, and the next day we set out for home, wherever that was. We had been ticketed to go to Paris, then London and home, but the U.S. air strike was still alive and it appeared that we could get a flight out of Paris more easily than out of London, so we postponed our trip to London for another time. We spent hours at a travel agency waiting for the flight we finally took, first class, into La Guardia, and then spent nearly a day waiting for a flight to Cleveland where we were to look for an apartment. We waited all evening, went to a hotel and back to the airport and suddenly the strike was over. All schedules were completely adrift, so while I spent most of the day reading three books, Elton stood in the stand-by line. We finally got an afternoon flight. This was not a great end perhaps, but this trip was by far the most memorable and enjoyable one we had ever taken, and one of the best we would ever take. And it looked as though it would be beneficial for our new business.

After two days in Cleveland, we located a reasonable, three-bedroom apartment on Fairhill Drive, not far from University Circle and Shaker Square. It was not the nicest place we've lived, but not bad and we ended up spending nearly five years there.

After clinching the deal, we flew to Hibbing and packed up, with all that that term includes, and by Labor Day we were ready to leave. I told Elton then, and meant it, that never again, under any circumstances, would I ever move back to Hibbing. And since I am now over 80 and in a retirement home, I think I'm safe in saying I will never have to go back to Hibbing. As Dora Carlson had promised, the year there wasn't too bad, since we were somebody, but that fact alone left me with a permanent sense of distaste for the town. And once Elton left Hanna, we were again nobodies.

Daille left with us and we drove to Syracuse, Indiana to see Tom and meet his parents and then Daille went back to school. Elton and I went on to Cleveland. The movers arrived on Wednesday and we began to settle in. Elton had located office space downtown in the Marion Building on West Third Street. He spent some time selecting furniture and office equipment and unpacked his many boxes. I helped too, so, between returning to the graduate school program and getting our apartment settled I was kept busy. Elton hired Jan Peterson, his former Hanna secretary, to work for MSI, and before long he was busy working out the corporate details. After getting the business organized, he followed up on the European trip and his many contacts. Jan stayed for only three months and we hired Carol Dray who was with us for nearly a year, with Marian Peabody, one of Elton's old Hanna friends filling in from time to time.

I did whatever I could, which included ordering stationary with the company logo that Gregg had designed. Elton had Peat Marwick, an accounting firm, draw up a chart of accounts and set up the books, and I took on the job of bookkeeper. I was always reasonably good in math but barely balanced my own checkbook. I knew nothing about accounting and made some really strange mistakes, but the accountants were very helpful. After the first audit in 1967 I had a pretty good idea what I was doing. I also started working part time in the office of the Dean of Adelbert College at Reserve, typing a little, filing, and performing other office duties, at all of which I was a real beginner. I thoroughly enjoyed the staff there and liked the work.

As to MSI, Elton proceeded with the effort to market bentonite but ran into a lot of problems, partly because of working with the Greeks, and probably partly because he was learning international business. We had one sale to Pickands Mather, and got paid for it, thanks mainly to the kindness of the manager, Hank Whaley, and took in a total of about $250,000 on the bentonite project over a period of a year. However, our capital was running low, and without any big jobs, it became necessary to come up with something else to make money. We established a program for computerized maintenance—very new—which was run by a New Yorker named John Viola and which had been sold to only two companies, but brought in a little income. The program was very simple but innovative, since computer technology was really new and not in wide use at that time. Elton began marketing consulting services and that was what kept MSI in business.

Meanwhile, on the home front, Daille was finishing her last semester in college, and in October we drove to Madison to see her and attend a football game. While we were having dinner that night, Elton asked her what she wanted to do when she graduated. She said, "Get married?" He hit the roof, as much as he ever did, especially in a restaurant, and spent the rest of the meal alternately scolding me because I'd "been pushing her into marriage," and Daille because she wanted to marry at all and especially someone unfit for her, which Elton thought Tom to be. She and I took turns going to the restroom in tears. When we returned to our motel room and had gone to bed, the manager knocked on the door to call Elton to the phone. It was Tom, apparently calling to lace into Elton. This was not a nice night at all.

We had always told the kids we would support them until they got a degree. After that they were on their own, so if Daille could support herself and she decided to get married, we pretty much had to accept it. Although Tom was a nice guy and I liked him very much, Elton and I had our doubts about his future and whether Daille, a highly structured, fairly rigid person, could get along with someone as laid back as Tom. Nevertheless, he made every effort to accept Tom and support the marriage. Like many parents, we misjudged our daughter and her chosen mate, and after nearly 40 years we couldn't imagine life without him.

In 1966, Daille and Gregg came to Cleveland for Thanksgiving, Gregg with a haircut so long we attracted stares wherever we went. It would be laughable now, because his hair was long after nearly three decades of crew cuts, but pretty short by standards since then. This year of 1966 was near the beginning of the baby boom revolution. It burgeoned over the next few years to be our national culture—boys with long hair, co-ed dormitories, wide-spread recreational drug use, coarse language, doing-my-own-thing, making love with anyone anywhere, uni-sex clothing, wandering all over the world looking for oneself, trusting no one over 30, and so on—habits the western world came to accept, though reluctantly. Besides the hair, Gregg had begun inserting four letter words into every sentence. I tried to ignore it for a few months until I decided I didn't have to and told him in no uncertain terms that he couldn't talk that way around me. He did censor his language after that.

Gregg came to Cleveland to spend Christmas with us, but Daille and Tom went to his folks in Marietta and then drove to Cleveland for a late-day gift opening and dinner. After Christmas, Daille and I began to make wedding plans for April 8. I had no idea that people reserved places for wedding receptions as early as two years ahead, so I spent more time looking for a location for the reception than for anything else. I finally located a motel on Warrensville Road. We had joined Plymouth Congregational Church on the edge of Shaker Heights shortly after we arrived and we scheduled a candle-lit wedding there.

1967

January 1, 1967 was the beginning of the first year for the new company and it looked like many difficulties were ahead. Elton stuck with it, however, and his board supported him all the way. The year brought many changes in our personal lives. In January, Daille completed her education and got her B.A. from the University of Wisconsin. Gregg and I drove up together. He was now the proud owner of a Volkswagen Bug, the only car he ever owned after his senior year in high school. He met me in Toledo and we drove to Madison where we met Elton. Gregg was driving and we were so engrossed in the story he was telling me about Woody Allen that he missed the road to Madison. We drove all the way into Milwaukee, but still managed to arrive in Madison in time for the graduation. This was typical of Gregg who could always find an interesting story to tell. We saw Daille receive her degree, attended the reception honoring the graduates and went to dinner. Elton, Gregg and I drove back the next day after getting Daille off to Iowa and depositing her belongings at the Greyhound Bus depot for shipment to Cleveland.

Tom was scheduled to graduate from Parsons College in August and was taking courses right up until then, so Daille decided to move to Fairfield,

Iowa to get a job and a place to stay until the wedding. Parsons College, by the way, was a college established on the premise that anyone who wanted a degree could get one. It had a student body of high-class kids, some with very well known names who **had** to get a degree because it was expected of them. Diplomas were not just handed out, but students could take courses over and over, if necessary, until they passed and eventually could graduate. The college was accredited, but lost its accreditation the week Tom was to graduate. It was not the major tragedy it seemed at the time. Tom had chosen Parsons because he had flunked at Marietta before going into the Navy for six-years. When he returned, he flunked again. His father and brother had PhD's, so Tom felt under some pressure to get a B.A. at least, but he still really didn't know what he wanted to do when he came out of college.

When Daille went to Fairfield, she got a job at the school that was to resume in two weeks. In the meantime, she came to Cleveland and we bought her dress, ordered the wedding cake, and arranged other wedding details before she took the train back to Fairfield. Toward the end of February, we drove to Fairfield with Daille's belongings to see her and the place where she lived. We then went to Colorado Springs for a few days. I remember two things clearly about that visit to my folks. When we arrived, we learned that Dad's brother, Ed, had died a few days earlier. No one had informed me, so I hadn't even been able to give Dad my sympathy. He was the first of my uncles to die, but Uncle Dick Skamser died only a few months later, in October.

The other memory is the evening we spent with Jack and Betty and the discussion we had with Jack before we left. These discussions became more and more frequent from then on—he was adamant and always right, insisted that questions be answered and he then set out to convince you that you were not only wrong, but stupid. As long as he got any response at all, he would not stop the discussion, no matter how frustrated I became. The subject was often of little importance and I recall that that night we were discussing the meaning of "love." Jack's dogmatism and refusal to change the subject left me angry and in tears through the next day. It took me several years and a lot of anguish to simply not answer when he asked me what I thought of something and until his death he never stopped his inquisitions.

When we left the Springs late that February day, we drove east through Kansas to Wichita where I spent the night and Elton left on a sales trip. I drove from there to Tulsa to see the Arnots, our Westlake neighbors of 1962. After spending the night, I drove to Lincoln for a nice visit with Aunt Phoebe, and then home via Fairfield.

April and the wedding arrived quickly, and much remained to be done. Among other things, I made a dress for myself, which turned out very satisfactorily. Dad and Mother drove from Colorado and Ethel flew from South Dakota. We had been back in Cleveland only a short time and most of our friends and relatives were far away, but we still had about 75 guests for the buffet dinner after the wedding. Daille was a lovely bride; the church was beautiful, my Dad sang a solo and the reception was perfect. The bride and groom flew to Chicago for a brief honeymoon.

As it turned out, all of Tom's groomsmen, except Gregg, were married within the year, including Dave Snyder who met Bonnie Young, a bridesmaid, that night and married her by the end of the year. One sign of the times was the joint occupancy of a room by a groomsman and his fiancée. Now it seems unbelievable, but in 1967 unmarried couples simply did not share rooms. I was proud that I accepted their arrangement without objection. Eventually I began to accept that sort of thing without a thought. Gregg brought a girl friend from Detroit, which thrilled us no end—we were not aware that he would never be married. Peggy was a darling, and we were sorry to hear later that she'd married a friend of Gregg's.

Now that the wedding was over, our parents had left, and everything was back in order, I was able to concentrate on our company business. In March, Elton had hired Bill Holland as Vice President, and we were looking forward to his contribution to the business. A year later, however, he had to be let go. Although Bill looked and acted like a good find, he was undisciplined, lazy and disinclined to do anything useful. He had the talent to put up a good front but failed to produce. He could have been a perfect middle manager for a large company, but we needed a real worker. Elton, meanwhile, was still trying to make a success of bentonite trading, and took further trips to Greece in August and December.

After their wedding, Tom and Daille were looking for a job opportunity for Tom and learned that the U.S. State Department was seeking people for its overseas communication division. That appealed to both of them, with their degrees in English and desire to see the world. Tom applied for an appointment. We were all pleased when he was accepted. After his graduation and their visit with us and with the Pettits in Marietta, Daille and Tom went to D.C. in September for three months training and the indoctrination program.

I was back in school by this time and signed up for a community service project—tutoring black kids in Hough. I was assigned a 14-year old girl and met with her at an old church on East 65th Street once or twice a week. I don't know that I was much help to her, but it was an interesting experience for the kids and us. This task didn't begin until my folks had left after a two-week visit, which had been very enjoyable for all of us. We went to an apple festival in Chardon and drove to Canton to visit the recently opened Football Hall of Fame.

In October, Elton and I flew to Montreal to visit Raman and Roxy Rao and their two girls and attend EXPO, Montreal's World's fair. Our next trip was to D.C. for Thanksgiving with Daille and Tom. Gregg flew down from Detroit and drove with us to Washington where we had a pleasant couple of days. On Friday, Elton announced that he had to be back in Cleveland for a meeting with some of his Board. We were all hurt, disappointed and surprised that a business meeting would be held on a Thanksgiving weekend. But we consoled ourselves and took an interesting trip to Dover, Delaware on Saturday. Gregg and I drove back to Cleveland on Sunday where Gregg caught a plane for Detroit.

In December, we had planned another big trip to celebrate the fiftieth anniversary of my Mother and Dad on the 29th. I spent the time between Thanksgiving and Christmas attending school and getting gifts and cards ready. Tom and Daille spent the second weekend in December with us to attend the wedding of Dave Snyder and Bonnie Young. Then they departed for their first post, Jerusalem.

That was a very sad day for me. Elton, true to form, left on the same Sunday for Greece at nearly the same time as Daille and Tom for Jerusalem. I was sad and lonely because my baby was going halfway around the world and I had no one to comfort me. I became really unhappy when I gathered the papers Elton had asked me to return to the office for him. I found a recent love letter, from Georgiana, after he had promised me the affair was in the past. Apparently, he had resumed this relationship when we got back to Cleveland. I realized then that his early departure from Thanksgiving in D.C. was to allow him to spend time with her.

I was desolate, but true to my form, I went about getting ready to go to Colorado Springs, taking time out only to buy a pretty red lounge suit. I planned to wear it when Elton came home and we would sit and talk. Like most carefully laid plans, it fizzled. Elton came home a day early and found me in grubbies and the apartment littered with wrapping paper, cookie makings and cards. I decided to postpone a confrontation and we went ahead with our trip to the Springs. Gregg flew from Detroit and the three of us flew to the Springs and had a very nice week. Christmas was fun, Jack and Betty were in their lovely new house where we spent some time, and the family was there for the anniversary, with the exception of Daille. We also briefly visited Dale and Mona's oldest, Nancy, who had married Jim Gerstner that fall. They too were living in Colorado Springs.

Gregg left the Springs early and Elton and I flew back to Milwaukee where we were to watch a major NFL game between Dallas and Green Bay. This was just a year or two before the Super Bowl began, and it was THE big football game of the year. We were to be with Iron Mountain friends at the game and afterwards drive to Iron Mountain for New Year's Eve before going back to Cleveland. This worked out fine except that the temperature on the day of the historic game was 18°F below zero and I refused to get out of the car and go into the grandstand. At the half, Elton and Marvel Greenly came out to see how I was, and to see if I'd kept the heater going so long that the car had run out of gas. Actually, I think they had had enough of the cold themselves. It was impossible to keep warm—thermal underwear and foot warmers were still in the future.

We all drove to Iron Mountain after the game for the New Year's Eve celebration. The next night on the way home I told Elton about finding the letter. We had a discussion that dragged on for days, in fact months, about whether or not he would give up his girlfriend. As 1968 began, we were not sure whether MSI would be successful or whether Elton and I would still be together when the year ended.

CHAPTER 9

THE END OF THE SIXTIES

1968

When people refer to the sixties, they're talking about the Cultural Revolution that began in the last half of the sixties but continued into the seventies. When I think of the sixties, I think of our first years in business and my introduction to business and finance. Elton's efforts to grow the business and make it successful, and our serious marriage problems required both of us to make adjustments. Our marriage difficulties affected our private lives but not business teamwork. We had always been able to work well together on any project, and building a successful company was a very important project.

Elton worked hard finding consulting jobs and it was a real break when a friend at Armco recommended MSI to Mr. Linhares, President of Compania Vale do Rio Doce (CVRD) in Rio de Janeiro, Brazil. He needed a technical consultant. In April, Elton went to Rio and Vitoria and was hired for an extensive three-year feasibility study and operations management project. It was a good job for us and kept us afloat for a couple of years. Unfortunately, their bill payments were slow because of their complicated accounting procedures. Contract and invoices had to be approved by the Brazilian Consulate in Pittsburgh, invoices had to be notarized, and the notary's signature certified by the County before an invoice could be sent to Brazil. More time elapsed before we received a check.

We had replaced Carole Dray in November 1967 with Virginia Risberg, who spent four months getting us organized. We hired another woman for a month and finally in April 1968, we hired Lyn Cameron who was with us for eighteen months. She was a real jewel. Elton fired Bill Holland in June; he had not contributed at all to the company. Elton then hired Frank Madison. After only a month, Frank decided that there was not enough business to justify his employment. Elton was alone in the office through much of 1969, except for a secretary and me.

Meanwhile, I continued my work for the Masters degree and other activities. I took two courses at Western Reserve, both semesters in 1968, and worked part time in Adelbert College of Western Reserve. I was there to witness the student demonstrations. They protested the war in Vietnam, demanded more control over their curriculum and threatened to take over the Adelbert building. This was like the demonstrations everywhere in the country. As I try to recall the mood of the demonstrations, I think it was typical of student "rebellions" but it was also clear that the participants demanded drastic changes. One day the demonstration was so serious that the University had to be evacuated. This was a year of historical significance—Robert Kennedy and Martin Luther King were assassinated and both deaths had a great impact on the U.S.

At the same time that Elton went to Brazil, I went to the national convention of the LWV in Chicago. It was a momentous and exciting meeting for the League, partly because it expanded its program to include Human Resources as well as its regular political and financial issues. I was elected Vice President of the Cleveland League at its annual meeting in June and spent a lot of time on League matters, including chairing a comprehensive study on "Housing in Cleveland" with a committee that included three black women. I asked them to work with me because they were members and interested in the housing issue. We had a good, hard-working committee, and it was the first time that black members were included in League activities.

Although our children were not with us, they continued to be an important part of our lives. We talked to Gregg often and heard regularly from Daille. She and Tom arrived in Jerusalem less than a year after the Six-Day War; living there was very instructive for them. They had no phone or fax, but she faithfully wrote every week, so we kept in touch. The U.S. Consulate employees were friendly as were the people in the other English-speaking consulates, and Daille and Tom were soon active in bridge groups and social events. They enjoyed their new experiences; however, I found out later that Daille was continually afraid of the unstable peace in that city. Luckily, this didn't stop them from thinking about having a family and we were very happy to hear in the fall that they were expecting a baby at the end of the coming April.

Gregg was still in Detroit during the first part of the year, going to love-ins and, I think, using drugs, drinking and taking part in sexual activities, all of which were occurring worldwide at that time. Gregg came to Cleveland several times during the spring. He quit his job in Detroit in June and went to "where the action was"—New York. He had no problem getting free-lance work, but he was hoping to get a job.

While Gregg was in New York, Elton had to attend an MSI board meeting in July. I went along and visited Gregg for a couple of days. We spent time in Greenwich Village and Central Park where dozens of happy, bare-footed kids—from 14 on up—sold paper flowers, love and drugs. Gregg took me to see *Hair,* the hit musical about the *Age of Aquarius.* The show did not appeal to me but it was typical of this new era where brief nudity was shown on stage. Gregg stayed at a friend's apartment in Greenwich Village and when we walked down the street together the gays called out and kidded him—that should have been a wake-up call, but it took me several more years to understand and accept what was going on.

Gregg was there only until September when he decided he would take a ship to England and tour Europe before settling down to another job. This is what the baby boomers were doing and although he was a little older than most, he wanted to share in all the fun. We heard little from him once he got to England, but apparently he enjoyed himself there and in France, Italy and Greece. When we finally talked to him, I told him that if anything bad should happen to him, I wouldn't know. He responded reasonably, "If anything bad happens to me, you'll know!"

From Greece he took a boat to Israel and when Daille and Tom met him, he was down to his last penny. He spent Christmas with them and in January 1969, he called and borrowed money from us to return to England where he had a job and friends waiting for him. He asked for $100, but we sent him $200. We did not expect him to repay us, but it worried him. Later, he bought us a lovely Hockney drawing, worth considerably more than $200. It still hangs in the living room today.

Although both kids were embarked on their new lives, Elton and I were still at a standoff in 1968. I started going to a counselor in May to help me decide what to do about our marriage situation. I had several problems in making a decision, one of which was finances. Until 1969, my services to MSI were gratis, with my agreement, but then I began to be paid part time. I was being paid also by Western Reserve; however, I realized that the small compensation I received would not be sufficient to sustain me. I was convinced also that I would not find another man and, as I said earlier, in our culture that was important. Above all, I really wanted to be married to Elton. He had never asked for a divorce, nor suggested he wanted one, and I guess he continued his double life. In any case it was I who had to make a decision.

The counselor was helpful in several ways. He told me immediately that I was very angry and suggested I write a list of all the things in my life that had made me angry. I did, and it was a long list. Just recognizing this helped me to make a decision. By July the counselor had persuaded me that somehow I could make it on my own but that I had to draw the line and insist that Elton give up the other woman or me.

In August I gave Elton an ultimatum—it had to be me or Georgiana. He felt he needed more time to think about it, so I took the car and headed west on an interesting trip. I drove through Illinois, listening to reports on riots and demonstrations at the historic Democratic National Convention which nominated Hubert Humphrey as its presidential candidate; I spent a couple of nights along the way, and then went to visit Ethel in Rapid City. I stayed there over Labor Day and had a nice visit, but as it turned out later, I left her believing that Elton and I were breaking up, without telling her anything of our relationship.

From there, I drove to Ft. Collins where I spent a night with my high school friend, Betty Stamper Roberts, and then on to Estes Park. I spent two days there, enjoying the Ponderosas and the mountains, meditating and communing with God. I left knowing I could deal with whatever might happen to me. The next stop was the Johnsons in Leadville. Nancy was there with her new baby, Dawn, born August 31, but with the sad knowledge that her young husband, Jim, was in hospital in Denver very near death. He was to die very soon, from cancer.

After a few days with Mona and Dale and the girls, I drove across South Park, which I have always loved, and into Colorado Springs. Mother, Dad and I had a good visit and quite a lot of fun, which included a ride up the Cog Road to Pike's Peak and a trip to Salida and beyond to see the Sand Dunes National Monument. While I was with them Betty went to Omaha to be with her ill mother. Craig was sick, so I volunteered to take over until he was better and stayed at their house for a week. While I was there, Elton called to ask me to come home. After a few days, I was on my way, elated! I spent a night in a motel in Denver, just to be alone, and watched the new TV show, *Laugh-In*. I stopped in Lincoln to see Phoebe and in Omaha to see Betty and headed east.

I didn't go to Cleveland immediately, but went on to Pittsburgh to spend a couple of days with the Madisons. When I got back to Cleveland, I met Elton as planned. I will never forget the great big smile on his face when he saw me drive up. We went to the airport and flew to Atikokan, Ontario, for a very good week, combined with business. And that was the end of Georgiana. Within a couple of years, she was married to Gordon Way. Ironically, he was one of Hanna's Vice Presidents.

Our reunion was a happy one and very welcome, but otherwise the year held plenty of problems. At some point in 1968 I read my horoscope that said it would be a good year for me. I often thought, "Thank God, it's a good year—I couldn't get through a bad one!" And the next major mishap in my life was falling and breaking my wrist. Elton was in Brazil—again for a long stay. At 11:30 one night I stepped onto a soft chair, at the same time reaching to adjust the curtains (don't ask why I was doing this at 11:30 p.m.) and fell with full force onto my right hand. There was no doubt it was broken—it was hanging sideways, at right angles, so I called the doctor. He asked if I could get to the hospital. I was sure I could so he said I should ask for Dr. Nahigian. I couldn't write the unfamiliar name so I said it over and over, got in the car and went to St. Luke's and asked for Dr. Nahigian.

It was a very bad break and Dr. Nahigian told me it would never be okay, but I knitted all the time my wrist was knitting, even with the cast on. However, when the cast was removed, the next six weeks were difficult and painful. By then, it was time to get ready for Christmas. I typed, wrote and knitted and my wrist healed and eventually became about as good as new. I had a wonderful time keeping the MSI books and writing checks with my left hand.

In October, Climax transferred Dale Johnson to Pittsburgh and moved the family, including Nancy and Dawn to a small town nearby. We went down to visit them as soon as they were settled and were glad to have them somewhat nearer. This move helped Ethel make the decision to come east also. We had Thanksgiving alone, but soon afterwards Ethel called and told us she was moving to Cleveland. She didn't ask what we thought about it, and would have interpreted anything but a warm welcome as our not wanting her. And, of course, I did not want her. I felt, selfishly, that I had just begun to get my life in order and could not or would not devote myself to her.

We were sure she thought we were getting a divorce and Elton would move in with her, but in addition to the fact that our marriage was, apparently, continuing stronger than ever, he would never have moved in with her. For these reasons and others, her move was a foolish decision. She had never lived in a big town, or the east, and the climate, culture, apartment living— everything would be strange to her. Further, she would have no friends, and, at 70 years of age she was not very adept at making them. She expected that she would see a lot of Elton, but he could not give up traveling, which was all that kept MSI going, and she resented his leaving town so often and for long periods.

At any rate, she drove to Minneapolis where Elton met her. He drove her to Chicago where I met them and brought her to Cleveland. She was with us until some time in January and then moved into an apartment on Lakewood's Gold Coast, a half hour ride from us.

Christmas was not a happy one. Elton called at 3:00 p.m. on Christmas Eve and said he'd be home as soon as he had bought a gift for me. I told him that no place would be open at that time except a dirty bookstore. Sure enough, in the morning, he had a paper bag with a dirty book. He also bought me some nice clothes. An old friend called after Elton had talked to me and asked him to meet for a drink. It was midnight before he came home. Ethel and I had supper and I survived, but I was not a happy camper.

One more unpleasant thing happened before the year was out. We had planned a New Year's Eve party in the building's party room, but there was a serious flu epidemic and half the guests couldn't come, the other half were not very festive and it was probably the least successful of any party we ever gave. But at midnight, the year was over and we could start a new one.

1969

In 1969, after Ethel had moved to her new apartment, I took her to P.E.O. several times and introduced her to several people who offered to take her to church. I'm not sure she went more than once or twice. We took her to church a few times, but it was difficult because of the distance, and we took her out to dinner when Elton was in town. I called her regularly, and in March, we took her to Pittsburgh to spend a couple of weeks with the Johnsons. I invited her to various League affairs and luncheons, but she rarely accepted, or she would back out at the last minute. One of these League affairs was a seminar on urban development. I was the M.C. and George Steinbrenner was the main speaker. At that time the Yankees were far in his future and he was president of American Ship Building. It was interesting talking to him, even without knowing that he would eventually become the nemesis of all Yankee-haters, including me.

During this time, I was working on my degree and League matters, as well as MSI. I also spent a lot of time with Nancy Wakeman who had four little kids and a traveling husband. I think I was reasonably nice to Ethel, but not nearly as nice as I should have been, and she certainly expected more. By June, she had had enough and moved back to Rapid.

Elton was spending a lot of time in Brazil. In late 1968, CVRD wanted an engineer to work with the company in Vitoria. Elton thought it fortunate that Bob Brandt was available and interested in accepting the job. Bob had worked in the Hibbing Lab under Elton after completing his MBA and his Masters in Metallurgical Engineering, and we had seen quite a bit of him and his wife Ramona when they were newlyweds. In fact, it was they who owned the piano we had borrowed in 1958. They now had five children and were living in Pittsburgh. Arrangements were made for the entire family to move to Vitoria, and Calvert correspondence courses were arranged for the children for home education. Bob commenced his employment with MSI on January 1, 1969 and moved his family to Brazil in February.

Elton spent a lot of time with Bob in Brazil and planned to go again in June, taking me with him. This would be soon after Daille's due date, which we were both excited about, and we decided that I should go to Brazil with him and then go on to Jerusalem to see the little family. I knew I could not be there when the baby was born because of all the complications of school, Elton's traveling and the uncertainty of the birth date. Kristin Margaret was born on April 28. Tom promptly wired his folks about her arrival, but in his excitement, forgot to let us know. Fortunately, Peggy called me to rejoice with me about our little granddaughter, so we did learn immediately about the birth. We were both thrilled at being grandparents and I looked forward to seeing all three of them. I spent a lot of time making plans for what turned out to be a complex trip, since Gregg was now living and working in London, and I would visit him there after leaving the Pettits.

Looking back, I am as impressed with the scope of this trip as I was then. I left North America to go to three other continents, South America, Asia and Europe, and I saw a good bit of a fourth when we flew over the northwest corner of Africa. I was in three of the oldest cities in the world—London, Rome and Jerusalem, one of the most beautiful, Rio, and the newest, Brasilia. And I saw spectacular and interesting things in every one of these places, the most important of which was, of course, our little Kristin.

We flew with Varig, the Brazilian airline, on this long trip, but with the time change, it was only two hours to Rio. We stayed in the Hotel Lancaster at the beach with a breathtaking view of the harbor and city, a view that you can get from almost anywhere in Rio. The Brandts drove down from Vitoria, where CVRD's facilities and port were located, and we spent two days touring Rio with them. We then flew to Vitoria, where we were lodged in a luxurious guesthouse for the two or three days we were there. We spent a good deal of time with the Brandts and I realized that Mona was really frightened to death by the foreign atmosphere and the language, though Vitoria is an ordinary, Brazilian, middle-class industrial city. Morris Brown was our major contact as he spoke excellent English, having had an English father. We did not realize until later that though he sounded like an American, he thought like a Brazilian. His wife knew no English but was taking lessons, and was a real doll who took me on a couple of auto trips along the beautiful coast.

One day we flew to Brasilia on our own, to see the very new city which was of international interest at that time. Unlike the capitals of almost all countries, this city was built in the nearly empty center of the country to encourage the country's development. When we were there in 1969, most of the major buildings were completed, in addition to the residential areas and the road system. The government had only recently moved there from Rio and this meant that the embassies and other foreign offices were required to leave their beloved Rio and they were taking their time—no one wanted to leave Rio. Brasilia was largely empty, but we were overwhelmed with the beauty of its buildings and the massive undertaking of its construction.

We spent a few days in Itabira at the location of the CVRD iron ore mine, about 300 miles inland. Again we were housed in a luxurious guesthouse, and the very nice wives of several of the mine employees entertained us. I had a lovely trip with four of them to the fascinating city of Ouro Preto, a town dating from the 1700's when gold was discovered in the area. The government buildings, churches and cathedral were gorgeous, heavily decorated with gold, and very interesting. The trip was fun. The women knew little English, but we managed to talk about a lot of things. Incidentally, this relatively unknown city was the location of the movie "*Moon Over Parador*" with Richard Dreyfuss.

Elton and I took the train back to Vitoria, and then we flew to Rio, where I spent a couple of days. When I checked in at the airport to go to Jerusalem, problems occurred with my ticket and reservation and frantic attendants were trying to return passports to the right people. It was a long flight to Rome, from about 1:00 a.m. to 4:00 p.m. I got a taxi to a hotel, settled in, had dinner and then walked around to see the Coliseum, the Forum and other interesting sites. The next day I left about noon and had a wonderful, fairly low flight, on a bright day across the northern shore of the Mediterranean. It surprised me that the view was exactly like the map! When I landed at Lod and passed through customs I saw Daille and Tom, looking proud as peacocks over their wonderful accomplishment, Kristin, asleep in her basket. I must admit that at that moment I was really happiest to see my baby again. She had been away for eighteen months. Then I became thoroughly entranced with their baby for the next two weeks.

I realized then that I had neglected my maternal duties by not being there when the baby was born—the time a woman needs her mother most. But Daille had been fortunate in meeting an American nurse, married to a Jordanian, who took over my role and she had survived all the little crises faced by the mother of a newborn.

I had a wonderful two weeks, enjoying baby and parents. They took me everywhere in what is surely the most fascinating place I'd ever visited. I felt there was something very spiritual in this city, sacred to three religions. The house the kids lived in was in Bethany and when we drove towards the city we could see the old wall and the golden gate. We went past the Garden of Gethsemane, a quiet, peaceful and holy place. One day we drove north and spent a night in Caesarea, with remains from the Crusades; then we drove to Nazareth and to the Sea of Galilee, where we spent a night on the hill said to be the site of the Sermon on the Mount. We swam in the sea and saw the Golan Heights in the distance. We toured the Old City and went to Bethlehem and the Garden Tomb—the place where I felt God's presence most strongly. And we drove to a seaside resort south of Tel Aviv where the kids swam in the Mediterranean while I watched Kristin.

We had a good time in Jerusalem too. Tom and Daille arranged several bridge and cocktail parties and a wonderful champagne party. It was my first experience with Foreign Service social life and I could see why they were enjoying it. But it was not a peaceful paradise. There were signs of unrest with the Arabs everywhere, heavy army equipment traveled the road to Jericho almost every day and the sound of guns could be heard in the distance. No matter where we went, bags were examined. I wrote to my mother that I didn't think the problems between the Israelis and the Palestinians would ever be resolved. It still appears, in 2006, that I was right. An El Al plane had been highjacked not too long before and the kids thought I was brave to fly to London on El Al, the Israeli airline. However, I had an uneventful and beautiful flight over the Mediterranean and the Alps. I was sad to leave, but looking forward to seeing Gregg and London.

My visit with Gregg was very different from my visit with Daille. He had not replied to my letters asking him if it was all right for me to come, and when I finally talked to him, he told me he would get a hotel room for me. He seemed glad to see me, but kept me completely away from his life so I met no one and saw him only in the evenings and at the weekend. Again, I should have recognized that he was living openly as a gay man and was afraid to let me know it. But we had a good visit—once I realized he didn't want to hear any more about my granddaughter—and I saw a lot of London and the surrounding country.

I felt at home in England the moment I arrived. The suburbs looked exactly like the places I'd read about in books. I stayed at the Prince of Wales hotel in a room on the ground floor, down the hall from the dining room, surrounded by empty storage and banquet rooms. As always, London was full of tourists and Gregg had probably had to scrounge to find this room where I was really alone. It was hot! London was suffering a very hot July, without air conditioning.

Many of the tourists were Boomers, boys and girls. Crowds of them gathered on the steps of the public buildings in Trafalgar Square and in front of the American Express building, waiting for money from home. Many of them were on the tours I took. The day tours included Stonehenge and city tours. I went by Tube to Kew Gardens, Buckingham Palace and Westminster. I saw museums and many other historic and interesting sites. We rented a car on the weekend and drove to Oxford, Avon and Coventry. Since Gregg's license had expired, I had to drive, on the **left** side of the road—an experience I'd hate to repeat. The only room we could find was over a pub and we did not have a very restful night. But we enjoyed seeing everything together and had a good visit. On the night of the moon landing, we were in the lobby of my hotel watching the event on a small black and white TV and we were just as thrilled as if it were in full color. Elton watched the moon landing with my folks in Colorado Springs, after a business meeting in Denver. Both he and I headed back to Cleveland the next day.

This trip had been important to me because it made me realize that our children were now independent and didn't need us anymore. It also made me realize that they would always need to know that we loved them and cared very much about them. From then on, I wrote regularly to them, whether or not we heard from them. And I added weekly letters to our mothers, too, for good measure. This paid off in a way—Gregg wrote a little more often than he had and it was obvious over time that he really liked hearing from me, and it made him feel closer to us.

When I got home I found that Elton had spent his six weeks in Brazil as well as Colorado where he had seen Jim Madison graduate from the Air Force Academy. I also learned about a 4th of July tornado in Lakewood that had done a lot of damage. I didn't have much time to get my act together before we were on the road again, or in the air, to be exact, this time to Rapid City and Custer for Elton's 30th high school reunion. We found that Ethel had moved into a new little house where she lived until she died in 1989. We met Ramona, Dale and girls in Custer. They proved to be a receptive audience for stories about my trip and, especially, about our granddaughter.

Once back in Cleveland, I spent a month or more getting my photos into albums—the first time I had seriously organized them. I went back to school and work in September. In October, Lyn Cameron gave notice, to my disappointment, because I really enjoyed working with her. She arranged for someone to take her place, but when Elton came back from a trip he was very annoyed and insisted I fire this lady. We replaced her with Jan Kruger who was with us for four years. She was a good secretary, but I missed Lyn and continued to get together with her.

Mother and Dad came to Cleveland for Thanksgiving and Elton and Dad left a day or two later for Brazil, a trip Dad was really thrilled about. Mother stayed with me and we got ready for Christmas. Elton and Dad had a good time together and had some very interesting experiences. By the time they got back it was the middle of December and Daille and Tom were to arrive soon for Christmas—their first home leave. Tom's next assignment was to be NATO in Brussels. We thought my parents might like to stay and see their first great grandchild, but Mother especially was lonesome for Jack's family and they left a few days before Daille was to arrive.

Daille and Tom went directly to Marietta and we also drove down to spend Christmas there. Elton had not yet seen the baby and I was dying to see her again. Fortunately, the Pettits had found a room for us next door—fortunate because Peg's housekeeping left much to be desired and really bothered Elton, especially when he observed Kristin crawling under a couch and coming out covered in dust. Christmas Day was enjoyable and we loved being with our grandchild and were happy to be together.

After Christmas we drove with Daille, Tom and Kristin to Pittsburgh to spend a day with the Johnsons, then we all returned to Cleveland. The family stayed with us until the end of January and we enjoyed having the opportunity to be practicing grandparents.

CHAPTER 10

THE EARLY SEVENTIES

1970

The year began well. Daille, Tom and Kristin were with us until February 14. We thoroughly enjoyed seeing Kristin grow and learn what we meant by "No!" and how to patticake. We enjoyed her parents' company equally. I was sorry to see them leave, as was Elton, but he was involved with MSI—primarily with the CVRD job. I continued in my roles as student, League member and bookkeeper. My MSI job had expanded to include filing and editing, but my major effort was directed toward bookkeeping. At about this time, I also took over from Roy Bierman some stockholder caretaking responsibilities. In other words, I made sure that the stockholders received, in a timely fashion, the reports they needed, dividends and interest payments on their debentures.

Elton and I flew to New York on the Easter weekend. We spent the night and had an elegant brunch at the Plaza. We watched the Easter parade, then Elton flew to Brazil and I flew home. Because he became involved with CVRD in completing a feasibility study and contract application, he was gone for six weeks. Several weeks were spent in Belo Horizonte, holed up with the engineers.

He was in Brazil at the time of the Kent State shooting, which was a complete shock to everyone in the Cleveland area and I think to most of the country. I'm sure the Boomers were especially shocked. They had been behaving as though they had the freedom to do whatever they wished and there had been an increasing number of anti-war riots and demonstrations all over the country for two or three years. The Kent students joined in by rioting at Kent and setting fire to at least one building. Governor Rhodes responded by sending in the National Guard, the result of which was the shooting of several students. I felt this outcome inevitable. It seemed remarkable to me that it had been so long in coming. Surprisingly, sympathy went out for the students, even among people old enough to know better. The general feeling was horror and gloom about the state of a country that could treat innocent people in this way. This was the beginning of the end of the demonstrations. They appeared to taper off, but nevertheless continued until the U.S. withdrew from Vietnam. The attitudes and emotions, however, did not dissipate. They lived on to cause problems well into the twenty first century.

Elton's absence also spanned Mother's Day, and that long absence changed the direction of my life. I was completing the final hours needed for my M.A. and, up until this time, I'd fully intended to work toward a doctorate in history. I had passed my language capability test, though barely (I really was not at all proficient in French but could read it well enough), and applied to the history department for acceptance. While Elton was gone I spent a great deal of time in the library and was pretty lonesome, despite my League chores and time at the office. I shared, of course, in the unrest and concern of the rest of the country. I decided then that I didn't really want to spend all my time studying, learning more and more about less and less and being away from other people so much. Consequently I gave up the idea of the doctorate. My only regret has been that I did not complete my plan to work on the theory of social Darwinism and its effect on immigration, using Hibbing residents as the prime example. I still think it would have been an interesting study.

I did complete my Masters' work and received my degree in June, 1970. Western Reserve University had just merged with Case Institute of Technology and had become Case-Western Reserve University. We were allowed to choose which of the two we wanted our diplomas to list. I chose WRU, since that was the school at which I had worked so long and hard. Though academically eligible, I was not admitted to Phi Beta Kappa, because I had too few hours at Reserve.

Jack, Betty, Carola and Craig came to visit us that summer, only the third trip they ever made to our home. Jimmy was in San Francisco, having gone there to attend art school, but he ended up as a non-studying, non-working, meditating flower child. Sally was working in Colorado Springs.

It was an unsatisfactory visit in many ways. Jack felt it was his vacation. He would sleep late, but we were expected to hold breakfast until he got up and then do whatever touring they (that is, he) wanted to do. Unfortunately, he slept every day until noon or after. Craig was only nine and bored sitting around, although we had a pool at our apartment house and he did swim a little. After a few days, they took a trip to D.C. and then returned to spend some time with us. We took them to Blossom Center on 4th July for the special concert, and we drove to Niagara Falls one day, managing to get Jack up a little earlier. Elton had been to one of the Caribbean Islands, St.Lucia, looking at pumice. He met us at the Falls and came home with us.

One night Jack and I stayed up until 3:00 a.m., arguing about Robert E. Lee whom he felt was the most despicable American who had ever lived because he had fought his country. I hadn't yet learned not to argue with him. I told someone we'd done that and she said "Why on earth were you talking about Robert E. Lee?" Good question. Jack would never go to bed and thought no one else should until he was ready. Elton, of course, went when he was ready. Jack was probably the most difficult guest we ever had and I guess I should be thankful they didn't ever come again. I felt sorry for Betty and the kids, but Betty and I had some good visits, and I guess the kids were used to having their father do as he wanted.

We had now lived in Fairhill Towers for four years and had a lease for five. Although I liked the location and really liked being a resident of the City of Cleveland, we had never been completely satisfied with our apartment, so I spent some time that year looking at apartments, and when Elton was in town on weekends we went together. We wanted something bigger and easier to get to with better bus or rapid connections. All the rooms were small and although we did some entertaining all the time we were there, it was always difficult. I think Elton really wanted to be on the west side, and although our place was handy to the university, it was not that handy to the office downtown. When they started building the Carlyle in Lakewood, we thought it was interesting, and when Gregg was in town for a few days in the fall we went with him to look at it and pretty much decided then to get a place there.

Gregg was able to come to Cleveland because he was in New York on a job and took the time to visit us and various friends. He was working in London, enjoying his job, and becoming an Englishman. Although his agency was in the process of a merger, Gregg was not left without a job, and it was very nice to see him. We enjoyed his visit.

In November my Dad had surgery for lung cancer. He had been a smoker. I flew to Colorado to be with him and Mother. He was in the hospital for a week or more, but the surgery went well and Mother also seemed to be fine. During my visit I went one day to Mother's storage closet for something and found there a portrait taken of Dad and Uncle Ed in about 1900. This had always hung in my grandparents' house and I hadn't known what had become of it after their deaths. Mother, who was completely unsentimental, said she was going to take it to an antique shop and sell it. Because the frame was bad, she was sure no one would want it. I was horrified and told her I would love to have it. Eventually, she gave it to me, although both Alan and Jack also wanted it when they found she had it. I had the frame repaired and it has hung in my living room ever since.

I returned to Cleveland in time to drive to Pittsburgh for Thanksgiving with Mona and Dale. Elton came home in time to fly with me to Europe where we were spending Christmas with Daille and Tom in Brussels. Tom was in the Communications Department of NATO. After the kids met us in Brussels, Elton went on to Sweden for a few days to make some business calls. When he rejoined us, he actually took some time off. I had a great visit with the Pettits, especially Kristin, now about one and a half. She enjoyed being read to and was chatting about "good toys" (any bicycle or motorcycle) and "ducks" (any bird). I knitted her some red mittens and she was so entranced with them she wore them to bed the first night they were finished. When Elton returned, he spent a whole day playing with Kristin and referred to it as Kristin's Day.

We did as much touring as possible. We visited Bruges and all the town squares in Belgium. We especially admired the beautiful square in Brussels, where we saw the Mannequin Pis, a sculpture which truly enchanted Tom. As in Jerusalem, there was much socializing and we all had a very good time. Gregg came for Christmas, arriving just at the tag end of a party thrown by Daille and Tom. He told us about the typically Gregg hang-ups he had in making what turned out to be a torturous trip. He had grown a beard which frightened Kristin enough that she wouldn't make up with him for days. We went to a Christmas Eve service in an English church where the pastor gave a sermon that made us all laugh. None of us ever forgot it, because none of us had the slightest idea what he was talking about. We had a lovely Christmas, except for a few little glitches when one or the other of us got mad about some minor issue. Elton and I remembered this Christmas as the best ever.

After Christmas Gregg went back to London; Daille, Tom and Kristin drove (with help from the Hovercraft across the Channel) to London. We took a train to Paris for two days before flying to London to join the Pettits and Gregg for New Year's Eve. Elton's Paris visit was very profitable. George Kauders had arranged for him to meet some people from a company that was mining iron ore in Mauritania. MSI got a major job as a result of the visit. We were happy in spite of a terribly hot plane trip to London and a terribly cold hotel when we reached it. Daille and family were already ensconced in the hotel. When we saw the room the Pettits had reserved for us, our first thought was, "We have to go down the hall to the bathroom!" The second thought was, "My God, it's cold." We turned the tiny heater as high as it would go and went to bed together in one twin bed with all the covers from both beds and our coats on top. The next day we moved to a room downstairs, kept the bathtub full of hot water, closed the windows when the maids opened them for airing, and we were still cold.

Despite the cold, it was a memorable few days. Gregg took us to lunch on December 30 with some of his co-workers and friends, one of whom was Jackie More. Jackie impressed me not only because she was a great gal, but also because she was a descendant of Thomas More. We went pub-crawling in the evening, leaving Kristin with a sitter. On December 31, after we'd realized that Gregg had sent out invitations for his New Year's Eve party and bought the liquor in Brussels, but had done nothing else, we bustled around getting the necessary provisions for a party of about fifty people. Our bustle paid off. It was such a smashing good party that Gregg's friends talked about it for years. We met some of the interesting people he had told us about, some of whom we still know.

1971

On January 3, 1971, the Pettits left for the Channel Hovercraft and home. We packed up and headed to the West Side Terminal. It was a cloudy, gloomy day and when we reached the Terminal, we learned that because all flights were cancelled, they weren't taking buses out to Heathrow. After more and more people turned up, they apparently decided they'd better move some of the crowd, including us, to Heathrow. Every single flight was, indeed, listed as "Canceled." We had planned to go to Madrid before I flew back to Cleveland and Elton to Mauritania to look at the iron ore mining property. Since our flight was canceled too, it looked like a long wait. But no . . . we were lucky. Most of the crowd waited nearly two days. After only a few hours, the "Now Boarding" sign flashed on for our flight and ours alone. It was loaded in record time. Everyone ran down the ramp; we had our bags stashed and seat belts fastened in no time and we took off immediately. We were happy to be on the flight, and relieved to get to Madrid safely, but we never did learn why only that one flight took off and no others.

It was unusually cold in Madrid, too. The streets were so icy that all tours were canceled, but I managed to get a cab to the Prado and to see some of its extraordinary paintings. Elton met his Spanish contact and potential business partner, Enrico Biel. The Biels took us to dinner that night, even though it was Twelfth Night—a big family holiday in Madrid. Dinner was at 10:00 p.m. We were nearly the only customers, and the restaurant had a flamenco show afterwards. Never have I struggled so hard to stay awake. The Biels, incidentally, gave us a real insight into Franco's Spain. They were Filipino, but had moved to Madrid to escape the crime and corruption in Manila. They were ordinary, law-abiding citizens and found it very comfortable for people such as themselves to live under Franco. We, of course, considered him a dictator anyone would wish to abolish.

The next day I flew back to Cleveland, encumbered by several bulky packages. I was sure they would not go through security. I was hand searched, but thankful that I didn't have to unwrap them. Elton, meantime, flew to Mauritania for the commencement of an interesting job and job location. He came home later in January to report on the project and on Mauritania. All of Mauritania is near desert; the northern part of the country is part of the Sahara. It was formerly French West Africa, so the main language is French. The company that was beginning to develop the program to mine and ship iron ore was a French company, but within a couple of years, all foreign companies were nationalized and the project became a Mauritanian project.

Mauritania is a Moslem country. At that time, the people were mostly nomadic and barely eked out an existence by moving their flocks from area to area. There are essentially no resources in the country that can bring in revenue, except iron ore, and that had not yet been developed. It was a desperately poor country, although stable politically. Ironically, it began to get international attention around that time and aid for the poor began to arrive. This brought many nomads into the "cities." Because the people could get some food and assistance, they stayed, multiplied and in time the poverty problem worsened. This is very old news, and things may have improved by now, but it is hard to see how very much improvement could ever take place.

The company needed consulting help on locating, mining, concentrating and shipping the ore, and MSI was given a contract for this. When Bob Brandt's tour in Brazil was completed in March, he and his family moved to Rocky River and Bob prepared to do a good bit of the work in Mauritania. He took French lessons which were largely a waste of time since he barely learned "*Oui*!" but he managed to travel between Paris and Mauritania for a year or so.

In the meantime, we leased an apartment at the Carlyle and proceeded to get it ready for occupation. We moved in on March 1. It was considerably larger than our Fairhill apartment and was built in a tuning fork arrangement. The master bedroom and bath were on one side of the hall; the other two bedrooms and bath were on the other. I loved that arrangement, as well as the view of downtown Lakewood and Lake Erie from our 13th floor. I arranged for Higbee's (Cleveland's wonderful department store, now dead many years) to help with the decorating. They sent a young man named Ken Nye. Ken worked with me on the Carlyle apartment, on the new office space into which we moved in 1975, and later our condo in the Meridian. He was very helpful, had good ideas and did not encourage me to spend a fortune. I finally got our carpets out of storage, had our couch recovered in blue, hung new drapes and was very happy with the result. We had quite a few problems arising from the construction, but eventually they were all solved.

I hated to leave our Fairhill location for one reason—it was located in Cleveland. I'd signed on to work at the polls during our first fall back in Cleveland and continued to work at almost every election for many years. It was fun being able to vote when Carl Stokes ran for mayor in 1968 and became the first black elected mayor in a major city. And I enjoyed going to City Council and testifying for League issues as a resident of Cleveland.

It was strange to be back on the West Side, but it was more convenient to downtown and we liked the area. I found that some of the people whom I had seen often either wouldn't come west or didn't want to, and I had to make a real effort to see Joanne Tilberry, a friend from my first year at Western Reserve, and Lyn Cameron. The Cumberlidges had lived in Rocky River since 1966. Although we'd always enjoyed their company, we hadn't seen much of them for years, so I was happy to be able to see them more often, and the Dick Smiths and Floyd Lees were also close by, as well as most of the members of my P.E.O. chapter.

Soon after settling into our new place, we went to New York for the annual AIME convention and had a wonderful time. The Wakemans were there, along with many others whom we knew. The dinner dance was on Elton's 50th birthday—a good way to celebrate an important day. A few days after we got home, Alan and Lui's son, Walt, came to visit us with his new wife, Marilyn, and spent a couple of days. Alan had adopted Walt early in his marriage, although Walt kept his father's name of Nelson. Alan had been the good and quite strict father young Walt really needed. He was always a nice, pleasant, and interesting boy, and I was happy to see him marry a girl I liked very much. They were still going to school as I recall, but soon afterwards, Walt began to teach at a Junior College in Denver. He taught there until he retired.

In the spring of 1971 we took a major step which we never regretted. We wanted to find a church closer to us than the one we'd been attending. Before trying any Lakewood church, we went to Old Stone Church downtown. It had been recommended by Dick and Mary Cass (Mary is a P.E.O. sister) and Donnie and Gil Gilbert, Cass' friends. We'd gone to a lot of churches in and around Cleveland. This was the very first one where we were greeted and made to feel welcome. We also thought it a beautiful church; we liked Dr. Lewis Raymond, the senior pastor, and we decided there and then to join. We never thought of joining another church in Cleveland. We expected to spend the rest of our lives as Old Stone members, and remain there into eternity. In 1991 we bought niches in the Columbarium for our ashes and my dear husband's remains reside there now.

We spent Easter alone together in Cleveland in 1971, but Elton was traveling most of the spring. He went to Brazil for CVRD and also for a job with a very wealthy and famous Brazilian named "Baby" Pignatari. He went to Mauritania, and in July became involved with a Mexican company which took him to Mexico City. This year we celebrated our 30th anniversary and my gift was a trip to Mexico with him. We were there for a week of business for Elton, tours for me, and wonderful places in the evening with Otto Gramp, Mr. Villanueva and others. I loved every minute of the temples, pyramids and scenery, and the night spots were some of the most interesting and fun we'd ever experienced. I had a day or two of "Montezuma's Revenge" though I tried to be very careful what I ate and drank. This didn't spoil a lovely trip for me, however.

In September, Elton went to Argentina for a job with some wealthy businessmen and was paid $10,000 in cash for his work. They wanted to go to Peru, however, to look at the port where the ore would be shipped and decided to drive over the Andes. Elton rode with the driver and the two businessmen rode in the back of the car. Going up was no problem, although the roads were barely usable, but when they started down they found an earthquake had damaged the road and knocked trees and rocks across it, making it impassable. Although the driver spoke no English and Elton spoke no Spanish, they both understood what had to be done. They cleared the rocks and trees, and using a fallen tree as a lever, managed to get down to the bottom of the mountains. The businessmen apparently sat in the back seat saying their rosaries! When they finally got into town and Elton could telex us, my first thought was, "What happened to the $10,000?" In a few days he returned to Cleveland—he and the money both intact.

His next trip was less memorable when we went together later in the month to Seattle, visited Alan and Lui and saw the World's Fair. We also took an enjoyable day trip to Victoria and had a pleasant and leisurely week seeing Seattle and the surrounding area. Our enjoyment ended, however, when we went from there to Colorado Springs for a week with my folks. We found my Dad very ill and much worse than Mother had ever indicated. He was obviously depressed and in need of some personal care, but my mother was sure he would be well eventually, that there was nothing much wrong with him. We drove them up into the mountains on Sunday to see the beautiful golden aspens. When we got back, having seen Dad's condition, Elton and I realized we must discard our somewhat vague dream of retiring to the mountains. It would be too impractical. We recognized how important it would become to be near hospitals and doctors when we grew older.

I spent most of the week trying to make Mother see that Dad was in serious condition and she would have to change her way of life permanently. She couldn't see it at all and I felt pretty discouraged about their future. I was really worried and didn't know how I could help much and I spent a long time Friday night praying that God wouldn't let him linger too long in his present condition. When Mother called me very early in the morning saying something was the matter with Dad, it turned out that he had died of a heart attack. It really brought home to me the great power of prayer. It was probably a good thing that Dad was gone. After calling 911, we went to the hospital, then called Jack, Alan and Elton and went home to make the necessary arrangements. Elton arrived about noon and Alan and Lui soon after. Mary Jane and Aunt Ruth also came for the funeral.

I stayed in the Springs for a few days, leaving with some misgivings, which later proved to be well founded. Mother was quite sick in December, but whenever Betty or I called and she didn't answer, we assumed she was out somewhere. It turned out that she had been ill and, I think, rather out of it. She had a much harder time than she admitted or any of us realized.

Back in Cleveland I resumed my bookkeeping for MSI and various jobs for the League, while Elton worked on the Miferma (Mauritania), Mexican and Brazilian jobs and pinned down others for Inco Sudbury, Ontario. Bob Sanden came to work for us in October, 1971, and Jan Kruger continued as secretary.

In October Daille, Tom and Kristin arrived for a visit and Daille and Kris stayed with us while Tom went job-hunting. They both liked foreign service, with the opportunity to travel, having had several trips around Europe, and the various perks, but Tom didn't like his occupation. Communications sounded okay, but the days of decoding and such activities were about over and the department turned out to be more stenographic—copying, etc.—than anything else. When he signed on with the State Department, he had not had to take the Foreign Service exam because the Department waived it for needed employees. Without ranking, however, there was no opportunity for promotion. Tom was unhappy with the work and the people with whom he worked, so he decided to look for something else. He went to various areas he thought he might like, but didn't find anything and returned to Brussels while Daille visited us and the Pettits. When he returned to Brussels, he took the FSA exam, and in his next post, he took the orals. Within a few years he became an administrative officer. Meantime, he continued in communications until after his next postings to Brasilia and Jakarta.

Daille left soon after her birthday and we entertained Dick and Jini Smith for Thanksgiving. With Christmas just around the corner, we made a decision that I've since regretted. Instead of going to Colorado Springs to join Mother for her first Christmas without Dad, we went to Rapid City and spent it with Ethel. Alan and Lui did go to Colorado Springs. We were home in time to spend New Year's Eve alone. We welcomed 1972 which was to be a busy and memorable year.

1972

Both Daille and Gregg continued to live overseas and we settled down to our busy lives at MSI. Although Elton continued his peripatetic life on airplanes and in foreign countries, I was working in Cleveland. In March, Tom developed hepatitis, just as he was about to close up shop in Brussels and move on to his next assignment in Brasilia, so he was in bed while Daille got ready to move. At the same time she had been told she had an ovarian cyst that needed to be removed. I found a gynecologist for her, a wonderful doctor and nice guy, a friend of our Dr. Harshman. Three days after they arrived in Cleveland she had seen Dr. Bunde and was in the hospital where she stayed for nearly two weeks. The urgency was not for medical reasons but to allow her time to recover before going to Brasilia.

Tom had to report to the State Department, so he left the day after Daille went to the hospital and poor little Kristin stayed with me. She hadn't known what to make of any of this but she accepted me and was as good as gold, and I enjoyed having her with me. Easter arrived while Daille was in the hospital and both my mother and Ethel flew in to spend Easter with us, and Tom returned from D.C. for the weekend. After our mothers left and Daille had a couple of weeks to recover, it was time for the Pettits to head south. As Kristin watched them pack she became more attached to her mother and when they left for the airport she was hanging on to Daille for dear life. Grandma was nice for awhile, but not for good.

In June of 1972, I was elected President of the Cleveland League of Women Voters and spent most of my time alternating between the League office on the 5th floor of the Marion building and MSI's office on the 2nd floor. I had a tough job taking over from Ilona Gram who had left the office flooded with multiple copies of everything except the papers I needed, most of which she took home with her. Most of the year I had the help of a young black girl supplied by CETA, a government program designed to give employment and experience to the poor. She was somewhat better than no one, but I had to do most of the office work myself. I did a great deal of sorting and tossing and arranged to have the earlier League documents taken to the Historical Society. I was President for only one year; however, the League accomplished several important projects that year and certainly the office was better organized. I felt I had done a good job.

Some of the national events of that year did not immediately affect us, but they were to have a great deal of influence on our future, especially the burgeoning feminist movement. Since *The Feminine Mystique* had been published in the late 1960's, many women (including me, although I never actually read the book) had begun to think seriously about their roles in society and to realize they were basically second class citizens. The Civil Rights movement intensified this realization as did such events as: the passage by Congress in 1962 of the Equal Rights Amendment, the ERA (never ratified by the necessary number of states), publication of the first issue of *Ms. Magazine* and, for that matter, the growing use of Ms. instead of Mrs. or Miss. While women such as I saw all of this as progress, men, including Elton, were unreceptive and largely opposed, naturally, to any change in the ranking of genders. To quote a speaker I heard, "Wouldn't you like to have your dinner ready and your shirts ironed?"

Ignoring all of this, Elton and I decided we should go to the State Fair in August. We were fond of county fairs, but had never attended a state fair. We went to the Fair in Columbus, and then drove to Cincinnati where we did a little touring and spent the night. We toured in Kentucky the next day and found some interesting things of which we'd never been aware. We had picked out a town where we would spend Saturday night, but as we drove through we realized it was "dry." Since we couldn't have a Saturday night drink, we drove 100 miles more to Portsmouth, Ohio, where we could. On

Sunday we visited various scenic and historic spots in Ohio before returning to Cleveland. We had a delightful three day trip which we intended to repeat, but never did.

This was a presidential election year and the Watergate scandal had begun to unfold. Nevertheless, Richard Nixon was expected to win easily over George McGovern. Elton and I spent Election Day in Paris, having voted absentee before we left home. Elton was going there on business and insisted I go along. Gregg had moved to Paris during the preceding year, and we wanted to visit him. He was living with George Roland who had gone there a little earlier. When we arrived on October 31, Gregg met us. We checked into the Celtic and then went down the street to a sidewalk café where we met several of Gregg's British friends. A pleasant few hours were spent trying to explain the U.S. electoral system to them, as well as the way we celebrate Hallowe'en in the States.

On the next Tuesday, our Election Day, the Hilton Hotel in Paris gave a party for people to watch the election returns. Gregg had received one of the invitations sent to many American citizens living in Paris and invited us to go along. We experienced one of the most interesting, memorable, and unpleasant, parties we ever attended. The ballroom was huge—it appeared to be as large as a football field—and was filled with hundreds of people. To add a political note, the management had decided it would be a good idea to have a donkey and an elephant join the milling crowd. Needless to say the animals' party manners were found wanting and very soon the floor of the room was a mess of paper cups, spilled drinks, animal feces and God knows what else. The time difference between Paris and the U.S. meant that no results would be seen until after midnight. Happily, Richard Nixon took an early and impressive lead, and we were able to escape the worst mess we had ever seen in a hotel ballroom.

Gregg was having a good time in Paris. He'd had only high school French, but a good ear for accents and a fantastic memory, so he simply ignored rules of grammar and seemed to make himself easily understood. This was fortunate, since he was the only non-French person in the agency. He and George gave a dinner party for us with a nice group of guests, and we took a couple of tours, met some interesting people, saw a lot of Paris and had a very good time.

And finally, after all the years of hints and ignoring unexplainable actions and events, I came face to face with Gregg's homosexuality. We were having dinner with Gregg, George Roland and George Kauders and I was talking to George Roland about art when I suddenly had a flash of realization; I knew that Gregg and George were gay partners. Elton had come to this realization earlier, but neither of us nearly as soon as we should have. This is hard to understand these days, but at that time, very few had heard of homosexuality. Although we were both aware of its existence, no one admitted openly to being gay. Those who were either hid it as best they could, often including marrying and becoming parents, or living as bachelors or old maids, or moving completely away from anyone who knew them to some place like New York or San Francisco. One member of my high school class, for instance, moved to, and disappeared in, San Francisco; Elton's Uncle Ord Geist pretty much disappeared when he reached maturity. Was he gay? Possibly, but no one ever suggested it. The very few who did admit to being gay were shunned by all "decent" people. I'm quite sure my mother and many others went to their graves ignorant of its existence. So I never considered the possibility in relation to Gregg. It came as a great shock, even though I had plenty of hints; perhaps I was somewhat prepared. I was very glad we left Paris in the morning. I was able to quietly absorb the fact as we traveled. Elton had become quite certain that Gregg was gay and this was the major reason he had wanted me to go to Paris with him. It was much harder for him to acknowledge, as it is for most men, than it was for me. I should add that neither of us ever considered disowning Gregg, or withdrawing our love from him.

Again we flew out by way of Spain, with a couple of days sightseeing in Madrid and the countryside before Elton flew to Mauritania and I returned to my various responsibilities and activities in Cleveland. Among the responsibilities were more and more MSI duties. Because this was the pre-computer age, most things were a lot more work than they are today; bookkeeping, for example, required much pencil work and ledgers. I did all the bookkeeping and financial reports, as well as the filing, and edited all reports. Our current secretary, Jan Kruger, was very good, and Bob Brandt was extremely precise in his letters and reports; Elton's reports, however, needed editing. I enjoyed this job, because unlike a lot of people he knew, I improved his reports and he'd allow changes with no argument. We had also added Bill Bronkala in the spring of 1972, primarily to sell equipment but also to lend a hand with any metallurgical projects.

Somewhere about this time we were expecting a visit from some of the Miferma (the Mauritanian job) group. We became concerned about the appearance of our unpretentious little office. We set about renting more attached space from the building and scrounged around all the second-hand stores for furniture. My office turned out to be in the far back corner, but that was fine. I liked the quiet and privacy and, since Elton was still hesitant to let people know that his wife was working for the company, he could ignore me when important clients visited.

My mother came for Christmas, but she was not very happy and the weather was dull, cold and dreary. It was not the most successful Christmas celebration we ever had. But in the meantime, we'd received happy news from Daille—she was expecting again in June.

1973

Karin Virginia's birth on June 26, 1973 was the major event of this year, but it was five months before we saw her. In the interim, we went to Chicago with the Bronkalas for the AIME convention in February and had a very good time, and we spent Easter with them at their home.

Some time in 1973 Dale Johnson was transferred back to Leadville after about five years in Pittsburgh. Nancy and Dawn had been with them when they moved there, but after a few months, Nancy had courageously decided to take her baby and go back to Greeley, Colorado, to get a degree. In due course, she graduated, met another guy, Mike Dermody, and married him. Vickie finished high school in the consolidated school near the Johnson's home and began dating David Araneicka. They began school that fall at the University of West Virginia at Morgantown, majoring in accounting.

Liz was the Johnson's only child at home and she went back to Leadville High School as a senior—not easy for a young person who had been gone for five years. She became involved with a young drop-out whom we all considered to be a real loser. Liz did not want to go to college, but her parents insisted she learn a skill she could use to support herself. She decided to go to beauty school—a very good decision, because she married Wendell when she graduated! For most of their marriage, which lasted about four years, she did support herself. As far as any of us could determine, Wendell had nothing going for him, but we may have been prejudiced!

Returning now to our lives, I decided in the spring to look into the possibility of a hearing aid. While I had needed one all my life, they were not feasible until the small, battery-operated products became available. It is a wonder to me now that I heard anything at all before I got aids. I realize that I did some unconscious lip-reading, because TV sounded louder when I looked at it! And I was very good (and still am) at responding correctly to what I thought people might be saying. But I missed a lot—music, for example. Music never sounded very good to me; I never heard birds singing, coyotes howling in the distance on Mt. Manitou, nor the call to prayer from mosques when I was in Israel. Even with hearing aids, I miss the punch lines of many jokes and humorous comments because people lower their voices at punch lines.

I made another major decision when I got the hearing aid—I cut my hair short! After wearing it in a bun or French twist for years, I recognized that only a few old ladies were still wearing long hair and buns, but mainly, I wanted to conceal the hearing aid. I was able to wear an aid only in my right ear because of a chronic infection and drainage in the left ear. I found it hard to get used to—I heard noises I'd never heard before, the click/click of the turn signal in the car, for instance. But I also found that it helped and now, many years and many hearing aids later, I am more and more thankful for them.

It probably is unnecessary to mention that Elton continued to travel. He made sales calls and worked on projects in Mexico, Mauritania, Brazil, Liberia and Canada. In April, we began a project in Oregon with Midrex, and 1973 turned out to be one of our best years up to that time. Jan Kruger left in June and we hired Antoinette Merritt, a Dutch girl who was capable but had a very hard time with Elton's dictation, especially when he used American lingo such as "upsetting the apple cart." In October, Lynn Zidd, whom I knew from the League, began working part-time and proved to be a real jewel. On a personal basis we spent an uneventful summer and fall but after sharing our Thanksgiving with the Cumberlidges and Bob Sanden and girl friend, we planned and set out on a trip to Brasilia to spend Christmas with the Pettits.

We flew to Brazil by way of Mexico where "Wild Bill" Villanueva had arranged for us to spend a weekend at Calado Caballo (Horsetail Falls), some 50 miles from Monterrey. He picked us up and took us there for three wonderful days, marred only by very cold weather, for which we were unprepared. The spot is beautiful, the hillsides were covered with blooming poinsettias, and the lodge was up-to-date and comfortable. We took a horseback ride up to the Falls. I became quickly convinced that, if I'd ever been able to ride a horse, I no longer was. Frank and Kathryn Madison, on a temporary stay in Mexico, came up and spent one evening with us. Bill came to get us and had a party for us in Monterrey. We took a plane the next day, flying by way of Guatemala City and Panama City, over a live volcano, and into Brasilia.

We were thrilled to see Karin, now five months old—a pretty, happy little girl—and to renew our acquaintance with Kristin. She was a happy 4½ year old, speaking Portuguese fluently, but knowing immediately who spoke it and who didn't. After directing a couple of Portuguese words to me, she spoke nothing but English. She had some pretty sensible ideas; she didn't, for instance, want to go to Cleveland; there was snow there and it was VERY cold; she wondered if we could send her a TV. They had TV reception in Brasilia, but it was all in Portuguese and Daille and Tom, both of whom managed the language quite well, hadn't wanted it; Kristin certainly did. I took gifts to both girls, but being caught up as I was in the feminist movement, I did not want to educate these little girls to be women! I'd taken trucks and things to Kristin, and pants and shirts. She really wanted pretty dresses—so much for that idea!

It was interesting to see Brasilia again after our visit in 1969 when settlement was just beginning. In those four years it had changed in many ways that really amused me. I became convinced of the accuracy of the law of unintended consequences and the impossibility of making grandiose plans with the expectation that a populace will follow. They won't! The city had been planned and constructed in large "super blocks," each with its school, church, shops and apartment houses, making each super block self-contained. Because people would need to travel little, except to work, there were no traffic signals and only entry and exit ramps to each super block from the highway. That is not how it worked. Each super block developed its own type of marketing; one block developed with butchers, another with clothing, still another with bread, and so on. Each block had its own specialty. The unintended consequence was that people drove all over the city for various services and traffic became a serious problem. The installation of traffic lights began very soon after our visit.

This did not affect us or our visit, which was really pleasant. We spent three weeks with the Pettits, except for a few days when Elton flew to Itabira to see CVRD. He called the airline to make his reservation and had trouble with the Brasilian clerk understanding his name until she finally realized, "Oh! Like Elton John!" There was a large group of Americans in Brasilia, including several from a foreign aid organization. As there was not much night life and everyone had servants, they had a continual round of parties and luncheons, in which we were included. Elton played golf with the men, I played bridge with the women, we ate at the Curascaria del Lago and one day we took an interesting trip to Cristolena. This was a town set in the middle of a plain, seemingly hundreds of miles from anywhere, with street after street of merchants selling the semi-precious jewels in which Brasil is so rich.

Our Christmas was very nice, all of us laughing at the very funny, but expensive, tree and Kristin enjoying every minute of the holiday. One day Daille was upset because the baby was missing from the creche. We were all relieved when Kris came home from school with it. She had taken it in for "show and tell." We were amused at the conclusion reached by Kris and a friend that, since there were no fireplaces for Santa to descend, he must be driving around in a Porsche and delivering through the door.

We took a plane on December 31 to Rio. It was awash with people who came to celebrate New Year's Eve in Rio's unique way. We thought we had hotel reservations, but found we did not because of the crowds. People filled the beaches, lighting candles and sending little ships out to the ocean with expensive gifts for the goddesses. Though it began to rain, the sight was spectacular, and we wandered around for a while taking in the truly romantic sights. Fortunately, we met a Hanna man. He took us to his apartment and found another traveling American salesman who was willing to give us a bed for the night. When we left for the airport in the morning, the beach was deserted and cluttered with nothing but scavengers. I might mention that there was at least one pickpocket in the New Year's Eve crowds. My bag had an open but narrow top and my cosmetics kit was apparently "lifted," but not my wallet, thank goodness.

1974

I began 1974 with a cold I caught before we left Daille's, and the evening rain in Rio had not helped. It got worse as the day went on, so the next few days were quite miserable. We flew to Caracas and spent two days there before I flew back to Miami and then home. Elton was making sales calls and had trouble with his air space, so he came later. I was miserable for some time so I suspect I had more than just a cold. Nevertheless, I went back to work to start finishing the year-end bookkeeping. Elton was still away when the funeral of Gordon Way, Hanna's VP of Engineering, took place. This was the job many people thought Elton should have had, and it was he who had married Georgiana Rhodin. I attended, but was annoyed to hear all kinds of comments about the wonderful contributions he had made to Hanna—for most of which Elton had been responsible.

Ralph Lestock came to work for MSI in March 1974, and was still with the company long after Elton and I retired. He was an engineer with a Peace Corps tour in Vietnam behind him, and a wife from Poland who added a lot of spice to everything she did. Ralph's first big job with us was an assignment in Liberia where we were helping with improvements in the Lamco pelletizing plant. He also worked with a young man from Brazil who spent several months with us studying various mining problems. He, too, had a lively young wife who became good friends with Gerta Lestock. Another young woman who entered our lives and joined the company in 1974 was Mary Margaret Coates, a geologist. She worked part time for us throughout the year and remained our friend after she and her husband moved to Denver.

The job for Lamco in Liberia was a major assignment for us and required that Elton make three trips to Liberia during the year. On one of these in May, he was on his way home when his PanAm plane taking off from Dakar had an engine failure; the pilot made an emergency landing. The flight had to be cancelled, and although there were no casualties or, apparently, any injuries, a serious problem was created for the passengers who were kept in Dakar for a day. Another flight was finally arranged, this one to Paris where there was a long delay because the French demanded that the passengers have French visas. This was clearly impossible as most of the passengers had not intended to go to France. Elton finally got an American flight to Cleveland and arrived two days later than planned.

In the meantime, I had gone to the airport to meet the PanAm flight he was to have been on, and found it had been cancelled. When I called PanAm for information, the operator told me, "That flight crashed in Dakar." "And what about the passengers?" I asked. "We have no information", I was told. I got no information for more than a day, and needless to say it was a worrying time for me until Elton was finally able to contact me when he landed in New York. Everyone who flies can tell hundreds of airline horror stories, but this is the only time in all our flying that I was truly frightened.

Between flights and trips overseas, we had a pleasant visit from Gregg in April. He arrived just in time to join us for a big party with a French theme which MSI put on in the Carlyle party room. We had an orchestra, dancing, drinking and a late supper and the guests all enjoyed it. This was the second of three parties we gave in the Carlyle. The first was a Las Vegas party the year before with gaming tables and all the fixings, and the last one in 1975 with a "Come as Your Secret Ambition" theme. We gave a few more of these parties in future years for clients, customers and business acquaintances, and although guests always enjoyed them, they were expensive, and probably not very effective marketing tools—and a great deal of hard work. Gregg left a few days later to spend Easter in New York with friends, but it was great having him around for that time.

Throughout the first half of 1974 it was nearly impossible to ignore the Watergate issue which was getting hotter and hotter. Unlike the liberal media, Elton and I did not consider any of what went on as sinful as it was made to appear. Unfortunately, my brother, Jack, got completely immersed in the issue and, even with the distance between us, we couldn't ignore his feelings. Nixon had replaced Robert E. Lee in his ranking of evil Americans and he ranted to anyone who would listen and wrote letters to us raving about how terrible Nixon was and castigating us because we had voted for him twice. I have never known why these letters bothered me so much, but they thoroughly upset me.

We got one of these letters in May, just before we flew to Pittsburgh for the graduation ceremonies at West Virginia University for Vickie Johnson and her fiancé, David Araneicka, and it upset me enough to spoil our visit with the Johnson's. They met us at the airport and we drove to Morgantown for the happy occasion. Afterwards, we had dinner with the Don Johnsons and then flew back to Cleveland. Within a few days, Elton and I flew to Denver for a meeting on the Carter Creek project (more about this later). We drove to Colorado Springs to see Mother, with an unpleasant stop at Betty and Jack's while Jack abused and raved at us.

Tom's tour in Brazil ended in June and they flew back to the States through New York. Tom went on to Washington, and Daille and the girls came to Cleveland. I met them at the airport, but went to the wrong gate. Daille was already trying to get the luggage, stroller and girls down to the baggage claim, where I finally caught up with them. I took Kristin with me to get the car and said, "I'll bet your mother said, 'where is that Grandma?'" Kris responded, "She said 'Oh, shit!'" This was not a good start, but we had a good visit anyway.

The Pettits were in the States on home leave before they began their next tour in Jakarta, Indonesia. After a visit with us and Tom's parents, they stopped in Denver, where we joined them, to visit the Colorado relatives. We covered a lot of ground, spending time with Walt and Marilyn and their one year old, Alan; going to Strasburg (Colorado) to visit Nancy and Mike; driving up to Leadville to see Dale and Mona and even visiting with Liz Johnson, not yet but about to be married. After Denver we went to Colorado Springs and spent time with Mother, Aunt Jo and Jack and family. Alan and Lui were in town and we had a memorable (typical Roeser) picnic. It was interrupted by a sudden downpour and we rushed to Jack's to finish the picnic. Being with Jack again turned out to be a continual rant about Nixon, and the day before Tom and Daille were to leave for Indonesia, he cancelled a dinner with us, because he had to watch the impeachment hearings. This annoyed me greatly. We had a good visit otherwise, and even got to Pike's Peak. Poor Kristin was disappointed, however, because she had been dying to see snow, but there was not a speck to be seen.

We flew back to Cleveland just in time for me to check into Fairview hospital for a hysterectomy. I had menopause symptoms for nearly three years, including hot flashes, but my periods had never stopped and I was suffering from continual bleeding. I put off seeing Dr. Bunde, but when I did he said I had to have a hysterectomy, so there I was in the hospital, and in bed, for over two weeks—a far cry from today when one is up and walking immediately and home in a day or two. I'm sure this method is better, because it took me a long time to recuperate. I was discharged from the hospital on August 8, the day Nixon resigned . . . . which did not put an end to Jack's vituperative letters, but they were eventually about other matters.

Elton took me to Toronto for Labor Day to celebrate my recovery and I enjoyed seeing the city, but not as much as I might if I had been completely recovered. He went on to Sudbury and I went back to Cleveland to more of the usual MSI work and League activities, which included an interesting trip to the University of Maryland for an LWV Solid Waste Conference. Ethel came to visit us in October. We entertained her as best we could with Elton gone most of the time and I involved in my usual activities. This year those included P.E.O. I was president at that time which used a considerable amount of my time.

Elton had to go to Sudbury the week of Thanksgiving, so I went with him and we had a Canadian dinner on Thursday to celebrate the day they had celebrated early in October. He left soon after that to work on the Portland project, and because he was going to be there a good bit, Alan and Lui asked us to come for Christmas. I arranged to meet Mother in Denver and gave her explicit directions for when and where to meet, but right along with the rule that things never work out as you expect, my plane to Denver was canceled after she had left Colorado Springs. I made arrangements to notify her and then caught a direct flight to Seattle, worrying every minute about her. As it turned out, she had gone to the wrong place and had not heard a public announcement addressed to her. Luckily, Walt had gone to the airport to see her, heard the announcement and got her on her plane. This was a hint of a kind about the Christmas celebration. It snowed heavily on Christmas day and in the afternoon the power lines to Alan's house went down. We shivered by the fireplace until the next day when a neighbor with power invited us in for the day. By the time we left, the power was on and planes were flying, but it was a colder and darker Christmas than we'd expected.

The year ended with dinner at the Hollenden Hotel with the Bronkala's, feeling rather glad that 1974 was behind us, and hoping 1975 would be a little less eventful and at least as profitable.

CHAPTER 11

MOVING AND CHANGING

1975

The year began with the move of MSI from the second floor of the Marion Building to the seventh floor. The new office was bigger and better arranged, with a conference room, several pleasant offices, and a very nice one for the President. The move was a chore, but we got settled fairly quickly, with the help of Ken Nye, who selected paint colors and wallpaper. Sally Bronkala was also a big help, and after we had moved in, she volunteered to come in weekly to clean the office.

This was a very big year for MSI, with more employees and outside consultants than ever, and jobs all over the world. The work in Itabira, Brazil was essentially completed, but we still had some Brazilian work with the Rio CVRD office. The Mauritanian job was still in the works as was work on the Mexican pellet projects. We were working with McKee on a large pellet project in Macedonia, Yugoslavia, with Bethlehem Steel on an improvement project for their Liberian plant, and we were completing our work on the Midrex metallizing plant in Portland, Oregon. We had worked on several Inco projects during the past two or three years, first improving the pellet quality for its pellet plant and then improving plant maintenance which extended to improving maintenance company-wide. Inco started a nickel plant in Guatemala that year and we did a great deal of work on this Exmibal project. We helped with the design and worked with them on the start-up. Elton was in and out of planes all year and I accompanied him on several trips.

The first of these was in January. Elton had to be at Allis Chalmers in Milwaukee for one of the pellet plants, and he arranged to have a Saturday meeting at O'Hare with some of the MSI Board, primarily on the Carter Creek project. This project involved an iron ore body in Montana, owned by Carter Creek group, which had done some initial developing work, and had tried to get leads on improving its technical information. For a price, MSI eventually acquired a lease on the mineral rights that were sold for a nice profit at the end of the seventies. There was considerable disagreement among the Directors as to whether to proceed with this transaction, and many meetings followed, including this one in January.

We had planned that I would join Elton at O'Hare for dinner on Friday; I would shop on Saturday while he was in the meeting and we would have dinner downtown with Dwight Jamar (a Board member) and his wife. Elton's Milwaukee visit went well, but we both were delayed by bad weather getting into Chicago—Elton from Milwaukee and I from Cleveland. Neither of us got to the hotel until midnight. I spent the weekend in the hotel because it was too cold and snowy to go downtown, and it was too icy for a cab to get us downtown for dinner Saturday night. On return to Cleveland on Sunday, we decided that the next time we were to plan a weekend in Chicago we'd spend it in Cleveland instead. In fact, it was more than 25 years before we were in Chicago overnight again.

My next trip didn't do much to restore my faith in flying. We went to the AIME meeting in New York in February and planned to spend Sunday in New York before the meeting. Instead, we spent all day Sunday at the Cleveland airport because of bad weather. We did get to New York, however, and I had one very nice experience. While Elton went to Europe, I went to an opera—a mediocre one I'd never heard of, but with Leontyne Price replacing the star, it was certainly worth attending.

Elton's trip took him to Kavadarci, Macedonia where he had an exciting experience. While hiking with a group through the wooded mountains to look at a possible pipeline the group got lost. They had a grueling day hiking, sitting out the night in a sheepherder's hovel and finally riding horses back to Kavadarci.

I flew to Guatemala with Elton in May on one of his trips for Inco on the Exmibal project and we spent a week in Guatemala City. The country was peaceful at that time and I took a couple of tours into the spectacular mountains, one to Chichicastenango, which was one of the most interesting places I'd ever seen, especially the Catholic church. Tiny people sat in the Cathedral, performing all kinds of primitive religious acts. One day Elton and

I flew into Tikal to see the historic Mayan ruins. The weather in Guatemala was wonderful, the people were friendly, the scenery was beautiful and the food was delicious. We flew back to Cleveland via Mexico City where Elton spent a couple of days on business and I toured.

There were more trips for me that year. We went to Iron Mountain to spend the Labor Day weekend, visiting and talking shop; we drove to the Mining Congress in Denver that fall, and in November, I went with Elton to Macedonia. Our trip to Denver included a visit with the Greenlys, now living in Oklahoma City, and a drive from there through Amarillo, Raton and Trinidad to Colorado Springs and to Denver. After the Mining Congress, Elton went his way and I went to Colorado Springs to visit Mother. Of course, I visited Jack and Betty too, and found Jack still giving me hell but, at least, no longer about Nixon. Mother and I had a nice week. We visited the Dermodys in Strasburg, Mona and Dale in Leadville, and Walt, Marilyn and Alan in Denver. I drove from Colorado to Rapid City with Mother for company. She flew home, while I had a short visit in Rapid before returning to Cleveland with Ethel for a few weeks stay.

Meantime, Tom's tour in Jakarta ended in June after just one year, a rather difficult year, since an infestation of termites required a move into another house, and the crowds of people everywhere in Jakarta overwhelmed them. Tom was expected to be in Washington D.C. for some further training before going to Yaounde, Cameroon, where their belongings had been sent. But his assignment was changed to Paramaribo, Surinam, formerly Dutch Guiana, in South America. They arrived in Cleveland after stops in Singapore, Hong Kong and San Diego, and spent a little time with us before Tom and Daille went on to Virginia to find a place to stay for a month. I kept the girls and took them to D.C. on a difficult journey. Leaving our apartment, Kris found that she was missing one of her Barbie dresses, and Karin thought her 'blankie' was missing; both howled all the way to the airport. When we finally got on the plane, I insisted on holding Karin (now two) because Daille had told me she wouldn't sit in a seat alone and I would have to hold her. After arguing with every official, I did put her in her own seat, and she sat very calmly and quietly for the whole trip. The family returned to Cleveland later in the summer for a very short time, and then went to the Pettits before they took off for Surinam at the end of July.

Looking back I wonder how I was able to do as much as I did between my trips and entertaining company. I managed to do what was necessary for MSI (still part-time) and a multitude of other jobs. I was president of the County League of Women Voters and of my P.E.O. chapter that year. I had also joined the Women's City Club the previous year. I had wanted to do this for some time, and was quite active in the organization for the next five years.

At the end of January, a meeting of prominent women and leaders of women's organizations was held to talk about celebrating International Women's Year, 1975 having been proclaimed as such by the United Nations. It was eventually decided to organize a three-day IWY Congress in October, including seminars, lectures, informational booths and major keynote and final sessions. All involved spent a lot of time planning the Congress and it turned out to be one of the highlights of my life, as it was for most of the other women. Those involved and attending came from every conceivable level of society and age—lesbians, pastors, nuns, secretaries, politicians, housewives, welfare mothers and many others. No group of women was unrepresented. After three wonderful days of inspiring meetings and presentations, we all experienced a real high at the closing ceremony, realizing that as women we were more important than any of us had ever felt before. We all concluded that "I am woman; I can do anything."

No one wanted this experience to end, so one of the leaders, Dr. Joan Campbell, and several others decided that we should call people together to discuss what we should do next. The upshot of these really fascinating meetings, again with all kinds of women represented, was Women Space, formed early in 1976. It set out to do all things for all women, and since this is obviously impossible, the organization eventually faded away after about twenty years; its accomplishments, however, were impressive. Jane Campbell, later elected Mayor of Cleveland, was the first Executive Director; I was a member of the board of about 50 women from the beginning, served as treasurer for a while, and was the third president for two terms, so I was well acquainted with its programs.

We were the first group to bring forth the problems of battered women, rape treatment and displaced homemakers; we had workshops on how to manage money, how to get along in the workplace and how to handle many other issues of particular concern to women. We also had a Help line that was a real lifesaver for many women. Most of all, we had the opportunity to learn to know and understand women from all walks of life. Today, it is hard to imagine that there were no shelters then and little knowledge of the special problems of a time when women were mostly housewives. Parenting and housework were generally the sole responsibility of women. I believe the services we offered were of extraordinary value, and I'm really proud of my work in the organization.

At the same time, my enthusiastic and even obsessive participation was very hard on Elton and our marriage—the damage nearly destroyed it. It was several years before my excitement about the increasing equality of women and my ideas about marriage partnership began to be more realistic and I could prioritize the issues in my life. More about this later.

Meantime, I did spend quite a lot of time, some of it on weekends and at night, on MSI work. In October, we finished a humongous report for the FENI (Yugoslavian) job, with the help of several consultants and secretaries Lyn Zidd, Chris Gilbert, Nancy Brandt and Martha Knight, who had started working for us in the fall of 1974, and became a very good friend. In November, Elton returned to Macedonia and took me with him. It was interesting visiting Yugoslavia again, getting acquainted with the secretarial staff and their ways of doing things, and seeing Macedonia, with many opportunities to note the differences between their society, still Communist, and ours.

We stopped for a weekend with Gregg in London on our way to Yugoslavia and for a week on our way back. The tax situation in France had persuaded Gregg to return to London, and George was there too, so they got a flat on Roland Gardens that was Gregg's home until he died. We had a good time with Gregg and stayed in his flat. This was not very comfortable, because it was heated only with gas logs and London was cold that November. But our visit included a great two-day auto trip to the lovely little city of Bath, Stonehenge and the Winchester Cathedral. It was a harrowing trip because Gregg's dyslexia made it almost impossible for him to know right from left, and I began to realize that Elton suffered from the same problem, so my directions to turn left or right led to confusing, but never fatal, mistakes. Our London visit came very close to tragedy when Irish Republican Army (IRA) terrorists blew up a restaurant to which we had planned to go one night. Many diners were killed. For some reason we had changed our reservations at the last minute to another restaurant. During the next few years Gregg was close to several of these IRA actions.

I did most of my Christmas shopping in London that year. I was home in time to prepare Thanksgiving dinner, write Christmas cards, finish preparations for Ethel's visit, and dine on Christmas Day with the Cumberlidges.

1976

There was considerable anxiety in the country early in the year about our 200th anniversary. Gerald Ford had become President after Nixon resigned and there had been continuing antagonism towards the Administration, especially when President Ford pardoned Nixon, eliminating the possibility of a long drawn-out trial. Because this episode was now officially in our past, the country began to relax a little and look forward to the 4th July. It turned out to be a day of joy and celebration all over the country.

This was also an election year with Gerald Ford running against Jimmy Carter, and the Cleveland League of Women Voters was able to sponsor a debate between Ford and Carter. This was an exciting event for Cleveland and for the League. Another exciting pre-election event, for me, was the arrival of Ronald Reagan and Jimmy Stewart at Lakewood Park for a campaign speech for Ford. They arrived late, and we were all milling around when the limousines drove up. Two tall men got out and I had to move out of their way. I was pleased, however, to be so close to those major movie idols! And, as it turned out, I was close to a future president. Since I've always been passionate about politics, worked at the polls from the time we moved to Cleveland, and had done some volunteering for the Republican Party, this was an important event for me.

One of the major changes for us in 1976 was the return of Tom and Daille to the U.S. Tom was transferred to Washington after a very difficult year with the Surinam Ambassador who was one of those bosses whom everyone hated for good reason. Tom was assigned to the State Department in D.C. and the family began a four-year stint there. We were happy about this move, even though D.C. was 350 miles away—at least it was reachable without an overseas trip. They bought a townhouse in Centreville, a long way from the city until the construction of Highway 66. They came to visit us before Tom started his job. They liked being in the States in some ways, but they missed the overseas perks and the extra spending money they provided. With house payments added to their reduced income, they were very hard pressed. Daille found several short term, low-paying jobs to help their finances, and to their credit they never asked us for financial help.

I was very busy as ILO (Inter-League Organization) president. The League board approved the publication of a cookbook, the work on which was left almost entirely to me. Lin Emmons and I each paid $1,000 towards the printing, though the ILO did manage to repay us within a few years. Most of the cookbooks were eventually sold. It was an attractive book and could have been a good fundraiser, which was its original purpose, but the Leaguers weren't good salespeople and neither was I. As president of the ILO, I also attended the National LWV convention in May in New York—again an exciting meeting. Later in the summer, I set up an office for the ILO in a cubbyhole that the May Company provided. It was isolated in a far corner of the top floor of the building and almost impossible to find. It was not pleasant, but at least it gave us a place to meet other than in various restaurants. I also managed to acquire some file cabinets and furniture.

May was an exciting month for another reason—I signed up to go back to school. I took the GMAT test (with a nearly perfect grade) to qualify for the Women's Program in Management, a new program at Case Western Reserve which was designed to provide half an MBA program to women who were in business but had no specific training and for women who would like to get into business. This was a direct outgrowth of the IWY celebration, because one of the women involved in the IWY, Dr. Betty Diener, taught marketing in CWRU's School of Business. The classes began in July with 25 women ranging in age from me at 54 to one woman of 22, and from degree holders to high school graduates. It was a great program that we all enjoyed and profited from, though it demanded much time and hard work. Our first course was marketing and we were divided into groups to work on a marketing problem. Our group consisted of five west-siders and we became fast friends.

Meantime, Elton and I made a major move in August, midway in my marketing course. We bought our first home, a condo in the Meridian. Elton had felt for some time that we should get out of rental apartments and buy a home, preferably a condo, and I agreed with him, except that I really loved our Carlyle apartment and certainly did not want to move again. I told Elton this was too busy a year for me to move. Since almost every year of my life has been busy, he reasonably ignored my protest, cashed in most of his Hanna stock for the down payment, and we spent several days looking at condos before we decided to stay on Lakewood's gold coast. To be exact about our moving, it was I who moved. Perhaps not intentionally, Elton went on a long trip, mostly for sales purposes, to the Philippines and other Pacific areas during the three-week period of packing and moving. The Meridian was new, though our suite on the second floor had been occupied for a year by a family of four and decorated by them. Everything (including their furniture) was yellow, a color I dislike, and the kitchen and bathrooms were papered in ghastly foil. I insisted on re-papering those three rooms. We had a great cabinet and closet built in on one bedroom wall, and we had our blue couch recovered in green so it fitted in well. It would have been foolish to throw out nearly new drapes, grass cloth and carpets, so we lived with the yellow while I gradually changed first one thing and then another; we finally got rid of all of it over six or seven years.

I might add here that I did what I had always done when we moved; I knocked myself out getting things organized so that the place would be livable when Elton returned. I finally realized (after nearly forty years) how foolish it was; he had no idea what was involved, and he could have helped if I'd left things undone. I hated every move we ever made—I hate the mess, the work and the decisions to be made about what to move and where to put things and getting used to a new place. I decided, and told Elton, that I was never going to move again, except into a nursing or funeral home. I don't think he believed me, because several years later, when he was thinking of retiring, he suggested Arizona and I said, "bye-bye," I wasn't moving. Now, as I write this in 2006, we moved once more and I've moved yet again by myself. But I managed not to move for 26 years. Thank God! I never see a moving truck that I'm not grateful someone else is using it.

While all of these things were going on in my life (and ours), Elton was busy working, either on continuing jobs or on efforts to obtain new ones. The Exmibal project in Guatemala was a big project. It required several extra consultants or short-term employees and also provided one of the most exciting experiences of Elton's career. In February, Guatemala City had a big earthquake, killing hundreds, and cutting off communication for a day or two. Elton was on one of the top floors of a high rise and had to get down the steps climbing over debris, but reached the ground unhurt. We had no news and Tom's embassy in Surinam hadn't even heard of the earthquake. We finally heard from someone in the mining business who had some contact with Guatemala that everyone was okay, but it was a long and worrisome day for me and others at MSI—not to mention for Elton.

Between school and moving and club activities, we continued our traveling with a trip in February to Las Vegas, via Colorado Springs, for the AIME meeting. This was nowhere near as much fun as the meetings had been when Elton was working for Hanna and dealing with many pedlars who entertained us lavishly in Vegas. We were not gamblers and thought Vegas fun to visit just once.

No sooner had we settled into our new home than we were shocked to hear that my very dear friend, Jini Smith, had died suddenly in Iron Mountain. We drove there for the funeral. Our next trip was in October when we went to Colorado Springs to join the Greenlys and Carl Nichols (Hanna's Executive VP) and his wife for a golf weekend at the Broadmoor. When growing up I heard about the luxurious Broadmoor, and it was quite a treat for me to stay there. I was able to spend quite a lot of time with mother while the others golfed.

We spent Thanksgiving in Centreville with the Pettits—the first time we were able to be with them for Thanksgiving since the first one after their marriage. We did quite a lot of touring of D.C. and enjoyed the break, except that Elton was about to have a hernia operation and was feeling a lot of pain. The surgery was scheduled for December 7, and he was in St. Luke's hospital for a week—quite different from today, when hernia surgery can be an outpatient procedure. I spent that week studying for exams, going to the hospital to visit Elton, and doing what had to be done at MSI. I also had to prepare for a big Christmas celebration. Gregg was coming, both our mothers and Daille's family. We picked up Ethel at the airport two days after Elton was discharged from the hospital. Ethel needed a wheelchair that Elton had to push, as I was in the car. That was not great for his healing. We also had a problem with my mother. She decided, more or less at the last minute, that she wouldn't come; she changed her mind when I got pretty hurt and angry. The holiday was a happy one, however, and everyone enjoyed Christmas Day.

Daille and Tom stayed in a motel, and Gregg slept in the hide-a-bed. Karin, now 3½, woke up the morning after Gregg arrived and couldn't find her mother and dad. She was upset until we hurriedly phoned them and they assured her they were here. She was an insecure little girl, having been moved from house to house and town to town since she was a year old and never going back to the same place. Although she was never an unpleasant child she rarely smiled or seemed happy. Her insecurity was made evident by what happened when they returned home after Christmas. She rushed from room to room exulting over the fact that "the curtains are still here, the bed's still here, my toys are still here" and thrilled that she really had a home!

We had an open house the day after Christmas, something we did often when we spent Christmas at home. We also had a group photo taken of the four of us. Then, they all went their respective ways and we were left to face a very cold January.

1977

The years of 1977 and 1978 were very cold and especially January 1977, which was the coldest month on record in Cleveland with a couple of really bad blizzards. There was a natural gas shortage, which resulted in people complaining in the buildings on both sides of the Meridian about our outdoor pool being open and using gas to heat the water. The building had been constructed with indoor/outdoor pools connected by an opening, but after that year, the outdoor pool was closed and from then on it was open only in the summer.

I remember one weekend in January when Elton was gone, I sat and did my homework, wrapped in a comforter, worrying about the fuel shortage, which didn't happen, thank goodness. As he had every year since he went to work for Hanna, Elton attended the Mining Symposium in Duluth that was always held around the middle of January. Although mining people claimed it was a great opportunity to meet people and get information, it seems to have been mostly an opportunity for drinking. At least they could stay warm that way. Meantime, in Cleveland, we slogged through the snow and ice and one-lane streets to get to the office to carry on and write reports that were our major product.

Getting a report out in those days was a much bigger project than it is now with word processors and fast printers. We were using typewriters for most of our work, using carbon paper early in MSI's history. Then, we advanced to whiteout for correcting mistakes in the late sixties, and finally, around the middle seventies, we used IBM Selectric typewriters with built-in correction ability. But we still had to make copies of what we wrote and if we made any changes we had to cut and paste the original. We had an elemental copy machine our first year in business, one which had to have a tissue sheet entered along with the paper and was very slow. We got more advanced machines as they were developed, but until the mid-eighties we had to make one page, one-sided copies and collate by hand. Copiers were constantly breaking down. One of the mechanics uttered what I consider an immortal line when I asked what in the world was the matter with a machine that broke down almost daily? He replied "It's got evil jujus in it!" It seemed to me that there were a lot of those little guys around.

One year we leased a fancy new Xerox, which broke down so often that I finally leased a Pitney Bowes and told Xerox to come and get their machine. We had all sorts of major Xerox people storm at us about giving up their machine, but we loved the Pitney Bowes, partly because the mechanic in charge of machines in our area was so devoted. One day when phone lines were down he stopped in just to make sure our machine was working because we couldn't call in for help.

From the time we started our business, I guess there were computers, but only very large main frames, and it wasn't until about 1980 that personal computers were developed and it became possible for small businesses to use them. Until then, all written work was done by typewriter and almost all accounting work was done by hand in ledgers, although calculators were available for computations. MSI acquired its first Commodore computer in 1983, which had very little memory. I bought VisiCalc, the first spreadsheet program, to enter some of my accounting figures. I am still amazed at a computer's ability to 'replicate,' i.e., copy, a formula or figures with the touch of a button, and its ability to have a correct sum for a column of numbers, no matter how often one changes the figures. No longer does a whole trial balance have to be rewritten in pencil if one or two figures are wrong.

Another "antique" item of business equipment was the telex. This was a machine on which a message was sent after punching holes in a tape that went by phone line to a telex machine somewhere else. It was certainly an improvement over the telegram, which required contact with Western Union, but it was hard to use, and it was not possible to make corrections. We bought a telex machine around this time and replaced it a couple of years later with an electronic machine that was somewhat like a fax, in that messages were typed in directly. All of this was replaced in the mid-eighties by the fax, a great improvement. And now, of course, it's the Internet!

Meantime, in 1977, we plugged away with the ancient equipment that was then state-of-the-art, worked hard at whatever we were doing and generally enjoyed our jobs that winter, despite the drop in business. Business was scarce in the years between 1976 and 1981, mainly because of the 1973 decision of OPEC (the mid-east oil producers) to raise oil prices. Pelletizing, which had become the primary method of supplying iron ore to steel makers, was extremely oil-dependent, so the cost of pelletizing went up and so did the cost of producing steel. We were directly affected, because the producers did whatever they could to lower costs. Both pelletizers and steel makers found that outside services and consultants were expendable and, therefore, were among the first to be cut.

We were still working on Exmibal and Kennecott, as well as Inco in Sudbury, and had a big job for the Mt. Newman iron project in Northwestern Australia. But there was not as much work as there had been, and Elton spent more time drumming up new business than he had since our early days in business. He got involved with Tom Schott, an engineer, in Pittsburgh. Tom had worked for Dravo on various Hanna projects and was now trying to promote a company called PelleTech. They and others met often, made various contacts and traveled to New York and other places to get the company off the ground, but nothing ever came of it, except a lot of wasted time and money. Elton also traveled to South America in May and pretty much toured the continent, Panama, Ecuador, Peru, Bolivia, Brazil and Argentina, researching various projects, including Marcona in Peru. In May he went to Mt. Newman. In August he was in Paris talking to the Socomine group and others and visited both ends of Canada, Labrador and Vancouver.

Early in the year, we had a request from a company called ORI, Ore Reclamation, Incorporated, whose sponsors wanted us to reclaim chromite from the sand used in foundry work in the Youngstown area, in the town of West Middlesex, Ohio. Our work on this project was a lifesaver, we thought, since we needed additional revenue and, with Elton's contribution, it kept Bob Sanden and Ralph Lestock busy for more than a year. But in the long run, it was costly and debilitating, and the people in charge used us and left us holding the bag in several ways.

Before the end of the year, our staff had changed considerably. Lyn Zidd left at the end of April, to our sorrow, Martha quit full-time employment in the summer, Bill Bronkala decided to seek greener pastures on the West Coast and left in July. Only Bob Sanden and Ralph Lestock remained with us. Before Lyn left she hired a woman to replace her, but we had to let her go after two months. While she was there, Elton returned from a trip to New Zealand with a report that had to go out and I did more of it than she did. To replace her, we hired Joanie Licht in August and she was with us for two years. I began working full time in 1977 for the first time since we'd been in business, and was finally being paid a salary, instead of part-time.

I was still working on my various activities. My course in management was completed in June, but our west-side group met regularly for dinner and up-dates. And we all attended the wedding of Dr. Marion Morris and Jan Heinlein who was the favorite of the whole class. Marty had been helping her (and the rest of us) throughout the course, so we were all fond of him too. Marty took a job the next year with Kimberly Clark in Appleton, Wisconsin, and we really hated to see them move; however, they visited this area often (Marty had family here) and "the group" made several trips to Appleton for great reunions.

As usual, Elton and I made several different trips together, the first one of the year to Atlanta in March for the annual AIME meeting. While there, we visited our friend from Hibbing, Jim Young, who was now with the IRS, and his wife, Sara, and we also had lunch with black friends from Cleveland, the Jackson's. Some of our mining friends thought it strange that we had friends who worked for the IRS and friends who were black.

When my mother came to visit at Easter in 1977, she went with us to spend the holiday with the kids in Virginia, and while we were there, we went to Alexandria to see the house she had lived in when Dad was at Ft. Belvoir during World War I. She flew back to Colorado from Washington and we drove home. We visited Daille and her family again in the summer and took a long drive in the Shenandoah mountain area. In November we met them again in Orlando where we visited Disney World and spent Thanksgiving. Disney World was almost as new as Disneyland had been when we visited it in 1956. The kids were delighted and we all had a lot of fun.

I also took a trip or two without Elton. Early in the year, I decided I would fly to Virginia for the weekend, since it was the first year the kids had been that close. It was not a blissful rest as I had hoped, since the girls did a lot of bickering and fighting, but it was, as always, nice to see them. Since Elton was out of town so much, I had the opportunity to see my friends, one of whom was Lyn Cameron whom I saw often for lunch or dinner. We had talked about taking a trip to England to visit Gregg and a good friend of hers, and in October, Lyn arranged the tour—a chartered flight (Evergreen Airlines) and hotel reservations—that sounded like a good deal. We had a tough trip—late leaving Cleveland, late leaving an unscheduled stop in New York and very late arriving in London—instead of 7:00 a.m., we arrived in the afternoon. This complicated our plans and our schedules, but nevertheless we had a great time. We did some touring, sightseeing, saw a lot of Gregg and Lyn's friend and really enjoyed the week. I should add that there were so many complaints to the tour company about our flights, both there and back—which included an unscheduled stop in Gander, Newfoundland—that later we each got a letter of apology and a small refund.

This year, the Pettits were going to spend Christmas with Tom's folks, so Elton and I decided to go to Colorado Springs. We went a few days early, spent some time with Mother, visited Mona and Dale in Leadville and Walt and Marilyn in Denver, and had a pleasant time until Christmas morning when Elton announced he had a flight out at noon to meet someone in Toronto the next day. I could not imagine who was scheduling such a meeting, but I was told it was important, so of course, he left. And, of course, I was furious. Christmas and the days after were a nightmare, though I managed to get through them. Alan and Lui were with Walt and Marilyn and their two little ones for Christmas and they all came to the Springs on the 26th. Even though these kids were her grandchildren, Lui held to her position that little kids were unpleasant, so while the adults watched football games, I played with the kids and tried to be as sociable as possible. Finally, I caught my flight home, still angry. The reason for Elton's departure was never really explained to me.

1978

Life went on and 1978 had its own pleasures and problems. We had another cold, snowy January, with a severe blizzard at the end of the month.

All through 1978, I worked at my League duties but they no longer included the presidency of the ILO board. However, I took care of membership for the Cleveland League and wrote, printed and mailed the newsletter, which I did intermittently for another 20 years, and became a board member of the League's new tax deductible Educational Fund. I also worked on various Women's City Club projects and added two new jobs during the year. One of these was as a Deacon at Old Stone Church. We had been members for 7 years and Elton had been made an elder while I attended one or the other of the women's circles, but we had not really been integrated into the church. The Presbyterian Church did not allow the ordination of women pastors or officers until 1971 and Old Stone did not allow women in the Diaconate, or the Session until about 1976. Even after they were permitted in the Diaconate they were not allowed to take up the offering (one of the Deacons' duties) until about 1980. Every man knew that women couldn't be trusted. The first two women who became elders had one function—to remove the cloth from the communion elements. None of this lessened my passion for women's equal rights or my involvement in anything that contributed to that end.

I volunteered to be on the Advisory Committee for the Board of Missions and for a few other activities, but the entire church and its activities were under the complete domination of Dr. Raymond. There was little any layperson could do, except the few chosen ones, who were long-term members and wealthy or prominent.

In the fall of 1978, I was chosen to be on the 1978-1979 Leadership Cleveland team, which was a great experience. There were fifty of us, including several important personages, and we spent a lot of time together, with an opening weekend and then a full day each month studying some phase of Cleveland life, e.g., schools, finance, government. It was during that year that Cleveland was declared in default under Mayor Dennis Kucinich and we were at the City Council meeting when this happened. It was an instructive and exciting year. I was also appointed to the Lakewood Planning Commission, a job I dearly loved and worked hard at until 1981 when a Democrat replaced the Republican mayor and the Planning Commission membership was changed.

With all of this activity on my own, I did not travel much in 1978. The only trips I took with Elton were to Denver, once for the AIME meeting in February, once in October for a board meeting, and the third time to Rapid City for Ethel's 80th birthday. When we went to the AIME meeting in February we stayed in the Brown Palace Hotel. This was always described as the epitome of luxury when I was a child growing up in the Springs, so it was a thrill to stay there, but I was not too impressed. We did not get out of Denver, but asked Jack, Betty, Mother and Aunt Jo to drive up for dinner one night. We saw one of Elton's cousins one day, and had lunch with Mary Margaret Coates (our erstwhile employee) and her little ones at the hotel.

We did not see Walt and Marilyn, because when I wrote to them and suggested a meeting, Walt wrote back that he was leaving Marilyn for one of his students. I was sorry about this and really angry with Walt. I spent a great deal of time during the next few years in commiserating correspondence with Marilyn. Walt got a divorce, married Jenny and tried for years to get custody of the children, which he finally did, to my disgust. Marilyn married a preacher, moved to Ohio and later to Maryland.

Our trip to Rapid City in November for Ethel's 80th birthday was really fun. Gregg joined us from London, and Mona and Dale were there. We celebrated Thanksgiving, and then had an open house for her birthday celebration.

One other interesting trip that year was short but memorable. We accepted an invitation from Tim Kirby, our Aetna representative in Pittsburgh, to join him and his friends for the Rolling Rock races. These were (and probably still are) steeplechase races that attract a big, select and important group of spectators. We spent the weekend in Pittsburgh, joined his group for the day and for dinner afterwards, and thoroughly enjoyed the experience, though watching steeplechase races is like watching a cross-country ski race—you only see the beginning and the end, especially on a rainy October afternoon.

As for Elton's business travels, except for a couple of trips to Australia and to France, Spain and Greece, his travels that year were mostly in Canada and the States, with many visits to West Middlesex, often by bus (a very exciting trip). We were not doing much work for Inco in Sudbury at the time, but he was there often, more than he needed to be, as it turned out, always staying at Cassio's.

We were still working for Inco's Exmibal project in Guatemala and made an unusual agreement with them in the spring. Because of international problems and rules in shipping, they asked us to purchase various equipment items and arrange for shipping. In order to do this, they transferred around $150,000 into our account. When the audit for the year (ending June 30) was completed, the auditor could not understand this fund, which was neither a loan, nor an advance, nor a payment. Peat, Marwick was our auditor at the time and they always sent young and inexperienced auditors to do the examinations and audits of our books. The one they sent that year was no exception and we went over the deal many times, but in the end, he booked it incorrectly and as a result, the auditors overstated our income for the year. When they finally realized this many months later they said they would have to drop us as a client because we had lied to them. Needless to say, we were incensed at this accusation and we were very happy to leave them and take our business to Arthur Andersen.

That year Elton became involved with Paul Revey and Chris Lorenz, two fellows who were to be important in our lives in the future. Paul worked for Inco and went to Australia on our behalf, then went to work for the Iron Ore Company of Canada before finally moving to Cleveland in 1981. Elton met Chris when he called on the World Bank, and they worked for several years to form a working partnership. Chris lived in Loudoun County, west of Centreville, where his wife worked with horses. When we were at the Pettits for Christmas that year, we took the girls to visit Chris and his wife one evening and were amused how the long stretch of road through heavy woods frightened the little girls—city folks by now.

We had a pleasant Christmas that year in Centreville and enjoyed having our family close enough to be able to see them although we missed Gregg, who was on a Christmas cruise with friends. We knew that Tom eventually would be sent on another overseas assignment, and I think they were anxious to go; meanwhile, we enjoyed and appreciated their present assignment in the U.S. It appeared that we were facing another bad business year as we returned to Cleveland with a sense of regret for the past and insecurity about the future.

CHAPTER 12

YEARS OF TRAUMA

1979

The year 1979 began with more cold weather and problems for MSI. The West Middlesex plant, being run by Sanden, Lestock and John White was a mess, and Elton spent most of January trying to get it straightened out. One of the major problems was Bob Sanden's inability to operate a plant, as well as the problems raised by the less than dependable owners. Elton also had further fruitless meetings with Tom Schott concerning PelleTech. In February, he spent some time in Liberia on a more fruitful and satisfying job, but the next month he was off to Egypt. That trip resulted in the loss of his baggage and little of worth from his contacts there. Everything looked pretty discouraging.

We flew to Washington for Easter at the end of March and then returned to our usual routine. Elton spent the spring and summer trying to make something of the ORI project in West Middlesex, and, more than anything else, trying to develop extra jobs in Sudbury and Toronto. I went to Dayton in June for the League's State Convention, and then we went to Colorado to celebrate Mother's 85th birthday on July 1. She had been somewhat put out—justifiably, I think—because we had made a big thing of Ethel's 80th, so we'd agreed to have a family party on her 85th. Alan and Lui were there and Jack and Betty and their kids, but neither of our children or Walt could come. Mother had arranged for a dinner in her apartment house and we all drank too much and got pretty quarrelsome, as Roeser's were wont to do, and it was not the most pleasant party. It was nice, though, to be with Alan and Lui, and before we left the Springs, I agreed (and I thought Elton did too) to meet them in London for Christmas with Gregg.

On our return to Cleveland, Elton made another fruitless trip to Sudbury. Joanie announced that she was leaving at the end of August because her husband wanted to move to California. We did nothing about replacing her because Elton told me he knew a woman in Sudbury, Jacqui Vesey, who had been Paul Revey's secretary; she wanted to move to the U.S. and might be interested in MSI. Since we didn't have much work to do all summer, I waited until she came down in September for an interview, decided she would be suitable, and waited until she could arrange to move in October. While she was in Cleveland for the interview, we asked her to lunch on Sunday. Afterwards, Elton went with her to look for a house for her and her three children. She finally decided on an apartment in the Waterford, two blocks away from us, and returned to Sudbury to make arrangements for her move.

Meantime, the Board of Directors had a tumultuous meeting in Ontario; it resulted in several board members resigning. They were dissatisfied with the company's results, insisted on a complete pay-off of the debentures and refused to consider a profit-sharing plan for the employees. As a result of this meeting, we used some of our reserves to pay off the debentures and buy back some of the stock.

Jacqui had scarcely started working for us than I realized that there was far more to this hire than I could have imagined. It became clear, eventually, that she had been one of the reasons Elton had spent so much time in Sudbury and was probably the reason for his sudden departure from Colorado Springs on Christmas day the year before. With Elton, she was much too friendly; with me, she was too stand-offish for a secretary starting a new job. She essentially refused to do anything for me, Bob Sanden or Ralph, and she was high-handed and unpleasant with Martha who was working part-time while expecting a baby in February. Further, she refused to let the members of the League use our copier, something that had been permitted for years. Apparently, she was not planning to be a secretary, or to work for anyone but Elton. I didn't know then and still don't know what Elton had told her about the job, or about his relationship with me. Whether he said it, in so many words, or simply gave the impression, she obviously intended to be an officer or aide in the company, and apparently intended to supplant me in the company and in his personal life.

In retrospect, I can better understand what happened. While I had been devoting a good deal of thought and energy toward improving the position of women in the world, I was certainly not devoting much attention to Elton's business and other problems. He was having a very difficult time. For one thing, he had been brought up in a male dominated culture and he never readily accepted new ideas about society. He had been obliged to accept Gregg's homosexuality and now I was asking him to accept my completely changing my role in life. He saw no virtue or point in my new feminist views, and I am sure he felt threatened by them.

Elton was always ambitious, but uncommunicative, and he never complained. Because I am not ambitious, but very task oriented, I didn't appreciate the blows his ambition had taken. He had hoped and planned to build MSI into a major company in the mining world. Instead, he had been able to bring in only enough work to keep us afloat—and barely that at times. His problems with the board must have been very disheartening, and I am sure he had some discouraging turndowns in response to his sales calls. He got little comfort from me, but Jacqui, apparently, had become fond of him and had given him sympathy and encouragement. She was also ambitious and she wanted to live in the United States. The outcome was probably inevitable.

I tried to ignore what I saw and did what I could to make her move easy, but as fall progressed, I found the relationship difficult to ignore. When Elton took a one-day sales trip to New York in October, Jacqui went with him. He had asked me to go, and I foolishly refused. I tried to pretend that things hadn't changed between us, and we went to Pittsburgh again that October for the Rolling Rock races. But it was less fun than it had been the year before, and he was less interested in what was happening. Later, when Elton and I went to the inauguration of George Voinovich as Mayor, followed by a reception at the Women's City Club, he invited Jacqui to accompany us. They kept each other company while I socialized. The worst experience, however, was at Thanksgiving. I asked her and her three children to dinner, together with the Cumberlidge's. John and Marsha were as embarrassed as I by Elton's fussing over, and solicitousness toward, Jacqui.

I had been looking forward to our Christmas in London with Alan, Lui and Gregg and had gone ahead with our travel plans. I had the tickets and everything was ready to pack. On our way home from a party the night before we were to leave, Elton told me that he would not be going to London. His reasons were nebulous—some possible meeting with someone—and we had a major argument. But he stayed in Cleveland and I went to London after telling him that I would divorce him when I got home. No doubt I left him to a pleasant week with Jacqui!

Gregg was very disappointed that his Dad had not come. He had made lots of plans for a perfect holiday; he had even taken down and replaced the first tree he put up because it didn't satisfy him. Alan, Lui and I had an apartment a few blocks away from Gregg, but we spent most of our time with him.

Despite Elton's absence and my anger (which I felt I should conceal), we had a great week of parties, dinners and excursions, topped off by a memorable New Year's Eve party in a night club. Alan and Lui left on New Year's Day; I went home the next day to face whatever 1980 might present.

1980

I certainly did not forget that Elton had not gone to London with me, but I had cooled off, reconsidered, and did not tell him to leave. I got through the next several weeks somehow, including a board meeting in Marathon, Florida at the home of Jack Kringle, one of the two remaining directors. Elton and I were civil to each other, but not much more. We did agree on some things, one of which was our dislike for Miami Beach. We spent the day looking at it while awaiting the arrival of Peter Riede, the other remaining director. The day after the board meeting, Elton had to leave for Paris and a meeting with SOCOMINE. I had a little break from our problems when Martha Kringle took me and some friends to Key West on a pleasant trip. Somewhat refreshed, I returned to Cleveland the next day.

After his return from Paris, Elton was in town for just one day before he left for Brazil. He took our little staff out for lunch and told us that there were some SOCOMINE executives coming to visit the next week, and Jacqui was to handle everything. She did so, without including any other person in the meetings; to me, she was downright nasty. While the French were here, we had a terrible snowstorm. I was happy to hear that it badly complicated things for Jacqui. The whole experience was just too much for me, so as soon as Elton returned, I packed up the car and took off by myself. I spent about a week in Pennsylvania, including two days in Philadelphia, and then drove to Daille's for a week, without telling him where I was or where I was going. If I had expected Elton to feel worried or bereft, I would have been disappointed. Reports from various friends indicated that he enjoyed the unfettered time with Jacqui.

While at Daille's, I developed water on the knee. I had foolishly bought some higher heeled shoes in order to look sharper and feel more competitive, and it was probably due, in part, to stress. Whatever the reason, I was in considerable pain. Realizing that I was accomplishing nothing by staying away, I drove home and told Elton that Jacqui must leave the company or I would. When he said he couldn't fire her after she had moved her family from Canada, I spent Saturday packing up all my belongings at the office, including a typewriter and other equipment, and moved out. I also took with me all the financial data, including the books and the checkbook. I was still unable to make a final decision. I felt that I had put too much into the company to risk Jacqui taking over the banking, so I spent three months at home, keeping the company books, writing the checks, becoming more and more discouraged about the situation, babying my painful knee, swimming, reading voraciously and continuing to be uncertain about what I should do.

Daille and her family were in Cleveland for the Easter weekend. Their visit should have been a bright spot in a dreary year, but it served only to make me feel more miserable. I think we all were glad when the weekend was over. I was in nearly the same position as in the sixties—I couldn't afford to break up with Elton and leave the company, and again, I didn't really want to; I still wanted to remain married to him. I told myself that I could at least have someone in bed with me to warm my cold feet. Now, however, I had some salable skills and work experience. I applied for several different jobs and had a few interviews, but didn't pursue any of them very seriously and didn't get any offers. I borrowed money from the bank in order to establish some credit of my own, and I also bought a small annuity. I persuaded Elton to get counseling, but it was unproductive because he had no interest in negotiating. I think he and Jacqui were enjoying their time together, and I believe she went on at least one trip with him.

Despite our marital problems, we kept up a public front. In May, we had a board meeting in Cleveland with the revised board, which now included John Greenly, Bill Aubrey and me. I continued as treasurer. This was a job I would not relinquish without a fight; the Board was happy with my work and had no idea of Elton's and my personal difficulties. In May, we went to Washington to meet with Chris Lorenz. We had agreed to set him up in an MSI subsidiary that he would run. We met with him, his wife and secretary. In July, Elton and I flew to Rapid for the Mines reunion—this one an all-class reunion. It was nice to see some of our old schoolmates and the guys who had roomed at the Geists' in 1941 and 1942, as well as Mona and Dale and their kids. But all-alumni reunions are not my idea of fun, and it was work, trying to pretend that everything was fine with us.

After Elton flew home, I went on to the Springs for a few days. When I got back to Cleveland, we agreed that I would return to the office, at least on a part-time basis. Meantime, Jacqui left "on vacation," but when she returned, we had some serious tangles. Finally, Elton agreed over Labor Day to let her go. Although she was in the office several days afterwards, she was no longer officially on the payroll. In some ways, it was worse after her departure, because I didn't know what either of them was doing. I heard from our advertising man, however, that she had found a job some time that year.

This was not the end of the affair by any means. Elton certainly saw her often, spent a lot of time with her, paid her phone bills and gave her money, all of which I suspected but couldn't prove. But I went back to the office and things settled down a little.

In the summer of 1980, Tom was assigned to an administrative job in the Embassy in Bonn. After he left and Daille had packed up and was ready to join him, she and the girls spent two weeks with us in July. Elton and I acted as though nothing were wrong; we spent a lot of time with them, much of it in the pool—one of the things my family and I liked best about the Meridian—and one day Elton and I took the girls on a boat trip up the Cuyahoga River. Although we had not seen the family as much as we would have liked, we had seen them fairly often and talked on the phone a lot while they were in Centreville. I was sorry to see them go abroad again, but they were pleased with the assignment.

With the family gone, I returned to work and also to some of my organizational activities. There was very little improvement in either my relationship with Elton or in the business. One of our problems was an ore dryer which Elton had arranged to purchase for the ORI project. This was to have been paid for by the managing group, which had already pulled several questionable financial deals while we were working on the project. They left us holding the bag for the dryer. Until it was eventually paid for, we were out about $12,000 each month—a huge drain on our budget.

We had received payment for the Carter Creek leases during the two preceding years, but were rapidly depleting these funds through the combination of a poor business climate, operating expenses and our losses on the ORI project. We did finally get the dryer paid for (more than $100,000). Bill Bronkala came back to MSI early in September, 1980 and one day in the following spring he, Sally, Elton and I drove over to West Middlesex. We cleaned up and painted the dryer to make its sale easier. We eventually sold it, but for much less than we had paid for it.

In the fall of 1980, with Bill back, Jacqui gone, and things in better order at the office, I set about hiring some dependable office help and found a highly qualified young woman. She turned out to be a very bad secretary! She was convinced that she knew it all and would accept no direction. She started in October, after I'd spent a month doing the secretarial work with the help of some temps. One of those temps was very good. Her name was Connie Sowl; she had been hired by Jacqui in a rare moment of doing something worthwhile. I was still doing all the accounting, filing and editing, and as a little additional contribution to the job, I was translating minutes of SOCOMINE meetings from the Mauritanian colloquial French into English. We hired a Frenchman to do one set of these minutes and found that although he knew English well, he didn't know the mining vocabulary, which I did; his translations were worthless.

During this fall, we prepared bids for several jobs in Africa which had to be written in the correct language and we hired Berlitz to do the translating for us. We spent Thanksgiving Day working on these bids and quit only to have dinner at the Bronkalas' house.

Christmas 1980 was quiet and depressing. Elton and I spent it alone, while Gregg went to Bonn to join the Pettits. We did, however, attend the New Year's Eve party in the Meridian party room.

1981

Still attempting an amicable conclusion to our stand-off, on March 5, 1981 Elton turned 60, and I threw a successful surprise party for him. I reserved half of the Pewter Mug and sent invitations which said we were having his favorite dinner at his favorite place with his favorite people. Dick Smith asked him over to Hanna and then suggested they stop at the Mug for a drink. He was really surprised and pleased at about the first birthday party he had ever had.

I prepared another, less pleasant surprise for Elton later in April. He was in Brazil with Ralph and Bill on a new and very welcome job on the Trombetas aluminum project in northern Brazil near the Amazon. I inadvertently opened his bank statement and found checks to Jacqui and a deposit from his mother. Apparently, he had borrowed money from his Mother to help with his gifts to Jacqui. When I checked his desk, I found several unexplained documents and one rather damaging contract between them. Apparently he had been giving her money each month and paying many bills. I decided that enough was enough, went to an attorney and prepared to file for divorce. I told Elton about it when he returned in mid-April.

He moved to a motel and was there until Mother came to stay with us before she and I left for Europe. I didn't want to tell her about our situation because she was strongly opposed to divorce. I never did tell her, but the pending divorce made our trip difficult for me. Mother had always been a little put-out that Elton had taken Dad on a foreign trip, so I thought I would even things up by taking her to London to see Gregg and to Bonn to see the Pettits; she was excited about the project. I spent considerable time getting this organized. For one thing, I feared that, because the town in which Mother was born—Hinckley, Minnesota—was destroyed by fire when she was two months old, I would have a problem getting a birth certificate and passport for her. However, the Minnesota state capital had her birth certificate and we scheduled the trip for April. She flew to Cleveland, spent the night, and we left, with a flight change in Boston.

Now that I have reached 83, I marvel at the fact that, at 86, Mother did so well. I realize now that I expected too much of her. It was a difficult trip in many ways: my ongoing unhappiness, the wait in Boston was much longer than scheduled and our trip across the Atlantic the fastest I've ever experienced. It was so fast that they had to stop the movie before it was finished in order to throw breakfast at us because we arrived several hours early. We didn't even have time to go to the restroom. From Gatwick, we took the train to London, and Gregg met us at the station. We checked into the hotel, but had to wait several hours before we could get into our room.

After a few days in London, with some sight-seeing but more walking than Mother could really manage, we took the train to Dover, where we boarded a ferry to Ostend and a train to Bonn. It would have been easier to fly both directions, but I had thought, mistakenly, that she would enjoy seeing more of Europe by traveling over land and water.

Kris and Karin met us at the station in Bonn and we went to their very nice apartment. We had a reunion with Daille and Tom and an enjoyable two weeks. We took a brief trip down the Rhine, went to Cologne and then took an overnight trip down the Mosel valley to Trier, where we spent a night before driving back through Luxembourg (notable because it was the only country I had seen that Elton had not). We had a good visit and Mother and I enjoyed the girls and Tom and Daille.

Instead of flying back to London as we should have, I thought Mother would enjoy seeing Paris, so we took a train through Belgium and France to Paris, where we spent the night. I was exhausted and I'm sure she was too, but she didn't know why we should go to bed in Paris while it was still light! It was after 9:30 p.m., but she didn't really understand the differences in time and longer summer days in Northwestern Europe. I had cashed some travelers checks in Paris, and when we walked out of the restaurant after dinner, I was mobbed by some little dark people (probably Algerians) who reached into my purse and took all my cash. Luckily, my passport and travelers checks were in another billfold, but it was very upsetting. Nevertheless, we enjoyed a cab ride through Paris to see the sights before returning to the hotel. The next morning, we took the train to the coast, where we boarded a Hovercraft to Dover and then a train to London. As we traveled, Mother had problems understanding many of the things we encountered. For instance, she couldn't see why we needed different currency in each country, and she had a lot of trouble with the languages. At a restaurant in Germany, she wanted vinegar for something, but no one knew the German translation—Mother couldn't understand why her vinegar never came!

We spent a couple of days in London, and on the day we were to leave, I called the airport for confirmation (later than I should have). I was told the flight had been canceled. I jumped in a cab for Heathrow, got us on another flight, hurried back to the hotel for Mother and the luggage and returned to the airport. After all this effort, the flight ended in Minneapolis, and we had to spend the night there. When we finally reached Cleveland, Mother flew away to Colorado Springs, with some relief on her part, I think, and certainly a lot on mine.

There is an amusing footnote to this complex trip. I'd wondered why Mother had taken so much luggage—which I had schlepped, with some difficulty, all over stations, ships, trains and cabs. When she got home, she said "You know, Doris, I don't know how it happened, but I had a batch of things for Good Will that I packed and took with me!"

Although my situation with Elton had preoccupied me a good deal on this trip, it was a good thing I had our travel problems to occupy my mind, instead of fretting about our impending divorce. Once home, I had to think about a secretary for the company, having laid off Debbie in frustration. So the first thing I did was look for someone more experienced and reliable, i.e., older. This time we dealt with an agency (government funded) which placed people over forty. They told me they had just the person I wanted, but it was a male. We had never considered a male secretary, but we had no objections, and certainly Elton was not going to have an affair with him, so we hired Lewis Swingley in July. We were never sorry. He was the best secretary we ever had and he became a good friend. I should note that Bernie Niehaus, the company's attorney, was highly amused by our hiring a man, after the trouble we'd had with a female. We hired another female, however, in August, when we got Bea Jordan from the same agency. She and Lewis were still with us when we sold the company in 1991, and they remained our friends.

I drove to a League convention in June in one of Ohio's southern cities (not Cincinnati, but I really can't remember where it was). Near Wooster on the way home, I had a serious problem with a bearing in one of the wheels. I couldn't locate Elton where he was supposed to be and had to rent a car, then return it in a few days and reclaim my car. While not an important event, it made me realize that I was really on my own. We were, by this time, living in the same apartment while the application for divorce was filed, and working together, more or less in harmony, and waiting to go to court.

While I had been on my trip with Mother, Elton traveled to Australia to work with Chris Lorenz on a study he was doing for the Union Bank of Switzerland. This turned out to be a major break for MSI, because the UBS person in charge was Heinz Hess, who was responsible for a great deal of MSI work in following years. On this first job, he liked the work Elton did and had him come to Switzerland, with stops in The Netherlands and France on the way. The trip to Australia turned out to be much more important than Elton had expected. It was a great boost to his self confidence and optimism.

He was also engaged that summer, as usual, in seeking different avenues for business, including buying and selling Alabama coal and working with various people to whom he had been introduced by John Magnuson when he went out to Denver in July. The Greenlys were now in Denver and John Greenly had arranged to get Elton and Magnuson together. In August, we both flew to Denver and I drove to the Springs for a short visit with Mother while Elton did some selling in Denver. The next day, we had a Board meeting, scheduled primarily for discussion of a possible profit sharing plan, which we finally agreed to establish for MSI employees. Once the terms were agreed upon, we had a nice evening with the Board and visit with the Greenlys, and then Elton and I drove to Estes Park. We had a very pleasant and harmonious evening and a nice day sightseeing before we returned to Denver and to Cleveland.

With our filing for divorce still in effect, in October Elton and I had our first court contact and were assigned a counselor. We met with her only a couple of times. Elton agreed to the terms she laid down, mainly not seeing Jacqui again and not giving her any more money; because we had been doing so well, I agreed to drop the application for divorce—hoping that the affair was actually over. We went on from there.

Although Elton and I seemed to have made his girl-friend his ex-, Bill and Sally Bronkala were embroiled in a similar situation. Bill met Alice in Brazil and at some point brought her to Cleveland for a month or two. He had all of us involved in trying to get her back to Brazil and out of Sally's hair. Bill spent much of his time collecting gifts to send her and gave her a lot of money, all of which I heard about in detail from Sally. This was not funny for Sally, but it kept the whole office amused. Apparently, they remained in touch until Bill died in about 1989. He left Sally with no inheritance. This was not entirely due to Alice. Bill was always disorganized and prone to chasing chimeras.

From a business standpoint, the rest of 1981 went well, with enough jobs to keep the revenue rolling in. When he returned from one of his trips to Brazil for Trombetas, Elton had the rather intimidating experience of smuggling $5,000 in gold into the U.S. because Trombetas had been unable to get our payments arranged in the normal way. They did have gold available, and we accepted it! Elton managed without mishap, i.e., arrest, and we sent the gold to the smelter in Denver to exchange for cash.

In November, Elton went with Hess to Wyoming's Powder River Basin. The Chicago Northwestern Railroad was looking for money for the shipment of coal from the Basin into Chicago. Hess went with Elton to Rapid City where they visited Ethel, then traveled through Wyoming. With a large group of people they rode the Railroad back to Chicago. Heinz loved the trip and all of the U.S. he had seen, as well as visiting Ethel. And Elton enjoyed showing it to him. This trip, like all of the work with UBS, required office staff to put out reports and arrange further trips, so it was a real boon for us.

We spent Thanksgiving and Christmas alone for the second year in a row, while Gregg again visited the Pettits. But at least business was improving and we were still together. I sincerely hoped our personal problems were behind us.

1982

As 1982 began, representatives of IBM and other companies were engaged in trying to sell MSI on the need for a personal computer (PC). At about the same time, Cuyahoga Community College offered a course for business people to acquaint them with computers—the only requirement being ownership of a PC. I bought a Commodore while Elton was on a trip to Australia, although I was a little concerned about whether he would agree that we needed it. The concern was unnecessary, because it was becoming more and more evident that we must become computerized. Bea Jordan, Bill Bronkala and I went to the class for a few weeks and began to learn how to use a computer. Like most older people, we were scared to death of it. Bea and I had some hilarious moments when we thought we'd lost all the data.

Gradually (very gradually), we learned how to use it and accept it. Somehow or other we found a strange young man—a computer nerd, as it turned out—who came and helped us, particularly with the accounting, which I immediately put on the computer. He had great ideas for an accounting program designed just for us, but we had so little computer memory it was impossible. After a while, he just disappeared. Maybe he eventually started one of those dot.com companies, made millions, and went belly-up in 2000!

In February, 1982, Gregg was in New York for a visit and we met him there. Elton was starting a trip to Australia (via Switzerland, Paris and Mauritania) and left the day after we arrived in New York, but I stayed for a couple of days. Gregg took me to visit his close friend, Lyle Heeter, who was to die of AIDS within a couple of years. Lyle was one of the first victims I'd heard about. As yet, AIDS had not even been diagnosed. Gregg and I had a good evening going to see *Forty-Second Street* and having dinner afterwards.

On my return to Cleveland, I got ready for a Board meeting to be held in San Diego (actually in La Jolla where Peter Riede lived) and where Elton was to arrive from Australia. I spent a few days in Colorado Springs with Mother, my last visit with her in her apartment before she died the next year, and we had a good and harmonious visit. I then flew to San Diego, where I joined Elton and the rest of the Board. We had a good meeting and a couple of days of pleasure, including a trip to the outstanding San Diego Zoo.

In May, Elton had a meeting with Armco concerning pellets they had sold to a plant in Pakistan. They hired MSI to check out the plant in Pakistan where the pellets were to be used. Elton was, of course, the person who took on the job, and he had a very interesting trip to Karachi, Pakistan. In June he went back to Brazil, first to Trombetas, and then to Rio to meet with CVRD.

While he was seeing the world, I stayed at home, doing my things. In June, I flew to Frankfurt where Daille and Tom met me. They had reserved an apartment in Diana Morena, a town on the Italian Riviera. I spent a week with them in Bonn before we all left for Italy. We drove from Bonn, all the way along the Rhine, with a stop in Heidelberg and a night in Freiburg. The next night we drove into Switzerland and through Geneva. As we drove into France on our way to the Mont Blanc Tunnel, we had car trouble and had to return to Geneva. With help from the U.S. Embassy, I agreed to rent a car to continue the trip. After arrangements were made to leave the Pettit's car for repair, we retraced our steps, got to the tunnel and drove south to our destination. We spent a week in the apartment, swimming in the ocean, touring the surrounding country, visiting Genoa and taking a one-day tour into Monte Carlo. It was a great trip. The girls were good company, and we all had a very good time. Kris was almost 13, a really pretty girl, and beginning to be very interested in boys. "Do you think he's cute, Grandma?" she asked me whenever we saw a teen-age boy.

When it was time to go, we drove back through the tunnel to Geneva, spent the night and picked up the car. The next day we drove east by Lake Geneva, up to the mountains and down into Italy over the spectacular and historic Brenner Pass to Milan. The next day I took a plane home while they toured Italy a little more before heading back to Bonn.

I had no more than arrived in Cleveland than Elton and I flew to Maine for a Board meeting at Bill Aubrey's cottage on Moosehead Lake. It was our first trip to Maine, and we found it as beautiful as we had been told it would be. We were disappointed that we didn't see a single moose, but we enjoyed hearing the loons on the lake and being with the Board members, who now included David Coolbaugh. We had a productive meeting before we flew home.

Our next trip was a short two days to New York where we were very happy to see Gregg again. He was on his way to Connecticut for a friend's wedding. While Elton talked to Rio Doce and lined up a nice market study, Gregg and I did a little sight-seeing and had lunch at the famous Russian Tea Room—Gregg in his jeans, boots and tieless shirt (this was before casual clothes were quite so omnipresent) but with a Rolex watch—which apparently works wonders on *maître d's*. He was working hard on a series of ads for Rolex which featured important people in all fields, and he was enjoying the contacts and the work and doing very well. It was a real treat having him in New York with us.

In September we decided to lease a new car, the first time we hadn't bought one, and we got a Buick Skylark. This was not a birthday present, but we got it about the time of my birthday. Sally Bronkala decided to have a surprise party for the sixtieth birthdays of Bill (October 3), Bob Sanden (September 29) and me (October 17). Needless to say, it was impossible to surprise three different people, but it was a nice party, nevertheless. I was really surprised and pleased when I received 60 red roses from Gregg.

There was plenty of work that fall of 1982. We were doing some work for Best Sand and Gravel, more work on the Chicago Northwestern Railroad job, another Australian coal study; the MIM Newlands mine for UBS and an 'Expert Committee' meeting in Mauritania. Then, in December, Elton was asked to help the Escanaba and Lake Superior (E&LS) Railroad in an attempt to take over the Hanna Groveland plant—now closed.

MSI's annual meeting was held in Cleveland at Quail Hollow in November, and then we all settled in for a winter that included a visit from Gregg for Thanksgiving. Because he had been doing a lot of work in San Francisco all year, it had been very nice for us to have him near—at least in the same country. Bea asked the three of us to her house for dinner. He was suffering from a very sore throat all the time he was here, symptoms of what was to come, but we were not aware of this.

1983

Gregg was to be 40 on January 12, 1983, and I decided to make up a book of his life, with pictures of him at various ages and lists of his addresses and other data. I spent quite a lot of time after Christmas (which Elton and I had again spent alone) getting the book ready and off to him. As it turned out, he was ill on his birthday and for quite a while afterwards with some kind of lung ailment. He also had shingles. Later we learned that these were symptoms of his being HIV positive, but at that time, few knew of AIDS or HIV. AIDS had first shown up in 1975 in Africa and spread rapidly until, by 1985, it was a full-blown epidemic in the gay community. However, it was not until Rock Hudson, the popular movie actor, died in 1985 that it became generally known. We were not aware of it at all in 1983. In any case, Gregg recovered that spring from his various illnesses and went on with his work.

During this time, Elton was doing a lot of work for E&LS and was trying to sell a maintenance program to a mine in Texas. He had appointments in February in the west, and I planned to go to Colorado Springs to spend a couple of weeks with Mother; we planned to fly to Denver together. The night before we were to leave, however, Elton got word that his mother had had a heart attack and was in the hospital. I rented a car and drove to the Springs; Elton flew to Rapid, and for the next two weeks, we were occupied with our mothers. A week or so earlier, my mother had apparently had a stroke or a heart attack (I never learned which); neighbors called an ambulance and she was taken to the hospital. The hospital was ready to discharge her in a few days, and Betty and Jack had found a nursing home bed for her. That's where she was when I arrived.

She was very confused, incontinent and nearly helpless and it was evident to me that she would not be able to return to her apartment, although, of course, that is what Mother wanted. I decided to begin closing up her apartment when I was not with her. I spent two weeks either with her or in her apartment, sorting, packing and getting everything ready to move out, and knitting frantically whenever I took a break—always my way when I'm upset. I carefully sorted things into Jack's, Alan's and mine, and arranged for her furniture to go to storage and my barrels to be shipped. Elton's mother was better, so he came for a weekend on his way to a job site somewhere. A few days after he left, I packed up the last things, went to see Mother, and left for home.

I had just arrived home when I got a call from Jack that Mother had died. Of course, we both flew out the next day. Alan and Lui were in New

Zealand on Alan's work and a vacation. It was hard to locate them, so the funeral had to be postponed for a couple of days after we arrived in Denver. We drove to Leadville to see Mona and Dale and spent the night, then went down to the Springs and stayed with Aunt Jo. We left for home the night after the funeral. I must record one nice thing about the funeral. Mother hated beards and mustaches, and except for Elton, all the men in the family had both, as well as long hair. On the day of the funeral, Craig shaved and had his hair cut for her.

It turned out that I had really done the wrong thing in shipping Mother's belongings to myself without her permission—actually stealing from her, I realized, and her executor was pretty put out. After the boxes arrived, I had to prepare a very careful statement for him of everything I took.

This was a sad time for me, as it is for anyone whose mother dies. And having to have a tooth pulled almost immediately didn't help, especially when I developed a dry socket and was really uncomfortable. The weekend after I got home, the Diaconate of Old Stone Church was having a retreat in which I took part. It was very good for my general state of mind. However, I felt tired and listless for several months. When I told a friend this, she said it was no wonder, "When your mother dies, it's like you're standing out there all alone." I think this is how most people feel, and I guess I did too.

Elton was back in Mauritania by the first of March for another Expert Committee meeting and celebrated his birthday in Nouakchott, Mauritania and Las Palmos in the Canary Islands, on his way back to Paris and then Bonn, where he had a nice visit with the Pettits. He then went to Milan and back to a meeting with Hess in New York. He barely had time to land in Cleveland before taking off for Silver City, New Mexico for a Kennecott job. In April, he was once again on his way to Australia for the UBS. On this trip, he had an interesting visit to the Argyle diamond mine, and spent some time in Brisbane for the Newlands and Collinsville coal projects. Again, as he had the year before, he headed back for a reunion with me and a Board meeting, this time in Mexico City, at the home of David Coolbaugh.

This was a great place for the meeting. We did all the touristy things, as well as hold a board meeting. Elton and I had an unhappy experience, however. Someone came into our room and stole items which had not fit in the hotel safe. One of those items was my hearing aid, which needed repair. I've often wondered what the thief did with it. They also stole a Navajo bracelet we had bought at the Grand Canyon in 1955 and, worst of all, Elton's camera with undeveloped pictures of the diamond mine. We complained to the hotel management and told them they had better pay for these things because we had our lawyer, Bernie Niehaus, with us to make sure they did. And they did. I was amused at this outcome. After all, doesn't everyone take their lawyer along when they travel?

Tom's assignment in Bonn was over in June, 1983, and after a stop in London to visit Gregg, they arrived in D.C. on July 4. They stayed in Centreville long enough to get organized and then drove to Cleveland as their first stop on a trip to Kingsford, Michigan, for the 20th reunion of Daille's high school class. Elton was in Iron Mountain at the time, having driven my car up for work with E&LS, and I drove up to Iron Mountain with the Pettits where we met him. Daille and Tom celebrated with the Kingsford class of '63; Elton and I celebrated our anniversary with friends at Spread Eagle (the resort area where most of the people we knew had summer homes) and saw many friends before we all headed back to Cleveland in the two cars.

The Pettits took off in a day or two to visit Tom's family in Indiana and Elton got ready for another trip to Europe for conferences with various people on a Kennecott job and for another SOCOMINE Expert Committee meeting in Paris. We were enjoying a pretty good relationship by this time and I felt quite certain Jacqui was in his past, although he still disappeared from the office almost every evening when he was in town—we seldom had dinner before 8:00. He also had some contact with the company she was now working for (as I learned from our advertising advisor, Jim Standford) but I had no real reason to think they were still involved. After I took him to the airport to go to Europe I planned my week and went about my business.

But a few days later I suddenly knew, for no apparent reason, that he was with Jacqui. I called her office and was told she was on a wonderful European trip with her boyfriend. I called Gregg to ask if she was with his Dad. He said, "I can't answer that," and I responded, "You already have."

I was miserable and as angry as I've ever been. I drove to Zanesville on Sunday to get some consolation from Kathryn Madison. The day before Elton was due to return, I saw an attorney and was advised to get a legal separation. When Elton arrived, he came from the airport by cab and sat down at his desk. I went in and asked if Jacqui had been with him. Of course, he said no, and I, for the first time, didn't blow my top. I did tell him what I thought of him and his lies, how angry I was and that I was going to file for a legal separation. He got a motel room. I postponed my action until after a visit with the kids who were due to arrive the next day. I told Daille and Tom everything. They had lunch with Elton and told him what they thought. While they were in Cleveland, he stayed in the motel except for meals with the family. I was decidedly cool towards him.

Daille and Tom left the children with us (with me actually) while they went to Centreville to begin unpacking and get settled, and I drove the kids to Centreville just before Labor Day. The day they started school, I drove back to Cleveland, determined to take legal action. This time, however, Elton took some positive action. He promised to come home after work and to break off with Jacqui completely. I agreed to postpone action on a separation. It seems that my being angry without exploding, his conversation with the kids, or his realization that I was really determined this time, persuaded him, because he kept his promise about being home and once again I believed he was changing.

As far as I know, Elton had no further contact with Jacqui and stopped giving her money. The next spring I told him I would not do the income tax return until I had a report from him as to how much he had given her, and that he could not do the return himself because I had all the data—which I asked the League office to hold for me. I soon received a report with a total of about $10,000 that he had given her. Although I continued to be angry for many months and, in some ways, was hurt for the rest of his life, he kept his promises to a large degree, and we gradually overcame our antagonisms and went on with our marriage. I saw Jacqui a couple of times after this—on the bus or in the store—but I was told by someone that she had moved away. In the nearly twenty years since, I have heard nothing of her.

One outcome of this long term affair was that, while it continued, I severed contact with anybody in the mining business, except for a few very good friends. I knew Elton had taken Jacqui to the Mining Symposium one year, to lunch with local friends and clients, and on at least this one major European trip. I can't stand pity, and felt for years that the people he saw in London and Paris would pity me, so I tried to avoid contact with anyone associated with the business and did my socializing with Leaguers, church people and other organizational acquaintances. The little entertaining we did was related to the company or church.

Elton went about his business, spending a great deal of time in Iron Mountain and Detroit, working on the E&LS case, going to the Mining Congress in San Francisco in September, and making another trip in October to the Powder River Basin with Heinz Hess. Daille and Tom came to Cleveland for Christmas and we enjoyed our first one with them in four years.

December 31, 1983, brought an end to what was the most difficult period in my life. I was happy to see 1984 arrive, bringing with it, no doubt, new problems and challenges, but certainly some exciting and interesting events.

CHAPTER 13

BETTER TIMES FOR GEISTS AND MSI

1984

Prior to 1984 I was concerned about my personal problems and those of MSI, but as always, I had time and energy for other things. I'd also been keeping up with my various activities, mostly WomenSpace, the League and Old Stone, and a few extra jobs thrown in. One of these extra jobs was my political activity. I worked at the polls for every election and I was on the County Republican Party's Executive Committee.

In 1979 I was approached to serve on a search committee for a new Executive Director for the Cuyahoga County government. It was an interesting experience that taught me an important lesson pertaining to collective wisdom. The committee was made up of prestigious people, heads of the Republican and Democratic parties, presidents of the local colleges, various business CEO's and a few other important volunteers. After many meetings, hundreds of resumes, many interviews and much hard work, we finally found the man for the job whose resume was perfect and who impressed us all in his interview. We recommended him unanimously to the three County Commissioners and they agreed to hire him. One month later he was dismissed for incompetence and another man was hired—so much for collective wisdom.

By 1984 I was just about through with active participation in WomenSpace but the experience had been rewarding. Among the interesting WomenSpace events was a program featuring Miss Lillian, President Carter's mother, and a trip to Philadelphia in 1980 with Linda Batway, our wonderful Executive Director, to visit the Philly women's group. We stayed in the home of a friend of Linda's, a typical flower child in a typical flower child home and neighborhood. It was illuminating, if not exactly my idea of living.

During my term as president of WomenSpace, I had found the organization's accounts in some disarray and spent a lot of time with the young and inexperienced bookkeeper. After my two one-year terms as president, I became treasurer for a couple of years and worked on various projects. I took all the financial data with me, including the books and the checkbook, and proceeded to get the finances in order. After Linda left in 1981, we selected a new Executive Director who later questioned my honesty. I was hurt and angry. I hung on for a while, but I was essentially out of it. In 1984, I was awarded their Susan B. Anthony Award for honorable service. The organization closed down completely in the early nineties. The end was inevitable. It had become clear that it is impossible to do all things for all women.

In 1981 I spent a lot of my time in the League as Ohio State LWV's ERA chairperson. The Equal Rights Amendment provided that "Equality of rights under the laws shall not be denied or abridged by the United States or by any state on account of sex. The Congress shall have the power to enforce by appropriate legislation the provisions of ratification." The Amendment had been approved by Congress and sent to the states, and by 1981, it was only three states short of ratification, Ohio being one of them, with the deadline for ratification set for June 30, 1982. We wrote letters, spoke to whatever groups we could round up, talked to our state legislators and stood on street corners passing out flyers and ribbons, but by June 30, we were still two states short and the Amendment died—for the time being. I still believe it should be adopted and will be eventually.

I found another organization to fill in the gaps left by WomenSpace and the ERA effort—the American Society of Women Accountants. I was held up in traffic one morning and picked up a woman whose car had to be left by the side of the road. I mentioned that I had to do the payroll at work that day and she told me I should join her organization. This organization had been founded sometime after WWII to provide a sort of support group for women who, at that time, were neither admitted to college accounting programs nor allowed to become CPA's; nevertheless, they were working as accountants and bookkeepers. I practically joined on the spot and became very active for the next few years, thoroughly enjoying the other members and the informative programs. As more and more young women became accountants, however, ASWA did not attract them and, at least in Cleveland, it became virtually inactive.

I continued to do various jobs for the League—whatever needed to be done, including the newsletter and being treasurer of the LWV Educational Fund. I took on the job of treasurer when we found that the treasurer hadn't filed the IRS 990 forms for two years and we were liable to fines of up to $500 a day for every day we hadn't filed. After much debate and correspondence with the IRS and lawyers we were forgiven for our lapses and I took on the job that I didn't give up until 2002. And I always filed the 990's on time!

In 1983 Old Stone's long-time minister, Dr. Lewis Raymond, retired, much to the sorrow and regret of most of the members, but not so much to us. He was a wonderful preacher in his prime but in his later years he preached less often and gave shorter and much less inspiring sermons. The congregation was quite elite and most members were the in-crowd, and we didn't feel we really belonged. We're not sure Lewis ever knew Elton's name, perhaps because he was out of town so much and perhaps because he wasn't a "somebody." The First Presbyterian Society (FPS), which controlled all the finances and owned the church property, was very secretive. We didn't know of its existence until the eighties.

On the other hand, we liked the building, the location, and the people we did become acquainted with, and I liked never having to work in the kitchen, which was a pleasant change from other churches to which we had belonged. The church had a cook and kitchen staff that provided lunches to the public at low prices and produced wonderful meals. When Elton finally became a member of FPS and was elected a trustee, in the late eighties, he found that the church was not obeying the employment laws for its kitchen staff and, in fact, was not even paying Workers Compensation. So, eventually, the meal service was shut down because it couldn't meet these requirements and be profitable enough to continue.

In order to get a pastor to replace Lewis, the Presbyterian Church required a mission study by the members and I was appointed to the study group as a female member of the congregation. We met often and eventually issued a report. The thing I remember most about the study was getting acquainted with Warren Scharf. He and his wife, Maggie, were the music director and organist and although we knew them by sight, they didn't know us. At that time, Warren was head of the music department at Baldwin Wallace College. During one of our discussions, he made a remark that I told him was pedantic. He definitely didn't want to be thought of that way and for the first time he became aware of me. We eventually became acquainted and then good friends, but I don't think he ever forgot (or forgave?) me for calling him pedantic.

There had been other events in the year leading up to 1984, most notably in the lives of Jack's family. Carola became pregnant, and the baby was due in April 1984. She was not married and didn't really want to keep the baby, but she decided against an abortion and to marry the father, a postman. Jack was violently opposed to abortion and he and Betty were anxious to have grandchildren, so I think we were all glad she didn't have an abortion and hoped a baby would settle her down. She had been on drugs and was possibly an alcoholic, and although she was working as an advertising salesperson, she had worked at a lot of different jobs, always briefly and always losing the job through no fault of her own. In any case, Jack, the Judge, married her to Chuck Tollefsen in a quiet wedding in December 1983, and Jacob, Jack's only grandchild, was born in April 1984.

At about the same time, Sally, now 33, announced that she, too, was going to marry. She had always said she would never marry, but when she met Max Laird, she began to change her mind. He was not an ideal candidate, having been married before (twice, as I recall) and with children elsewhere. But because Max promised to do all the cooking and housework and take good care of her, she succumbed. She had had a serious backlash injury some time before and still had problems related to that, so she really liked the idea of someone taking care of her. The wedding was on February 18, 1984. We were invited, so we flew to Denver, rented a car as usual, and drove to the Springs after a night with the Greenlys. Since the Roesers couldn't put us up, we contacted our friends Ray and Evelyn Chard and they were thrilled to have us stay with them and we had a good visit. Betty complained about how busy she had been with the wedding plans, but Sally and Max planned and paid for everything. As far as we could see, the only thing Betty and Jack did was invite Walt, his new wife and us for drinks and potato chips and attend the wedding and reception. Jack performed the ceremony. The wedding was small, the reception was well done and we were glad we were there, but we did not feel welcome.

The marriage was quite brief. Max and Sally divorced several years later. In about 1987, Chuck Tollefsen died of carbon monoxide poisoning, either accidentally or by suicide. Carola raised Jacob somehow and, somewhat surprisingly, he has turned out to be a nice young man. When he was little, Jack enjoyed him, but bemoaned the fact that he didn't have more grandchildren. He was not even especially pleased that Jacob lived in the same town and he could see him any time—something I would have loved.

In the meantime, we were busy making a living and, although we were in Colorado in February 1984, for the wedding, Elton couldn't afford to take more than a few days off. He flew from Denver to Bahrain to work with Bob

Young of McKee to start up a steel plant (owned by a private corporation) using Brazilian iron ore and Arabian oil. While Elton flew to the Mid East, I returned to Cleveland.

Sometime around the end of December 1983, Paul Revey had lost his job at the Iron Ore Company of Canada (IOC), and he and his wife moved from Labrador to Cleveland. We were pleased to have Paul available to do some work for us, and we both liked Caroline. We were shocked when she became ill in January, went back to Toronto for medical treatment and found she had inoperable liver cancer. She died in July, leaving Paul bereft and lonely. He was without a job, so he began working for us full time in the summer.

We were to see a lot of the Pettits in 1984. After they returned to Centreville in August 1983, Daille went back to school, the University of Maryland, to get her M.A. in library science. Tom worked on temporary assignments, and in April he began a year's assignment in Africa as temporary administrative officer in whatever country needed him. At the beginning, he was pleased with the job, because he wanted to see some of Africa. By the time he completed his year, he had experienced a year full of adventure and trauma, primitive conditions everywhere, and warlike conditions in some of the countries to which he was assigned.

Before Tom left for Africa we drove to Centreville for a visit early in March. Sadly, we saw them later that month when Tom's mother died unexpectedly on March 22. They drove to Syracuse, Indiana, stopping with us for the night on the way. I drove alone to Syracuse for the funeral and brought the girls back to Cleveland afterwards. Tom and Daille came the next day.

After Tom had gone to Africa and school was out, Daille and the girls came to visit us and went on to visit Dr. Pettit. When they returned to Cleveland, we had a visit with them that spanned Karin's birthday on June 26. They also visited us for a couple of weeks in August, which included a trip to the Ohio State Fair. The summer Olympics were being held at the time and Karin spent a lot of time making a scrapbook for her Dad, a major project for an eleven year old, since she knew he would be interested and probably wouldn't (and didn't) have access to the news. In September, with Elton gone on one of his jobs, I drove to Centreville, via Charleston, West Virginia, to see if there might be a better route from Cleveland to D.C. I ran into nothing but truck traffic up and down the hills. It was the last time I tried that. The girls, Daille and I had a good visit that included a trip to Harpers Ferry. We took their dog, Beau, despite Daille's objections, but the girls wanted him and promised to clean up if he got sick—which he did and they did. But we all, even Beau, had fun anyway.

At MSI we continued with our different projects, including insurance jobs. Paul Revey, Bea Jordan and two or three of the people who had assisted Frank Zorko managed these. This project got under way in spring. Zorko, an engineer, had been doing investigative work for insurance companies that needed expert opinions on certain cases (e.g., arson, walls collapsing). He persuaded us that this was something we could do and it turned out to be a big chunk of our business and was quite lucrative. Zorko worked only part time and Revey and Bea did most of the work with the help of other outside engineers. We also did a job or two for UBS and had more work on the Mauritanian project. The Bahrain project required at least two more trips for Elton.

As always, I had distractions from family and work this year. A most worrisome discovery was made that the bookkeeper (one of my friends) of the League Education Fund had written several checks to herself and was unable to repay the funds. We did not press charges against her—for one thing her husband had lost his job and they had spent everything they had (and Ed Fund money) to get a new business started. We knew we could not collect any of it and didn't want to take her to court. I lent her $1,000 to repay the Ed Fund. We fired her, of course, and I was never repaid.

In July, Elton had to make a trip to Mauritania for the plant's official dedication and we decided that we would both go to London and spend some time with Gregg, then Elton would go on to Mauritania and we would meet him in Paris when he got back. This was a very pleasant trip and we enjoyed all the time with Gregg. While Elton was there, we went down to see Brighton and in the days following his departure, Gregg and I did a lot of touring of London and the London area. When we met Elton in Paris he was quite ill—either from the primitive food and conditions in Mauritania, the god-awful heat there, or some bug. We were in Paris on Bastille Day and Elton spent the day in bed, but Gregg and I saw the parade. We thought it was very dull by U. S. standards. It was just military equipment, bands and music with no floats or high school bands or, above all, no Sousa! But it was interesting to see the crowds and watch how they celebrate in Paris. Elton had to attend some meetings in Paris and Gregg had to go back to work, so we flew to London. I had a day or two shopping and visiting museums, and then returned to Cleveland.

MSI's annual meeting was customarily held in the autumn and, from the time of our board meeting at Kringel's in Florida, we'd had two board meetings each year in some interesting place—the reason we'd been in Mexico, San Diego, Moosehead Lake in Maine and other spots. The meeting this year was in Denver at the Oxford Hotel, a very old hotel just renovated. We picked the place because we could combine it with family visits and we picked the time so that we could fly right from Denver, through Rapid City, to Washington, where Kris, bless her heart, was planning a surprise party for her mother's 40th birthday. We saw all the relatives in Colorado Springs and Leadville and flew to Rapid City to spend a day or two with Ethel before going on.

We got to Washington at an awkward time—too early to go to the Pettit home, where Kris was expecting guests at 6:00. Unfortunately, Daille picked us up and suspected something was going on when we wanted to stop for a drink, the drug store, and wherever else we could manage, to delay our arrival—she knew this was not at all like us. So the party was neither a surprise nor a howling success, but we thought it was very sweet of Kris to do this for her mother and the people who were there enjoyed themselves.

We were back in Cleveland long enough to have our Thanksgiving Day dinner at the University Club and get ready for another trip to Washington. Tom had returned for a home leave between his tours in Chad, Guinea Bissau, Kenya and other exciting African countries. We were there for Daille's graduation, some business with the World Bank and Heinz Hess, Christmas and whatever else we could squeeze in. It was an interesting trip. Elton went ahead and I joined him for dinner with UBS's Wetzler. We stayed the night at a hotel before going to the Pettits. When I arrived, Elton was at a meeting and I checked into the hotel and asked for a key to Elton's room. The clerk refused to let me in without a marriage license. I thanked her for thinking I was young and sexy enough to be a pick-up, and I was able to persuade her to break the rules.

The next day, we went to Daille's to go with the family to her graduation. It poured all day, through the services, through lunch and through a couple of stops for drinks. Elton was planning to go to New York the next day for a meeting with Hess, but during the night he fell down the stairs to the basement and knocked himself out (partly due, no doubt, to all those stops for drinks, but the hall and door arrangements were also rather tricky.). When he came to and woke me up, I realized that he had to be taken to the hospital to have the cuts on his face and head stitched. Tom took him to emergency while Daille and I cleaned up after him. Luckily, he had no broken bones or concussion, but he certainly wasn't able to keep his date with Hess.

That day was Christmas Eve and we spent it and Christmas Day with our usual activities. The day after Christmas we left for Florida, to visit Bob Young and his new wife, a trip I was very reluctant to take. Bob and his second wife, Ann (who had been his secretary until he divorced his first wife) had lived in Lakewood for a year or two; we'd seen quite a lot of them and I'd become very fond of Ann. After Lakewood, they went to live in London, where I had visited them when I spent Christmas 1979 with Gregg. A year or two after that visit we got word that Bob was divorcing Ann and, you guessed it, marrying his present secretary. I was disgusted with Bob and sorry for Ann who was miserable and died of breast cancer within two years. Her death, I'm convinced, was at least partly due to her unhappiness. Consequently, I had no desire to visit Bob and Avril, and although she was pleasant and they were hospitable, I was very glad when the two days were over. Elton, of course, enjoyed it more than I did.

We flew back to Cleveland just in time to welcome Heinz and Renate Hess. We took them to see the Cleveland Ballet's Nutcracker one night, attended the New Year's Eve party at the Meridian the next night, and saw them off on New Year's Day after we had welcomed 1985. I was looking forward to going back to work and getting a welcome respite from the frivolities.

1985

Elton took several trips during the next few months, including another one to Bahrain, and I continued bookkeeping and running the office when he was gone. After trying to keep books with the minimal capacity of the Commodore computer, I began to research other computers and had several appointments with different dealers. Like our other employees (none of us under 60), I was rather frightened of computers. I was really impressed with the astonishing potential of some of these systems. I finally decided on a Wang because I felt the word processing program was the best I had seen and, even now, long after Wang had gone belly up, I still think it was the best. Also, the sales, training and maintenance people we dealt with in this company were all women—this really impressed me! Before the year was over, we had it installed and the office staff (Bea Jordan, Lewis Swingley, Connie Zalenka, Jane Gehring) and I attended several all-day training sessions. We used the Wang as long as we were in MSI, and when Elton and I left the company in 1991 and started Geist and Geist, we continued to use Wang equipment and systems. It was a real blow to me when Wang went out of business and we lost all the information we had carefully backed up on floppy discs.

In April we drove to Washington for Easter with Daille and the girls, thinking we'd finally see the cherry trees in blossom. Instead, we arrived after a windstorm had blown off all the blossoms. Nevertheless, we had a good visit that included seeing *Godspell* at the Ford Theater, and attending Easter services on a lovely day in their Centreville church. Tom was still in Africa suffering harrowing experiences in several different countries, though his tour there was to be over in June.

We had looked forward to 1985 because Kristin would turn 16 in April and we had promised her, when she was little, that we would take her to her birthplace when she was sixteen. We realized that no one in his right mind would take a sixteen-year-old girl abroad, but despite some misgivings, we proceeded to make plans for a June trip to Jerusalem and began to look forward to it. We were back in Centreville on June 13, prepared to leave on "The Trip" on the 15th. Since Kristin wanted to take a Mediterranean cruise, we included a three-day Aegean tour in our plans, and flew to Athens via Amsterdam. We spent a day and a half there at the Grande Bretagne, sightseeing and shopping, mostly for some dressy clothes for Kris whose mother had failed to see that she had packed some.

The next evening, Monday, we went aboard the Stella Oceanis for the three-day cruise. The three of us shared a cabin and were assigned a pleasant middle age couple as our table companions for meals. The cruise was really quite comprehensive for such a short period. It included a trip to Crete where we spent most of Tuesday and a late afternoon stop at Santorini. On Wednesday, we stopped at the Isle of Rhodes, and on Thursday, we took a bus trip and tour of Ephesus, Turkey. We landed at Piraeus early Friday morning. Kris was not too excited about the sightseeing and there weren't many young people on the ship to get excited about, but she did go ashore with a few boys one afternoon. After they got back, they apparently got drunk—at least Kris did—and the steward came to report to us that she had passed out in one of the halls. I got her into our cabin and to bed and was simply furious with her for a couple of days.

When we returned to Athens, we went back to the Grande Bretagne and spent the next two days touring every place we could, from Delphi to Corinth. Kris was interested, of course, in meeting some boys, which she didn't, but she was pleased that she attracted a lot of attention with her blue eyes, blond hair and cute 16-year-old figure. This was especially true in Jerusalem, when we got there on Monday. The Arabs were all quite taken by her and we got some very interesting offers for her. The best offer was thirty camels. One afternoon at the American Colony in Jerusalem she spent a lot of time by the pool with two young men, in their twenties. They asked her to have dinner with them and she couldn't understand why I said No, but the young men understood. She was so taken by this invitation that we hid the room key after she went to bed and was asleep, thinking she might get up and sneak out. We realized later that this had not been very likely.

We rented a car when we arrived in Israel and went to all the major points of interest, including the Dead Sea, which was off-limits to visitors at that time, but which we could see from a distance. We went to Bethlehem, and our favorite spot, the Garden Tomb. We could not remember how to get to Kris' first home, but we spent a lot of time in the Old City shopping. Altogether, it was fun and interesting, and we saw things that we would never be able to see again. We were worn out when we arrived back at Dulles on June 27, but we felt the trip was a success.

Neither Kris nor we were finished with long-distance traveling for that year, since Tom was to be posted to Tokyo in fall and we used some of our bonus air tickets to visit them there in November. During the summer they spent six weeks in intensive Japanese language sessions, and made their plans for their next assignment, while Elton resumed his business travels. I went back to Cleveland to spend innumerable hours learning to use the computer. I interrupted this long enough to fly to Rapid alone for my 45th high school reunion. I rented a car and drove to Custer where I stayed in a motel. On my way back, I stopped to visit Ethel, but did not stay with her. I never really forgave her for her nasty reaction to my letter telling her I'd filed for divorce. But the reunion was fun. There were several people whom I had not seen at earlier reunions and whom I never saw again.

We left on November 14 to fly to Tokyo for an interesting week. Daille and Tom were working and the girls were in school at the American School in Japan, so we did some touring on our own, and Karin spent the better part of a day showing us around—at this point I have no idea why she wasn't in school. The girls loved it there—they liked the school and had a long trip to and from, by subway, bus and walking, but they especially liked the fact that they were perfectly safe and could wander around anywhere.

Actually I didn't like Japan much. This probably stemmed mostly from WWII and was pretty irrational since the late autumn weather was lovely, the city beautiful, clean and safe. People were very polite and pleasant and there were many beautiful and interesting things to see. I suppose my major objection was the food, most of which I found inedible. But all in all, we had a good visit and enjoyed being with the girls and Tom and Daille.

We got home just in time for Thanksgiving, which we celebrated in a restaurant. Soon after, we began to prepare for our next trip to Rapid City for Christmas. Gregg came from London via New York to go with us, and we had a great trip. We spent a few days in Rapid, then flew to Denver, rented a car and drove to Leadville for a night with the Johnsons, then back to Colorado Springs for two days with the whole Roeser family. Alan and Lois were there from Seattle, Walt and Jenny and their three from Denver, Carola and her husband and Jacob, Sally and Max, and even Jim from San Francisco. We had a festive party at Jack and Betty's before we headed back to Cleveland the next day and Gregg left for New York. A very full and eventful year came to a close and everyone was looking forward to 1986.

1986

Although we'd spent a large part of our time, effort and money, traveling during 1985, we had also put a lot into MSI projects and 1986 proved to be an important year for the company, with many changes. The company had been founded to market materials for the mineral industry but it soon became evident that this was going to be almost impossible for a small company. Elton had taken on consulting to keep the wolf from the door. This had been increasingly profitable with several major, continuing customers, but with the completion of two or three major projects, we were again looking for additional sources of work and income. Elton decided on a project that was a return to our original purpose, and it was a real boon as long as it lasted.

With the help of Bob Prittinen, a Minnesotan retiree from Republic, Elton had talked to the major pellet producers and steel companies and had finally gotten agreements from several on a new plan for selling pellets. Because of complex contracts and agreements among the major companies, several steel companies had an excess supply of pellets that they couldn't sell, and some of the smaller steel companies couldn't get the pellets they needed. MSI was to sell the pellets at a lower price and get a commission. The first sale was in the fall of 1986 and we felt we were rolling in money when we received a check in January 1987 for several hundred thousand dollars. We used a lock box arrangement—a new process for me. The project brought in a great deal of money for us and caused a major upheaval in the industry. Unfortunately, the project came to a close when LTV declared bankruptcy.

In order to better manage the work of the company, with the added job of the pellet sales, it was decided to change the company's name and its purpose. It became Midland Standard, Inc., and a new corporation was formed retaining the name Mineral Services, Inc. This of course entailed two sets of books with income tax returns for each company. As bookkeeper I handled all the accounting for MSI, the Employee Stock Option Plan, the Profit Sharing Trust, and now I was keeping the books for another company. We had upwards of 25 consultants in any given year, some of them real experts in their fields. This too, created a lot of paper work, payments, record keeping and IRS 1099 forms and reports. The latter must have been too much for me, because I got a notice from the IRS a few months after we formed the second company that we hadn't made any deposit of employee withholding. When I recovered from the shock, I realized that the employees were no longer with Mineral Services, for whom I had been making the payments, but were now employed by the new company. The IRS made the transfer with little trouble.

In addition to the pellet sales, another major change in the workload of Midland Standard was work with Reading Anthracite in Pottsville, Pennsylvania. Our connection with them began when the company went to UBS for a loan. They retained us for consulting when UBS backed out. For most of the rest of the 1980's, Reading was our major consulting client—a mixed blessing. The company was headed by Jim Curran who had little idea of money (though he always had a lot), or time, but he was one of an interesting cast of characters in Pottsville.

Pottsville actually resembled Hibbing, in that they were convinced the world could not run without them. The Iron Range had supplied the world with its essential iron for decades while the Pottsville area had supplied the U.S. with anthracite coal when that was far and away the fuel most in demand. Neither area was ready to accept its decline when other iron and steel producing countries supplanted much of the U.S. production, and oil and gas took the place of anthracite for heating. Reading was trying to find other uses for its vast reserves and MSI worked on many projects, mainly cogeneration plants in the Pottsville area. But in addition, Elton accompanied Jimmy and his coterie on trips to Frankfurt and to Japan for tours of heating plants and sewage disposal, among other things. We had two new employees working on the Reading job—John Magnuson in Pennsylvania and Otto Gramp, in Cleveland. We also hired Jack Hollister to work with Bob Prittinen who was elected a company director.

While taking on all these changes and new projects, we decided we needed more space and we were doing well enough to afford a more prestigious location. So, in the fall of '86 we decided to move the office from the Marion Building to the Illuminating Building. Of course, I had to manage that **and** do much of the bull work besides. The move didn't take place until August 23, but we worked all summer preparing. Luckily Elton was in town on moving day, so for once he could see how difficult moving was. The worst of it was that the Illuminating Building management had promised to have the space completed according to our plans by the day we moved. When I arrived to welcome the movers, I found every single office space unfinished and full of ladders, trestles, and other building paraphernalia. I was fit to be tied for a week, but we did eventually get everything where it belonged and we settled into what was really a nice office.

Not all changes in our lives were caused by relatives or business. We made two personal changes that fall—we replaced our leased Buick with a second one and, more importantly, I got a new eardrum. As I mentioned earlier, my left ear had been damaged when I had the mastoid surgery as an infant and I had a perpetual infection and no eardrum. When I talked to a new audiologist about the aid for my right ear, he suggested that I should have the Warren Otological Clinic examine the left ear. He said the clinic was world famous, which I questioned, but when I went there I found that it was widely known and had an excellent reputation. I was told they could replace the eardrum which they did that fall. I spent one night in the Warren hospital and had no ill effects at all, except that I couldn't bend or lift for a week. The surgery improved my hearing somewhat, but mainly I got rid of an annoying, unpleasant and, sometimes embarrassing, lifelong problem and was able to use a hearing aid in that ear.

Elton was traveling all year in 1986, as usual, not only in the States but also in Europe and Australia. We had no major family trips, but we went to New York in the spring for a weekend with the Hess'; we flew to Iron Mountain for Marguerite Miller's wedding and drove to Zanesville for Liz Madison's wedding. I went to Pottsville with Elton for a few days and we had an MSI board meeting in Phoenix. In Phoenix we stayed at the Camelback Hotel—a place that had always sounded to me like the epitome of wealthy living, mainly because my high school friend, Betty Stamper, had worked there in the winters and described it as such. Although it was elegant in a southwestern way, it failed to meet my expectations and I really don't like Arizona and all that sand. The weather, however, was wonderful, the board was congenial, the meeting was productive and, all in all, it was a successful affair.

One of the things that changed for us that year was communication. When we started work on the Reading project there was one minor, but important, outcome—the acquisition of a fax machine. Although faxing had been used since WWII, new ways to send faxes had only recently been developed. Since we had no fax machine and needed to send and receive many documents between Cleveland and Reading, it was necessary that we use a fax-machine-owning-middleman to send and receive for us. It was costing us upwards of $15 per page. When a salesman came to the door and said he was selling fax machines, I jumped at the chance and ordered one on the spot. This really changed the way we did business. Later, of course the fax was largely supplanted by e-mail, but for ten years or more, the fax was in constant use. A nice side effect for us personally was the ability to stay in closer contact with our kids overseas.

Daille and Tom were in Japan, and after June, Gregg was in Dubai, in the Arab Emirates, so the time differences made phone calls almost impossible. Daille was always good about writing letters, but Gregg was not and we'd go months without hearing from him. He wrote a lot more once we had the fax. He was in Dubai on a temporary job, partly because it sounded exciting and interesting, and partly because he felt that, since he was now HIV positive, he should leave his life in London to avoid infecting others. Most of the countries in the Far East were at that time trying to avoid AIDS and were getting very suspicious of people who might be carrying the virus, so Gregg felt this was a good area for him to be celibate. There were several other Brits he knew in Dubai and he really enjoyed the job and the desert weather and life there.

We did not see the Pettits that year, but we had a short and pleasant visit from Gregg in the spring before he went to Dubai and we also had a visit from Alan and Lois, who were returning to Seattle from a golf camp in Florida. We always enjoyed seeing them, and the visit seems even nicer in retrospect, because this was the last time they came to see us. Alan had many medical problems, including surgery for an aneurism soon after they got home, and his heart continued to fail until he died in 1992. We did not see any of our other relatives during 1986, and spent Easter and Thanksgiving with the McCuaigs, Christmas Day alone, and New Year's Eve at the Meridian party. At least, Gregg and Daille were together. He had flown to Japan and they had a great time.

CHAPTER 14

Our Last Years with MSI

1987

In 1987, twenty years after the company's founding, business looked very encouraging and we approached the future optimistically. We received our first check from Shenango Steel for pellet sales in January, 1987 and were working for Reading and some projects for UBS. We took a break in January to fly to Rapid City for a week with Ethel. We spent several days on a trip to Deadwood with Ethel and her friend, Elsie, and visited Elton's Custer classmates, Ray Chard in Custer, and Mary Ellen Brady in Spearfish. When we flew back through Minneapolis, our plane arrived too late to make our connection to Cleveland. We were distinctly annoyed that the only flight we could get was the next morning, so we had to spend the night in Minneapolis. When we got to the airport in the morning, we were amused to learn that the flight we missed the night before had been unable to land in Cleveland and had to return to Minneapolis. Those passengers spent the night in Minneapolis, too.

With Elton out of town most of the winter on one job or another, I must have decided that I didn't have enough to do and joined still another organization, Altrusa. Many of the members of the American Society of Women Accountants, ASWA, belonged to Altrusa and made it sound like a great group. I left after two years, however, because, even more than most organizations, it demanded complete participation and undivided attention, and I had a lot of other things in which I wanted to participate.

One of these was Old Stone Church. Along with Elton's increased participation in the church, I was also becoming more involved under Malcolm

McCuaig's new leadership. This year I was moderator of the Deacons, and the first woman to have this "prestigious" role. The Church planned a retreat for the Deacons at the Presbyterian camp at the Highlands and carefully chose a weekend in April—the one that had a traffic-stopping snowstorm. The snow kept most Deacons away, but the few of us who arrived early managed to have a good meeting for the 24 hours we huddled together in the cabin.

Later in the year, in November 1987, I was elected to the search committee for an Associate Pastor for Old Stone. It was a committee that failed so completely we were finally asked to resign in the spring of 1988. By that time, we had become completely stymied and ineffective due to the fact that some of us felt it important to choose either a woman or a black person—neither of which had ever served at Old Stone. We found the perfect candidate—a black woman—only to find that the other half of the committee was determined to consider neither a woman nor a black person. There were still objections to women as pastors and, as always, racism. So much for Christianity in practice, or the lack thereof, but it was also a clear reminder of the continuing prejudices and obstinacy of humankind.

But long before this we had a wonderful trip around the world—the one and only time for me. Elton had done it several times when working on some of the Australian jobs. We went first to Los Angeles and then to Tokyo where Kristin was to graduate on June 7 from the American School in Japan. We spent a few days with the Pettits, celebrating Kristin's successful conclusion of her high school education and touring some areas of Japan. We made a road trip to the foot of Mt. Fuji which all the Pettits had climbed by then. Elton and I were happy they had already climbed it and we wouldn't have to do so. Daille, Tom and Kris were all at work after the graduation exercises, so Karin took us to the part of the city where teens could buy anything; she also took us to a tea ceremony. This had the same effect on me as the strip tease show to which Elton had once taken me. I wanted to yell, "For gosh sakes, take it off and be done with it." At the tea ceremony, I wanted to say, "Pour the tea and get it over with" instead of taking so many intricate and deliberate steps through the long ceremony.

We flew from Tokyo to Hong Kong where we had a long wait and a change of planes. This was the second time I'd landed in Hong Kong, both times at night, so I can't even claim to have seen it. In any case, we flew directly from there to Dubai. Gregg had been there for several months on a temporary job and, after a few days with us, had gone back again in June to work with a new agency. It was a little scary arriving there, because Gregg had to be in attendance to vouch for us. Although he was in the airport, they took considerable time examining our papers and interrogating us before they let him in to greet and claim us.

We spent four or five very interesting days in Dubai. Gregg had a lovely apartment and a nice young Pakistani houseboy. He, like many others, was brought in by the governing Sheik from Pakistan to water the center strips of the boulevards. The water was obtained by desalinization and was plentiful, but it was very expensive for the user—it cost more per gallon than gas. This is a desert country, but the boys watered the boulevard center strips every morning and they were lovely and green. After their watering chores, the boys had other jobs, many of them as houseboys. They had to return to Pakistan regularly to renew their work permits and Gregg also had to go there for that purpose, so he rode on airplanes with a lot of these "boys." They must have been exciting trips, because Gregg reported to us that the boys had little charcoal burners with which to heat their food in the planes.

Dubai and Bahrain had the most lenient governments of the Emirates, even allowing the sale of liquor in certain places. Censorship of movies and television, however, was quite strict. The soap operas, for instance, were allowed on their TV channels, but were a little hard to follow because so much had been cut. An article in *The Smithsonian* in October 2003 describes Dubai as working toward becoming the Singapore of the Mid East. What we saw in 1987, although impressive, was simply a microcosm of what the Emirate was to become under its ruling monarchy, with a system of hotels, beaches, shops, businesses and shipping that staggers the imagination.

While we were there, we took a car trip one day, through desert and shimmering heat, to Oman and a lovely resort where we had lunch. One day we drove to the port, full of dhows, but no sign of the containers which now fill it; we went out to what we knew as the Persian Gulf (now the Arabian Gulf) and swam in the beautiful clear, warm water. We also took a trip to the neighboring Emirate of Sharjah where, the newspaper informed us, they were having a revolution. This seemed to be manifested only in blockage of the highway and a detour on a nearby side road. We visited a mall there which looked exactly like Victoria Station in London, and went to a carpet dealer who had sold Gregg several carpets. We bought a beautiful blue and white silk carpet and had it shipped to Lakewood. I am still using it and loving it.

Gregg loved Dubai and the job there, but by the time we arrived, the agency was folding and the whole staff was going elsewhere. Gregg had a party for us and his fellow workers, most of whom were moving out a few days after we left—Gregg to Jakarta. We had one more interesting experience when we visited a gold souk (a market). We saw shop after shop with so much gold jewelry displayed that it looked like junk; there were heavily veiled women, wearing sandals, whose feet were decorated with make-up and much gold jewelry. Gregg bought me one sample of gold (a chain) for my neck, not my feet.

We took Jordanian Airlines from Dubai to Cairo, which was in itself an interesting experience. We had a layover of a few hours in Amman and then boarded another plane full of heavily veiled women and little girls, dressed to the hilt in fancy clothes. No one obeyed any of the boarding instructions and I'm quite sure we alone buckled our seat belts for take-off. When we landed in Cairo, we were surprised to find the terminal looking like a large, unfinished warehouse. It was full of money-changers and Arabs and luggage arriving on antique carousels. No cabs were available so we had to take a shabby van that was not allowed at the front door of the Sheraton when we arrived downtown. When we departed three days later and took a cab to the airport, we were dropped at a clean, bright, modern terminal. It was hard to believe we were in the same airport as the terminal at which we arrived, but we were. Obviously, this terminal had not been built in three days. Apparently, it was used for European and American airlines, and the other for Arab lines.

While in Cairo we did not go up the Nile, except for a short evening boat trip, but we took a couple of tours, saw the pyramids and other historical spots and did some shopping—the exchange rate was terrific. We had to cut short our visit to the museum for the King Tut exhibit because I had a quick bout of the Cairo equivalent of Montezuma's Revenge. Although we found the ancient sites fascinating, we were repelled by the really dirty condition of the city. It was certainly the dirtiest city I'd ever visited.

We flew Swiss Air from Cairo to Zürich (no complaints about that trip) and spent a couple of days with the Hesses in Bern. Heinz took us on a road trip up into the mountains. We had a pleasant time with them before we took the last plane of the trip back to JFK, then Cleveland and back to work.

Gregg flew in from Jakarta in July for a few days, and on August 5 we began two weeks of constant coming and going. Everyone except me arrived and departed every day or so for one or another reason, and I felt I'd spent the whole month on the road to the airport.

In September, Elton and I went to San Francisco for the AIME meeting. We had a good time seeing old friends, meeting Raman Rao's new wife, Liz, and doing the town. From San Francisco, I flew to New York City, where the national organization of the ASWA (accountants) was having its September Joint Meeting. It was held at the Waldorf and was a good meeting with interesting side trips.

The annual meeting of MSI was held in October in Cleveland, and it was a good meeting, with little bad news to report. As soon as the Directors were gone, Elton left for Gabon, and I flew to Tampa to spend a weekend with Kris. She was going to school at St. Leo's, a small Catholic college in a virtually non-existent town, some 80 miles northeast of Tampa. The school was chosen partly because Kris was not the best student and partly because the American School in Japan took pride in the fact that all its graduates go on to college and she could be admitted at St. Leo's. Furthermore, it had a restaurant/hotel management program in which she was interested. She was in a dormitory and appeared to be having a good time. We shopped and ate and talked and I was glad she was in the States where we could be together and do all those things.

She did not join us for Thanksgiving, because Elton had a meeting in Toronto with UBS that week, and we decided I should go with him and spend our holiday there. It really did not seem much like a holiday, as Canada celebrates Thanksgiving in October, but it was fun shopping and eating in Toronto, and it was a change from the usual.

When we got home I plunged into Christmas preparations which I had to finish early because we'd decided to spend Christmas in Jakarta with Gregg. We left on December 17 for Los Angeles on the first lap of the very long trip. We spent one night in Singapore, then went on to Jakarta for a visit as interesting as Dubai had been. It was certainly not in the desert, but in a tropical equatorial setting; the weather was hot and sunny, except for some rain and clouds on Christmas Day.

Gregg had rented a gorgeous house with large rooms, all wood paneled, shiny wood floors and an enclosed garden with its own waterfall. We found that although Indonesia was primarily Muslim, all major religious holidays were observed, so Gregg was to have Christmas off. Christmas decorations and ornaments weren't in great supply and those we found had been really picked over since it was only a few days before Christmas. We all wanted a Christmas tree, but we could find only some kind of live evergreen in its own pot. We bought this, decorated it with red ribbon bows and then realized that the pot was full of ants. They poured out of the pot in a steady stream all the while we were there. Gregg planned a party on one evening and needed glasses, so we spent a harried hour or two rushing from store to store to buy an adequate supply. He had also planned on a goose for Christmas dinner. He had found a goose, but we had some difficulty coming up with the proper ingredients and accompaniments, and while he was cooking the goose he had a small explosion in the gas oven. He had asked another couple to join us and in spite of the setbacks, the dinner was fine and the day an enjoyable, but certainly different, Christmas Day.

We had been invited to a Christmas Eve party and dinner under the stars with ex-pats from various English-speaking countries, and we did a little touring of the beautiful countryside. We visited Gregg's office and really enjoyed being with him for Christmas. We returned to the U.S. via Los Angeles, where we spent the night, and then headed home to the cold winter weather in Cleveland, work and a quiet New Year's Eve. And an end to 1987, an eventful and enjoyable year.

1988

This was an election year in which George Bush easily won. I attended a Bush rally in April and had my picture taken with him. It was the closest I have ever been to a President! For us, in retrospect, this was a year full of entertaining, visitors, short trips and organizational work. It seems that we had dinner parties all year and the usual visitors—that is, family. As always, I was deep into my organizations. I was elected president of the accountants group, ASWA, in 1988 and served until the summer of 1989. I was also working on the doomed pastoral search committee for the church, and throughout the summer, spent a day every week on an analysis of the work of the Old Stone Session and Deacons and the number of people needed to do this work.

My real work at MSI seemed to be mostly a continuation of work already begun. One of our continuing concerns had been, and still was, finding someone to take Elton's place as head of the firm some time in the future. One person favored by all the board was Rod Stone. We had a board meeting in Sarasota in February, and one of the major subjects was the selection of a vice president. The decision was made to offer the job to Rod.

While we were in Sarasota, and, in fact, the reason we chose it for the meeting, was so that Elton and I could visit Kris at St. Leo's. We took her and a friend back to Sarasota with us. The next day, the whole crew took a bus to Disney's Epcot. After a day's sightseeing, we were ready to return and could not find the girls. We spent an uneasy hour or so, but they finally showed up, indifferent to the worry they had caused. When it was time to return to Cleveland, I drove up to St. Leo's again, to pack up Kris and her friend to take them with us for their week's spring break in Cleveland. It was a hectic week because of their activities, but fun, nevertheless, for them and for us.

In April, Easter was followed by a sad day when Bea Jordan's husband died. We closed up shop to go to his funeral. Rod and Jane Stone came to Cleveland at the end of the month for Rod to talk about his Vice Presidency. I spent a day showing Jane around the city and getting acquainted with her, and we all had dinner at the Silver Quill in the Carlyle. Soon after they returned to Duluth, Rod decided he would accept the job with MSI.

At the end of April, Kris came to Cleveland for her summer break. She and I spent a week going to Sharon, Pa. to our favorite shoe store, to Great Northern Mall for clothes, and then she left to join her parents. In early May, in my role as President-Elect of the Cleveland Chapter of ASWA, I flew to Seattle for a conference. After the three days of meetings at the Downtown Hilton, Alan drove into town and picked me up, and I spent three very pleasant days with him and Lui before returning to Cleveland. Actually this turned out to be the last time I visited them. One day we drove to the location of the Mt. St. Helen volcanic eruption two years earlier. We were very impressed with the amazing regrowth of the area.

At about the same time, Tom completed his tour in Tokyo and flew to Indiana to spend his home leave with his Dad before checking in for his next assignment. Daille and Karin stayed in Tokyo until school was out at the end of June, then they flew to Hawaii and on to San Francisco. Tom and Kris met them there. I remember that the day they were all to arrive in San Francisco I expected a call from them, telling me they had arrived. Having heard nothing from them, I went to the Old Stone picnic and worried all through the picnic and for the next couple of days until they finally called. I knew they planned to rent a car and go touring, but if they were to go off the road, or meet with some catastrophe, no one would know where to find them. Obviously, worry was useless (aren't most worries?), and I don't worry much ever, but then I felt it was justified. The fact that they were usually very good about staying in touch increased my concern. Gregg never was as good about this as Daille, but he did keep us posted about his move in the spring to an assignment in Kuala Lumpur. He wasn't there long and went from there to Hong Kong. Both of these were places we'd like to have visited, but he was in both too briefly and we couldn't manage the time.

Daille and the girls took a couple of weeks to get to Cleveland. They toured the west and visited relatives; Tom left them in Denver to go back to Washington. They were to be posted next to Santo Domingo and were to spend two or three months in D.C. on language and orientation. Daille and the girls arrived in Cleveland on July 3 and we spent nearly three weeks shopping, going to ball games and Geauga Park, taking Karin back and forth to her friend Amy's place in Hudson and generally having fun. Tom came for one weekend and joined Daille at her 20th Westlake High reunion. By early August, they were all in D.C., where they rented a small apartment in Roslyn, across the river from D.C. In August, Kris returned to St. Leo's, and in September, Karin started school in Arlington. We drove to D.C. for a visit on my birthday, a visit I scarcely remember because I had a really terrible cold. About the middle of November, they left D.C. for Santo Domingo.

Rod Stone moved to Cleveland in the middle of July and Jane moved soon after. They joined us for the MSI summer board meeting in August in Quebec City, where we stayed in the picturesque and beautiful Chateau Frontenac. The assembly was sobered before the meeting when John and Marvel Greenly got word that their daughter, Ann, in her early thirties, had died of a heart attack. This was especially sad because she had been a real *sixties'* child, trying everything the other boomers tried, including having several children with a black father without marriage. All of this had alienated and devastated John and Marvel, so her death was even more shocking for them. Of course, they returned to Oklahoma immediately.

The rest of us proceeded with the board meeting, which was uneventful. As usual, we spent our time before and after the meeting seeing the area. We found it interesting to be there in the midst of Quebec's push to make the province French-speaking. We had more trouble communicating with the natives of Quebec than we had in Paris and we knew that most of them knew English. We had a lovely tour to the magnificent cathedral where, some people believe, the bones of the Virgin Mary's mother are enshrined. My feeling is that if you believe that you'll believe anything.

Meantime, I had been elected president of ASWA, and in September, I led a delegation to the national meeting in Indianapolis. One of the other members drove and we had an interesting trip, a good meeting and enjoyed the city.

Elton, needless to say, was traveling this summer and fall, including another trip to Australia for UBS. We continued to work on a job which lasted through 1989. Elton was retained by a legal firm representing certain railroads which were suing the major mining companies and other railroads for price fixing on shipped iron ore pellets. This involved a great deal of data analysis of all the ore that had been shipped from Minnesota from as far back as there were accurate records. We hired several people to input the data, including both Karin and Kris who spent several days in July working on the project. Elton spent much time on the project, mainly with the attorneys.

Elton's mother's 90th birthday was November 29, so she planned a big party, with some help from Ramona and Elton, and, of course, we went to Rapid for the celebration. Actually, because the 29th was five days after Thanksgiving, we flew out on Wednesday. We thought it would be too much for her to have to plan Thanksgiving, so we told her we were arriving on Saturday. I decided that this would be a good time to take a side trip to Colorado Springs, so I called Jack and asked if they'd like us to come for the holiday. He gave me a brusque "No"—they already had the day planned and didn't want anyone to drop in. Because they celebrated all holidays with their kids and no other company, I'm sure our presence would have caused little disruption, but he made his feelings quite clear. Interestingly, he called later and asked us to come and see them on our way home, which we couldn't do because of business commitments. After their earlier turndown, I don't think we'd have done so anyway.

We got a room at the Alex Johnson Hotel, which had seemed the epitome of luxury when we lived in Custer, but it was certainly not that in 1988, although it was at least a Grade B hotel. We had Thanksgiving dinner in the hotel, after spending the morning touring the southern hills, including a visit to the Mammoth monument in Hot Springs. This was a really interesting site; the remains of mammoths and other prehistoric animals had been only recently discovered. On Friday we checked out and did some more touring to Deadwood and Lead. We spent the night in one of America's historic hotels, the Franklin, in Deadwood. It was certainly historic or at the very least, antique. Walking down the hall, we felt the floor would collapse; the bed and bedding seemed genuinely ancient, and taking a shower meant flooding the bathroom. While not the worst hotel we'd ever been in (it was clean), it was an adventure.

We finally showed up at Ethel's, then picked up Ramona, Dale and Liz at the airport. We spent the rest of Saturday getting ready for the party. It was held in a party room above the city's main bank. The party went very well and there were many people there, most of whom we didn't know. The number of friends she had was really astonishing to those of us in her family. When with us, she spent most of her time suffering, at least verbally, and we didn't think many people would remain her friends when her health was usually her only topic. Apparently, she found other things to talk about with friends or she wouldn't have had so many. In any case, she had a fitting and happy celebration of her ninety years.

Kristin was going to Santo Domingo for Christmas, but I flew to Tampa early in December for a brief visit to see how she was doing. With the Pettits in Santo Domingo and Gregg in the Far East, we planned Christmas at home. However, the Stones asked us for Christmas dinner, and that was a pleasant change. We spent New Year's Eve at a party at the McCuaigs' home. We were then launched into another year.

1989

We had looked forward to 1989 with both anticipation and trepidation. It was the year of Karin's 16th birthday and her trip to her birthplace. Karin had had boy friends from the time she started school; boys always liked her. We were, therefore, a little nervous about how to avoid trouble with male attention. We solved this problem by spending considerable time in planning a trip through Brazil.

Before Brazil, however, we had a trip to Santo Domingo in February. Again we planned an MSI board meeting to facilitate a visit to our kids and found the trip very interesting. We flew by way of Puerto Rico and stayed in Santo Domingo, not far from where Daille and Tom were living. The meeting was, as usual, productive and uneventful. We had several excellent meals in various places, and visited a casino one evening. Never interested in gambling, Elton and I watched the others and I was struck by the fact that, even though people refer to gambling as fun, there wasn't a smile to be seen. Fun? We stayed an extra day in the city to be with the kids before returning to Cleveland.

In March, I was asked to join a Federation of Community Planning committee called Council for Older Persons or COOP. This was an advisory group, made up mostly of professionals in the field of aging, with a few active lay people. It was an interesting activity for me, though I didn't contribute much until I was elected chair a couple of years later. It was customary to have a lay person head the group. In the meantime, I was happy to be a member.

Although it hasn't been mentioned often in this history, there always seemed to be some sort of employment problem in MSI, as I expect there is in most companies, and we had an unexpected one in the spring of 1989. We had had a wonderful, dependable clerical staff for several years with Lewis Swingley, Bea Jordan and Connie Zalenka, and for a few years we had Jane Gehring. Jane was neither as dependable nor as good as the others, but she was satisfactory. She was the widowed mother of 6 children, and two of her daughters worked for us from time to time. One of the daughters, Debbie, was a joy. She was a good employee and a very sweet girl who tragically died of uterine cancer in 1988, at the age of 24.

Jane Gehring also had a son, John, whom I put to work after Debbie was obliged to quit, and, with great difficulty, got him to do the computer input for our bookkeeping. On the day before we left for Karin's trip to Brazil, he told me he had AIDS. He was not very ill but was so shaken by the diagnosis that he really couldn't produce. He and his mother moved to

Virginia later in the year to be with other family members. After we returned from Brazil, I got a member from the AIDS task force to come and talk to the staff, because most people were very fearful of AIDS at that point. One of those we had hired for the data input on the railroad job, Mary Ann, was willing to take over from John, and she did some of the bookkeeping until we left the company.

Meantime, Kristin finished her year in school in April and spent a few days with us before leaving to join her parents. She returned early in June to see if she could find a job in Cleveland, and went to work for a temporary agency the week before we left for Karin's trip. We left Kris alone with some trepidation, without a real job and with no friends in Cleveland. I think she had a lonely time of it while we were away on our very interesting trip to Brazil.

We had a Brazilian travel agency arrange the trip and we were delighted to discover that they had booked not only all the flights and hotels, but arranged for a guide in each city who picked us up, helped with money exchange, got us to hotels and took us on tours of whatever city we were in. This made the trip much easier, and we needed all the help we could get, because we covered six cities in less than two weeks.

MSI's case with the railroads vs. mining companies was going to court in Baltimore just as we were about to leave on our trip, so Elton spent two days giving a deposition, which apparently won the case for the railroads. The case was settled later in the railroads' favor. He then flew to Miami. Kris took me to the airport in Cleveland, and I left to meet Elton and Karin in Miami. We took a flight out that arrived in Belem at about 1:00 a.m. Karin was very quick to tell us that, in Santo Domingo, she had a new boy friend in whom she was very interested. This eased our minds about her looking for boyfriends. She talked a lot about Cyril and didn't seem very interested in any other young men. We spent two days in Belem, at the mouth of the Amazon, and left in the evening for our next stop, Manaus, which is in the Amazon jungle. We stayed in a huge hotel there. Obviously, it had been an elegant place in earlier years, when Manaus was the rubber capital of the world, but it was somewhat shabby, musty and very damp. The next day we took an all day boat trip on the Amazon and were astonished at its immensity. We had a side trip into a bay, or lake, with enormous water lilies, and saw a boy with a sloth, apparently a pet. We saw no other animals, and we heard none. The jungle was very quiet, and this surprised us.

The next day, we did a little shopping and bought a suitcase for Karin—hers had come apart when we landed in Belem—and went into the city.

Unfortunately, the opera house, which had, apparently, been world famous when Manaus was the world's rubber capital in the mid 1800's, was closed for repairs. We checked out of the hotel that afternoon and spent hours at the airport with hundreds of people with duty-free purchases. We finally boarded our flight to Brasilia and flew for several hours over the vast unsettled expanse of Brazil. We were met in Brasilia that evening by the best guide of all. Jão, in fact, was the best guide we ever had anywhere. We spent the next day touring the city, including a visit to the hospital Karin had been born in, and the apartment house they had lived in, as well as all the gorgeous buildings and a magnificent monument to one of Brasilia's founders. It is a truly beautiful city and we had a lovely day.

We were up **very** early the next morning to get our plane to Belo Horizonte. We asked our guide there to take us to Ouro Preto, one of my favorite cities. It seems to be clear out of the world, but it was the center of mineral development in Brazil, and the churches and buildings are beautifully decorated with gold and semi-precious minerals. The town is full of gem merchants and we bought quite a few for us and for Kris, most of which we later had set in rings in Cleveland. One interesting thing about the entire trip was the fact that the country's financial state was so precarious that merchants were not only willing to use our credit cards, but were willing to accept personal checks—anything but their Brazilian currency!

From Ouro Preto, we returned to Belo and had supper. Early the next morning, we went to Sao Paulo. It is a big industrial city and not very interesting, although we toured an unusual reptile garden and spent time in a mall which was as upscale as any I had seen in the States. We were there on June 26, Karin's 16th birthday, and celebrated over an elegant dinner and buying her some gold earrings. While in Sao Paulo, she called a woman who was a friend of Peg Pettit's when she had been a girl living in Brazil. The next morning, we caught a plane to Rio, one of the most beautiful cities in the world. We were warned by everyone, however, not to walk around alone, because of thieves. We stayed on the Copacabana and had a nice two days which included meeting Theresa and Roberto for dinner. They were a Brasilian couple who had spent some time at MSI in the seventies.

Returning from Rio to Cleveland via Miami turned out to be a real adventure. At check-in we were told we didn't have space reserved, and we spent a couple of worried hours before they told us we could board the plane. Finally on the plane, we were just getting settled when everyone began to get up and get out and we eventually learned that there was a bomb scare and we would have to go back to the terminal. We were there for several hours with Karin, scooting around, trying to spend the rest of our Brazilian money, until they invited all of us out onto the tarmac to pick out our luggage, get back on the plane, and take off for Miami. Apparently, there was an important TV star on the flight, and the bomb scare turned out to be a false alarm. Daille, meanwhile, had flown from Santo Domingo to meet us in Miami. We were about six hours late, but she had seized the opportunity to get some extra sleep. The next day, July 1, Daille and Karin took off for Santo Domingo and Elton and I to Cleveland, where we found that Kris now had a job staying with an old lady not far from us.

We had barely reached home when Daille called to tell us Tom's Dad had died on July 2 and Tom was leaving for Maine, where his father, John, had been living with Tom's brother, and that she and Karin would be flying up in a day. Since the memorial service for John was to be in Syracuse later, they decided not to go to Maine. We celebrated July 4 with Kris and lunched at the Watermark.

Daille arrived on July 8 and stayed with us while waiting for Tom to arrive. We went to a movie on the 13th, arriving home in time to receive a call that Elton's mother had died that day. Elton had talked to her in the morning; she told him she was doing okay, but apparently, she felt bad enough to call a friend to take her to the hospital. She died en route. We immediately made reservations to go to Rapid the next day; Daille and Kris with Karin—who had just arrived from D.C. where she had been visiting friends—drove our car to Rapid, arriving there the following day. Because we had a layover of several hours in Denver, it seemed to take us as long to get to Rapid by plane as it had taken Daille and the girls to get there by car. Mona and Dale picked us up when we finally arrived.

Ethel had her funeral all planned and all we had to do was go to the funeral home and make those arrangements. She was to be buried in the V.A. cemetery in Sturgis with Sam, who had originally been buried in Custer and was moved to the V.A. several years later. All of Mona's family arrived; only Gregg was missing. The funeral was on the 18th and was very well attended. We all left the next day, in spurts, with Daille and the girls driving to Indiana and on to Cleveland. We retraced our flights via Denver.

Kristin was through with her job as caretaker and went to work for us at the office. For the next few days Elton was on business in California while I tried to do a little catching up, partly dealing with the problems of John and Jane Gehring. Everyone had problems that hectic summer and one of ours was the disposition of Ethel's property, so on July 26 we flew back to Rapid.

We spent two or three days with Mona and Dale, sorting and packing Ethel's things and finding a real estate agent to sell the house. None of us needed or wanted her furniture and appliances, except the TV and VCR, which we took. Mona and Dale selected a few things, too, and we asked Ethel's friends to come and choose what they wanted. It all went very smoothly. The house was almost emptied in a few days and it was sold within the month.

In one way, the timing of Ethel's death was fortuitous, since we finished the house just before the 50th reunion of the Custer class of '39. With Mona and Dale, we went to Custer for Gold Discovery Days and a reunion that was more fun than any of the previous ones. As someone said, "At your 20th and 30th re-union, you're trying to impress everyone; at your 50th, we're all the same." We had planned for months to have an MSI Board meeting in the Black Hills following our reunion, so we moved again, checking out of the Custer hotel and into the Sylvan Lake Hotel, where we had reserved rooms. The meeting was followed by a day-long tour of the Black Hills, including Mt. Rushmore, after which we departed for Cleveland.

Meanwhile, Daille and Tom had been to and from Syracuse, spending part of the time with Karin. She wanted to take driver's training and get her U.S. license before she went back to Santo Domingo, so she stayed in Cleveland most of the next few weeks. Kris got a job at the end of July, working at Camp Cheerful (for disabled children) and liked the job and a boy she met there, but when Daille and Tom returned from Syracuse about the middle of the month, they found she was really sick. They picked her up, brought her to town, took her to a doctor and learned that she had seriously infected tonsils. They were bad enough that she went right into the hospital and had the surgery on Saturday. This meant that Elton, Karin and I went to the cottage of our friends, the Niehauses, for a day at the beach without the other Pettits. Kris was quite sick and took some time to recover.

By now, Daille and Tom had finished cleaning up the Pettit house in Syracuse, leaving it in the hands of an agent who would sell whatever was left, including the house. They had brought the rest of what they were taking with them, as well as Tom's Dad's 1978 Chevy Impala. They had decided to give it to Kris to drive back to St. Leo's and have a car while in school. In retrospect, Elton and I felt that this was a serious mistake, though it seemed wise at the time. The three Pettits left on the 20th to go back to Santo Domingo; Kris left the same day in her "new" car to head south. However, she did not go alone. Her boyfriend from camp, David Folta, and a couple of girls decided to go with her. The night before they left, David spent the night on our couch and seemed like a nice enough boy, but his history was pathetic and ominous.

His mother had left him when he was a baby and he had been more or less raised by his father and various step-relatives, all of whom left him with real personality and character problems, which soon became evident.

We thought it possible that, if Kris hadn't had the car, David would not have gone to Florida with her. Unfortunately, when they got there, her life took a real turn for the worse. She moved into her residence while he got a place in Tampa and a job waiting tables. After taking a trip to Cleveland for a few weeks, he returned to Tampa and she moved away from St. Leo's to join him in an apartment in Tampa. She continued to go to school, but David turned out to be excessively possessive and drove out with her to the school each day until she simply dropped out. She came to spend Thanksgiving with us and we were shocked by the changes in her personality. Instead of her usual bubbly self, she hardly spoke and seemed more dead than alive. She spent a lot of time on the phone with David, and when the Stones came for Thanksgiving dinner, she was not only unsociable, she was downright rude. We sent her back to Florida with a great deal of trepidation and any time I called her, I had to talk to David first—apparently, he would not permit her to talk on the phone except to a select few. We were unable to draw from her what was going on and we were extremely worried.

By Christmas, Daille and Tom were concerned too, and when they had Kris come to join them in Santo Domingo, they paid for David to come with her. This turned out to be a wise move. He was like a fish out of water in a foreign country and committed all kinds of social gaffes. Although they had to feel a little sorry for him, they believed Kris grew discouraged with him. Nevertheless, she stayed with him after Christmas, apparently because, like other abused women, she wanted to leave him but didn't know how she could, even though he was extremely possessive and abused her verbally (though apparently, not physically).

We worried all winter but had no idea what we could do, and it wasn't until spring that Daille solved the problem. Tom's tour in Santo Domingo was to be over in June 1990 and they expected to be in D.C., so after they'd found a house and Daille left Santo Damingo in May, she called Kris and told her she was coming to take her to D.C. She rented a U-Haul trailer and arrived after David went to work, helped Kris pack and they started off to Washington. This was the end of David, except for bills he continued to run up on her credit cards and, more importantly, the injuries to her emotional well-being and personality. She was in a very fragile state for a long time after she left him.

Life had gone on for us after they'd all left Cleveland the previous fall. We tried to recoup in September from the very hectic summer and spent a few days trying to pull our home, our business and ourselves back in order after all the goings and comings, and, at least on my part, enough disturbance and upsets to result in a summer-long case of diarrhea, which eventually disappeared as things settled down.

But before this occurred, Elton and I flew to Zürich for the wedding of a UBS employee, Tony Affentranger, and his long time love and live-in, Melinda Spitzer. We had a pleasant three or four days which included a visit with the Hesses, a couple of nice tours into the countryside and the wedding in a small German chapel, without a word of English. The reception was fun. Although we could converse with only a few people, everyone was friendly and welcoming.

We returned to Cleveland in time for me to work with the auditors and for Elton to get back into his various jobs, the major one being with Reading.

In September, Mona and Dale visited Vickie and David in Pittsburgh. We drove down for a few hours to see them, and then they bussed to Cleveland to spend a night with us. In October, my Custer classmate, Herb Heidepriem, with his wife and daughter, Nikki, spent one night in Cleveland. They were on their way to Washington to deliver Nikki for a new job. We had a pleasant evening with them. We also had our usual annual meeting of the MSI stockholders in October, with all the work, discussion and sociability these meetings entailed. This was the last meeting David Coolbaugh's wife attended. She died of cancer a few months later. One other visitor this fall was Dick Greenly, who came to ask Elton's help on a project. It was nice to see him and to find that he had turned into a really fine young man, good father, husband and citizen—a real blessing for John and Marvel after the heartaches they'd suffered with Ann's death.

We had Christmas with the McCuaigs, while Gregg celebrated the holiday in Jakarta, where he had gone back to work earlier in the month, and the Pettits were still in Santo Domingo. But we spent a couple of days with the Pettits between Christmas and New Year's when we drove to D.C. to be with them while they looked for a place to live when they got back to D.C. in June. It was not until spring 1990 that they found a place they wanted to buy. Meantime, we saw out the 1980's and welcomed the 1990's at a New Year's Eve party at the McCuaig's.

Elton and Bill Bronkala
MSI, 1973

Gregg, 1973

Christmas 1976

Elton and Chris Lorenz,
about 1977

Grandmother Cora Roeser
with Gregg, in London,
May 1981

At Liz Johnson's wedding, Vail, 1990

Our 50th Anniversary, July 1991

50th Anniversary, 1991

Elton and Doris, Alaska cruise, 1994

Elton, Antarctica, 1997

Celebrating renovation of Old Stone Church, May 1999

Renovated Old Stone Church
1999

At Old Stone Church, Aug. 5, 2004 after Elton's interment
Back Row, L to R: Tom Pettit, Daille Pettit,
Doris, Kristin Sheppard, Steve Sheppard
Front Row, L to R: Tim Sullivan, Karin Sullivan holding Cassidy,
Aaron and Carolina Sheppard

CHAPTER 15

THE EARLY NINETIES

1990-1994

What would be a momentous decade began, as most do, with things as usual. We could not know that the next four years would be years of great sadness, as well as joy, for us; dramatic changes would take place in the lives of our small family. But all of this was ahead of us in January, 1990, our work at MSI continuing much the same as it had in the past.

We had jobs with Best Sand in Geauga County; Liberia and Mauritania in Africa; Hamersley and Mt. Newman in Australia; Fundidora in Mexico; CVRD in Brazil, and Carter Creek. We were also doing some work with Reading, and in March, Elton flew to Saarbrücken, Germany with Michael Clark and Jim Curran to investigate the procedures for supplying district heat. And in the spring of the year, we prepared a procedure manual for Kerr McGee.

We had begun to think of retirement and to look for a buyer for the company and had one potential buyer who backed out in May. Also, in May, in the midst of this busy year, Lewis retired. He had been an exceptional secretary—the best Elton ever had and a real addition to our office crew. He was somewhat temperamental and had a violent temper when he got mad, but he could always be depended upon and was always there and on time. He had a great sense of humor and was well-informed and knowledgeable and he and I had interesting conversations about everything when everyone else was out of town (and even when they were not). We had not really replaced him when we left the company in 1991, but Connie Zalenka, who had been with us since 1985, took over most of his work.

My activities in the League, ASWA and Old Stone continued; one of the major League activities was a search I did with Joyce Wallace for a Cleveland location for the State League convention the next year; I put out the League newsletter every other month, and kept the books; and I was also treasurer of the Women's City Club Foundation. This was an interesting job; one of my major roles was to invest the reserves, and during this period, interest rates were in the 16-17% range so we knew we'd be making a good return. I was in the Old Stone Diaconate and on a couple of nominating committees. I handled some of this extra activity in the office where I usually went on Saturday and on Sunday after church. My office workload increased, multiplying with the amount of business. I did most of the accounting, worried about the cash flow, edited every report and managed the office. And a note in my diary said, "also got the photo albums up to date in September!"

Elton and I were part of a new bridge club with the McCuaigs, the Scharfs, Frances and Howard Wilder and Kathryn Cotts. This was fun, although I'd sworn years before never to play bridge again—I'd liked the camaraderie and visiting, but really didn't like playing cards, especially with committed bridge players. However, Malcolm was persuasive and we liked the company. Malcolm, Kathryn and the Wilders were all quite expert, but we had not played for years and were very rusty; the Scharfs turned out to be completely out of their element. They worked hard at learning the rules, but unfortunately, they are people who expect to be good and expert at whatever they do, and we spent a lot of time trying to get them up to speed. Needless to say, I suppose, the club pretty much petered out after a couple of years, but we had a good time while it lasted.

In February, the MSI board had a meeting in Palm Desert, California. I dislike all deserts but I was glad to go there because my cousin Mary Jane Roeser Biehn had lived in one of the neighboring towns for twenty or thirty years. We spent a very enjoyable afternoon with her between the meals and meetings of the Board. After the meeting, while the other MSI people went their separate ways, we flew to Salt Lake where there was to be an AIME annual meeting. We were met by the Raos and stayed with them. Liz and I had a good visit while the men went to their meetings—both AIME and with Kennecott, concerning their various projects.

Back home, I was happy to have a new cleaning lady, Maria Perez, who stayed with us for 11 years. She was very dependable and did the laundry as well as the cleaning, making it much easier for me to do my work and cope with all our entertaining. We both enjoyed the presence of the Stones in Cleveland. Rod was a major addition to the work force, not only on the board, but also working on our projects. We saw a lot of them and shared our Easter dinner with them this year at the University Club.

The first sad news of the decade for the Roeser family was the sudden death, on March 3, of Carola's husband, Chuck. Apparently, his death was accidental, but he and Carola had been drinking and fighting and there was some question as to just what happened. In any case, poor little Jacob was without a father at the age of six.

Elton and I had another, more pleasant, surprise that spring when we had an unexpected windfall of $50,000 from an insurance plan which had provided Elton with generous life coverage as long as he was at MSI and under 70. This was cancelled because he would be 70 the next year. We decided to use this extra money to buy a high class car. I suggested a Mercedes or BMW but he felt there was too much danger of something like that being stolen, so we settled on a Buick Park Avenue. We did not trade in our Buick Century, but gladly gave it to the Pettit family. The new car was quite lovely, despite problems that developed in Colorado Springs. A truck's slipping cargo caused the loss of a tire which was not immediately replaceable by the local Buick dealer, and our windshield wiper system went out during one of the rainiest weeks ever experienced in the Springs. We had to drive to Denver to get it replaced on one of the few days when it didn't rain.

We were in Colorado Springs in June primarily for the happy occasion of the wedding of Liz Johnson and Dean Koll in Aspen on July 7. At the same time, we included a Roeser family reunion and many visits and get-togethers. We saw lots of our favorite people and old friends, but the high point of the trip was the presence of Gregg and Daille who flew to Colorado for the wedding.

We had expected to meet Gregg in our hotel when we got to the Springs, since Alan and Lois were to be on their way from Ft. Collins and were to pick him up at the airport. But Alan had a serious heart attack and was taken to the hospital in Denver and Jack went to pick up Gregg. The next day we drove to Denver, visited Alan in the hospital, went to see Walt at his house, picked up Daille at the airport and went on to Leadville and then to Vail. It was really fun, all four of us together, and Liz's wedding was lovely, as weddings always seem to be.

After the wedding, we went back to the Springs. Daille and Gregg arranged to go to Denver together to catch Gregg's flight to Indonesia and Daille's to D.C. We stayed in the Springs for a few days, took trips to Denver and around. We visited old friends, including Alice Petheram Martin, with whom I'd played when I was a child but hadn't seen for years, and Marie

Keller, our old friend from Virginia, Minnesota. Late in the year we heard that Marie had committed suicide. I've always wondered if we inadvertently encouraged her decision. Leon had died a few years earlier, and she had been very ill with a brain tumor. She was apparently recovering, but she was very sad to see Elton and me still together.

We also visited with Jack and his family, Aunt Jo and Barby, and, after he was discharged from the hospital, Alan and Lois. This was the last time I would see my dear brother, Alan. He died in February 1992, but was in very poor health during his last months. It was also the last time we would see Aunt Jo, Dad's sister, who died in the summer of 1991.

When we left the Springs, we drove west and spent a night with Mona and Dale, stopped in Gunnison to visit Craig Roeser at Western State, then Telluride, which we had not seen since we moved away in 1951. What a beautiful area it is! Our stone retort house was still standing, as was Gregg's grade school. It was a nostalgic visit, but it was refreshing to see those mountains and beautiful forests again. From there we drove north to Wyoming and east to the Black Hills and Custer. We spent one night in Rawlings, Wyoming and ate in the restaurant that we think was the most accurately named of all those in which we have ever eaten, "The Bum Steer."

My fiftieth class reunion was held at the Blue Bell Lodge in Custer State Park. Most of the alumni who were still alive were there and we had a wonderful time visiting them for a couple of days and reminiscing over old times. We hated to leave, but set forth from Custer to another place we hated to leave—Iron Mountain. After two days there, Elton returned to Cleveland while I drove to see the Morris' in Appleton for a reunion with Jan, Fran Zimmerman and Peggy Robinson. From there I drove home. It was a memorable trip, not least because we saw so many people we would never see again—not only Alan and Jo and Marie Keller, but some of my class and a few old Colorado friends. As it turned out, this was our last reunion, too. Herb Heidepriem, who spearheaded all of the reunions, died on a trip to Peru in 1994. We all missed him, and no one had the heart to schedule another reunion.

After our return to Cleveland in mid-summer, we settled down to tending our business, which seemed to have been long neglected. This included, among other things, holding our annual board meeting in October at Quail Hollow, a resort east of Cleveland. The people at the meeting included Paul Revey who had recently been remarried to a local woman named Tina, and their presence was interesting to say the least.

As I said earlier, the Pettits returned to D.C. in June and settled down with both girls in a 3-story town house in Arlington at Ballston—the first Metro stop west of Roslyn. They still owned the house in Centreville, and it was decided some time that summer that Kris should live there, find work and, perhaps, some roomers to help with the expenses. This was a large order for a 21-year old with little work experience who was still suffering from emotional shock. She worked at a variety of jobs that fall, including some as a temp and one job for a company that folded while she was there. She got some food stamps, and tried to recover from her trauma with David.

While Kristin was getting settled, and as soon as she herself was settled, Daille looked for a job where she could use her library degree. In August, she went to work for the American Hotel and Motel Association as an information officer. She was very happy to be working again, and since they lived two blocks from the Metro, both she and Tom, back at the State Department, could ride to work and not have to drive in the always difficult D.C. traffic. Meanwhile, Karin went back to Arlington High for her senior year.

The four Pettits drove to Cleveland for Thanksgiving and we put on a formal dinner with the McCuaigs as guests. In December, Elton and I went to New York and the Waldorf for a dinner party hosted by Jim Curran, of Reading Anthracite (RAC). He had a big party every year in New York for selected Pennsylvanians and others, both those living in New York City and those from Pennsylvania. This year it was to be at a restaurant, but the guest list grew so fast it was moved at the last minute to the Waldorf Rainbow Room. It was an elegant affair, except for the cocktail reception at which the appetizers were plebeian servings of chunks of cheese and crackers. I figured that even the Waldorf couldn't round up enough people with one day's notice, one week before Christmas, to provide fancy canapés!

On the next night, Jim took us to a VERY exclusive club for cocktails. On our way out, I picked up my coat in a cloak room so busy and crowded that I accidentally left my wallet. Three blocks away, I missed it, but by that time the attendant had left, with my wallet, and apparently went shopping for her family with my credit cards. I had a nice letter of apology from the manager of the club, and wasn't charged for the several hundred she spent. But so much for very exclusive clubs!

We flew back to Cleveland and then drove to Arlington for Christmas with the Pettits and Cyril Callas, Karin's boy friend who came from Santo Domingo. We had a pleasant week before we returned to Cleveland to spend New Year's Eve with the McCuaigs and the Scharfs at the Ritz, in formal attire and with dinner, champagne, and the works—very plush. For once, Elton got good use out of his tuxedo this December.

But our New Year's celebration and our outlook for 1991 were clouded by the disturbing news we'd received a few days before. We'd returned from Washington to find that our lives were to be changed more than we could imagine. Elton had gone to Dr. Harshman about a tremor in his right hand, and was told that he probably had Parkinson's disease. I, and others at MSI, had been aware of the tremor for several months and I had asked my current internist about possible causes. She suggested several things, including Parkinson's, but whatever the cause, I felt he had to get a diagnosis and pushed him to go to the doctor. Harshman recommended a neurologist whom we soon visited; he confirmed the diagnosis.

Elton was really devastated, as I was too. We went to the library to check out the disease, but really couldn't find a lot of helpful information. Many years later I realized that the information was then and still is pretty skimpy. This is partly because the disease affects every patient differently and there is a wide variety of medication, none of which was at all effective until El Dopo was developed in the late sixties. This replaces the material missing from the patient's brain and is the one essential drug which helps, but doesn't cure, and must be taken regularly. My Dad had Parkinson's, and took El Dopo, but information about the disease at the time he died in 1971, and the probably inadequate medical knowledge of the doctors in Colorado Springs, kept him from receiving proper medication and care. In any case, from the little he knew, Elton was sure it would be necessary for him to quit working entirely, so he decided to speed up his plans to sell MSI. The new year, 1991, began with his informing the board of his decision and beginning the effort to sell the company, which culminated in June of that year when a consortium headed by Dick Smith bought our baby.

The beginning of the Gulf War in January was disturbing to all of us, but on February 2, 1991, we left on a long-planned vacation trip to Indonesia to visit Gregg. The trip began with a flight to L.A. and then to Honolulu, where we spent two days. This was my only time in Hawaii (Elton had stopped there briefly a few times before) and I found it as lovely as reported. I've always hoped to return. From there we flew to the airport at Bali, where we were to take a local flight to Jakarta. Our change of planes there was interesting. Language was a problem and it took some time for us to find where the local terminal was and how to get there. None of the porters spoke English and the transfer involved a long unlit walk with men with whom we could not communicate. I was very impressed with how easy it would have been for them to do us harm and steal all our baggage. Instead, they delivered us safely with a smile. This experience helped to confirm my conviction that most people everywhere are pretty decent.

When we arrived in Jakarta in the middle of the night, Gregg met us and told us he was putting us up at the Hilton because he was covered with some kind of bites he thought might be from bed bugs and he didn't want us to suffer. As it turned out, his problem was dust mites and his place was eventually cleaned of them, but we spent nearly two weeks at a lovely tropical Hilton with an Olympic sized swimming pool and gorgeous surroundings. Since Gregg had to work most of the time we were there, we were usually on our own. We were happy to find CNN, which was just beginning to be a major news source, and since the Gulf War was going on, we spent a great deal of time trying to catch up on its progress. We were thankful for CNN because we could watch the war's progress on television in English.

We did a lot of touring while Gregg was at work, and saw volcanos and caves and native dancing and a lot of beautiful country. We liked Indonesia, except that I didn't like the food and was happy to find that the restaurants served spaghetti and meatballs as well as the native fare. I ate spaghetti almost every day.

On the weekend, the three of us took a boat to the island of Putri Pelangi Perak, in the Java Sea. The island was small enough that we could walk around it in an hour. We had hoped to swim, but even though we were some distance from land, the water was too polluted for swimming. The scenery was lovely but we were startled while we were sitting on the porch to see a huge lizard, as big as a very large dog, scoot by. We are sure it was a Komodo dragon, an animal native to Komodo Island, up to nine feet long and about three feet high. We had no idea how it could be on this island, or keep out of sight the rest of the time we were there. The Tsunami of 2004 made me think of this island, but I've not been able to find any information about whether or not it survived that disaster.

On Monday, Elton and I flew to Bali after seeing Gregg's workplace, meeting his friends, eating in his lovely home and driving around with his chauffeur, Tardi. We spent a week in Bali, with Gregg joining us for the weekend. We took many tours and, everywhere we turned, there was something different and interesting to see. Among the more interesting sites was a small park with trees full of bats and dozens of monkeys milling around. The scenery from almost any point was breathtaking and overall, Bali is beyond description—beautiful, interesting, full of one of a kind animals, native religious dancers and programs, and wonderfully friendly people. It should be noted that, like nearly all Indonesians, the people were desperately poor and exploited, while the president lived in incredible wealth. After Gregg left us in Bali, we began our long trip home. We stayed overnight in Guam, then another night in Los Angeles, where it was very damp and cold. We had taken the chance and left Cleveland without warm clothes so, as I've done in many cities, I bought a sweater and we made it home the next day without freezing to death.

We had the opportunity to warm up later in March when the next MSI Board meeting—and, as it turned out, our last—was held in Cancun. Cancun is considered a tourist's paradise, with big beautiful condos and hotels, a beautiful beach and lots of activities, but I could not ignore the contrast to the squalor of the natives living in shacks on the edge of town. I thoroughly enjoyed a bus trip to Chichen Itza, the Incan ruins, and, as always, enjoyed the company and the shopping, but I had no desire to stay longer than the three days we were there or ever to go back.

We had not been home long when Martha Knight's husband, Tony, died of colon cancer. He had been seriously ill for a month or two so it was not a surprise, but very sad. Martha had worked for us for some time and had become my good friend, and Tony was only 40. The funeral was on March 30, the day before Easter, and we spent most of a few days with Martha and her kids and had Easter dinner with them at the University Club. I spent a lot of time the next few months with Martha and I was disturbed when she began to date another of the Cleveland Orchestra's bass players who had recently lost his wife. They jumped into a marriage on Valentine's Day in 1992. It was nearly as sad as Tony's funeral had been, with all of the children crying, and all of the guests convinced of its foolishness. Needless to say, they were divorced within two years.

After Tony's death, we revved up our planning for a 50th anniversary party on July 9. Elton had always said he wanted to have a really big party with everyone we knew and that's what we planned. We had talked to Gregg about invitations for the party and he was designing these while we made the other arrangements. At the same time, we were working on the sale of the company and when it looked favorable, we set June 30 as the date of our leaving MSI. We decided that we would form a new company, Geist & Geist, Incorporated, and Elton would work as long as he was able, and we had to find a location for this company. As at so many other times in our lives, we had all these major projects to plan and put in place at the same time. Fortunately, we always liked working ourselves into the ground.

Our number one priority was our anniversary and we arranged for it to be held in the hotel on Public Square in Cleveland. The hotel has lived under several names and, at one point in about 1978, it was closed. Several city leaders chipped in to buy, remodel and update it, and when we held our party it was the Sheraton—a really gorgeous place. We also planned a dinner party in the Meridian party room the night before the big party for our out-of-town guests. There were many of these, including Heinz and Renate Hess from Zürich, Tom Probert from Australia, Raman and Liz Rao from Salt Lake City, several people from Iron Mountain, Mona and Dale Johnson and their girls from Colorado and Dale's brother, Don and his wife, Vesta, from Florida, and, of course, Gregg from Indonesia. My brother Jack came, but without Betty, and Alan was too ill to come. We asked over 100 and had about 75.

It was a spectacular party, with music provided by Maggie Scharf at the piano, toasts to both of us from many of the guests and a surprise by Fran Zimmerman's Sweet Adeline barbershop quartet. Many of the guests told us it was the best 50th they had ever attended.

Our party somewhat overshadowed Karin's earlier graduation from High School on June 1, but we were there to help her celebrate. It also overshadowed the farewell party given for us by the MSI crew. A highlight of that party was a picture of Elton and me, painted by a friend of Bea's from a photograph. Bea was delighted with the picture, but it had both of us with brown eyes (Elton's were very definitely blue and mine somewhat hazel). We were not happy with it, although we tried to hide our disappointment. We hung it for a few years and then gave it to Daille.

Before our anniversary, we had located and bought a one bedroom condo in Winton Place, the next-door condo to our Meridian. We did a little redecorating before we moved in soon after our party and officially began Geist & Geist, Inc. We moved what we owned from MSI and put what we couldn't use in a storage locker, and then set out to provide desks, tables and bookcases, as well as the Wang system, a fax and a copier. We bought most of the furniture from Office Max and had to put it together—a terrible job, because of the instructions written in "japlish" (i.e., undecipherable language written in English by someone who didn't know the language). Some had no instructions at all. But perhaps the worst part of it was that much of the work had to be done on the floor, and my arthritic right hip had begun to be exceedingly painful. Most of the work we did together, but I recall the summer as one round after another of trips to Office Max, working with hammer and pliers, going back for more, and suffering every minute.

In August we drove to Hibbing for the wedding of George Kotonias' daughter. George had come to our 50th, but Pat had been busy with the wedding and couldn't get away, so we agreed to go to their big celebration. We drove north through Chicago on a blistering hot day, spent the night in Eau Claire and then drove through Duluth to Virginia where we stayed with Bob and Elaine Prittinen—Bob was one of MSI's former board members. We had a good time with them, enjoyed the wedding, saw friends we hadn't seen for years, and stopped in Appleton to visit Jan and Marty on our way home. It was an altogether very satisfying week. We spent an interesting few hours north of Virginia, out in the middle of the Minnesota forest, at a casino run by the local Indian tribe. We had not been aware of the recent establishment of casinos on reservations all over the country, and we were astonished to find it full of people, on a sunny, summer Sunday, when one would expect Minnesotans to be, as they always had been, fishing or swimming at the lake.

Meantime, Karin had decided to go to college at Marquette University in Milwaukee. We are still not sure why she chose this college, but on August 18, she and her parents stopped at our place on their way to Wisconsin for her enrollment in school. At the end of October, Elton and I drove up to Milwaukee for Parents Day and had a visit with Karin, and then took a few hours to visit Sally Bronkala. She and Bill had moved to Wisconsin a few years earlier and Bill had died of colon cancer shortly after, so we felt we should see her, since we were so close. Our visit with Karin was quick and somewhat unsatisfactory but we wanted to do as much for her as we could.

Before this trip in September, I rode with another ASWA member to Chicago for the ASWA annual meeting. Our group of delegates was very compatible. We had a good time at the meeting and seeing Chicago, but I was in pain all the time, and when we had to walk back to the Western Hotel from Navy Pier, I wasn't at all sure I could make it. On returning to Cleveland, I finally went to see a member of an orthopedic clinic. I was assigned to a young doctor who really wasn't interested in old ladies. He prescribed exercise and a new medicine which required a monthly check to see if it was affecting my liver, and told me I shouldn't hurry into surgery. When Elton told Dr. Harshman about this, he highly recommended a doctor whom I finally saw in February and who scheduled me for surgery. More about this later, but meantime I continued to be miserably uncomfortable.

I had felt that I would have more time for volunteer work after I left my full-time job at MSI, but Elton continued to work full-time for MSI, largely on projects he'd been on before we left, mostly UBS and Kennecott, so he was gone a good deal. I spent quite a lot of time in our new office, doing everything, although we hired part time secretaries for awhile and used a typing service for big projects. In October, I had an abscessed tooth, a difficult root canal job and a new crown. With my aching hip and a case of the flu in November, I felt generally lousy and spent a few months finding it difficult to keep up with anything.

We had a pleasant break when Raman and Liz Rao spent three days with us in November, and later the Pettits, and Cyril came for Thanksgiving. I picked up Cyril at the airport early Wednesday, and later he and I went to pick up Karin. They immediately began fighting and I thought we would have a really unpleasant few days, but the rest of the family arrived late in the day and they seemed to settle their problems to some extent. The Stones joined us for Thanksgiving and I think everyone enjoyed the holiday.

Elton and I drove to Arlington for Christmas, spending the night en route at Breezewood. It was not the happiest holiday we ever spent together. I felt terrible and Kristin was not in the best of spirits, partly because of the job situation and partly because she had so much car trouble, which led to her parents and Elton spending time with her, selecting a new car. Karin was there briefly but she left for Santo Domingo to spend Christmas with Cyril Callas and his family. I think everyone was happier when the holiday was over and we'd gone back to Cleveland. It had been a memorable year, with some sad times and some pleasant times. We felt we'd accomplished a lot with our new business and looked forward to beginning our next 50 years together. We were happy to leave 1991 behind us and move on to 1992.

1992

In January, Geist & Geist began a program for Inco to manage maintenance in its many combined operations near Sudbury, Ontario. We, but mainly Elton, worked on this program in various stages throughout the nineties. He spent a week in Sudbury in January, some time in Salt Lake and Oklahoma City, and I hobbled through my various responsibilities until the middle of February when we left to drive to Phoenix for an AIME meeting. We went through Tulsa, where we spent the night with the Arnots, our friends from our first year in Cleveland, then spent a day with Ken Richards of Kerr McGee in Oklahoma City before heading through New Mexico for Phoenix. We were there for four or five days, attending meetings, visiting one of my Custer High classmates and we did some touring around the area.

We went to the Greenlys for dinner. I had looked forward to this—I thought of Marvel as one of my best friends. I was really disappointed when she was rather unwelcoming. I suddenly realized that, in the past, she had had to be friendly because of our business relationship with John and she no longer had to be. John certainly behaved in a friendly manner, but Marvel made her feelings quite clear, and I was sad about the situation.

Rather unhappily, we left the next day and drove northeast to the Four Corners, where Arizona, New Mexico, Colorado and Utah meet—the only place in the U.S, where one can stand in four states at the same time. We went from there to spend the night in Cortez, Colorado, and then drove up through Silverton to Ouray, through the San Juan Mountains, and over the Million Dollar Highway.

After coming down from the mountains, we drove to Grand Junction to spend two or three days with Mona and Dale. They had finally moved from Leadville and were in a condo there. It was not as nice as their house in Leadville and I think Grand Junction is a rather dreary town, but at least it's not as high or cold as Leadville. The first afternoon we were there, I had a call from Jack, telling me Alan had died the day before, February 29. He had been ill for so long that his death came as no surprise, but I loved him dearly. We had had a good relationship always and his death hit me pretty hard. Lui did not have a service planned and she did not want anyone to come out. I think this was mainly because Jack had antagonized her so much by needling Alan the last time he'd visited, she absolutely never wanted to see Jack again. I felt Lois needed someone, although she would never have admitted it, and after we got home a week later, I flew to Seattle and spent several days with her.

First, of course, we had to get home. We went from Grand Junction to Golden for a brief visit with another of the MSI directors, David Coolbaugh, and his wife Ruth, then on to the Springs where, as usual, we stayed in a motel. We were never invited to stay over with the Roesers, except when I was there just before mother died. At least, Carola had a dinner party for us and to celebrate Elton's birthday, and she had the family in. It was very pleasant, but we were up late and Elton insisted on getting an early start the next morning—always a matter of honor with him. This resulted in a short, but nerve-wracking 500 foot, 60 m.p.h. drive down a ditch in Nebraska when he went to sleep while on cruise control. Luckily, there was no traffic and no damage was done. This didn't seem to change his determination to always get an early start, but it did convince him he shouldn't use cruise control.

We spent a night near Lincoln and the next night in Joliet, then drove to Milwaukee to see how Karin was getting along. After a night there, we came home through South Bend where we spent a miserable night in a motel, chockful of noisy kids, then on to Cleveland for a few days before Elton left for Sudbury. I went to Seattle to see Lui. I spent most of my time there counting coins and putting them in wrappers—Alan, it seems, had been saving coins in his dresser drawers and closets for years, without Lois' knowledge. Although Lois would never admit to affection or need, I think she was happy to have me there—if only to do the coins.

Back in Cleveland our various activities took us up to Easter, when Karin arrived for the weekend and joined us for Easter dinner at Jim and Jean Cooke's. By this time, I had seen Dr. Helper (he obviously had to go into medicine with that name) and had been told that I should have my hip replaced and should actually have both knees and the other hip replaced too. I settled for having the most painful hip replaced first and we set May 13 for the surgery at Saint John's hospital. I was in the hospital for about a week, and then Daille arrived and spent a week or so with me at home. Therapy is absolutely essential for proper recovery from joint replacement and is required by Dr. Helper, and I had a very nice young therapist come to see me at home three times a week for six weeks. I particularly enjoyed my conversations with him because he was a strong and ardent supporter of Ross Perot, who had declared his candidacy and was running against George H.W.Bush and William Clinton for President in November. His candidacy ensured Clinton's election, which we considered a real mistake for the U.S.

Somehow, Elton always managed to have business out of town as soon as I got home from a hospital stay and he set off for Sudbury about the same time Daille left, but with the help of Jane Stone and other friends, I managed, and was well on the way to recovery when we got a shocking phone call from Gregg in Indonesia telling us he had been diagnosed with a brain tumor. He had been having various health problems for some time and George Roland had come out from England to be with him. He was in the hospital in Jakarta and they were preparing for surgery when they did some more tests and found he had several "tumors." With this discovery, they decided surgery was impossible and he should go back to England as soon as possible. This meant a plane trip on a stretcher with an attendant at a cost of $10,000. Fortunately, I had invested some of Mother's bequest in a $10,000 municipal bond which had just come due and we immediately wired the money. The wire transfer could not be completed in time for his departure but his Indonesian friend, Heidhy Margangun, put the expense on her American Express card and with that kind action earned our everlasting gratitude.

Meantime, George had arranged for Gregg's belongings and furniture to be packed up and shipped to England, and he flew back with Gregg. I was happy that George could do so much for Gregg, since it was obviously impossible for us to go to Indonesia. Elton was in Sudbury at the time, also worrying, and I spent one of my longest nights knowing Gregg was on the plane all night in very serious condition and wondering if he would make it to London alive. We were very relieved that he did, and happy to learn that he was diagnosed with toxoplasmosis soon after his arrival. This is a bacterial disease which can attack any organ and is usually contracted from cat feces. While easily treated and cured, it is hard to diagnose. He immediately began to improve, but the disease had already caused brain damage which affected his mobility and left him subject to epileptic-type seizures; and the doctors now realized that he had full-blown AIDS. He remained in London, in George's flat, and in George's care, very close to the main hospital where AIDS was being treated. From this time on, he was seldom out of our thoughts.

Despite my still gimpy hip and concern about Gregg, we proceeded to keep our promise to our friend and pastor, Malcolm McCuaig, to come to Prince Edward Island to visit him and Marion at their summer home. We drove there in July, and spent a very pleasant, but chilly, week with them, seeing everything on the island and having a good visit. When we left them, we took a ferry and a long drive across Nova Scotia to Halifax, where Elton had some business with Sydney Steel people, and we spent a couple of days touring this interesting and beautiful city. We drove back through New Brunswick and Maine, spending a day with the Aubreys at Moose Lake.

I had been concerned about traveling with my new hip, but it all went surprisingly well, so I was willing to spend a week in Sudbury with Elton in August, returning home in time to entertain Tom and Karin on their way to Karin's second college year. Kris came along and spent a few days with us, and in September, I took her back to Virginia. She needed a minor surgical procedure which she was very worried about and I went with her to the clinic in Arlington when she had it done. We were relieved that no further treatment was needed.

Since Gregg's return to London we had wanted to visit him, so the next trip Elton and I took was to Europe, partly, of course, to see Gregg, but also to use the gift the Hesses had given us for our 50th—a weekend at the Jungfrau Hotel in Interlachen. We flew first to Zürich. On arriving there, we spent a day with Renate and Heinz, who then took us to Gstaad for a night in their chalet and then on to Interlachen. They left us in one of the most elegant hotels in the world. We spent three days there, taking a train trip to the top of the Jungfrau one day and a boat trip across the lake on another, and enjoying the plush accommodations and elegant meals. We took the train back to Zürich for a day before going to London for a ten-day visit with Gregg.

In London we stayed at the Cranley Gardens Hotel. This was a block or two from Gregg's house and we divided our time between the two, as well as going to the Tower on a trip one day, and spending some time at Harrods—that wonderful department store. Gregg was in reasonably good shape and we were able to go with him to a play, *Grand Hotel*, and a movie, Clint Eastwood's *The Unforgiven*—the last play and movie we were to see with him. We had several good meals out with his various friends, including a dinner to celebrate my 70th birthday. One vivid memory I have of that trip was his comment when we walked somewhere, I with my still-healing hip and bad knees, Elton with his slowing gait, and Gregg with his hesitant walk, calling us "the three limpies." He had a variety of serious health problems, but my poor boy always said he was soldiering on. And he managed to retain his sense of humor. As always, we loved being with him, but were sad to leave him, obviously ill, when we headed back to the States.

I spent the next month or so doing a long-delayed redecorating of the den, including acquiring a new TV and sound system, new bookcases, carpet and wallpaper. I had it all in order when Gregg arrived on December 1 for Christmas. We had several social occasions with different people and enjoyed the holiday with the rest of the family. He stayed over New Year's Eve, when we had the Scharfs and McCuaigs to help us celebrate, and left for London a few days later. We loved having him with us, but we remembered the last few months of that year and all of the next year and a half with sadness and regret. Gregg was an interesting, bright, funny companion, a good person and a good son. His long illness and ultimate death in 1994 was the worst blow we had ever suffered.

1993

As the year began, one of our concerns was Kris. She had continued to have problems with her house and with men. She had a few renters and had trouble with payment and misbehavior, and she dated a few guys, somewhat indiscriminately, I felt, since some were good choices and some were bad. But when she got home after spending Christmas with us, a fellow who had been staying with her next door neighbor for a month or so introduced himself as Stephen Sheppard and made a date. They really hit it off and had something of a whirlwind romance. Daille and Tom decided they'd had enough problems with the house and with Kris living in it, and Kris was ready to move out, so they decided to sell the house. Steve and Kris moved into a hotel—supposedly with a third party who never materialized, but with the dog Kris had owned for some time and Steve's cat.

Steve was from Charleston, S.C., and had come to D.C. with a friend to start raising and selling fish for aquariums. This fell through in a few months and he went to work at an army PX. He was obviously from a good family (one of the old Charleston families, as it turned out) with good manners and social graces. It also turned out that he was the spoiled only child of a divorced couple who had gotten his own way all his life. *His way* included dropping out of education. Nevertheless, he and Kris got serious very soon, and when they came to Cleveland to visit in May, he asked her to introduce him as her fiancé. Kris told her parents in June that she was pregnant, and they planned a wedding for August 28, 1993.

Although Tom was perturbed with Steve for years because he had no education, no ambition, and no real desire to work, one of our perpetual worries lessened that year. When Steve's father died in 1998, and left Steve a sizable fortune, Tom no longer had reason to object to him. However, like most fathers-in-law, Tom continued to have a problem accepting him.

With Gregg in London being cared for by George, and Kris beginning to see the light ahead, we felt a little less urgency about family problems. We decided to buy a second car, a Buick Skylark, to accommodate our diverging activities (and difficulties of busing), and concentrated on Geist & Geist. Our job with Inco in Sudbury was huge for a 2-person firm, and Elton spent at least every other week flying to and from Sudbury. We had found a part-time secretary, Rosemary Starkey, who was with us for a couple of years and was a big help. I continued with my various projects and League and Old Stone jobs and since I no longer felt obligated to be in the office most of the time, I again became active in P.E.O., which met in the afternoons. When I was with MSI, I had all but dropped out of the organization.

In April, I went to London to visit Gregg. George took advantage of my being there to visit another friend who was also slowly dying of AIDS. Gregg was able to take care of himself, but I helped with the cooking, keeping things in order, and keeping him company. When I left, he wanted me to take some of the glass objects he'd made during glass-blowing classes in 1980—paper weights and a few glasses and bowls; he also insisted on sending his favorite of Ethel's quilts and the afghan I had knitted for him. In June, Daille went to London for a visit with Gregg, despite the decision of Kris and Steve to get married in August. She had begun to make the wedding arrangements before leaving for London.

The wedding was a major event for us, but we were also happy to help celebrate the 50th Anniversary in June of Tony and Vi Osojnicki in Iron Mountain. This was a long trip, as Elton had driven to Sudbury. I flew there to join him and we then drove to Iron Mountain. We took another roundabout trip when we went to Arlington in July. We began by going to Sharon, Pennsylvania to the *World's Largest Shoe Store,* then down to West Virginia and thence to Daille's. While we were there, we went with them to Bryce, in the mountains west of D.C., where they had purchased a vacation house. We were scarcely home from that trip when it was time to go back for Kris' wedding.

Elton was in Sudbury and flew directly to D.C. and I flew from Cleveland. We were happy that Gregg was able to fly to D.C. from London and, although he was not able to do much partying, he enjoyed being there. We were happy he was able to come and that he felt Kris' wedding important enough to make the effort. The wedding was lovely and there was a very nice reception in a Holiday Inn near the Pettits' house. We enjoyed meeting Steve's parents and were happy that Vickie and Liz came to represent the Johnson family. John Pettit, Tom's brother, and one of Tom's cousins were there, and the Sheppard family was well represented. Kris and Steve left the next day for a quick trip to Paris, Gregg stayed on with Daille for a day or two before returning to London, and we flew back to Cleveland.

Elton continued his commute to Sudbury throughout the fall, and in October I flew back to London. I stayed in the Cranley Gardens Hotel, but spent most of my days and evenings with Gregg. While I was with him one day, we had the sad news that Lois, Alan's widow, had died (on my birthday). I was not too surprised. When I had been with her in March 1992, she was barely eating enough to stay alive, and although she wouldn't let herself show it, she was absolutely devastated by Alan's death. Her whole life had centered on him and there was nothing else that really interested her. I might mention here that Walt went to Seattle and picked out a few things he wanted, and then had the house and its contents sold. Gregg was as saddened by the news as I, since he'd always loved Lui's wise-cracking, ironic manner and he found it just one more blow to bear.

One of the difficult things about AIDS in the early years of the epidemic was the way many people suffered and died quickly. Gregg had lost several dear friends in the past few years. He was obviously failing, but he was still able to manage quite well alone. He had always loved Hallowe'en, and his friend, Sue Young, planned a Hallowe'en party which we attended. He chose that night to display and present me with a portrait of himself that he'd had painted for Elton and me. He left London with me early in November to come to Cleveland to visit and the portrait accompanied us on what was a difficult trip, because it was so hard for Gregg to get around. I think he had intended to stay through Christmas, but he was suffering from several painful problems and had little energy. He decided to go to New Orleans, meet George and spend Thanksgiving with him. He was there only a few days when he decided he had to go back to London to get some medical attention. Both of those trips were very difficult for him. We spent that Thanksgiving with the Pettits, Cyril and the Scharfs at our house and then we went to the Pettits for Christmas. Kris was happily awaiting her first baby and the anticipation of a new baby added an expectant and happy touch to a sad holiday. On December 31 in Cleveland, we joined the McCuaig's and their friends to say goodbye to 1993 and greet 1994.

1994

When the year began, Elton was doing some work for Kennecott and intended to go to Salt Lake to talk to Raman Rao, so we decided we would drive out and see the family on the way. We left on January 18, the coldest day in Cleveland's history (-25°F). It was a cold trip all the way to Kansas, where it warmed up and it wasn't too bad in Colorado. We spent a night in Denver and had dinner with Walt, then spent two days in the Springs (in a motel, of course!) before going to Vail to see Liz and Dean. We spent the night in Eagle, a tiny, dreary town, and the Kolls took us to a restaurant they'd heard was good. It wasn't. And the motel was the worst we'd ever stayed in. We were amused in 2003 at the trial of Kobe Bryant, a famous basketball player, in that miserable little town of Eagle. At least we were able to leave soon. In the morning, we drove through Glenwood and had lunch at the hotel which had seemed too plush to even eat in when Mom, Jack and I spent time there in 1934. It certainly didn't seem so plush this time. From there, we went to Mona and Dale's and spent two days with them before driving on to Salt Lake for a very good three-day visit with the Raos. Throughout this trip I was knitting a denim sweater for Gregg, knitting furiously to keep from thinking about him too much.

We left Salt Lake on February 1 and drove across Wyoming to Laramie, with a freezing prairie wind blowing straight south across the plains and the mountains. Even with the heater going full blast, it was a very cold trip. After a cold night in Laramie, we drove to Lincoln for a night, then to Joliet, and the day after that to Milwaukee for a visit with Karin and a stay in the Pfister Hotel. When we got back to Cleveland, Elton left for Sudbury. He stayed only briefly, because we heard from George that Gregg's condition had worsened and he had moved into Mildmay Hospice. Elton came home and we left on February 20, flying through Newark, and arrived in London, where we checked into the Cranley Gardens, and then met with George to visit Gregg.

Mildmay is in the east end of London, much too far from the Cranley Gardens, so we moved the next morning to a big hotel at the end of the Tower Bridge, where we stayed when we weren't at the Hospice. During the first few days, Gregg was conscious, but very weak. I think he was glad we were there and we spent several days sitting by the bed, holding his hand and talking to him when he was awake, and praying. I sat and read and did a little needlepoint when he was asleep. I have no idea what I was reading, but as always, I had to have something going into my head to keep me going.

Gregg's friends, Veronica, Sue and Jackie More came in and, of course, George, but Elton and George were always at loggerheads, so he was not there when we were. We brought Gregg some food, but he wasn't able to eat very much. The Hospice was simply marvelous—all of the attendants were wonderfully kind, gentle and caring.

We had lunch one day with Father Timothy Dean, Gregg's friend, whom we had not met previously. He had left the priesthood for a while and worked in advertising with Gregg in Dubai, and he loved Gregg dearly. He was now back in the order and would give the reflection at the expected funeral service, so we talked about what he would say. But the eulogy I will always treasure was his very true comment, "Gregg always made everything fun."

In a few days, Gregg lapsed into a coma. We spent two nights at the Hospice, knowing that he had little time left, and twice postponed our return home. But Elton had postponed his return to Sudbury and felt he had to get back; I couldn't let him go alone. I was sure the people at Inco would have accepted his reason for delaying his visit, but I believe he couldn't bear to see Gregg go, so on the morning of March 2, we packed up and left on an interminable trip and change in Newark. When we finally got home and called the Hospice, we learned that Gregg had died at 6:00 p.m. that day.

CHAPTER 16

LIFE AFTER GREGG

1994

The day after our return to Cleveland following Gregg's death, with very sad and heavy hearts, we went around trying to pick up the pieces and doing what we had to do. Elton took off for Sudbury and I made preparations for a return to London for the memorial service, receiving and returning phone calls, letters and words of comfort. I also had the unpleasant task of replacing the items in my purse that had been stolen while we were eating lunch in the hotel restaurant two days before Gregg died. This was not the tragedy it could have been because my passport and ticket were in our room in the hotel, but it seemed like the last straw. Now, I had to have a new driver's license and credit cards and replace everything else I'd had in the purse. Needless to say I was in no shape to deal with all this.

While we were in London we'd been in daily touch with Daille because Kristin's baby was due about the first of March. Carolina Daille was born on March 10, a bright spot in that sad month. I was able to see her when she was only a few days old because Gregg's memorial service was scheduled for March 19. While Elton flew to London out of Toronto, I flew to D.C. and spent a night and got acquainted with Carolina. Then I flew with Daille and Tom to London where Elton joined us the next day. Tom had arranged with the State Department for a car and an apartment for us, and all I know about its location is that it was very hard to find, far away from everywhere, but somewhere in London.

George had organized the service that was held in the chapel in Brompton Cemetery. In fact, he had even sent out notifications of Gregg's death to everyone listed in Gregg's address book. The day of the service was a lovely, sunny, spring day and the chapel was full of flowers. Daille read from Romans and Gregg's favorite piano music was played. It was a sad and touching service. He was cremated the next day and his ashes placed in Manor Park Cemetery in Forest Gate, London. After the ceremony, Sue Young had a reception. The next day we had an unsatisfactory visit with George, did some shopping and left London. We took the train to Oxford and spent the night with the Clarksons, friends of Tom and Daille whom we had met in Brasilia. He took us to Gatwick the next day and I returned to the U.S. with Tom and Daille, while Elton flew to Sudbury.

We had a memorial service for Gregg at Old Stone the week after we returned from London with a memorable eulogy from Malcolm. We (especially Elton) did not want him to talk about Gregg having been gay or having had AIDS; Malcolm skirted the issue and gave a touching memorial.

We had another special and happier service at Old Stone two months later when Carolina was baptized. Kristin wanted the baptism at Old Stone, since she had been going there whenever she was in Cleveland, as far back as she could remember, and she and Steve had not yet become involved in a church in Arlington where they were living. Ordinarily, non-church members were not baptized there, but because of our membership and the fact that Kris and Steve were church members, Dr. McCuaig agreed to do it. So, on Memorial Day weekend the family, including Steve's family and the godparents, and friends of Kris, attended the service after which we had brunch, catered in the Meridian party room, for family and friends. I should note, for historical purposes, that the day before the church service, the men went to an Indians game in the new stadium, Jacobs Field, which had opened that spring.

We were planning an Alaskan cruise in July with Tom and Daille. I think Elton felt it would be good for me to go somewhere, though I really didn't care much what I did. We had also been talking for some time about having our kitchen redecorated and, since there was a couple living down the hall from us who did this for a living, we talked to them and arranged with them to do our kitchen while we were away. This was a wonderful plan. Not only did they tear out the old dark brown cupboards and put in new white ones, they even took everything out of the cupboards and put a lot of it back. I had to rearrange some things later but I didn't have to be there during the worst of it. A little later, we had a beautiful blue ceramic tile floor installed and blue and white wallpaper, making it a really pretty kitchen. It was a great improvement over the yellow we had lived with since we moved in. I was bothered later when we moved and sold the condo to learn that the new owner hated blue and tore up my pretty floor.

We left Cleveland for Alaska on July 27 and flew to Toronto where we spent the night. The next morning we boarded the cross-Canada train for a 3-day trip across the continent. We were in a first class car with an observation car next to ours. It was a very interesting trip across the wooded, glacier-eroded country of Ontario, the flat farmland of Manitoba and Saskatchewan and through the spectacular mountains of Alberta and British Columbia. We arrived in Vancouver early in the morning, hired a cab and checked our bags in at the dock, and then toured the beautiful city until it was time to board the ship in the afternoon. We met Daille and Tom there, did the requisite milling around and signing in, embarked, had our lifeboat drill and finally set sail just before dinnertime. The ship was very nice—not too big, but big enough—and our cabins were roomy and comfortable. We sailed up the coast and stopped for tours in Juneau, Skagway, Nome and Sitka and debarked at Anchorage.

We enjoyed being with Tom and Daille and we were dinner partners with a nice couple from Jackson, Mississippi. The entertainment and food were good, the service excellent, the tours well organized and the scenery spectacular. From Anchorage, Daille and Tom returned home, while we flew to Fairbanks where we spent two nice days and celebrated our anniversary. We took the bus back to Anchorage through Denali Park—but did not see Mt. McKinley because of low-lying clouds—and flew back to Cleveland. My memory of the entire trip is a little vague; I was still numb from Gregg's death and had constant pain in my two bad knees.

Soon after our return to Cleveland, we flew to Rapid City and drove to Custer for Elton's 55th high school reunion—always a pleasant experience. When we got home, I organized my nice new kitchen, went to the Red Cross blood bank to give blood for use if needed during or after my upcoming knee replacement surgery, and tried to catch up on everything else before checking into St. Luke's for the surgery. I had decided to do both knees at once as all doctors and nurses recommended. Most other people thought it was too hard, partly because the post-surgery therapy is too painful. Because I developed a bladder infection, I had a slow start with the therapy. I was at St.Luke's for nearly a week and was then transferred to Metro General for therapy. These proved to be two hard weeks. Elton was gone most of the time I was there and, although I had many visitors, I didn't have a roommate and spent most of my time alone between therapy sessions, reading a book a day. God knows what I read. I felt very down and sad and I was happy to finally go home, with Daille there for a few days to help me.

I went for therapy twice a week for a month and had a wonderful therapist—a woman, about to retire, who had started in physical therapy when it began after WWII. Largely, I think, because of her treatment, I was walking pretty well by November and without a cane before the end of the year. I had people say, "I have a friend (mother, brother, etc.) who needs to have her/his knees replaced, and I tell them I know this woman at church who had both her knees replaced and is doing wonderfully." I always wanted to be famous, but not because I had my knees replaced! I remain grateful to Dr. Helper for his fine surgery and to that wonderful therapist.

Daille and Tom spent a few days with us over Labor Day and then we concentrated on Elton's work in Sudbury. I tried to get caught up with finances, filing, and all the other work I'd been letting slide—not only for Geist and Geist but also for the League, for ASWA, for the Old Stone Foundation, which Malcolm had reinvigorated with our help, and as chair of Old Stone's Board of Missions.

Malcolm had also proposed some sort of special commemoration of Old Stone's 175th Anniversary in 1995. Marla Heideloff was appointed chair, and Warren Scharf and I assisted. We planned and executed a comprehensive series of programs, beginning in September 1994 and ending with a spectacular dinner and program September 1995. Each month had a different feature, including a variety of musical programs, meals with lectures on various subjects and a Lolley the Trolley tour of Cleveland's oldest churches. There were many glitches, but all in all, Marla made it a successful undertaking.

We were invited to Steve's mother's house in Charleston for Thanksgiving. We took the long route by way of Arlington and the Pettits' and a couple of days on the way visiting Rod and Jane Stone in New Bern, North Carolina. Rod had decided to retire from MSI not long after we left the company, and after spending a year or so looking around the country, they had decided on a development with a golf course in New Bern. It's a charming little town and they had a lovely new house. We enjoyed our visit with them. From there, we went to Carolina Beach, just off the coast of Wilmington, North Carolina for a happy day with Joe and Marnie Jamison. Marnie had been a member of P.E.O. chapter AE and one of my first friends in Cleveland.

The next stop was Charleston where we had some trouble finding Frances' house or David's, mainly because we'd forgotten to bring the map David had kindly sent us. We finally found David, got settled into our hotel and went to Frances' for dinner with all the family. We had Thanksgiving dinner with Frances' brother and his wife and the next day we toured Ft. Sumter and the City of Charleston. We left on Saturday to drive home through West Virginia to Cleveland. Besides seeing Charleston and spending time with Carolina's grandparents, I had one really insignificant reason for enjoying our visit to Charleston. I had realized during one sleepless night in the hospital that I had spent at least one night and eaten at least one meal in every state except South Carolina, Delaware and New Jersey. Now I had subtracted South Carolina from the list, and will probably never remove the other two.

We drove to Arlington for Christmas which was made memorable by its being our first Christmas with a great grandchild who, I must admit, was not too excited about any of it, but was adorable anyway. It was also our first Christmas without knowing that our dear boy was somewhere enjoying his favorite holiday.

1995

I was glad that 1994 was over, and 1995 turned out to be a big year for Cleveland, full of excitement for the city as well as for us personally. We were looking forward to at least one momentous event in 1995—the Scharfs and we had decided at some point to go to Europe and travel on the Orient Express. We spent months planning and arranging for a June 22 departure. As for the city, this was the year the Rock and Roll Hall of Fame opened and attracted interest and visitors from all over the country. ASWA had a national meeting in Cleveland in the fall and we had our "fun trip" to the Rock and Roll Hall—the one and only time I visited it. This was also the first year in several decades that the Indians had a winning baseball team. The whole area had World Series fever when the Indians won the division championship and almost won the Series. We had parades and played *Take Me Out to the Ball Game* on Old Stone's chimes and everyone had great fun. Everyone was terribly disappointed when we failed to win the Series.

These special events were especially important for Cleveland in 1997 because it was its bicentennial year. There were all kinds of observances, including an ongoing series of city-wide women's meetings, discussing a paper written in 1895 about what life was like then in comparison to life in 1995. I did some writing on this and attended some sessions, but I became pretty annoyed generally. Most of the women seemed to think things were now much worse—ignoring such important changes as advances in medicine, women and minority rights, transportation, technology, and much else.

In the midst of all the city celebrations and before we took our trip to Europe, Elton did his usual traveling, and also took a trip to Indonesia to Ujung Paurang, Inco's nickel project, and, of course, made several trips to

Sudbury. When he was in town he worked hard as chair of Old Stone's recently established Capital Asset Program (CAP) that was undertaking a complete renovation and restoration of Old Stone. Money had to be raised and plans made, with a great deal of work on both.

All of Elton's work meant some work for me too. This wasn't easy, because I was still learning Microsoft Windows, which we decided to use when Wang went out of business. As mentioned earlier, we had chosen Wang when we set up shop, and now I had to learn a new operating system—never easy for me. I contacted a computer expert, Robert Abbott, who installed computers for Parma South Presbyterian church and he was most helpful. I also took a couple of classes on Windows. Not only did I have to learn all this new stuff, but we also had to have all new equipment, including a printer. Coincidentally, Rosemary told us she wanted to retire, so we hired a gal named Nadine Browning who had never been a secretary and had no idea about how to set up a letter. She learned, however, and was dependable and willing to spend time every day, even if we were gone.

Kris and Steve brought Carolina to town for a brief visit in February when Kris introduced Carolina to the Meridian swimming pool, which Kris and she loved. I did too, and I swam often. We had another guest when Menno Friesen, an Inco employee who worked closely with Elton, decided to visit us for three days in April. Elton and I drove to Virginia later for a quick visit with the Pettits.

We were home in time to welcome Karin for Easter. She was due to graduate in a couple of months and was very concerned about what she would do. She was also concerned because she was getting involved with another guy but had not yet broken up with Cyril who had almost become a member of the family. He had been at every important event, including Carolina's birth. Despite my not very comforting reassurances that, no matter what decision you make in life, you take a risk, Karin fretted about both of her major problems and worried that she might make the wrong decision and be sorry. She was similarly reassured when I gave her a message from a rather strange woman whom I picked up often for church—she was something of a religious nut. I told her of my granddaughter's concerns and she said, "Tell her not to worry. In 2000 Our Lord is coming." We thought this very amusing, considering that we had the next five years to contend with, even if she proved to be right. Karin still was not reassured and continued to be worried.

We asked Martha and her children for Easter dinner and had a nice day. When Karin left I think she had decided the answer to one thing. Cyril soon seemed to evaporate and Tim Sullivan took his place. When we drove to Milwaukee for her graduation in June, however, we did not meet Tim—he had taken a trip west with some friends. Of course, Daille and Tom were at the graduation, as were Kris, Steve and Carolina. Before our trip to Milwaukee we bought a Cadillac. We had not been able to get as good a deal from Buick as we thought we should have, but I think Elton really wanted a Cadillac. It was a very nice, comfortable car. We stayed at the Pfister in Milwaukee and went there for lunch after the ceremony, then spent most of the day sitting around drinking and trying to help Karin get her bearings.

As it turned out, she got a job in Milwaukee, where Tim was working, and she moved with him into an apartment. He was from a fairly large Chicago Irish family, had graduated from Marquette in 1994 and was working as an IRS agent. He liked the outdoors and enjoyed hiking and backpacking. In fact on one of their early dates, he had taken Karin on a camping trip that she thoroughly enjoyed, and she asked her parents why they had never taken her camping. They had taken her to many countries and major world capitals and some of the most famous museums and historical sites in the world, but that apparently didn't compare with a night in the woods! Elton and I met Tim later in the summer when we drove through Milwaukee on our way back from Iron Mountain, where we had gone in July for the celebration of the Chippewa Club's 100th Anniversary.

Before the trip to Iron Mountain, however, we had our big trip on the Orient Express. One of my jobs was to make hotel reservations for the trip, but we were discouraged with my planning at our very first stop in London. I'd chosen the Elizabeth Hotel that was old and strange and shabby but whose big advantages were that it was not too expensive and it was close to Victoria Station where we were to board the Orient Express. It was not an impressive first night.

Maggie came down with a bug that first night, and Warren, Elton and I spent the next day without her. We had lunch with Veronica, one of Gregg's friends, and then we had a close view of a huge gay rights parade because our taxi could not move through the traffic, and we followed the parade for some time. It made a lasting impression on me, because there were so many people in it; amid the clowns and perverts of all sorts, there were hundreds of serious, determined men and women. One of the men in particular I will always remember. He was middle-aged, decent looking, decently dressed and feeling, I'm sure, that this is who I am, this is what I am, here I am in plain sight and it's okay. Elton and I were still adjusting to Gregg's homosexuality and I don't believe Elton ever really accepted it.

We finally got to the hotel, met Maggie who was feeling better, and we had dinner with Jackie More after cocktails at her house. The next day we packed up to go to the train. We boarded in time to be served an elegant lunch, and then got off at the Channel, took the Hovercraft and got on the Express in France. We spent two days and one night on the train and arrived in Venice about dinnertime on the second day. It was fun and elegant and we enjoyed all of it, although the men found it tough dressing in tuxedos on the train. To avoid carrying them further, we shipped the tuxedos back to Cleveland at great cost.

Our hotel in Venice was the Gabrielli Sandwirth that Elinore Barber, the Scharfs' friend, had recommended and which was better than the Elizabeth. We were there for two days and had a wonderful time. We toured with a young woman who was married to the organist at St. Mark's. Maggie had made contact with her at Elinore's suggestion and she even made it possible for us to go into the choir loft. I find there are two strong opinions about Venice—it's a magical, romantic city, or it's smelly, dirty and run-down. The Scharfs loved it; Elton and I leaned toward the other opinion. But it is certainly beautiful and interesting.

We took a train from Venice to Rome and stayed in a small hotel close to the many sights to be seen in Rome. This hotel was my suggestion—better than the one I made for London. We tried to see everything and visited the most important sights, including the Vatican. The third day we took a taxi to Tivoli and from there to Gregg's favorite place in Italy, according to George—the Ristorante Sibilla. In a shaded portico on a hill it was very lovely and, understandably, could very well be anyone's favorite place in Italy. I felt very comforted to be in a place dear to Gregg.

The next day, Sunday, we took the train to Florence and had attractive rooms in a hotel on the river. We were to leave on Tuesday and I was unhappy that we'd scheduled our trip to include Monday when the museums are closed and we could not get into the Uffizi. But we took a couple of tours, saw the cathedral and loved the whole area. I would like to have stayed longer and always hoped to return, but we were scheduled to take a train the next day through the very beautiful Italian Alps to Salzburg for two days in Mozart's birthplace. The Scharfs were excited about this city and we enjoyed it too. From there we went to Vienna where we finished our journey with two elegant days. They persuaded us to hire a car and driver instead of taking a city tour, so we spent a day in comfort—the rest of the time we were on our own. We attended a service in the very famous cathedral. Unfortunately for the Scharfs, who had hoped to hear some good organ music, the service was a special one for a large group of deaf people. The next day, we did a little shopping, celebrated our anniversary and then returned to Cleveland.

This trip was the first we'd taken with another couple and we enjoyed the many misadventures, the fun and the company. As we should have known, both Maggie and Elton liked to direct things, which led to a few bumpy moments for Elton—and perhaps Maggie. But we had a great time, particularly with the railroad trips.

After our return to Cleveland, our next trip was certainly less spectacular and very different. We went to Arlington for the Labor Day weekend and I stayed with Daille and Tom and took care of Carolina while her parents went on a brief vacation to Holland and Brussels. After one day in Bryce, Elton left for Canada and we went back to Arlington. Carolina was sweet as could be and I loved the chance to be with her. We were back in Arlington for Thanksgiving with the family, and at Christmas, they all came to be with us in Cleveland, including Steve's parents, Frances and David, and Karin, but not Tim.

The year ended with Cleveland having a big New Year's Eve celebration of the Bicentennial in Public Square and we kept Old Stone open with music in the sanctuary and music, cocoa and coffee in fellowship hall. It was very cold, and people enjoyed warming up at Old Stone. The Scharfs and we took rooms at the new Marriott Hotel and spent the night. So ended 1995, and we welcomed 1996 with breakfast together.

CHAPTER 17

TRAVELLING AND TRIPS

1996

Our business activities in 1996 were almost entirely related to work on the computerized maintenance programs for Inco, not only in Sudbury but also in Thompson, Manitoba. Elton suffered from the Parkinson's, but the medication was generally effective, though Dr. Mann changed it from time to time. He was in good enough condition then, and for the next two or three years to travel, to walk to and from our condo to the Winton Place and to fly to and from Inco locations. He rented and drove cars while there.

Meantime, I was still preparing the League newsletter, keeping books for the Ed Fund and with Old Stone. I also spent a lot of time on COOP for the Federation of Community Planning which I was serving as chair. This should have been an easy position, except when the Executive Director retired. The Federation muddled along for a while with different leaders and finally retained Eric Fingerhut who had lost his Congressional seat and needed a job. I guess he was a good legislator, but an ineffective manager, and he wanted to get rid of COOP and other committees. I talked to a lot of people and had many meetings, but to no avail, and I was out of a job before very long. A couple of years later COOP was reborn and I was on the board for a year or two before I decided to retire for good in 1999.

This was an election year and many of our family and friends were really fed up with "Wafflin' Willie" Clinton and his annoying wife who had put together a humongous universal medical plan which, luckily, was not approved by Congress. Bob Dole, however, who opposed the still popular

Clinton, was a rather unprepossessing candidate and we were to have four more years of Willie.

Our personal lives went on about as usual until March when Elton turned 75. I planned a surprise birthday dinner party for him and used the Club at the Marriott, thanks to Malcolm McCuaig. The party surprised me, too, because it was a real surprise for him. Daille, Tom, Kris, Steve and Carolina arrived and stayed downtown (and visited the Rock and Roll Hall), Karin and Tim came from Milwaukee and Erik Aikia flew in from Sudbury. They all walked in together and really overwhelmed Elton. The next day, we celebrated Carolina's second birthday at our house. We had a really happy and lovely weekend.

In March, we drove to Milwaukee to visit Karin and Tim. I asked them ahead of time if I could bring anything. They said maybe I could bring some sheets and bedding which I did, fortunately. As it turned out, they slept on the hide-a-bed and gave us the bed, but they had no pillows, sheets or blankets to put on it. They showed us a good time and we had a lunch date with Marty and Jan Morris who drove down from Appleton, and dinner at a German restaurant. We learned a little more about Tim, including the fact that he was a good housekeeper.

It is always interesting to visit newlyweds and discover how much I have learned over my lifetime. This visit was no exception. They had an old refrigerator with the freezer section chock full of ice because they had never heard of defrosting a refrigerator (probably no one born after 1970 has). Their plants were dying because Karin carefully watered each of them with only a few drops of water. They were basically happy in their old, but nice, apartment and with their jobs—Tim was an IRS auditor and Karin worked for a company that provided the courts with data on individuals charged with crimes.

We left for Cleveland on April 1, April Fool's Day, a dreary, cloudy day without snow. At a stop close to Cleveland, I heard, with amazement, that snow had made the driving very ugly in Cleveland. We found that they had five inches overnight, just in Cuyahoga County. It caused the cancellation of the scheduled baseball opener, leading to a lot of jokes about the April Fool snow.

Later in April, Erik Aikia's girl friend invited us to a surprise birthday party in Sudbury for Erik. We flew to Sudbury, but her plans had omitted details about where or when the party would be; she left no message for us, so we missed the party. Nevertheless, we had a pleasant, if cold and dreary week in the apartment set aside by Cassio's for Elton's use while he was there.

We had decided to sell our Buick to Karin and she came to Cleveland in May to pick it up. Then we drove to Daille's for Memorial Day weekend. It was an unpleasant weekend, weatherwise, but we had a picnic at Rock Park, with Kris (again expecting in October), and Steve and Carolina. At least the visit was more pleasant than the weather. After Karin took our Buick, we concluded that we still would need two cars, so we got a three-year lease on a small GEO.

In July we took another trip with the Scharfs. After our trip to Europe, we had agreed that we would make our next tour together an auto trip west. Elton wanted to show them the real west, whatever that was! They would be driving to Denver for a meeting and would then meet us in Grand Junction, where we would visit Mona and Dale, and we would drive on from there. After the disagreements Elton and Maggie had in Europe, Elton was determined to have the schedule down to hours and minutes and spent considerable time on it, so for him, at least, things worked out better. We flew to Salt Lake at the end of July and spent a couple of days with the Rao's, then to Grand Junction where we rented a car. Elton and I drove to Telluride to see the mountains, spent a night and then drove back to the Johnsons to await the arrival of the Scharfs.

In the Scharf's car, our trip was aimed primarily at Yellowstone, but we stopped at Dinosaur Park in Colorado, then Jackson Hole, where we spent two nights and enjoyed a rodeo. We toured Yellowstone for two days and saw almost everything, including many bears, elk, moose and deer. I enjoyed seeing it all again, but I was upset by the forests, which had experienced a mammoth fire a few years before and the burnt trees had been left standing, acres and acres of them. When Dad was a forester, every effort was made to extinguish every forest fire, however small, and for years he had spent many days and weeks working with fire crews. Then, in the seventies, the practice of letting fires burn had developed from the foolish idea that this made forests healthier. This upset me throughout our tour of the Park, despite the beautiful scenery.

From Yellowstone, we went north and west to Montana and took the magnificent Red Lodge Road over the top of the mountains. We spent one night in Montana, then drove east through Montana and Wyoming to Devils Tower, and on to Rapid City. We had arranged for two nights at a P.E.O. bed and breakfast, which turned out to be run by a woman whose husband had an advanced case of Parkinson's, with considerable trembling and exaggerated motion. This was a real downer for Elton and for all of us, but the accommodations were fine and we had a chance to tour the Hills, with a brief stop in Custer to see the Chards.

Going east from Rapid, we saw a little of the Badlands, stopped, of course, at Wall Drug, and then drove north where we turned east to head across North Dakota and into Minnesota and Michigan, spending nights at Bismarck, Bemidji and Duluth, after a side trip to Hibbing, before arriving in Iron Mountain. We spent some time with the Millers and other friends at the lake, and had brunch with the Millers. From there, we went to St. Ignace and across the bridge and took a ferry to Mackinac Island. We walked around for a few hours, but did not stay the night; we went back to the shore and headed home the next day. Whether we saw the real west is questionable, but we had a good time, saw some beautiful scenery and interesting sites, and got home willing to try another trip another year.

For several years, Jim and Jean Cooke had entertained us, the Scharfs, the McCuaigs and others on Labor Day and we were planning our Monday dinner there when, on Saturday, I got an urgent call from Kris. She had been having some problems with her pregnancy and was supposed to have bed rest, but when she went in on Friday, they put her right into the hospital. On Saturday morning, they told her that both her vital signs and those of the baby were such that they would probably have to take the baby that day. Tom and Daille were in Chicago for the weekend, but Kris knew only that they were at a Holiday Inn and she couldn't locate them. She was panicky, of course, and I told her I would be there as soon as I could. I was able to get a plane within the hour to either National or Baltimore, costing three times as much to fly to National, so I got a flight to Baltimore, rented a car and was at the hospital before noon. Kris was really happy to see me and I was glad I had been able to come. Steve was taking care of Carolina, and his mother was to arrive the next day. Of course, he couldn't stay at the hospital.

I spent the afternoon and evening with Kris and very late Saturday night the doctor decided they should not wait any longer. Frances had arrived and stayed with Carolina, so Steve was able to come to the hospital and they took Kris into delivery. She had a Caesarean and tiny Aaron Kirkwood was born on August 31. He had to be in prenatal care, since he was more than two months premature and he was there for two months. He did not do as well as expected, and for a couple of weeks we were very concerned about him. They finally found that he had some sort of fungus in his blood, which they were able to treat by injecting medication into his poor little head. He finally began to grow and develop. Kris was in the hospital for a few days before she was released and I went home the next day.

In mid-October I was back in Virginia to help Steve and Kris move. They had leased a townhouse in Centreville and had planned to move after

Aaron was born. They hadn't planned on his early arrival and his essential prenatal care. I told them I would help and Frances did too, but I seemed to be doing most of it—at least it seemed that way to me. Frances kept Carolina entertained, Steve ran errands, and I packed what I could. I ended up with the job of draining the water bed—a job I would never elect to do again. The movers came late in the afternoon and I took Carolina back to Daille and Tom; Steve took the cat and dog to the house, and Frances and Kris stayed with the movers who didn't get to the house until nearly nine. By then, Carolina was upset, wondering where her mommy was and everyone was worn out.

Frances and I spent the night with Daille and Tom and went out the next morning and worked hard all day. We both left about supper time and I took a "one-hour" flight to Cleveland. It was late, and we had a change in planes, then we stopped in Newark where we had another delay and another change. I came close to spending a night in New Jersey, but finally arrived home about 1:00 a.m. What a day!

My problem with flights continued on our next one, a trip to London. Elton and I had long planned this visit, using frequent flyer miles for a free, first class trip. I met him in Toronto and, because of airline problems including a change of planes and a very long delay, we spent the evening in the lounge and didn't take off until after midnight. We arrived in London late in the morning. But, we traveled first class which, presumably, made up for all the delays and changes.

We stayed in a suite in the very plush Intercontinental Hotel, near Hyde Park, and spent the week visiting Gregg's friends and sightseeing. We also managed to do a little shopping at Harrods. On a sad but memorable day, we visited the cemetery where Gregg's ashes were buried. It is far enough from London that we could not be there in time for his service. We found no marker, but the cemetery administration had a record of the location. We were glad we had seen this lovely cemetery and the hydrangea bush he had asked to be planted, and we arranged for a marker to be placed on his grave.

On one day, we caught an early train to York and spent the day touring this fascinating and historical city. Back in London, we went to a play in the restored Shakespeare Theatre on the south side of the Thames. We had lunch at Veronica's place and dinner with Sue Young, her mother, her daughter, Saskia, and her fiancé. Between times, we saw two or three small museums, new to us, and enjoyed sightseeing in central London. Having spent a whole week together, we hated to leave at the end of the week to return to Cleveland.

We spent both Thanksgiving and Christmas with Daille and Tom in Arlington and visited Kris, Steve and kids in Centreville. Aaron was home but on a monitor and still very, very tiny and fragile. Carolina was thrilled with this baby at first but he required a lot of care and she soon asked her mother if they could take him back to the hospital. It wasn't long, however, before she became attentive and protective. During Thanksgiving weekend, he was baptized at the Lutheran church in Arlington where Daille, Tom and Kris were now members.

Frances and David were in Virginia for their grandson's baptism and Tom, Elton and I took David to D.C. to see the new Korean War memorial. He was anxious to see it because he served in Korea. The monument was impressive, as was the parking ticket I got. Since we were driving a car we had rented in Baltimore with a Pennsylvania license, and I lived in Ohio, I ignored the ticket until they caught up with me six months later and I still had to pay $100.

This was the last time we saw David, by the way—he had suffered from cancer of the throat and mouth for some time and died the next March. He was a nice guy and dearly loved his only child and his family. He was aware, I think, that he and Frances had not raised Steve as they should and, I think for this reason, he spent his retirement days working on his investments so that he could leave Steve well provided for—which he did. While no one in the family knew just how much he left to Steve, it was obviously a substantial amount. Although Kris continued to work, they had money for nice cars and a lovely home a little later on, and they apparently had guaranteed funds for the childrens' education, which Steve was determined they would have, even if he had chosen otherwise himself.

We spent Christmas with Daille, Tom and Karin, and Tom's brother, John, and his wife, Betty. Their daughter Ann also arrived for a few days. John and Betty were difficult guests. Betty was always hard for us to get along with—a deeply committed, outspoken Catholic and a strong environmentalist. Elton and I were not made happier by our arrival back in Cleveland on Sunday when we had to attend a called congregational meeting at Old Stone at which Malcolm announced that he was resigning to take a church in a Philadelphia suburb. We hated to see him go because we felt he was a wonderful minister, and thought of him as a close friend. We felt so close to him, in fact, we were a little hurt that he hadn't given us even a hint of his decision to leave.

1997

The old year ended with a rather subdued New Year's Eve celebration with the Scharfs at a Cleveland Heights restaurant, and 1997 began with two unhappy tasks. One was the dreary process of saying farewell to Malcolm and getting an interim pastor, while the church began the requisite mission study for proceeding with a pastoral search. The other unhappy task—for me—was helping the League recover from a fire in the building where its office was located. It had not burned the League office but left everything smoke-damaged. East Ohio Gas offered the LWV temporary quarters. Until the office was cleaned and everything restored or replaced, I spent a lot of time doing my usual job with difficulty and helping in the unpleasant task of sorting through the material in the smoky file cabinets.

Malcolm's resignation led to a lot of work for the church and its members throughout the year. There was much anger mixed with sorrow in the congregation over Malcolm's leaving, but the Session realized we had to have a farewell party for him. Though none of us wanted anything to do with it, we reluctantly planned the party and attended it. Somehow a spirit of love and good will settled on us as we proceeded with the activities and it turned out to be a wonderful gathering. Nevertheless, we were disheartened when Malcolm preached his last sermon and he and Marion left.

The situation was particularly difficult because we were in the middle of the restoration project, initiated by Malcolm, and trying to raise the money needed to complete it. It was planned to return the church to the way it had been when it burned in 1857 which meant, along with a great deal of interior work, cleaning the surface stone as well as replacing the original steeple. There were objections to cleaning the church, since it had been black for so long many believed that that was the way it was supposed to be. However, the stone was whitish. The black soot had settled into the stone and moisture had caused expansion and damage to the stone, so it was essential that it be cleaned.

The other questionable proposed restoration was the steeple which was wanted, but certainly wasn't as necessary as the cleaning. It was to cost nearly half a million dollars. Many felt this would be an extravagant waste of money, so we had not gotten very far with the fund-raising. On the night of Malcolm's farewell party, I heard Alex Meakin telling someone about a woman he knew at his former church. He thought she might be interested in paying for the steeple. Alex introduced Elton to the woman and she ultimately donated the whole amount anonymously.

A step that needed to be taken immediately was the appointment of an Interim Search Committee. I was appointed to this committee and Jim Cooke and I were made co-chairs of the Mission Study. The Search Committee met soon and often and we were diligently looking through resumes when someone suggested a retired pastor of the Church of Christ, formerly in

Avon Lake, who might be willing to take the job as interim. We liked him, got the Presbytery's permission and the church's approval and Dick Bucey was in place by the end of March. He was very good and was a great help in a difficult time. June Begany had to take over everything and was a godsend, but we were happy that we had found an interim so quickly.

The mission study we undertook was a complicated procedure using prepared material outlining all necessary steps and involving a comprehensive survey of the congregation, the church and the community. There were not only special committees but also study groups looking at the church and its future. In October we had an overnight retreat at a center east of Cleveland and agreed on a mission. A pastoral search committee was elected the next month.

In the spring, Elton had a pleasant surprise when he heard from South Dakota School of Mines that he had been named one of SDSM's 100 most important graduates. He was also invited to the 1997 commencement to receive an award as one of the 50-year graduates. Of course we went to Rapid in May for this affair, which was very nice and he enjoyed seeing two or three of his fellow graduates in metallurgy. We spent several days in Rapid looking up the few people we knew there, looking around the town and, of course, climbing Dinosaur Hill. The day after the ceremony we drove to Custer and spent two days with the Chards. Elton was interested in planning a 60th CHS reunion in 1999. We visited the few 60 year graduates still around Custer; all assured us they would come to a reunion if they were still alive.

When we were back in Cleveland, Elton spent a lot of time in Sudbury and I was spending a lot of time on League business, including putting the Ed Fund's books into a new computer program, QuickBooks. I hate learning new computer programs, and this was about the fourth bookkeeping program I'd attempted. I had nothing but trouble with it and spent many long hours that summer swearing at the computer. I finally got it under control, but when I resigned as treasurer, several years later, I gladly gave up QuickBooks.

Not having enough aggravation with the computer, I decided that this was the time to clear out our storage lockers. We'd rented one when we moved out of MSI, put our stuff in it and after taking out what we needed for G&G, we added items regularly. By that time, I had no idea what was in storage and I was tired of paying $40 a month, so I was determined to go through it and give it up. I also had to sort through the storage at the Meridian to find room for the things we wanted to keep. Eventually, I got everything sorted and organized, and as it turned out later, it was the smart thing to have done.

While I was battling with the computer and cleaning out our belongings, Elton was having some serious urinary problems. In July, he had to go into the hospital to have his urethra reamed out. He was in the hospital for two nights and was released on the third day. He had a very difficult time getting his system back in working order. He spent a few uncomfortable weeks, because I think he was convinced he would never operate properly again, but, of course, he did.

While Elton was recuperating, I flew to New Orleans on a very quick trip, with less than twenty-four hours there, to see a special exhibition at the New Orleans Museum of Art. George Roland had been working there for some time and he and the museum were presenting an exhibition of the art works he and Gregg had collected. I learned in New Orleans that Elton and Daille had had a serious falling out with George in London over Gregg's possessions, most of which became George's, and neither Elton nor Daille would have anything to do with him thereafter and they never told me about this. I felt that if Gregg had not been gay and George had been a woman, they would not have been so angry. For a while, I was very angry myself with them—not with George. Anyway I had a nice, if short, visit with George and another of Gregg's dear friends, and enjoyed my brief visit at the Museum.

We drove to Washington for Tom's August 14 birthday and to visit Kris and her family. Soon after returning to Cleveland, we drove to Colorado to celebrate the Roesers' 50th wedding anniversary. Mona and Dale and Jack and Betty had been married a week apart, and Sally had a party for Jack and Betty, but the Johnsons didn't invite anyone to celebrate with them. Dale was always somewhat anti-social and didn't believe in gift exchange or entertaining, so, true to form, he and Mona had no party but instead went to Hawaii with their girls and their husbands. After we arrived in Colorado for Jack and Betty's party we spent several days visiting friends, Walt Nelson and his two lovely children in Denver and Golden, and a few days in the Springs.

The party was small, with about 30 guests, most of them relatives, and neither Jack nor Betty was very sociable or festive. We were not asked to the Roeser's home, but Carola had a party on Sunday. It was nice to see the kids and my cousin, Mary Jane, which was great. Mary Jane had always been especially fond of Jack, and he respected and admired her, so he was always on his best behavior when she was around. But after she left, the night before our departure, we took Betty, Jack and the four kids to dinner, and Jack, who always had extremely conservative views, went out of his way to start an argument with me about homosexuality. This left me very angry, disturbed and guilty about feeling this way. Unfortunately, this was the last time I saw him.

Some time that summer, Tim and Karin moved to Boston; Daille and Tom helped them pack and they spent the night with us on their way to Boston. Karin had decided she wanted to go to law school and, after much searching and many applications and tests, she was accepted at Suffolk Law. This was much harder for Tim than for Karin. Except for going away to school in Milwaukee, he had always been close to Chicago and had no coping skills for being in a new place. Of course, Karin did, and she got into the swing of law school right away. Tim, however, had a hard time finding a job and was not very happy for a long time.

The biggest international event in September 1997 was the death of Princess Diana of England. We could not believe the fuss made over this, but her death seemed to be the most important event of the year, at least the way the media played it. And rather to our astonishment, and judging from what we heard and saw, many Americans treated this as the tragedy of the century.

It certainly didn't compare with Diana's death, but I had an important occasion in my life in October when I turned 75. With Daille's help, Elton planned a surprise party for me—a catered dinner at the Meridian. I was really surprised. Expecting to go out to dinner with the Scharfs, I walked into the lobby and saw Daille and the little kids. It was a great party and I was very pleased.

The really important trip of this year and, in fact, of our lives, was the trip Elton and I had planned for November to Antarctica. We spent a lot of time in the midst of our usual tasks, planning and shopping for this trip. I was a little concerned about taking the trip in my poor physical condition and, when I met Tammy Lyons, the personal trainer of Mary Lou Giffels (one of our neighbors and a P.E.O. sister), I thought she might be able to help me and perhaps Elton too. We asked Dr. Mann about Elton hiring a trainer and he pooh-poohed the idea, which was fine with Elton since he didn't want to do it anyway. This annoyed me and I still feel he would have benefited from working with her. Nevertheless, I decided to hire her that fall and she became my trainer, as well as my friend, and she did improve my physical condition.

Elton had wanted to go to Antarctica for some time—since he had visited his sixth continent and thought he should go to all seven. Tom was also anxious to go, for the same reason, so they had talked about going together. Although I was not too interested—there being no museums, shops, or people and lots of animals and birds about which I am not too enthusiastic—we both felt that Elton should make the trip while he was still able. However, because

Tom couldn't go at this time, I decided to accompany Elton, knowing the Parkinson's would eventually catch up with him.

We chose a trip sponsored by Elderhostel because their schedule and costs sounded better than any of the other tours we had researched, and we were very happy we did because the tour was exceptionally well managed. We had a lot of information ahead of time, including a list of the clothing and other things we should pack. We were told to bring layers of clothing, not bulky wool sweaters. We were also told we needed waterproof jackets and knee-high waterproof boots. The boots turned out to be essential but were hard to find, at least inexpensive ones, and we didn't want to spend much because we knew we would never need them again. We finally found them at the Army and Navy store. At the end of the tour we left them on the ship so we wouldn't have to carry them home.

The official trip began with a flight out of Miami on the Saturday after Thanksgiving, so we drove to D.C. and spent the holiday with the kids, including a boat trip up the Potomac on Friday. On Sunday, we flew to Miami to catch the plane, with most of the tour group, to Buenos Aires. We were scheduled to fly from there to Ushuaia at the southern tip of Argentina, but when we reached Buenos Aires we were told that the ship we were to board in Ushuaia was in the Port of Buenos Aires, having pulled in there for necessary and now-completed repairs. The only way to get to Antarctica on this trip was by ship from Buenos Aires and, weather permitting, we would get there. Bad weather was always possible, and even likely, in that part of the world; if it were to become too bad, we would not reach our destination. We really had no choice, but hoped we'd reach our goal and we all voted "in favor." We embarked late in the afternoon and went to sea.

We were on the ship from December 1 to 11, and despite my reluctance to go, I had a wonderful time. The ship itself was a Russian research boat, with a Russian crew and there were about six Canadians who worked for Elderhostel. In some ways it was a more interesting trip because we spent about three days more on shipboard than expected. There were about fifty people on the cruise, including many interesting and likeable folks. Every morning and afternoon we heard lectures on biology, geography, history and politics of the continent and we even had a session or two on the Russian language. Between lectures and socializing, we read. By virtue of the ship's library of books left behind by passengers, I became reacquainted with my favorite historian, Paul Johnson. I was fascinated by the Port of Buenos Aires with its many hundreds of cargo carriers, the days on the ocean without land in sight, the birds, and the lectures.

On about the third day at sea, we saw our first iceberg, and a day or so later, we saw a pod of fin whales. How exciting! On December 7, we arrived at Moon Island and went ashore. This was not an easy process; we had to don our waterproof clothes and life jackets, pile into zodiac boats and land as near shore as we could—which explained the need for the knee-high boots. We enjoyed seeing the icebergs up close on our way to shore and hundreds of penguins on the island. The next day we arrived at Deception Island with fine weather—cold, but sunny and clear. With the weather holding we sailed the next day to Paradise Bay on the Antarctic Peninsula. We took the zodiacs to shore, waded through four or five feet of snow and spent an hour or two on the continent itself. Hallelujah! We made it!

Because of the ship's scheduling, we had to start back that same night and we sailed to Ushuaia where we bussed through the city to the airport and caught a plane to Buenos Aires. Our stay there was much longer than we anticipated because of plane problems. After spending the night in the hotel we had to check out of our rooms at 10:00 a.m., with no flight to take until 1:00 a.m. the next morning. The crew arranged tours and meals but it was a long wait in a hotel lobby. We took off eventually and got back to Miami and Washington, both of us feeling we had had the experience of a lifetime. I have never regretted taking this most interesting trip of my life.

Daille met us at the airport and we spent a day with them and then drove back to Cleveland, with only a few days left to get ready for Christmas. Kris and family arrived first and helped me set up the tree and get everything ready for celebrating with Daille, Tom and Karin, when they arrived. We had a happy day and a good family get-together and approached the end of 1997 looking forward, as always, to another interesting year in 1998.

1998

I spent most of the first few months of '98 in meetings. I had become more active in P.E.O. I was on Session and chaired the Spiritual Life Committee that took the place of the old Worship Committee. I was on the Mission Council for the Presbytery, which involved monthly meetings, each at a different church. I also continued to be treasurer for the County LWV, as I had been since 1993 and was still doing some things for ASWA. Elton and I gave several small dinner parties—something we had always done when we were in town. We were also in our second or third season attending The Cleveland Orchestra concerts. We enjoyed these, Elton especially, since I am not a great music lover, and really liked dining in their lovely restaurant before the concerts.

We spent Easter in Arlington in 1998 with Tim and Karin. It was a beautiful weekend and we had a great time. I helped Kris and the kids dye Easter eggs, inadequately, because Kris had nothing but the eggs and dye and none of the aids like vinegar, but the job was fun anyway. We took a trip south with Daille and Tom on Saturday and thoroughly enjoyed the lovely weather, the beautiful dogwoods which were out in full bloom and a brief tour of Quantico.

In June, Menno Friesen visited us again for a few days. Just after he left, we attended one of the strangest graduation ceremonies ever when Andrea Knight, my goddaughter, graduated from Cleveland Heights High. The ceremony was held in the Music Hall with about 300 graduates. The graduates and the audience were absolutely out of control. They waved and yelled at each other, graduate to graduate, graduate to guest and guest to guest, as they were ambling in (certainly not marching in), after they were seated and throughout the ceremony. We have never seen anything like it. They managed to get diplomas handed out, but we were dubious as to whether they would ever get the job done. The class was mixed, probably half black, the rest Hispanic, oriental and white. The spectacle was so disturbing that the next year when Scott Knight, Andrea's younger brother, graduated, he wouldn't go to the ceremony.

By this time, Karin and Tim had been living in Boston for nearly a year and we felt it was time for us to drive to Boston to see them and to celebrate Karin's birthday with her. We spent a night en route at an inn in a little town in New York that the Scharfs had recommended as a "charming little hotel." Obviously, it had been a long time since they'd been there. In Boston we checked into a good hotel downtown for one night, met the kids and went to a restaurant that Karin said was one of the best in Boston. We found nothing about it really outstanding, except the cost, but it was a lovely place, a good meal and we enjoyed the evening. The next day we picked them up and began a long, slow drive to Cape Cod—the traffic was horrendous. During that day and the next, we saw the Cape Cod peninsula that Elton and I thought was highly overrated. We always find the ocean a poor substitute for mountains, so our judgment can't be considered impartial. We got back to Boston and stayed in a hotel close to Karin and Tim, then left the next morning for Philadelphia to visit the McCuaigs in Abington, near Philadelphia.

The trip to Philly was quite nice, once we got through Connecticut. We by-passed New York City and saw some beautiful Hudson River country. We got to the McCuaigs in the afternoon and spent only one night with them and left about 24 hours later. We had dinner, visited Malcolm's new church and town and had a very good visit. Malcolm was thrilled with the church but Marion wasn't too happy with the town or her house. We drove all the way home, non-stop—that is, I drove—and it was a very hard drive, with rain in spurts between spells of bright sunshine. Until the sun finally set, the drive west was miserable.

The summer of 1998 was hot and dry and this was the summer the Meridian chose to tear up the entire driveway and parking lot and replace the surface. The process was noisy and dusty and made life distinctly unpleasant. It was a relief to get away from it by taking a trip to D.C. for the July 4 celebration. We had perfect Fourth weather and saw a wonderful parade and the fireworks in the evening from one of the Potomac bridges with the Washington Monument as a backdrop.

In August, we drove north to visit the Upper Peninsula once more. We drove all the way to Eagle Harbor, at the northernmost tip of the state, to visit John and Nancy Wakeman, after spending one night in St. Ignace. The Wakemans were happy to see us and to provide us with a room and a couple of meals.

On the way south from Eagle Harbor, we stopped to visit Bob Sundquist at his lake home. Elton had worked closely with Bob, a Bechtel employee, in San Francisco in 1954 and had been responsible for getting him together with his wife who had died in about 1972. We loved Bob and were devastated when Inga-Britt died. It was the last time we saw him. He died near the end of 2000. We spent a couple of hours with him and covered a lot of conversational ground while he prepared lunch for us. The whole U.P. was beautiful and we loved being back in that country and driving south to Iron Mountain.

We spent a couple of nights with Buck and Jane Miller and then drove to Appleton to visit Marty and Jan Morris. We knew she was in the hospital but we had no idea how ill she was. She had had surgery for cancer earlier in the summer and some implement was left in the incision that caused serious problems and they had to operate again. We visited her in the evening and then went back in the morning to find her in such serious condition they had called her mother to come, and Marty was near collapse. We had to leave them but were very concerned all the way home as we drove through blistering weather to the still unfinished driveway. Jan did recover in a short time, but the cancer was never cured.

Whenever he was in Cleveland, Elton worked diligently on the restoration project at the church and work was proceeding on the sanctuary. The floor was very bad and something had to be done with it. The Scharfs were very anxious to get rid of the carpet and replace the floor with a hard surface, preferably wood, to enhance the acoustics. They had considerable support from the musicians in the congregation, but opposition from the CAP Committee, headed by Elton. It would have involved enormous expense and the sanctuary would have to be closed for at least a year. Others and I opposed it because we objected to people walking on a noisy floor. This disagreement was especially difficult for us because of our friendship with the Scharfs.

When we left at the end of September on a trip north to Manitoba, the argument continued, hot and heavy, and became one of the two major issues I fretted about for weeks. The other one was a letter I had received from Jack asking for our help with Carola. He wanted us to buy her house so she could go on living there. He had never asked me for anything, but we could not imagine buying a run-down house in Colorado Springs, and I knew I would have to write and tell him no. Both of these issues were settled in a few weeks. I wrote to Jack and he accepted it without argument. The Scharfs eventually gave up their quest for a wooden floor, but I did a lot of worrying about both issues. Apparently, Elton didn't fret too much.

Elton's work for Inco at this time was primarily at their property in Thompson, Manitoba. Thompson is about halfway between Winnipeg and Churchill, the famous winter home for the polar bears in Hudson Bay, and Elton had suggested that I should go to Thompson with him and we would take the train to Churchill to see the polar bears. We spent several days in Thompson and then took the train to Churchill. I enjoyed Thompson; the wives of several of the people with whom Elton worked at Inco took me on tours and invited us to lunches and dinners. We enjoyed the train trip, too. The distance to Churchill is about 200 miles, but it took us nearly 24 hours to get there because we stopped so frequently. We had dinner and a sleeping car, but realized that berths were a mistake. As both of us had to go to the restroom during the night, we were obliged to get dressed to do so. On the return to Thompson, we got first class seats and slept dressed and sitting up.

In Churchill, we rented a room and scheduled a trip through the tundra to see the bears. We drove miles and actually saw only two. Arriving at the end of September turned out to be too early for the polar bears. But the whole trip was interesting. One of my more memorable encounters was on the train when a young man asked me if I knitted. He had bought yarn and needles and wanted someone to show him how to use them. I showed him how to cast on and how to knit and he was knitting along quite well when we arrived in Churchill where he departed for his job. I had not shown him how to cast off and I've had visions since of his knitting on and on, making the longest scarf in history.

When we got back to Thompson we stayed a day and then returned to Cleveland, rather reluctantly on my part, since I was scheduled to have an operation. I had a bad hernia, mainly because my Caesareans and hysterectomy had left me with no abdominal muscle strength, and my doctor had x-rays taken which showed that I also had some gall stones. When I called to check on the tests, the doctor's office girl told me I had to have the gall bladder out, but she said nothing about the hernia, and I was told the doctor didn't talk to patients on the phone so I would have to come in to see her. This made me angry, since I felt it was her job to communicate with me. When I got there and said as much to her, she yelled back at me and we had an astonishing screaming argument. Needless to say, I saw no more of her, but I did go to the surgeon who removed the gall bladder and repaired the hernia. In the process, however, no supporting screen was used for the hernia because doing the surgeries at the same time makes infection too likely. The upshot was that, eventually, I had to have two more hernia surgeries.

I was in Lakewood Hospital overnight and then home. Daille arrived and spent five days with me while I was recovering. After she left, I had a couple of weeks to get back on my feet before Kristin arrived with her two kids for a few days. This was a little tiring for me, but not too bad until we took them out to the airport on Sunday to fly home. She was on stand-by—not wise on a Sunday. We moved from check-out to check-out trying to find a flight with three seats. She finally located a flight for about 9:00 p.m. We went home for an hour to have supper before heading back to the airport and seeing them off. The kids were a joy, staying cheerful despite their long hiatus at the airport. Aaron was particularly fun—playing the part of a serious traveler. So the afternoon was interesting, but I was exhausted by the time they left and we got home. Alone again, we prepared for the holidays and also prepared to receive our new minister who had finally been selected. We had the Beganys for Thanksgiving dinner, and we drove to Arlington for Christmas. Tim and Karin drove down from Boston—much closer than Milwaukee. We all had a joyous Christmas. And at the end of 1998 we were beginning to look forward to a new century and the last year of the 20th century hoping, as always, for a great future for all of us.

CHAPTER 18

TURN OF THE CENTURY

1999

One of the major concerns of 1999 was the way it would end and the next year would begin. Perhaps this is true of every last-year-of-the-century. There was worry and fear worldwide that there would be widespread computer failures, disrupting everything; many believed the end of the world and/or the second coming of Jesus would take place. One woman I met at a cocktail party held by Dick and Mary Cass, just after January first, already had her basement full of bottles of water, kerosene stoves, lamps, and other necessities for use when everything failed on December 31, 1999. My amusement at this idea annoyed her and she broke off our conversation when I told her I thought there would be no problems. And I was right. I wonder what she did with all that stuff.

Regardless of how it would end, this turned out to be one of the most exciting and pleasant years experienced in our married lives. In a way, it seemed that several things wound up in 1999. On the national scene, for one, President Clinton was acquitted after his impeachment in 1998 for lying about sex with Monica Lewinsky. This affair and his actions after the accusations were made left a bad taste in the mouths of many and confirmed our opinion about his lack of character. We looked forward more than ever to the election of a new president in 2000.

Our personal lives were changing, as always. Although Elton continued consulting for Inco into 2000, our work with the company was drawing to a close, and his ability to continue working was becoming questionable. Old Stone also changed considerably with the restoration of the church, completed in 1999, including the exciting and eventful raising of the steeple. And the music program we had known since we joined Old Stone came to an end with the retirement of Maggie Scharf as organist and Warren as music director.

Work on the interior of the church was in full swing at the beginning of the year, and for six months, we held our Sunday services in the fellowship hall, the new minister, Dr. Kornell, sitting on a stool and the congregation sitting at tables. This was nice in some ways; the peace exchange became more intimate and everyone was more sociable. Nevertheless, most of us were happy to return to the sanctuary when the work was completed. We couldn't have an Easter service in the hall, of course, so we had it in the Grand Ballroom of the Renaissance Hotel on Public Square. We entertained Alex Meakin and his son for Easter dinner after the service. The retired pastor of Parma South church, Alex had become quite active in Old Stone, especially in the restoration project and, as mentioned earlier, he was indirectly responsible for the steeple. He and Elton had become quite friendly, and we were sad to see him suffering with cancer.

We were very proud of the steeple, raised in May, especially since Elton was in charge of the project. There had been a steeple on the original church which collapsed when the church burned in 1857, and was never replaced. When plans were made for the restoration, a steeple was included, but there were vehement objections to the cost of $500,000 with no known source for that amount of money. Alex had told Elton about a woman who had quite a lot of money, and wanted to make a contribution to some lasting memorial. She contributed, anonymously, the entire cost of the steeple. Elton and I had become acquainted with her and we then became good friends. At that time, she was 98 (but admitted to being only 94), and was a childless widow. The members of her family were Clevelanders, ordinary, frugal, working people, and there were only two or three children born to the family of six or seven. As her brothers and sisters died she had inherited money and become much wealthier than she had ever expected to be. As of 2005, she was still living alone in an apartment, taking care of herself, and bright as could be. We very much enjoyed our lasting relationship with her. And we greatly appreciated her gift which made Old Stone's steeple possible. A sad note to this project was the death from prostate cancer of Alex, her good friend, as well as ours by now. He passed away only a month or so after the steeple went up.

The steeple itself was manufactured by a Wisconsin specialty company which brought it to Cleveland in parts, reassembled it on the sidewalk in front of the church, and then raised it in three parts with giant cranes. There were crowds of onlookers, and there was much publicity. What an exciting moment it was when the cross was placed on top! We threw a party at the Meridian for the participants in the project and for our Virginia kids. I called it an Erection Party, but sent out invitations in more genteel language. The McCuaigs were not in Cleveland for the party, but they came to visit on Memorial Day to see the results of the restoration he had initiated. They stayed with us and we had a good visit—unfortunately, the last we were to have with Malcolm.

Earlier in the year, Elton and I had attended another party, quite different, when we flew to Centreville in March for Carolina's fifth birthday. We flew by small plane, which was enjoyable because we could really see the landscape, but it was our undoing coming home. There was a huge snowstorm the night before we were to leave and all flights were cancelled. Larger planes were flying the next morning, but we spent all day at Dulles, returned to Kris' for the night, and took the bus to National the next day to finally catch a flight Tom had reserved for us. Our baggage preceded us to Cleveland by many hours. The birthday party, however, which was held at a wonderful children's play center (later bankrupt), was fun, and we had two good days with Kris and family, and a happy evening with them and Tom and Daille, who returned the day after the birthday from a short trip to the Bahamas.

With the Erection Party behind us, we left in May on our next trip, planned for a year—a barge trip through France with the Scharfs. We left on June 1 and flew to Paris, where we spent a week before going on to Lorraine for the barge trip. We stayed at an interesting hotel in Paris, the Hotel Elysees Ceramic, not far from the Arc de Triomphe, and saw a lot of Paris. Unfortunately, we chose the one week when all museum employees were on strike, so we couldn't visit the Louvre or any other museum. We were disappointed, but the Scharfs, who were in Paris for the first time, were less so, partly because they are not very art oriented and they were able to spend a lot of time going into some of the many churches, looking at organs. We saw many other sights, including Versailles, to which we took a tour. The metro was also on strike for two days, so we did a lot of walking, mostly along the Champs Elysées, did a little shopping, ate in some very good places and had a fine old time. We spent our last night in Paris in the Hotel Regina, and in the morning, took the train to Strasburg where we were taken to the barge, along with the other 20 passengers. We were greeted with the bad news that the Rhine was so full from flooding upstream that boats were not allowed—we would have to stay in the canals; however, this did not upset us too much or spoil the trip. We stopped at several interesting places, enjoyed the barge life and meals and experienced one of the most interesting engineering events we'd ever seen—a cable lift of the barge up the mountains to another canal. At the end of the week we took the train back to Paris, spent one more night at the Regina and then flew home. We all agreed the trip was lovely, interesting and most enjoyable.

It certainly was much more enjoyable than the next event in this eventful summer. I had to have a second hernia operation, this time to insert a screen. This went well, except that it took a month or more for the wound to heal completely and when we took our next trip, I was still treating it. We went to Custer next for the 60th reunion of Elton's high school class. We stayed with Mona and Dale at a motel on the hill, behind Custer high school. The first night of the reunion we had cocktails at the home of Agnes and Allen Kline, then visited with the Chards. The next day was the parade, with a special float of 39'ers, lunch wherever we wanted, and then a dinner. On Sunday we went to a picnic at Chuck Mateer's. The weather was gorgeous (after all, this was Custer in July!), and we all enjoyed each other and had the opportunity to see two or three of the class members before they died. This was the last reunion for us, although those who were still around had a small get-together in July 2004, just before Elton's death.

We were back in Cleveland for only a few days before we left on the next trip—a Baltic cruise. Tom and Daille had wanted to take this cruise and be on the ship for Tom's 60th birthday. Although this seemed to us like a lot to undertake after the rest of the summer, when they asked us to join them, we agreed. We flew to London a few days ahead of them in order to spend some time with Gregg's friends. We stayed in the Basil Street Inn (a hotel we loved), recommended by Jackie More, on a quiet side street, just a block or so from Harrods. It is very English, not new, but with all the amenities and a lovely dining room where we entertained Veronica and Jackie. Daille and Tom (referred to henceforth as the IT's—Indefatigable Travelers) joined us in a couple of days and we all took the train out to Gregg's resting place. The next day, we took the train to Dover and boarded the ship, the *Norwegian Dream*. The ship sailed through the Kiel Canal which was fun, but it was scarcely wide enough for the ship and, in fact, this was the widest ship allowed. There were bystanders greeting us from the shore and bridges all along the way. We stopped on the German coast, where we rented a car and drove into Berlin, and met a friend of the IT's with champagne to drink under the Brandenburg Gate.

After lunch and a quick tour of the city, where the IT's had spent some time when they were posted to Bonn, we left in the late afternoon to sail to St. Petersburg where we docked for only 24 hours. But it was the most exciting day I have ever spent. We took a tour in the evening and another all-day tour the next day, with a wonderful guide. We saw enough that I felt I had been in what, to me, is the most interesting city in the world (because of my Russian studies at Reserve and all the reading I've done since). Elton did not feel up to the all-day tour and it was almost too much walking for me, but I made it.

Our next stop was Helsinki, Finland, with an all day tour, then on to Stockholm for another day. Because we had spent time there in 1966, Elton and I took a taxi into the center of the city to do some shopping, but spent most of the day on the ship while the IT's toured. That night, we docked in Copenhagen and went to the Tivoli. I'd heard for years about Tivoli as an enchanting amusement park; it certainly was an amusement park—very busy, but not very enchanting. The next day we had an all-day tour of the city. From there, we stopped at Oslo and had what I thought was a rather dull tour. I'd always wanted to see Norway, but this small taste of the country was disappointing.

We sailed back to Dover and had a real adventure, certainly unplanned. We were to dock at Dover in the morning, but at 1:00 a.m. there was a terrific crash, and the loud speaker told us to put on our warmest clothes and life jackets and get to our assigned lifeboat posts immediately. A cargo ship had rammed the *Dream* and had done considerable damage. It was feared that the damage included leaks that would require everyone in lifeboats. We waited on deck until it was decided we could get into Dover safely. To the passengers shivering on deck from cold and fright, the waiting time for that decision seemed long, but in a short while, they sent us back to our cabins and the ship limped into port in the morning. This was big news in England, so, as soon as possible, we all contacted our relatives in the States to assure them that we were all right. What we heard, with small variations was, "Oh, really? Your ship was rammed by a cargo ship?"

We rented a car to take us past London to a small town near Heathrow. We stayed in a hotel over night and headed to the airport in the morning. We went our separate ways, the IT's to Dulles, Elton and I via Toronto to Cleveland and home to rest up after a wonderful, exciting and memorable summer.

Warren turned 70 in 1999 on October 4, and Maggie did the same on December 26. We decided to celebrate Warren's birthday with a party. The Cookes agreed to have dinner at their house, and we would take care of invitations and various other items. It surprised Warren, especially since we included his son, Will, and his love, Cynthia, on the guest list. Will and Cynthia were a hot item for a few years, and his folks sincerely hoped it would result in marriage and children, but a year or two later, it was all over . . . . not that this had any effect on the 70th birthday party.

Later in October, Fran Zimmerman and I decided to go to Appleton to visit Jan and Marty. We flew up on Hallowe'en and came back on November 2. Despite her on-going cancer and complications, Jan was up and around, but that was about all. Although we were happy to see her and she to see us, she really was not up to much company.

In November, Elton and I flew to Sudbury for his final trip on the Inco job. We stayed at Cassio's, spent a lot of time talking to the Cassio sisters, Melinda Dozzi and Chris Young, had dinner with Menno Friesen and returned to Cleveland. We were sad to see the end of a long-term, mostly satisfactory, and certainly lucrative, relationship and job.

Since we had surprised Warren with his party in October, Warren planned a surprise party for Maggie's birthday the day after Christmas, a miserable day for a birthday. We were having the family for Christmas that year, including the Sheppards and Steve's mother, Frances, so we helped to work out Warren's party by having an open house catered in our suite; Warren's party was afterwards, with most of our guests going upstairs. Our party was a successful affair, with the help of Tom and Daille, Karin and Kris, and Maggie's party was a fitting conclusion.

With Christmas behind us and everyone gone, we, and everyone else in the world I guess, prepared for the New Year's Eve that many predicted would bring chaos. The Scharfs threw another party to celebrate, and together, we watched the celebrations all over the world on TV and the fireworks in downtown Cleveland through their windows. Those of us who were there were not at all surprised when the celebrations went off without a hitch. The only problems facing us were the normal ones associated with adjusting to a new year. We would discover that this year would be the beginning of what would become, in many respects, a new world.

2000

Our lives continued as before. On January 10, I had a cataract removed in the simple process that has become so commonplace now. We were working with the decorator on our bedroom, so we had meetings with her, and, of course, both of us had our usual round of church and other meetings—although Elton was definitely slowing down. We kept the office open while Elton finished up some work. In February, Pat Sweet resigned as Executive Director of the League Ed Fund, because her husband had become President of Youngstown

University. I knew I would miss Pat a lot, but we all felt it was time for new blood. However, it was more than half a year before we found a permanent replacement.

One of the saddest days of our lives was in February when we learned that Malcolm McCuaig had died from an allergic reaction before he could get to the hospital. This was an agonizing loss for both of us. We both loved Malcolm dearly, and his death was so sudden and unexpected. And we had another blow the same day (ironically, Valentine's Day) when we heard that my dear friend Jan Morris had died of cancer. Jan had had cancer for more than two years. They had tried everything without success, and she'd known for some months that she was dying. We knew it too, but it was still a shock. Fran Zimmerman and I decided to fly to Appleton for Jan's funeral, and were glad we did—Marty was suffering so terribly. Actually, he never recovered and the last time I had contact with him, before he disappeared, was two or three years later. Jan was such a wonderful person, it was, and always will be, hard to accept her death.

Old Stone had a service for Malcolm some time after his death which had not only overwhelmed us, but had left Marion on the verge of collapse. She had to arrange services at their church in Pennsylvania, in Ottawa and here in Cleveland, get out of her house with all the work that entails, and get their affairs in order. I talked with her several times every week. We met her at the airport and brought her home with us when she arrived for Malcolm's service and interment in Old Stone's Columbarium on March 30. Her nerves were in a really bad state.

The early part of the year had brought much sadness, but still, life went on. Daille and Tom came to Cleveland for Elton's birthday, and later that month, we flew to D.C. for Easter with the family. Although it was early (March 23), the weather was nice and we had a lovely drive to Fredericksburg and vicinity, dogwoods in bloom all the way. We were not separated from the family for long after that weekend, because on May 19, we all went to Boston for Karin's graduation from Suffolk Law School. This was a big weekend in every way, with tours of the school and meals in interesting places and, particularly, the graduation ceremony with the whole family in attendance.

With her law degree in hand, Karin was looking for a job, preferably in a state where she would not have to take another bar exam. Tim really wanted to return to Chicago, and it turned out she could get a job in the Cook County Prosecutor's office, contingent upon her passing the Illinois bar exam. Some time in June, therefore, they packed up and moved to Chicago where they found a very desirable apartment on the lower floor of a two-family duplex.

Their relationship was still on live-in status, despite continuing objections from their families. When Daille and Tom had remarked a year or two earlier that they believed the kids should be married, Tim said, "But it's the Nineties, you know!" Our reaction was "So?" Actually, however, he did buy Karin an engagement ring about this time.

With Karin's graduation behind us, I finally had my left hip replaced, because it was bothering me more each day. The surgery took place on June 6. I returned to Dr. Helper for this. St. Luke's had been closed and Dr. Helper was practising at St. Vincent's downtown and Euclid General. For the convenience of Elton and our west side friends, I chose St. Vincent's. I was there for about five days and then transferred to Lutheran Hospital for a week of therapy, followed by more outside therapy in Lakewood for six weeks.

One night in July while I was home recovering, and still in therapy, I was surprised to have a phone call from Fairview Hospital asking us if we could get in touch with the Scharfs' children. Maggie and Warren had been badly hurt in an accident and both had been admitted to emergency wards, Warren at Fairview and Maggie at Lakewood. The only number the hospital could find was ours. They had been returning home from a trip west and coming from the airport their cab was hit by a van. We helped locate kids and friends, of course, and as soon as possible, and often thereafter, went to see them in the hospital. They were both in very serious condition. Warren had only a ten percent chance of survival; Maggie had several bad breaks in her arm that were serious, especially because of her organ playing, and there were other injuries. She was transferred to Fairview in a few days, and they were both there for more than a month. They were incapacitated and needed help and much therapy for several months afterwards. They both recovered completely, but it was a long and difficult haul for them and a great concern for us.

In the meantime, Elton had continuing problems with the Parkinson's. Through July, the Parkinson's medication prescribed by Dr. Mann was doing quite well, but during the summer, Elton began having a great deal more involuntary motion, which made it harder for him to eat and quite uncomfortable. In August, we went to Richmond for the wedding reception of Nancy Johnson's daughter, Teresa Dermody. I did most of the driving, and we had a fairly easy two-day trip to Daille's, with a stop in Morgantown, West Virginia. The next day we drove to Richmond—Tom and Elton in our car, Daille and I in their car. Although Elton had some problems speaking and eating (mostly chewing and swallowing), he managed quite well through the evening and the next morning. After a night in Richmond, he and I went on to Williamsburg to visit the Stones. We had a reasonably good visit, with Elton contributing about as much as ever, and being able to eat his dinner with no particular problems. Throughout the summer, however, he was having more and more difficulty staying dry all night and this was a problem when visiting people. At this stage, I was doing all the driving. When we left the Stones, we drove to Daille's. We picked up the little ones and went to Bryce, the 'girls' riding in one car with Carolina regaling Daille and me with one of her long stories. We had a pleasant evening and a nice day, spent mostly washing both cars and playing cards. The next day, Elton and I left to drive to New York and Lake Canandaigua to visit Jim and Joanne Tilberry. We drove north through Pennsylvania, then west through New York, in lovely country, most of which we had never seen. We drove two days to the Tilberry's and spent two nights with them.

At this time, as I remember, Elton was having some involuntary movements in his neck and shoulders, and some trouble speaking, but he could still manage to join in a conversation and eat without too much trouble, get from one floor to another and manage satisfactorily, using a walker at night. We had a difficult time one night at the Tilberrys'—the toilet backed up because of the septic tank. We felt we were to blame, and we had a hard time cleaning up the mess. It wasn't much comfort to be told later that this happened often. Our room was down a flight of steep stairs and Elton managed the stairs without too much trouble. All in all, we had a really pleasant time. The drive home from the Tilberrys' was long and tiring, even though it was through picturesque country. The driving was made more difficult because it rained all day and we were on back roads, not throughways. Although I did all the driving, we were both pretty tired by the time we got home.

Probably because this trip had been somewhat tiring, the jerking in Elton's neck and head seemed to increase and become more painful, and he was having more and more trouble getting around. We were happy to see Dr. Mann early in September but we were disappointed when he told us it was okay to use heat and liniment, but he really didn't know how to improve Elton's medication to decrease the debilitating motions. He suggested we try to get an appointment with Dr. David Riley, the best neurologist in the area. Warren Scharf arranged for us to go to the masseuse they use through their alternative medicine group. We had about 6 or 8 appointments with her, and these massages relieved the pain somewhat, but didn't have any effect on the motion itself. We also bought a very nice wheeled walker, which helped him get around at home.

He was beginning to have a lot of trouble chewing and swallowing and I tried to use more and more soft foods—mashed potatoes, cooked cereal and eggs and anything else I could think of—but he couldn't really eat much and was beginning to lose weight noticeably. By the end of September, when we had a pot luck meal at church, he was considerably worse. He spoke less clearly, was definitely thinner, and made less effort to move around and mix. Several people at the affair were really shocked at his condition, one of them being Dr. Wilder, who said he would see if he could help us get an appointment with Dr. Riley. He did, and the appointment was set for October 31.

Through October, it became more and more difficult for him to eat, and when the Scharfs took us out to dinner for my birthday, he ordered just soup, and did not eat all of that. He was hardly able to join in a conversation and continued to have trouble eating and swallowing. He was not dry at night and continued to experience involuntary movements. Perhaps none of this was getting worse, but it was certainly not getting better.

We finally had the appointment with Dr. Riley who, with his assistant, Christina Whitney, spent two hours examining and testing him, and then gave him new prescriptions. He took Elton off Tasmar, which he had taken for more than two years and which had helped tremendously during the early stages, but obviously, wasn't helping any more. Dr. Riley changed the Sinemet dosage, kept him on Permax and added Amantadine, and set a schedule for the medication. We were most encouraged when we left his office, and by the end of the week, almost all of Elton's symptoms had decreased.

Unfortunately, the next Monday he had a cataract removed. This was a setback for him in two ways. First, some mistake was made in the surgery (which Dr. Statesir never did acknowledge) and Elton could barely see at all. Second, since the onset of Parkinson's, he had kept control of his own medication. Unfortunately, it was some time before I realized how poor his vision was and I did not step in as soon as I should have to help him select the correct medication. I suspect that his dosage was probably off for a week, and at the end of the week he was having some adverse reactions. Nevertheless, with advice from Dr. Riley's co-worker, Tina Whitney, he stayed on the medication as prescribed, except for a reduction in the amount of Amantadine, and as far as the PD symptoms were concerned, he was better than he had been before seeing Riley.

Elton's cataract surgery was the day before the Gore vs. Bush election, and on election night we went to the Scharfs for dinner and the election returns. The Sykoras' were there, and some trouble that Mary Jane was having with her legs and eyes helped to disrupt the dinner which was further disrupted by the election returns. We'd planned to stay at the Scharfs until the final result was known, but we didn't wait for the three or four weeks for resolution by the Supreme Court of the Florida mess. Thank God George W. Bush was declared the winner! But those intervening weeks were very uncertain and disruptive for all of us—more so for Elton than for others (except Gore and Bush). Because he couldn't read at all, he spent his time watching vote-counting shenanigans on television. This was almost full time and became deadly dull. He was frustrated and worried about his eye, which didn't improve, even though Dr. Statesir told him cheerily at each visit that it would get better. He really was not doing as well as he should with the new medication. This is the way he remained throughout November and the first half of December.

In the midst of arrangements for Christmas, I obtained two tickets for a Browns game on December 17 for our poor son-in-law who still had never seen a major league football game. He flew to Cleveland to see the game and then drove with us to Virginia for Christmas. Sadly for Tom, the weather on Sunday was so blizzardy and cold, he left the game after the first half. He was shocked when he saw Elton's condition. He was much worse than he had been in August, although he was considerably better than he had been in mid-October, before seeing Dr. Riley and having the PD medication adjusted. When Elton fell entering a restaurant the day before we left Cleveland, Tom attributed it to his inability to stand. I thought it was a combination of the wind and trying to use the walker on the bumpy, snowy ground.

We got to Virginia with no problem, Elton in the back seat, sleeping most of the time. We spent most of December 23 at Kris and Steve's place, then went back to Daille's and met Karin who arrived just in time for dinner. After dinner, Elton went upstairs with Karin. He had a brief blackout and fell down about 6 stairs to the landing, half scalping himself. Karin screamed to us to call 911, and he and I went immediately to the Emergency Ward at Arlington Hospital. We spent several hours in emergency where he had several X-rays, MRI's and CAT-scans, had his head sewn up miraculously well, and finally was put into a room at about 4:00 a.m.

The Arlington cardiologist recommended that a pacemaker be installed since blood tests had indicated that his heart had stopped briefly and a pacemaker would keep this from happening again. He was moved into the ICU unit on Christmas Eve, and on Christmas Day a pacemaker was implanted. Two days later he was moved out of ICU and into another room. Because he was unable to travel or go home, it was essential that we find some place for him to stay until we could make arrangements in Cleveland. The hospital made arrangements for him to be transferred to a nursing home called Sleepy Hollow, and he was taken there by ambulance on December 28.

Meantime, the Arlington neurologist who saw Elton before he went into the ICU, thought he was moving too much, possibly due to too much Sinemet, and he cut the dosage way down. What he should have known, as a neurologist, is the basic fact that without Sinemet a PD patient becomes immobile. This doctor did not see him after we left the hospital, but he would not hear of changing the Sinemet dosage, even though the people at Sleepy Hollow who were familiar with Parkinson's patients agreed with me that he needed more. It may have been wise to cut back the dosage until the pacemaker was installed and his head wounds had been stitched, but the doctor did not increase the medication even after these were done. This was, in my opinion, absolutely wrong. I thought then, and still do, that I had a good basis for a malpractice suit, but I didn't want to go through the kind of hassle necessary to accomplish it. Later, in February, I wrote to the doctor and told him what I thought. The fact that he called me and apologized, confirms my belief that he knew he had done the wrong thing.

In any case, Elton's three awful days in the ICU unit were also awful for me and the rest of the family. I spent Christmas Eve and Christmas at the hospital, except for an hour or two Christmas Eve at Kris', and dinner at Daille's on Christmas Day. I read three books from the time we left Daille's in the ambulance, grabbing one on the way out, but I have no idea what I read. The rest of the family also spent as much time as possible at the hospital. The nursing home, Sleepy Hollow Manor, is on Columbia Pike, a 30 minute drive west from Pettits' residence in Arlington. Elton became more and more comatose because of his lack of Sinemet and since the doctor at Arlington Hospital was still in charge of his case and I couldn't get any more medication for him until we got out of there, I grew frantic. But with two holidays to contend with, and all that meant—time off and vacations for employees—it was very hard to make any arrangements for change.

2001

So 2001 began with Elton comatose and I at my wits end. There didn't seem much reason to celebrate. I spent most of New Year's Day with Elton, as I had every day since December 22 when he'd fallen down the stairs. Kris and Steve came to Sleepy Hollow in the afternoon with the kids and I went home to have dinner with Daille and Tom, but otherwise it was like all the other days. Elton could eat little and I'm not sure he could even see any games, though Kris had brought over a TV. He didn't seem to be interested. The rest of the week was the same. Tom came in the mornings, and one day their very nice little Associate Pastor came to see Elton; Daille came in after work and Kris came nearly every day. I would go home, help with supper, do my laundry, etc, and watch a little TV. We finally made arrangements, with the help of Jean Cooke, Bill Wilder and Chris Whitney of Dr. Riley's office, for Elton to be admitted into Hanna House at University Hospital in Cleveland, and Kris made arrangements for a first class flight. Finally, on Sunday, January 7, he was discharged and we flew home to Cleveland. It never looked so good to me before.

Elton and I took an ambulance van to National, where Kris met us and saw us off; we were helped onto the plane and were met by a van in Cleveland. Meanwhile, Daille and Tom drove my car, with our luggage, to Cleveland. They left an hour or so before the van came to Sleepy Hollow, and Elton and I had quite a long wait at the airport, so Daille and Tom reached Cleveland while Elton was still being checked in at Hanna House.

Daille and Tom stayed until Wednesday to help me. I went to the hospital every morning, and they came over later for a visit. Chris and Dr. Riley were in to see Elton early on Monday morning, thank goodness, and immediately changed his medication schedule. We were very impressed with Chris, especially, since she came into the hospital several mornings to make sure he had the proper medicine at 6:00 a.m. From then on, he gradually became more mobile, but his long stay in bed had shrunk and stiffened the tendons in his legs and ankles; walking was almost impossible. He was started on therapy the first day, including swallowing therapy, and he improved in every way; he was eating and swallowing a little better by the time he left, and once home, I stopped using the water thickener (awful!) entirely.

But when I took Elton home, he was in a wheelchair. He needed help going anywhere and some help eating (only soft foods, and, at this late stage in his life, he learned to like oatmeal), so I hired Lois Oliver from an agency to come in for some home nursing—eight hours a day for the first ten days, then four for a couple of weeks. She was good with him, and knew what she was doing, but I couldn't stand her (she talked all the time about nothing), and I was glad when I felt he was doing well enough that I could manage alone. Also, after a week or so, the hospital sent a physical therapist and an occupational therapist, and they both helped a great deal. Once Lois Oliver was gone, I got my friend, Armaida Miller, to come in to be with him in the evenings and daytimes so that I could attend various meetings. The at-home therapist worked with Elton until some time in March when he discovered that we had stolen away (to the Play House); he told us we were not allowed to have in-home help if we could go out.

We got prescriptions from Dr. Golovan for therapy at Lutheran and Elton began regular sessions, two or three days a week. I also took him to the Cleveland Speech and Hearing Center and happened to arrive when they were about to start a Lee Silverman Speaking Program for Parkinson's patients. The program had just been approved for Medicare reimbursement. They had trained personnel ready to provide the program and were anxious for patients to try it. We agreed, and in April, Elton commenced the month-long intensive therapy program—one hour each, four days a week (half at University Hospital, half in Euclid) with a nice young therapist named Leanne, and the same thing at home, alone, on the other days. The program turned out to be a tremendous help. From speaking nearly unintelligibly, he improved to the point where he was able to speak quite clearly. On completing the program, he was told he must do the same things every day for the rest of his life, and he did so quite faithfully as long as he was able.

In addition to taking Elton to and from therapy until May, I worked on closing down Geist and Geist and moving out of the space. This was a tremendous job. It seemed endless and exactly like Hercules' Augean stables. Every morning when I went in, I could see no dent in the work. I would work a few hours, run home to help Elton and then return next day, and so on. After starting this in February, I finally got the last things out on May 22, but it was a bear of a job, and at least in the early days, I felt I could not be there for long periods.

Elton's recovery and therapy and our disbanding of Geist and Geist should have been enough to do in the first months of 2001, but all this occurred in an important year in our lives—Elton turned 80, and we celebrated our 60th anniversary. We planned a small dinner party in the party room for his birthday, had a caterer, the kids came, and it worked well, except you could guess that I was not in the best shape when, an hour before the caterers and bartender arrived, I realized that I had no appetizers. I called the Scharfs and it turned out they had shrimp and crackers and other things; I was saved, but no one will ever allow me to forget this near disaster. Elton was barely able to talk or get around, but he enjoyed the visit and party anyway. I think most of the guests did too, despite his condition. Then we had the 60th Anniversary to deal with.

First though, I had to see about finding space in our apartment for everything we needed to move from the office. When the family was here for the birthday, they helped some with the office. They moved the étagère from the office to home, took some things with them and decided what they wanted to be shipped to them. I shipped some items to the Sheppards at the lovely new house they had moved into at the beginning of the year. These included the chests of drawers from our guest rooms and our double bed, which we replaced with twin beds with motors. Elton was sleeping so restlessly now we felt we needed to make the change—a change we later regretted, since we both missed the intimacy of the double bed. Throughout our marriage, we had slept nude in a double bed, even when we were having marriage problems. Perhaps this is what kept us together.

When the chests were gone from the guest room, we had drawers built under the windows, all of which involved moving things around and pitching some. We had new wallpaper, carpet and curtains put in the guest room and all this continued through March and April. We didn't put the Winton Place suite on the market to sell, since it took me until May 22 to get everything out, but some time that month, Bill Heideloff told Elton he would like to buy the suite from us for $40,000 (we'd paid slightly less), so we simply signed the necessary papers and we were paid. It couldn't have been easier. It was a good thing, because nothing else had been easy those first six months of the year.

For one thing, there were all my outside activities. During all this time, I was doing my continuing jobs as LWV Ed Fund treasurer, scheduling door hosts at church, doing a job for the Presbytery's COM., trying to edit the Old Stone personnel manual and get it completed, having Bible study at our home every other week and being an elder. And of course, I was trying to get the office cleared out and the party arranged, as well as taking Elton to his various therapists and doing what was needed to be done for him at home.

By the end of May we were approaching our next project, our 60th anniversary. After that, I was scheduled to have hernia surgery (again!) on June 27. When Betty Roeser called me about June 10 to tell me Jack was in hospital and was not expected to live, we felt it was impossible for us to go to see him. When he died on June 16, we did not go out for the funeral. I had had problems for many years with Jack, and rarely had a conversation with him or letter from him that had not upset me. But he was my little brother, and now I was the only one left of the Roeser family of five. I was not as upset as I had been when Alan died, but nevertheless it was very sad for me.

Our anniversary kept us from traveling, because we had a major affair planned and felt we could not change it or be gone before it could take place. We had arranged, a year earlier, to have the Fellowship Hall at the church for a brunch after the church service on Sunday, July 8, and we invited everyone in church to attend. We also asked many others and our family was here (including Vicki and David Araneicka from Pittsburgh). More than 200 attended. We decided to work with the Scharfs on a program. It involved pertinent photographs from our sixty years made into a slide video, accompanied by my narrative and appropriate piano music by Maggie. It was good, and the very successful program was enjoyed by everyone, as was the paper we passed out. I had written this earlier about what life was like when I was growing up. Of course, a great deal of work and time went into the planning. I was exhausted by the time of our anniversary. This didn't stop me from doing too much, and, as usual, I had bitten off more than I could chew. After all I'd done I felt there was a lot of cleaning still to be done. In June, I was cleaning bookcases and china cabinets, even though I had to stop every 45 minutes or so to rest a few minutes.

It's no wonder that, after all the foregoing, I had a very difficult time with the surgery. Daille came on Friday for the weekend, thank goodness, because although I was in and out the same day of the surgery, I was very ill the next day, went back to Lakewood Hospital for some ineffective overnight treatment, was discharged again, and then became so ill that Elton, his caregiver and Paula Keating, Old Stone's Parish Nurse, took me to Lutheran Hospital's emergency room. Daille, reluctantly, went back home to her job after arranging for full time care for me at home. I was in the hospital for ten days, very, very ill, and when discharged, I was ordered to do nothing for at least two weeks.

We were able to get several different women to come in for various shifts, though we had no one during the night for two weeks, and then some help for a couple of weeks after that. We managed; I did, literally, nothing but read, watch TV and talk with the help for two weeks. Then my wonderful PEO sisters brought in food for a couple of weeks. By the beginning of September, I was up and around, but very weak for a long time afterwards. Realizing that I had to cut down on my extracurricular activities, in the weeks that followed I resigned from several organizations, notably the Presbytery's COM and as treasurer of the League of Women Voters.

Elton was still coping with his many problems, one of which was his vision, which he had never regained after his cataract operation the previous November. Warren Scharf arranged for him to see his ophthalmologist, Dr. Reinhart. This doctor had seen Elton while I was in the hospital, and a month afterwards he easily corrected the problem Dr. Statesir had not recognized. On October 23, Elton had the other cataract removed, and in December, we both had our eyes examined and were pronounced healthy by Dr. Reinhart. In addition to his many problems, Elton now developed another—sores on his head. Following his hospitalization early in the year, after he was "scalped" in his fall down the stairs at Daille's, the aide at the nursing home had failed to remove all the stitches after his head injury, and this was not determined for some time. As a result, Elton developed a continuing relationship with the dermatologist, Dr. Carney. One appointment with Dr. Carney that I will never forget was at 1:00 p.m. on a most historic day, September 11, 2001. This day was to live on as "9/11" but we were late learning of the disaster. Because we had not had the TV on that morning, we knew nothing until Ralph Lestock called about a plane flying into a building in New York. Like everyone else, we were horrified and wordless. Just as we were leaving to go to the doctor's, Daille called, very upset, to tell us how frightened she was after the Pentagon was hit and that she was home safe. We found Lakewood streets and the doctor's office almost empty of people, and those we did see were like zombies. That evening we had dinner with Joyce Hackbarth and her husband, Darrel. She was one of my PEO sisters who had made the date some time earlier because she didn't cook and couldn't bring me a meal. I am sure that dinner date is unforgettable for all of us. No matter what the conditions—war, peace or terrorism—life goes on, but I felt then, and still feel, no adult living through 9/11 would ever be the same again.

Daille and Tom drove up to Cleveland on October 4 for the weekend, Daille still very shaken by the events of September 11. We took them to dinner and a play at the Play House, had a lovely autumn drive on Sunday, and they left Monday morning. Through October and November, we went on with reasonably uneventful lives, except for the continuing concern about September 11. I was trying to get back into my church and civic duties, and Elton was working with Old Stone trustees and a Friends of Old Stone organization which had been instigated, and then left in the lurch, by Dr. Kornell.

We had Thanksgiving dinner at our house with the Sheppards, Pettits and Karin. By this time, Karin had passed the Illinois bar exam and was interning in Cook County in the Prosecutor's office. Tim was working with the IRS and they were FINALLY planning a wedding—the next Memorial Day weekend. Karin stayed with us a day after the others left on Saturday morning, and she went with us to buy a new hide-a-bed and chair to replace the old leather couch and my chair in the den. She fixed supper for us that evening.

Despite the problems we had the year before in Virginia at Christmas, we returned for another Christmas Day. I drove there in one day, with no problem, and arrived early in the afternoon of December 20. Kristin had reserved a motel room for us, close to them, but hard to get to from their place. One of the results of Elton's fall was a real phobia about stairs which, along with his physical difficulties, made it impossible for us to stay at either

Kris's or Daille's—there were stairs at both places. We were at Daille's for Christmas Eve and another meal, but we spent most of our time with Kris and Steve and the kids and with Frances, Steve's mother, who was there for the holiday.

Daille and Tom drove back to Cleveland with us, taking their car, because Tim's aunt had invited Daille and me to a shower for Karin in Chicago on December 30. This seemed like a bad time, but it was good for all of Tim's cousins and sisters who were home for the holiday. So Daille and Tom drove back to Cleveland with us, in tandem, and Daille and I flew into Chicago on December 29. We stayed in a hotel and had a nice time, including a good time at the party with a lot of people. Tim's cousins, sisters, aunts and other relatives all seemed to me to be the same age, coloring, height, and, I thought, personality. I found them all to be friendly and hospitable. We flew home the next day after talking to the person who would do the flowers for the wedding. Daille and Tom stayed with us for New Year's Eve and we went to the party, which was again at the Scharfs'. They left the next day and we started what we hoped, as always, would be a less painful year.

2002

It seems that whenever we started a year with hope that things would be better, we were doomed to disappointment. This year had its problems, beginning again with Elton's health. Since he had registered with the Veteran's Administration to obtain his medications the year before, he was required to see a V.A. doctor twice a year. He had an appointment early in January. The doctor there indicated that he might have some colon problems and he should have a colonoscopy, so he had this procedure early in February. The colonoscopy showed signs of cancer, and we met with the surgeon, Dr. Lee, and arranged for surgery on February 28 at Fairview Hospital.

The surgery went well, but he had some problems with recovery because of his Parkinson's medication, which always seems to be too much for hospital staff. The first day out of surgery he suffered an onslaught of such involuntary motion I spent three hours physically holding him down and as still as possible, before the nursing staff finally gave him a muscle relaxant. After two days the hospital lined up Dr. Good, a neurologist who was a life saver, prescribing the proper medication and making sure the nurses stuck to the schedule. In a few days the PD was as much under control as possible and Elton began to recover. Once again, I was spending my days at the hospital, knitting, reading, writing letters—all those fun things—and doing the necessary life-continuing jobs at home at night. Elton celebrated his birthday in the hospital and was discharged about March 9 after being told by Dr. Spiro that the cancer in the colon had been completely removed but that he had cancer cells in the lymph glands which would require chemotherapy. When he heard this unwelcome news, he thought a bit and then said, "I'm going to buy a new car." In April, he went with Warren to the Cadillac dealer and settled on a new black sedan, with OnStar, which we really wanted.

On April 15, Elton began eighteen weeks of chemo—one treatment on six successive Tuesdays, then a week off, with two repetitions. This turned out to be easier than he'd expected and he had little or no adverse reaction throughout the period. We both spent Tuesday mornings at the cancer center and fitted our lives into the other days for the next six months.

While this treatment continued, I continued to keep up with some of my activities, which included reading to kindergarten children at Cleveland's Tremont School every other Friday afternoon. I never did anything I enjoyed so much and was happy to have the opportunity. And, of course, church work went on. Dr. Kornell had been there for four years and was rapidly losing support for various reasons, one of which was that he could never be found, and he really couldn't be trusted. He could not get along with the Chair of the First Presbyterian Society Trustees, Bill Heideloff, and at a Joint Staff meeting (essentially the church's personnel committee) in January, he told us that we must get rid of Bill or he would leave. Since there was no way we could get rid of Bill, Dr. Kornell began in the spring to look for another job. We were not told this, but some of us rather suspected it. I was an Elder and he had made every effort to emasculate the Session, so there was not much pleasure in working at the church at all, but Elton and I continued with what duties we had. We began a Wednesday morning Bible study at our house, and this was a high spot in each week for both of us. Another high spot was my twice-a-week session with Tammy Lyons who had a baby in July. She continued to work out with me up until the time her son was born and again soon afterwards.

Easter was early this year (March 31) and we spent a very quiet day alone, Elton recuperating from his surgery. Daille and Tom came for a weekend in the middle of March and we saw a great deal of the Scharfs who were very helpful in many ways. We had lunch occasionally with the Floyd Lees who had moved to North Carolina when he retired 17 years earlier and had now moved back to Akron because three of their children lived in the area. We had also resumed our relationship with Frank and Kathryn Madison in Zanesville in the past year after years of little or no contact, and we met them for lunch several times during 2002 at the tavern in Zoar, about halfway between Cleveland and Zanesville.

Karin's wedding was certainly a big event in the offing, and with Daille doing most of the planning, we kept up with what was going on. In May, we took a trip to Nordstroms in Beachwood to buy a dress for me to wear to the wedding and then another trip to Sharon, Pennsylvania to buy shoes to wear with the dress and several other pairs of shoes for both of us.

The wedding itself was to be at 4:00 p.m. on Sunday, June 26, Memorial Day weekend. Daille and Tom arrived a few days early on their way to Chicago, and then Steve and Kristin and children arrived on Thursday. We drove two cars to Chicago, stayed at a motel in Joliet and spent from Friday afternoon to Monday morning enjoying the company, trying to find our way around and going to the rehearsal dinner and the wedding. There was an abundance of Sullivans and their friends and relatives, but not very many Pettit friends and family were able to be there. One highlight for me was the presence of Sally Roeser Laird who had come by bus with a friend, and my cousin, Helen Skamser Curfman, from Lincoln. Several of the Pettits' good friends from Brazil came, as did our friends, the Scharfs. The wedding was outside, in a spectacular garden on a perfect day. It was not only beautiful but interesting. A Lutheran pastor and a priest jointly performed the ceremony. We learned later that the priest had been defrocked, or something, and was really not qualified to perform the ceremony. It was a good thing there was a dependable Lutheran present. Karin was lovely, the reception was done very well, the dinner was good, and all was well.

After the wedding, it was home to Cleveland and, after the Sheppards left the next day, we returned to our routine of chemo one day a week, rarely interrupted by any special occasions, except a very nice weekend trip to Chicago with the Scharfs. We had been disappointed not to have visited the city when we were at the wedding, so they urged us to go. Warren drove our car and they made reservations at a hotel just off the Loop. When we arrived, it turned out that the hotel had no handicapped rooms and there were some other problems. The next morning, Maggie and I went to a neighboring hotel and we checked in there. We had a good time, sat at the sidewalk café and watched people go by, ate at a famous German restaurant, and the next day went to Karin and Tim's for Tim's very special, remarkable gourmet dinner. We saw their honeymoon pictures and had a pleasant visit. The next day, we went to church at Chicago's famous Fourth Presbyterian, then met Tim and Karin for lunch, a visit to the Navy Pier and a boat trip. It was a lovely afternoon and a lovely weekend.

The next bright spot in a generally pleasant summer was the annual visit of the Cumberlidges to see their daughter, Ann. We had them for dinner one night and had a very nice visit as we always do. In September, a plaque commemorating Malcolm McCuaig was put up in the church and Marion, Malcolm's brother, Ian, and his wife, and Marion's friend, Betty Mull, arrived for a special ceremony and reception. It was nice to see Marion again as well as the others.

Since I had a party for Elton's 80th birthday, he felt he should have one for mine, though I really wasn't interested in a celebration or a big party. Nevertheless, he planned a dinner—actually, Daille did most of the organizing and arrangements—at the Hyatt in the recently renovated Old Arcade. Elton called this a "non-birthday party" since I'd protested having a birthday party. Daille and Tom arrived on Tuesday and the party was on Thursday. It was a nice affair and everyone seemed to enjoy the occasion.

We were really shocked to hear on September 8 of the death of Dale Johnson, long ill with lung problems. And we were again shocked on October 21 to receive a call from Zanesville that Frank Madison had died suddenly. It had been only a couple of weeks since we had had lunch with them. Although we knew he was very ill, we had no idea he was so bad. Kathryn insisted she did not want us to come to the funeral, so we didn't, but I am still sorry we didn't. In addition to Frank's death, there were several more that year of Old Stone friends and of Shirley Babitt who had been my League leader for several years.

We were also made unhappy by events developing at church with our relationship with Dr. Kornell. November began with a letter from him to the congregation announcing his resignation and an unbelievably critical letter to Session which he read aloud at the meeting without an opportunity for rebuttal. It was a letter guaranteed to cause anger and antipathy and it soon developed that he had collected a coterie of people to challenge the government of Old Stone and, apparently, do their best to destroy the church. Although nearly everyone was angry, it was not until the annual meeting in January that the full intent of this group became known. Nevertheless, it was enough to make the rest of the year, and several more years, unhappy for most of us.

We got away from all this by driving to Virginia to spend Thanksgiving with the Pettits. We didn't succeed, however, in getting away from controversy. We stayed with Daille and Tom at Bryce, which was difficult because their stairs were very hard for Elton. It was controversial because Tim (and Karin, but particularly Tim) apparently had no idea how to be a guest at his in-law's home. In addition, I'd developed a really nasty cold and I felt terrible all the time we were there. I think we were glad when we were on the road home again.

But it was out of the frying pan into the fire. December turned out to be a miserable month for us. Elton developed a cold too, and found he had severe fluid retention. After visits to Dr. Golovan and the V.A., he started on dehydration pills to get rid of the fluid. He began to be really confused and have hallucinations. One day he called me into the bathroom to tell me the baby was crying; I assured him there was no baby there, but I was amused to think afterwards that I should have told him to do something for the baby! He didn't drink water, never had, and was never thirsty, but he had to have water now, so we spent hours with my saying, "Have a sip" and he would take one sip. We got his medicine adjusted somewhat, but this problem continued for a couple of months, and his dehydration problem actually continued to the end.

A few days before Christmas, I tried to help Elton up from a fall and pulled my back out. I was in agony for a week until I went to a chiropractor who relieved it a little. Elton developed several other ailments and on top of everything, we both began to lose keys, hearing aids, glasses, shoes, even his partial plate; I was spending every minute looking for something. After a couple of weeks, I swore I wouldn't look for anything, and after that we found things more easily. But never have I had such a miserable time.

We were both too miserable to go to the Christmas Eve service and we had the Begany's and Karl and Ruth Johnson for Christmas dinner, which I barely remember, and I have no idea how I prepared the meal. Daille and Tom drove up two days later for what had become our annual New Year's Eve party. We had appetizers at the Scharfs, a catered dinner in our suite, and back to the Scharfs for champagne. With all that, we were finally through a very difficult year.

CHAPTER 19

OUR LAST DAYS TOGETHER

2003

As the year got under way, Elton began to suffer from an ever-increasing problem with the Parkinson's, together with the new problem of fluid retention. I had finally persuaded him to use a trainer whom Tammy recommended. Robb Powers began to come twice a week at first and then less often as it became obvious that Elton could not handle very much exercise. Elton wanted to continue as a Trustee on Old Stone's FPS, but I finally convinced him that he just couldn't manage it, and we sent in his letter of resignation. This was a very difficult step for him to take. He was having more and more trouble speaking and used the walker more and more, but he continued to make every effort to get by and never, ever complained. We continued to go out for dinner with various people, to the Scharfs' concerts at the Baldwin Wallace chapel once a month, to church and, of course, to doctors. The Meridian had begun to hold a coffee hour every other Wednesday afternoon. Elton really loved this, and we were urged to come back even after we moved away, so we often did and always felt welcome.

The winter weather was not too bad, but there was quite a lot of snow and slush. When we went to see Penny, our audiologist, early in the year, and stopped at Wendy's for lunch first, Elton slipped and fell twice and was helped up by kind strangers in both cases. He had always worn heavy shoes or galoshes in snow, but he had disposed of all his work shoes and getting galoshes on now was impossible, so we visited the Terminal, had lunch in the Ritz's new Century Club, and bought him some new heavy shoes to wear outside; these helped a lot. He didn't like the appearance of the shoes—a sort of suede—because he had always been proud of his shiny shoes. For years he had spent some of every Sunday afternoon, when we were at home, shining all of his (and my) shoes. Now, I'm afraid mine don't get shined at all.

I tried not to go out much this winter but the church was embroiled in a controversy and I was on the Interim Pastor Search Committee, so I was very much involved in the whole affair and had some meetings and many letters and conversations. I was also reading to kindergartners at Tremont, and loved it, and still had several other commitments, so I lined up a few people to come in and be with Elton when I had to be out for a while. When I did have to leave him alone, I was concerned about him, because he had fallen several times at home when I was there. Unless he was close to something with which he could pull himself up, I was unable to get him up, and called 911 at least twice for help.

Daille had insisted we get the Helpline, but we didn't find it very useful. I have always slept very soundly, and without my hearing aids, I could hear very little. One night, Elton fell and became wedged between the bed and the nightstand. He couldn't waken me, so he got in touch with Helpline, they called the Scharfs who had our key. They came down, got him up and into bed. I slept through the whole thing!

The winter was full of worries, not only about the church situation, but also about the start of the war in Iraq. In the church, one group of people was protesting the existence of the FPS and writing letters, sending petitions, and generally causing trouble; another group (most of the older members) were trying to keep things as they had been and were fighting back with the same tactics. As for the Iraq situation, we always supported President Bush, but we were unhappy with the vitriol he faced from his opponents. But my most immediate worry was Elton.

His water retention problem eased up somewhat, but his balance was poor and he was still a little confused. Around the first of March, I woke up and thought, "We've got to move to where I can get some help." This was the last thing I wanted to do. I'd sworn I would never move again, I liked Lakewood and our apartment on which we'd spent a lot of time and money, and I couldn't face the whole prospect of moving, but I knew we had to do it. When I mentioned it to Elton, he thought I was going to put him in a nursing home and was very upset and bothered about it. He had seldom been with me when I'd visited people in senior residences; he thought they were all just old-fashioned nursing homes. However, I did a little calling around, and when Daille and Tom came for his birthday, we went out and saw a few places and ended up looking at a vacant apartment at the Renaissance. Elton had been resistant, angry and worried until he saw the place and the apartment. He obviously thought it quite nice and I signed a contract that day.

Moving there, however, turned out to be even more difficult than I had anticipated. We had to have physical exams, which were delayed for various reasons, and when they were completed, we were told we could not have the apartment we'd looked at but must go into Bridgeview. This was a new, poorly-developed program which used a specific part of the building for couples consisting of an independent spouse and one who needed help. They did not have an available two-bedroom apartment in Bridgeview and I had paid for two bedrooms and wouldn't settle for less. They had not told us anything about this when they signed me up, although they had to have known it was about to be put into place. I was really angry.

They finally persuaded Lucy Krsek, a lovely 95 year old widow, to move out of her two-bedroom and offered it to us. It was, of course, about twice as much money down and higher monthly fees, and after I threatened to get a lawyer, we arrived at a settlement with a reduction in the amount of extra money we would owe. All of this took time and it wasn't until July 17 that we could move in. Altogether, I feel we got a pretty poor deal, but I guess it was the right move and Elton would have the help he now needed.

In any case I began the horrendous job of sorting our belongings and getting ready to move. I spent many, many hours for three months going through the file cabinets and all the drawers and closets, sorting, discarding, giving away and keeping things. Someone told me that moving involves hard work, emotional feelings and decision-making, all three of which, individually, are exhausting. They certainly were, and I grew more tired with each passing day. Daille and Tom came at the end of March and again in May when Daille and I went through my precious books, one by one. I gave about 500 to the Lakewood library, probably threw out 300, got rid of others one way or another, and still had far too many.

Because I had been using the drawers in the built-in cupboards, we had a need for dresser drawers, and Maggie and Warren offered to give us a two-piece set they had. I got in touch with the Nesting Company, a marvelous company made up of two women who help with every aspect of moving, and by measuring the new apartment, they helped me decide what we could use and what we couldn't. Kris and Steve came to Cleveland in April and took a lot of my dishes, silver, and other things; and Carolina was delighted to take about ten long beaded necklaces. She was so delighted, she wore all of them all the time they were in Cleveland. Daille and Tom took a lot of things home with them too, including some plants.

We put the condo on the market and borrowed enough from the bank to pay the Renaissance. The condo didn't sell until the next January, but at least we weren't paying on two places at once.

Daille and Tom were a wonderful help; it would have been impossible without them. They came back a couple of days before the scheduled move and helped pack all that day and the next. We were given the use of two guest suites for them and for us and it was a good thing, because the moving van had mechanical problems on its way from the Meridian and didn't arrive until after 4:00 p.m. They couldn't finish unloading until after 11:00 p.m. and we would have had no place to sleep without the guest suites. We no longer had a hide-a-bed, and the beds were not made because rods had not been put in the one usable closet, and all the clothes were stacked on the beds.

Daille spent Friday getting the dishes and kitchen things unpacked and put away, and Tom did whatever he could and they left Saturday morning. When I started unpacking the big boxes of lamps, pictures, etc., on Saturday, I realized I didn't have the strength to lift heavy things out of the big boxes and knew I needed help. I called the Nesting Company and Linda and Beth were both available on Monday and Tuesday, and they were here through Wednesday, unpacking, hanging pictures, putting books in the bookcases and doing everything else needed. They were wonderful. Beth's husband even came and hooked up the computer and they also delivered things to Good Will.

Tim and Karin flew in the next weekend and rented a U-Haul. On Saturday we went to the Meridian and got the things we'd promised them. These included the piece of furniture we had used for liquor—our old phonograph-radio which we'd bought in Telluride and I had refinished in the sixties. This turned out to be a mistake. When we realized we had no place for liquor, we had to go out the next week and buy a nice piece of furniture. Clothing storage was a real problem in our very narrow closet. Every time I looked for something, I came out feeling as though I'd been on a trip through a jungle. We finally decided at the end of the year to buy an armoire for Elton's suits and other clothing, and this made things much easier. We bought two dressers to match and sent the Scharf's furniture back to them. But for months I was struggling with the clothing problem.

For anyone who has ever moved, this all sounds very familiar, and I'll skip the other problems of getting settled, which we eventually did. The apartment was pleasant, once we got everything in place. We had sunlight in the morning and afternoon and Elton had a good place for his desk and chair which he used a lot.

We were rather shocked by the fact that dinner service started at 5:30 and although there was a bar—which was one thing that made the move palatable to Elton—we rarely used it, except when we had company. A nice thing about the dinner service was that they seated people with others who were already in residence or, if we were seated alone, they'd ask if the so-and-so's could join us. This helped us become acquainted soon with several nice couples, and Elton enjoyed talking to others every night. This was something we couldn't do at the Meridian unless we had people in or went to a restaurant. Most people were friendly and two of my P.E.O. sisters lived here, Mary Dixon and Mil Davies, and they, of course, were friendly. We invited many of our friends to come and have dinner or lunch with us, and we entertained old and new friends, neighbors from the Meridian and many church members. We took most of them to the bar before dinner and asked them to come to our apartment afterwards. The residents seemed to do very little, if any, visiting in each others' apartments.

All of this made Elton feel better about moving, because he was having more human contact. The men had a meeting every Monday at 11:00 a.m. and I persuaded him to go, though he was not enthusiastic, but he really liked it and went religiously after the first time. Apparently, they just sat and visited, and he enjoyed that.

We hadn't been here long—perhaps a couple of weeks—when Elton fell out of bed, cracking his head open on the night stand. We pulled the call button, got nurses in, and then got the fire department to take him to Fairview Hospital. He was examined, his head was stitched and he was discharged. The staff had to come in each day to check his head, and we finally concluded that we should get some help in regularly, especially since we were paying $600 each month for it! So an aide came in every morning to help him dress and get ready for the day, and later they helped him exercise, although Robb came regularly all year.

We were paying for four hours of aid each day, which generally included their giving medications, but I insisted on doing that myself. For one thing, Elton had pills to take at 6:00 a.m., and I really didn't want the aides coming in at that time. The upshot was that we got, at most, one hour of aid a day for the eleven months before he entered the hospital. We were told in no uncertain terms that they did not have enough help for sitting. Of course, he could call for help if he needed it, but essentially, I was left exactly where I was when I moved in—I had to either take Elton along with me, or leave him at home alone when I went out. It was awkward for me to lift his walker into and out of the car; he didn't mind waiting in the car, however, while I shopped or ran an errand. We usually stopped for a Dunkin' Donut or ice cream, which was pleasant. But when I couldn't take him along for some reason, I did a lot of hurrying and worrying.

We were sorry to hear that my brother Jack's wife, Betty, died on November 3 after a long illness and several months in a nursing home.

Elton's health was not going downhill as fast as it had been, which was most encouraging, and the colonoscopy he had in November showed no problems. The Sheppards came for Thanksgiving, which turned out to be rainy, snowy, cold and just miserable. They had a new puppy, Scooby Doo, and had to bring him and Caesar, so they stayed in a motel and brought the puppy over here on Thursday and Friday while Steve spent some time in the motel. I had done scarcely any cooking since we had been at the Renaissance, and I fixed dinner, which turned out all right, except the turkey could have been cooked a little longer, and I forgot to put sugar in the pumpkin pie! I made sweet potatoes, and left them in the oven through dinner. That didn't matter much, because only Elton and I ate them anyway. We had breakfast in the Bistro both days and went to the Olive Garden on Friday night. Since it was too nasty to go out or go anywhere, we brought jigsaw puzzles in from the game room and what with the puzzles and the kids' books and puppy and gameboys, we had a pleasant visit in spite of the weather. They departed on Saturday, leaving us to prepare for Christmas.

I didn't decorate much for Christmas, so it wasn't as much of a job as it had been in the past, but sending gifts and doing the cards was a chore. I knew Elton would really feel bad if he couldn't buy a gift for me, and I didn't see how he could, so I suggested to Kris that she offer to buy gifts for him to give me if he would send her some money. He wrote one of the last checks he would ever write and sent it to her. I sent her a list of things I wanted, so he managed to have some gifts for me, and this made him happy. The Begany's came for Christmas dinner, brought some of the food, and we had quite a pleasant day.

Daille and Tom arrived after Christmas so that we could spend New Year's Eve with the Scharfs and Lonsdales as we had done for several years. We went to Cass's for a drink before we met the others at Bucci's in Berea, to celebrate the coming of 2004. Between Elton's eating and drinking problems, my hearing aid problems and the lateness of dinner, it was not the best party. That it was to be our last New Year's Eve together makes for sad retrospection.

2004

This was to be the saddest year of my life. But at least Elton was finally released from Parkinson's and had an end to his continuing efforts to overcome and conquer the disease. The year began, however, with little evidence of what was to come. His problems appeared to be the same as they had been, without any significant increase, until February.

Meanwhile, there was good news for other members of our family. Tim and Karin had announced much earlier the very good news that they were expecting a baby in March. They also became home-owners, after they'd lived in their rented apartment since going to Chicago. Tim's grandmother had died earlier in 2003 and the family had decided to sell her house to Tim and Karin. They moved at the beginning of December and were happy with their new home. And Karin was still happy as a Cook County Prosecutor.

Daille also had a major change in her life. She had begun a job in the fall at James Madison University in Harrisonburg. She was in the Library department, in charge of acquisitions and collection management under the direction of a boss whom she found difficult at first, and they were in the midst of a complicated reorganization of the library—a headache for Daille.

At the time she applied for the job, she was a candidate for national president of the Special Librarians Association and knew that would keep her busy if she were elected, but she wanted to be active in the field and her status in the SLA was a factor in her being hired. When she found early in 2004 that she had not been elected, she was very disappointed, as was the rest of the family, but she got very involved in her job and enjoyed being back at work again, even though she had a commute of thirty plus miles, mostly over hilly two-lane roads. They had planned a trip to Ireland in March with ex-pat friends from their time in Brazil, and what with those plans, her SLA commitments and the new baby, she had little free time. We saw them only once before July.

Meanwhile, Elton and I went on with our lives, which meant asking friends in for dinner or lunch and going to church every Sunday, except for one very snowy day—the weekend Saddam Hussein was found in Iraq. That day we watched the news. We saw quite a lot of the Scharfs, both at the Renaissance and elsewhere, and attended concerts at Baldwin Wallace and the coffee parties at the Meridian. Less pleasant was the continuation of meetings related to our church problems which were exacerbated by a meeting of the FPS in January at which the members voted not to have the congregation elect FPS members—the one thing the petitioners insisted upon.

In the fall of 2003, I had begun to attend a Bible study every Wednesday morning at the Renaissance. It was led by a woman minister from a nearby Lutheran church; she introduced a different slant on some aspects of the Bible than I'd been accustomed to, but it was a good class. And I enrolled in a CWRU-sponsored Living Room Learning (LRL) class, which met on eight Tuesday mornings. We studied James Madison and I enjoyed it very much. Elton had also started a new activity, playing cribbage on Monday afternoons. He loved this, having played cribbage since he was three years old, but sadly found that he couldn't really remember much and was very slow. We were both sorry he hadn't started with this group sooner.

We also continued with visits to doctors and dentists. Elton needed a new partial plate, after having lost his old one—the only lost item we never found. So we had visits to more than one dentist, because he also had to have a root extracted in March. And I had a serious problem which was growing much worse—weakness in my upper arms that prevented me from lifting my arms above shoulder level. I had been taking medication for high cholesterol for years (ever since the unfortunate discovery of cholesterol) and had to be taken off one medication due to much cramping in my legs. I then started on Pravachol, which I took for several years. My arms had been gradually getting weaker, and when the condition worsened, I decided it was the Pravachol and stopped taking it. I refused to take any more of the statins, high cholesterol or not. In March, I went to Dr. Golovan and he prescribed therapy, so I had six weeks of therapy in addition to my usual exercise routine. I did improve, but continued to have great difficulty lifting things, which did not help much in my care giving.

Early in March, Elton began to develop shortness of breath. Dr. Golovan was with the Indians at their spring training in Florida and when he got back we went to see him. He thought Elton should have an electrocardiogram, so we scheduled one for March 8 but postponed it so that he could play cribbage that afternoon. The next available date was March 12. We had just arrived home, after a quick stop at the bank, when Erin from Dr. Golovan's office called. A doctor had looked at the pictures and found a "mass." Of course, this scared both of us and Dr. Golovan told us we should go to a pulmonary doctor at Lutheran Hospital and have another chest x-ray. Since it was too late on Friday to call anyone for an appointment, Elton called Paula Keating and she suggested a Dr. Chadwick at Columbia and Lake of whom she thought highly. I decided to call him Monday. We were worried, but spent a fairly calm weekend.

Dr. Chadwick saw us immediately, but found no mass, only that the lungs were full of fluid. He scheduled surgery to remove the fluid, a fairly simple procedure on an in-and-out basis, but when we went back in for a checkup he said the fluid would build up again and it was unwise to do the surgery every time. He suggested a cardiologist and we made an appointment with a Dr. Vlasteris on April 23. Elton had never been to a heart doctor before and although he said little, I could see that he was simply scared to death, because of his memories of his Dad's bad heart. I finally told him that he was not going to die at 52 of a bad heart, so worrying was ridiculous and he snapped out of it quite well. When all was said and done, he was told that his heart was in pretty good shape.

His heart was okay and he still had a lot of strength in his arms and legs but with the lung and tooth problems, his worrying and increasing difficulty in swallowing and speaking, he was obviously getting weaker. When I tried to work with him on his speaking exercises, I realized he was unable to do them. Toward the end of May, we had a lovely lunch that we both enjoyed at Pier W with the Bucey's and Ingrams, and he managed to eat and speak quite well. But a couple of weeks later, when we had lunch with the Giffels, Elton's speech was almost completely unintelligible. I could understand a little and deduce some of what he was trying to say, but from then on it was very difficult. This was most frustrating for him and saddening for me.

At least the spring brought us good news from the family. Karin's baby, Cassidy Grace, was born on March 17, a good day for the daughter of an Irish father. The Geist relatives had rather hoped she would not be born on St. Patrick's day, since the Sullivan's were so strongly Irish, but she was a healthy, pretty, blue-eyed baby and turned out to be a happy baby, despite the fact that Karin could not nurse her.

I also received some surprising news in May. The League of Women Voters had voted to choose me and Kathy Barber as the 2004 recipients of the Belle Sherwin Award for "Democracy in Action." This award had been given to a woman every year, for about ten years, on August 28 (the date of the ratification of the 20th Amendment giving women the right to vote). The recipients had included some very prestigious women, and I was surprised but honored to be one of them. They needed a photo of me, so I located a photographer not too far away and went in one day in May to have it taken. I took Elton with me, and the photographer suggested she take a few of the two of us together. As a result, I have a photo of him that doesn't look much like the guy I remember, but was quite good for his condition.

Tim and Karin wanted us to see Cassidy and there was no way we could go to Chicago, so they drove from Chicago with her on the weekend of June 5 and 6. I thought this was very sweet of them, and I know Elton did too. Daille and Tom had been to Chicago a few days after she was born, and went out again, with Kris and children, to Cassidy's baptism on the Memorial Day weekend.

Throughout June, Elton was obviously getting weaker, less clear in his thinking, and unable to exercise much. About the middle of the month, we had lunch with Karl and Ruth Johnson after church and they began an argument about the church and the FPS. I didn't let it go on too long—Elton wasn't up to it and I was in no mood for it. That same week, Lyn Cameron and her friend, Chris Von Biedermann, came to lunch. We hadn't seen them for years. It was nice to see them, and we both had a lovely time with them—just about the last time we had a pleasant social occasion.

On June 21 we had an appointment with Dr. Riley, who told me sadly that there was nothing more they could do for Elton, and no other medication they could try. We had an appointment three days later at the V.A. and when we got in to see the doctors, they told me the same thing. The Parish Nurse, Paula Keating, who had kept in continual close touch with me, talked to me that morning and said she thought we should think about hospice; the V.A. doctors said the same thing.

I was discouraged, but I don't really know how aware Elton was of all this. On Friday, Betty Goulon, the nurse in charge of Bridgeview, came in while Paula was here and we all decided he should go into the Health Center and probably into Hospice. What happened then, I will always regret and be angry about. Betty called the Health Center, got a room and a wheelchair, put Elton in the chair and rushed him down the hall to the Health Center. No doctor was available until Monday and the room was really not ready. There was no reason he could not have stayed with me until Monday; we could have talked and I could have prepared him for giving up his walker (his lifeline), leaving me, and being in the hospital. I am sure that Betty simply wanted to finish up one of her cases and had no thought about how he would feel.

As it was, he was absolutely miserable and very angry about being in a wheelchair and away from home. I left him on Saturday afternoon because Ralph Locher (a long-time Old Stoner) had died and I felt I absolutely had to go to the funeral which turned out to be the most interminable funeral I had ever attended (one speaker gave a 45 minute eulogy), and I was gone all afternoon. I spent most of each day with Elton from then on, going down to his room sometimes in time to help him with breakfast, sometimes eating lunch or dinner with him, and occasionally going out for an errand. He was very angry at first, lashed out with his fists at everyone, including me, but as time went on he became a little calmer. He slept a good deal and seemed to be somewhat comatose when he was awake.

Daille and Tom came for the weekend of the 4th and we all spent a lot of time with Elton. I was knitting a dress for Cassidy and when I finished that, I started knitting long furry scarves which were all the rage. I think I knitted six while I was there. I read, watched the disorganized management of the health center and tried to make Elton feel a little calmer. Twice he wanted desperately to say something to me, and finally got out "Money." I assured him as always that we were okay and our finances were in good shape. Money, and the lack of it, was very important to him. For a year or two he had not really been able to have any say over our finances, though they were about as secure as they could be. And one time, he clearly said he guessed we'd broken up. Poor baby—nothing but his death could do that, and I believe that even his death has not separated us. I hope I convinced him; at least he seemed a little quieter after that.

Tom and Daille were going to a family reunion in West Virginia the week of August 2. The reunion was scheduled for Monday through Friday. Since Daille's schedule was tight, they had originally planned on going to the reunion mid-week and then coming here for the weekend of the 5th. However, when I asked if they could come earlier because I was concerned about Elton, they decided to drive up for the weekend of the 24th. I was really glad they came. Elton recognized Daille and was very, very happy to see her and to have her here, so I greatly appreciated her changing her plans.

We talked about putting him in the hospice, but I didn't decide to do it until one day before his death, July 28. That day in the hospice, Nova Kordalski came in the morning and spent all day. I'd lost a front tooth and had to have a root removed before I could replace it; my appointment was that morning, so Nova was there while I was gone. Elton was asleep most of the day and very quiet in the afternoon. Rev. Myers stopped in briefly and then Bill Heideloff came in, and after Nova left, with Bill still there, at 5:00 p.m., I realized that Elton was no longer breathing.

What is there to say about his dying? It had taken me a long time to realize it was coming, but now I was glad he no longer had to bear the difficulties he'd gone through. But I was very sorry we hadn't been able to say goodbye, or to have the chance to talk about what was happening. It had been weeks since he had been able to say more than a word or two, so we wouldn't have been able to discuss it in any case. I think he was aware of the situation and had come to accept it. He had continued nearly to the end to go to church and to listen when I prayed, and I know that he believed in life after death. I believe that, to the degree he was able to know what was going on, he had also grown to accept his coming death.

Although my life was not over, even though Elton's was, in a very real way the story of our lives was over, whatever the future might hold for me. For many months there were few moments when he was not in my every thought and I'm sure this will always be true to some extent. But from now on, my life is my life only. I began this history originally as a story of our marriage, then, for the sake of those who will read it and might wonder about our families and our childhoods, I added the early chapters. But to go on with *our lives* from here would put everything in a different perspective. From this point on, *my life* is a different story and with the greatest reluctance, I say *Finis* to this one.

EPILOGUE

2005

Elton died peacefully in the late afternoon of Thursday, July 29, 2004, while I was sitting with him in the Hospice at the Renaissance. He had visitors earlier, including our interim pastor and Bill Heideloff who was with me at the end. After we talked to the nurses we went to my apartment where I called Daille and the girls. Bill took me to dinner and the next day other friends took me out to every meal and to the funeral home, so that I wouldn't be alone. Between trips out, I made many calls. Daille and Tom arrived late Friday evening.

Neither of the girls could come for the funeral before Wednesday, so after Tom helped in the various ways he could, he went back to West Virginia to a family reunion he and Daille had planned to attend. Daille stayed and helped me make plans with Rev. Robert Bates and took care of some of the many necessary tasks. Tom came back Tuesday night and the girls arrived on Wednesday.

The service was actually a memorial service with a short interment service in the columbarium of the church afterwards. The service was beautiful with more than 200 people attending. I was touched by the fact that Raman Rao flew in from Salt Lake and Marion McCuaig drove all the way down from Prince Edward Island. David and Vickie Araneicka represented our families and Jim Cooke, Floyd Lee and John Cumberlidge gave touching eulogies. Daille gave a heartfelt tribute to her Dad.

Before they all left on Saturday, Daille wisely suggested that we go through Elton's clothes so the three men could take with them what they could use. This was difficult, but easier if done quickly. Daille also helped with writing notes and letters and doing whatever needed to be done. When they all left I was exhausted and spent days reading something, anything, trying to sleep, writing letters and trying to deal with my life. This was made more difficult than it need have been, because the Renaissance Bridgeview contract required my moving out of Bridgeview within a month. It was a terrible provision, which I protested in every possible way and it was later changed. But in the meantime, I had to move and I agreed to do so by October 1. The move was to a similar apartment, paid for and arranged by the Renaissance, but it was, nevertheless, yet another move in my life.

I was distracted from mourning and moving by the League of Women Voters' program presenting me with the Belle Sherwin Award, a very special occasion, on August 28. Daille and Tom returned for the program, then Daille flew back to work and Tom and I drove to Virginia. Kris had persuaded me to go with them to Saluda, North Carolina, to visit Steve's mother who lived in a small house in the woods with three dogs. We drove in the van, with another two dogs, and spent a few hectic, haphazard days with Frances, seeing the sights and visiting. Back in Virginia, I visited the Pettits and then came back to Cleveland. A little later in the month, I drove to Pittsburgh to the Araneickas to see them and Mona and Liz, who had not been able to come to Elton's service. I had a nice visit with them, unfazed by a nine-inch rain caused by Hurricane Jeanne. They drove up on Sunday to a nice program held by the church, after the service, to honor Elton and me.

It was great seeing Mona, and there was an additional benefit to the meeting. She read the first part of this book and told me more about her parents. Furthermore, she had quite a lot of letters and things her mother and other relatives had written and I asked her to send them to me so I could make copies for my records. This gave me a lot of information about Elton's early life. At the same time, I made up a *memory book* for Elton in order to keep a record of the wonderful things people had said about him.

The fall was busy and disturbing in several ways. There was the need to get used to a new residence and this made it harder to become accustomed to being without Elton. Then there was the ever-present vitriol of the upcoming election. I feared Kerry's election because all the plans he spoke about were nebulous and I didn't trust him, but until I woke up at 5:00 a.m. on the day after the election, I expected him to have won election. One activity which should have been pleasant was another Living Room Learning lesson on *From Dawn to Decadence* by Jacques Barzun. Barzun's negativity about the present was unnerving, and I felt the leader wasn't up to the job of covering this huge tome.

I did a lot of knitting, including a sweater that I patched up from yarn and a partly knitted sweater given me by a friend, and long fuzzy scarves—all the rage that year, but which I neither liked nor used. I read, as always, and got ready for Thanksgiving with the Sheppards, following a weekend trip to the Greenbrier in West Virginia with Daille and Tom. This weekend was my gift to them for all the help they'd given me. I went to Virginia again for Christmas, this time at the Pettits', with the Sheppards and the Sullivans with their little Cassidy. Christmas was in the Pettit house in Basye which they had hoped to have vacated by then. However, the house they were building in Harrisonburg was not ready to move into until February, 2005.

Once again I spent New Year's Eve with the Scharfs and their friends, this time at a potluck in the Meridian. Surrounded by friends among our group and the Meridian residents, I found the night less sad than I'd expected and reached the end of 2004 hoping I'd gotten over the worst of missing Elton. I know now that it takes much longer than six months.

In the many sleepless nights and sad days I've spent since his death, I've remembered the good and the bad days of our lives. I believe I have discovered many things I had never consciously known about Elton or myself, including the many influences affecting our lives, singly and jointly, and explanations for the mistakes we made while we were together. Certainly, both of us failed to fulfill the needs of the other in many ways and we were both untrue to our vows in one way or another. But I know that neither of us could break apart from our relationship and, despite everything we went through, we remained the mates we had subconsciously known we would be that fall day in chemistry class at Custer High in 1938.